CONDEMNATION PRACTICE IN CALIFORNIA

Authors
Norman E. Matteoni
Henry Veit

Editor
Donald R. Briggs
CEB Attorney

December 1990

Supplement to California Practice Book No. 59

CONTINUING EDUCATION OF THE BAR ▪ BERKELEY, CALIFORNIA

Book Authors
Paul E. Anderson
John B. Anson
Thomas G. Baggot
Irwin M. Friedman
Burton J. Goldstein
Richard L. Huxtable
Norman E. Matteoni

Book Editors
M. Reed Hunter
Davidson Ream

Library of Congress Catalog Card No. 72–619711
© 1975, 1977, 1979, 1981, 1982, 1983, 1984, 1986, 1987, 1988, 1989, 1990
by The Regents of the University of California
Printed in the United States of America
ISBN 0-88124-348-5

RE–30683

CONTINUING EDUCATION OF THE BAR ▪ CALIFORNIA

Governing Committee
Luther Kent Orton, San Francisco, Chairperson
Warren E. Schoonover, Special Assistant, Division of Agriculture & Natural
Resources, University of California (Oakland), Vice Chairperson
Nanci G. Clinch, Nevada City, Liaison Governor
Edward E. Kallgren, San Francisco, Liaison Governor
Catherine C. Sprinkles, San Jose, Liaison Governor
William A. Carroll, Director, Continuing Education of the Bar
Paul F. Dauer, Sacramento
Professor Edward C. Halbach, Jr., University of California
School of Law (Berkeley)
Barbara K. Mizuno, San Francisco
Joseph A. Pastrone, University Controller, University of California (Oakland)
Keith Sexton, Dean, University Extension Programs,
University of California (Berkeley)
Barry A. Weiss, Irvine

Joint Advisory Committee

State Bar Committee Members
Raymond J. (Jerry) Coughlan, Jr., San Diego, Chairperson
Marcia Haber Kamine, Los Angeles, Vice Chairperson
Nanci G. Clinch, Nevada City, Liaison Governor
Edward E. Kallgren, San Francisco, Liaison Governor
Catherine C. Sprinkles, San Jose, Liaison Governor
Malvina E. J. Abbott, Chula Vista
Phillip S. Althoff, Martinez
Janyce Keiko Imata Blair, Gardena
Arthur H. Bredenbeck, Burlingame
Adryenn Cantor, Beverly Hills
Michael B. Carroll, San Francisco
Donna M. Dell, Walnut Creek
James C. Hagedorn, Sacramento
John F. Hartigan, Los Angeles
Barbara R. Johnson, Inglewood
Kathleen A. Knox, Pasadena
Craig Labadie, Oakland
Susan T. Levin, San Jose
Palmer Brown Madden, Walnut Creek
Gerald F. Mohun, Jr., Mammoth Lakes
John W. Noonan, Pleasanton
Mary V. O'Hare, Burbank
Peter C. Pang, San Francisco
Thomas A. Papageorge, Los Angeles
Richard Pearl, San Francisco
Elaine M. Profant–Turner, Eureka
Bruce E. Ramsey, Modesto
James J. Scherer, South San Francisco

EDUCATION OF THE BAR

Anthony F. Sgherzi, Los Angeles
Willie J. Smith, Fresno
Richard Neil Snyder, San Francisco
June T. Summers, San Francisco
Stephen E. Traverse, Los Angeles
Leslie L. van Houten, Oakland
Gary L. Waldron, Fresno
David M. Zeligs, Fair Oaks

Law School Dean Members
Dean Scott H. Bice, University of Southern California Law Center
Dean Paul A. Brest, Stanford University
Dean Benjamin Bycel, Ventura/Santa Barbara Colleges of Law
Dean Jesse H. Choper, University of California (Berkeley)
Dean Charles E. D'Arcy, Lincoln Law School of Sacramento
Dean Michael H. Dessent, California Western School of Law
Dean John A. FitzRandolph, Whittier College School of Law
Dean H. Jay Folberg, University of San Francisco School of Law
Dean Arthur N. Frakt, Loyola Law School
Dean Nels B. Fransen, Humphreys College of Law
Dean Seymour Greitzer, Glendale University College of Law
Dean Kenneth Held, University of LaVerne/University of LaVerne at
San Fernando Valley Colleges of Law
Dean Fred Herro, Monterey College of Law
Dean Chris Kanios, New College of California School of Law
Dean Jeffrey Kupers, John F. Kennedy University School of Law
Dean Robert Leahy, Empire College School of Law
Dean Mark Owens, Jr., San Francisco Law School
Dean Anthony J. Pagano, Golden Gate University School of Law
Dean Janice L. Pearson, San Joaquin College of Law
Acting Dean Mary L. Perry, Western State University College of Law of
San Diego
Dean Ronald F. Phillips, Pepperdine University School of Law
Dean Perry Polski, University of West Los Angeles School of Law
Dean Susan Westerberg Prager, University of California (Los Angeles)
Dean Franklin Thompson Read, Hastings College of Law
Dean Gordon D. Schaber, McGeorge School of Law,
University of the Pacific
Dean Wade V. Shang, Northrop University Law Center
Dean Kristine Strachan, University of San Diego School of Law
Dean Leigh H. Taylor, Southwestern University School of Law
Dean William H. J. Tiernan, National University School of Law
Dean Gerald F. Uelmen, University of Santa Clara School of Law
Dean Marcia B. Wilbur, Western State University College of Law of
Orange County
Acting Dean Bruce A. Wolk, University of California (Davis)

Preface

This supplement, like most CEB publications, is a product of and for members of the California Bar. Members of the Bar wrote and edited it, and the problems were discussed with California lawyers.

We would like to consider this supplement a part of a dialogue with our readers. Another supplement next year, cumulative of this one, will give us an opportunity to make corrections and additions you suggest. If you know something we did not include, or if we erred, share your knowledge with other California lawyers. Send your comments to:

Supplement Editor
Continuing Education of the Bar—California
2300 Shattuck Avenue
Berkeley, CA 94704

CEB is indebted to the authors of this supplement, Norman E. Matteoni, of Matteoni, Saxe & Nanda, San Jose, and Henry Veit, of Lerner & Veit, San Francisco, who wrote Chapter 12. CEB attorney Gordon Graham acted as consultant for this supplement.

Legal research assistance was provided by Bonnie Lamb, Kenneth Scudder, and Martin Weis. Copy editing and production were handled by Inge Leonardos. Special editorial assistance was provided by Nila Kanzaria, Melanie Lawrence, Cynthia Roberts, and Pat Theard. The indexer was Robert W. Burke, Jr. Composition was performed by CEB's Electronic Publishing Staff.

William A. Carroll
Director

Contents

Cutoff Dates

We completed legal editing on this supplement at the end of September 1990.

We have checked:

Case citations through:

—Shepard's California Cumulative Supplement vol 71, no. 6. Cutoffs were 49 C3d 1229, 215 CA3d 1502, 106 L Ed 2d 615, 889 F2d 1109, 724 F Supp 984.

—Shepard's United States Cumulative Supplement vol 88, no. 12. Cutoffs were 107 L Ed 2d 570, 893 F2d 348, 727 F Supp 635.

—Shepard's Federal Cumulative Supplement vol 80, no. 2. Cutoffs were 107 L Ed 2d 570, 893 F2d 348, 727 F Supp 635.

California statutes for amendments and repeals through Stats 1990, ch 1168.

Federal statutes for amendments and repeals through 104 Stat 726.

We try to add significant statutory and judicial developments, subsequent histories of cases, and other matters such as new forms and regulations after legal editing is done, but you should not assume that all developments after the listed cutoff dates have been included.

Selected Developments

CONDEMNATION PRACTICE IN CALIFORNIA
Supplement December 1990

Since Previous Supplement: On a beneficiary's entitlement to condemnation proceeds from property subject to a prior land sale contract, see Supp §2.10.

See Supp §4.70 on owner's alternatives when a redevelopment agency fails to acquire property subject to the plan within three years.

See Supp §8.8A on a condemnee's remedy from an order granting prejudgment possession.

On the applicability of legal or market interest rates to security deposits see *Redevelopment Agency v Erganian* (1989) 211 CA3d 166, 259 CR 213.

The United States Supreme Court has upheld the imposition of user fees that are imposed to reimburse the government for the cost of services. See Supp §13.22N.

Since Publication of Book: This Supplement includes an updated contingency fee contract. See Supp §1.17.

On the effect of hazardous waste, see Supp §§1.17 and 2.20.

See Supp §4.61 for considerations in valuing goodwill.

See Supp §5.22 on the effect of electromagnetic radiation from power lines on valuation.

Special verdict forms may be necessary to permit some appeals. See Supp §5.32.

See Supp §6.25 on challenging a resolution of necessity under the Political Reform Act.

An owner is not shielded from nonrecognition of gain by IRC §1033 if the replacement property is acquired before condemnation but in anticipation of it. See Supp §12.5.

The rule imposing absolute liability for interference with land stability proximately caused by a public project as deliberately designed or constructed is modified in flooding cases. See *Belair v Riverside County Flood Control Dist.* (1988) 47 C3d 550, 253 CR 693, discussed in Supp §13.17.

A public agency that is sued in an inverse condemnation action may cross-complain for equitable indemnity against an entity undertaking the work giving rise to the claim of inverse condemnation. See Supp §13.29A.

The *Agins* rule on nonavailability of the remedy of inverse condemnation for land regulation cases was effectively overruled in *First English Evangelical Lutheran Church v County of Los Angeles* (1987) 482 US 304. See Supp §§13.22B, 13.22K.

Tax changes continue. California has completed its steps toward conformity with the Internal Revenue Code with the enactment of the California Personal Income Tax Fairness, Simplification and Conformity Act of 1987 and the California Bank and Corporation Tax Fairness, Simplification and Conformity Act of 1987. See "Note: Legislative Changes" at the beginning of Chapter 12 and App C.

The California Administrative Code is now called the California Code of Regulations.

The Tax Reform Act of 1986 (Pub L 99–514, 100 Stat 2085) made several changes that affect tax issues in condemnation. See Supp chap 12.

The legislature has prescribed a new method for calculating interest on compensation awards, which is based on "apportionment rate" based on earnings of the Surplus Money Investment Fund. Interest on inverse condemnation awards is also subject to the new interest rate provisions. See Supp §10.24.

Appellate courts have reviewed the grounds for recovery of litigation expenses based on pretrial offers and demands (see Supp §10.23A), determined that the specific statutory authority for condemning property must be stated in the complaint (see Supp §8.23), ruled that a prior commitment to take will remove the conclusive presumption from a resolution of necessity (see Supp §6.19), and held that a resolution describing the public project is conclusive and may not be contradicted in trial to decrease or avoid severance damages (see Supp §§5.12, 6.18). Additionally, the trial court has been held to have the inherent power to fashion a procedure after trial and pending appeal to increase a deposit made for prejudgment possession. See Supp §10.19A. Relocation assistance has been held to apply to a property owner displaced through inverse condemnation as well as one displaced through a direct taking (see Supp §4.54).

The courts have considered the recovery of attorneys' fees under contingent fee contracts in both direct (Supp §§1.17, 8.33) and inverse (Supp §13.30) condemnation cases, the loss of value of business inventory (Supp §4.61), the right to inverse condemnation damages from a fire caused by the negligent construction and maintenance of a public improvement (Supp §13.13), and the federal income tax treatment of interest paid a landowner as a result of property acquisition from condemnation or threat of condemnation (Supp §12.14).

The Internal Revenue Code has been amended to preclude partnership interests from qualifying as "like-kind" property. See Supp §12.17.

The Revenue and Taxation Code has been amended to provide that, unless the Franchise Tax Board provides otherwise, a proper tax election filed in accordance with the Internal Revenue Code must be considered a proper election under the Revenue and Taxation Code. See Supp chap 12.

The California Supreme Court held in *Baker v Burbank-Glendale-Pasadena Airport Auth.* (1985) 39 C3d 862, 218 CR 293, that a public agency that did not have the power to condemn air easements nonetheless could be liable in inverse condemnation for damage from airplane flights over plaintiffs' homes. See Supp §13.3.

Notable decisions have discussed the effect of tax benefits on valuation (Supp §4.1), recovery for loss of inventory caused by inverse condemnation (Supp §4.52A), and the exchange of valuation data before trial (Supp §9.14). The courts have also ruled on the recovery of attorneys' fees and costs by condemnees in contested federal actions (Supp §11.23), the taxpayer's right to depreciate condemned property (Supp §12.3), and the right to inverse condemnation damages because of a municipality's negligent maintenance of an improvement (Supp §13.3).

The United States Supreme Court upheld a scheme to condemn portions of large estates to transfer title to lessees. See Supp §6.5.

The Eminent Domain Law (CCP §§1230.010–1273.050) that went into effect on July 1, 1976, was a comprehensive revision of prior condemnation law and procedure. The new law was a product of nearly ten years of effort by the California Law Revision Commission, culminating in the publication of its Recommendation Proposing The Eminent Domain Law, 12 Cal L Rev'n Comm'n Reports 1601 (1974). Although it made some important changes, it was primarily designed to recognize, restate, and codify existing California condemnation law at the same time it enlarged the substantive elements of compensation such as goodwill losses. It also made many changes of a technical or corrective nature and eliminated numerous statutes that were duplicative or inconsistent.

The litigation concerning the city of Oakland's attempt to condemn the Oakland Raiders football team (discussed in Supp §6.6) has brought condemnation law some unaccustomed notoriety.

Decisions concerning the effect of blight and precondemnation activity on property values have appeared in the wake of *Klopping v City of Whittier* (1972) 8 C3d 39, 104 CR 1. See Supp §§4.7–4.7A. Disputes over pretrial demands and offers and their effect on recovery of litigation expenses, including attorneys' fees, are noted in Supp §§9.14A, 10.23A. On the right to relocation assistance, see Supp §§4.53, 11.18. Federal legislation has liberalized the income tax rules on replacement of a condemned residence and introduced an election to exclude up to $125,000 of gain on disposition of a residence. See Supp §12.31.

In the area of inverse condemnation, a source of continuing litigation is the conflict between a community's desire to regulate growth through zoning, planning, or other controls and an owner's or developer's desire to be compensated for loss of vested rights as a result of the government controls. See Supp §§13.22A–13.22O. The State Bar Committee on Eminent Domain has adopted recommended jury instructions for use in those actions. See Supp §13.33.

Statutory changes have been made in a number of areas, such as the authority of private property owners to exercise the power of eminent domain (see Supp §6.6A), the offer that a condemnor must make before it adopts a resolution of necessity (see Supp §7.4), proration of property taxes (see Supp §10.15), payment of judgments (see Supp §§10.21–10.21A, 10.24–10.27), reduction in income tax rates, adoption of the accelerated cost recovery system (see Supp §12.14), and extension to two years for replacing an involuntarily converted personal residence (see Supp §12.31).

1

Attorney's Initial Contact With Condemnation Action

ASSESSING POTENTIAL LAWSUIT

[§1.3] Should Condemnee Retain a Lawyer?

Code of Civil Procedure §1255.410 replaced former CCP §1243.5 on obtaining an order of immediate possession.

[§1.4] Validity of Agent's "Offer"

Compare *Hilltop Props., Inc. v State,* cited in Book §1.4, with *Santa Monica Unified School Dist. v Persh* (1970) 5 CA3d 945, 953, 85 CR 463, 468, in which the court denied estoppel against a school district that failed to honor its offer to purchase. The offer had not been ratified as required by former Ed C §15961. Under existing case law, estoppel does not apply to a municipal agency that has not complied with statutory requirements for the exercise of its power.

Education Code §15961 was amended and renumbered Ed C §§39656, 81655 in 1976.

Preliminary Investigation of Value

[§1.6] Precedent Knowledge of Client and Lawyer

The general rules of evidence concerning market value of property (Evid C §§810–823) have been extended to all property valuation cases, including those for eminent domain, except cases concerning ad valorem property tax assessment and equalization. Evid C §810. The practitioner in eminent domain must now take note of developments in the rules of evidence through divorce, property division, contract, and other cases.

COSTS AND DELAY OF LITIGATION

[§1.8] Court Costs

Defendants with a single, unified interest are allowed only one cost bill (*City of Downey v Gonzales,* cited in Book §1.8); but if there are two or more estates or divided interests in property sought to be condemned, the costs of determining apportionment of the award (see Book chap 10) are borne by the condemning agency. The cost of determining any issue of title between competing defendants is taxed to defendants. CCP §1268.710 (replacing former CCP §1246.1).

The procedure for abandonment now appears in CCP §1268.510; recovery of litigation expenses and damages on dismissal for this or other reasons is provided for in CCP §1268.610. Recovery of costs by a successful plaintiff in an inverse condemnation case is now governed by CCP §1036; former CCP §1246.3 has been repealed.

Code of Civil Procedure §§1255 and 1255a have been repealed.

Government Code §68093 has been amended to provide a witness fee of $35 per day and 20 cents per mile for mileage actually traveled, both ways.

The subject matter of former CCP §1032a regarding deposition fees, including videotaping, and of CCP §1032.5 has been incorporated into CCP §1033.5 without substantial change. Effective January 1, 1987, CCP §1033 was repealed and replaced with a new CCP §1033, which provides that costs shall be determined under CCP §1034 when the prevailing party recovers a judgment that could have been rendered in a court of lesser jurisdiction. New CCP §1034 provides that prejudgment costs and costs on appeal shall be determined under rules adopted by the Judicial Council. See Cal Rules of Ct 870 on prejudgment costs and 26 and 135 on costs on appeal.

In 1988, extensive revisions were made to the law governing jurors under the Trial Jury Selection and Management Act (CCP §§190–236). Jurors' fees and expenses are now set forth in CCP §215. Unless a higher fee is provided for each day's attendance by county or city and county ordinance, the fee for jurors in superior court civil cases is $5 per day for each day's attendance as a juror and, unless a higher mileage rate is provided by statute or local ordinance, superior court jurors shall be reimbursed for mileage traveling to court at $.15 per mile for each mile actually traveled to attend court as a juror.

Reporter's fees must be paid in advance of each day's trial by deposit with the clerk of the court or with the reporter. Govt C §69953. Initially, the parties must pay the fees in equal proportion and then amounts paid can be taxed as costs at the conclusion of trial. But the state, a county, city, district, or other political subdivision is exempt from initial payment under Govt C §6103, and Govt C §6103.5 specifically excludes recovery of what would have been the public agency's share of such costs in a condemnation case.

See Supp §10.23A regarding condemnee's right to recover its costs.

[§1.9] Attorney's and Appraiser's Fees, and Other Litigation Expenses

"Litigation expenses" are defined in CCP §1235.140 (formerly CCP §1255a(c)) to include all expenses reasonably and necessarily incurred in preparation for trial, during trial, and in posttrial proceedings; the term specifically includes reasonable attorney's fees, appraiser's fees, and fees of other experts, whether incurred before or after the filing of the complaint. This definition is referred to throughout the Eminent Domain Law (CCP §§1230.010–1273.050). See CCP §§1245.060 (entry for survey), 1250.325 (disclaimer), 1250.410 (settlement offers), 1255.030 (increase or decrease in amount of deposit), 1258.290 (exchange of valuation data), 1260.120 (dismissal on objection to right to take), and 1268.610 (expenses on dismissal or defeat of right to take).

A property owner, whether testifying as an expert or otherwise, cannot recover fees for time spent in preparing and presenting testimony, because that time does not qualify for compensation as litigation expenses under CCP §1235.140. *County of Madera v Forrester* (1981) 115 CA3d 57, 170 CR 896.

In 1975, former CCP §1249.3 (now CCP §1250.410) was enacted to allow the court to award defendant in a direct condemnation action the reasonable litigation expenses necessary to protect his or her interest if the condemnor's final offer was unreasonable and the property owner's final demand was reasonable. The final offer and demand must be served and filed at least 30 days before the trial date. Expenses are awarded on defendant's motion, which must be made within 30 days after entry of judgment. The offer and demand are to be "viewed in the light of the evidence admitted and the compensation awarded in the proceeding." CCP §1250.410(b). See Supp §10.23A regarding posttrial motion for recovery of litigation expenses and discussion of case law interpreting the above standard.

In *City of Los Angeles v Beck* (1974) 40 CA3d 763, 115 CR 569, attorney's and appraiser's fees were not allowed under former CCP §1246.3 (now CCP §1036, granting successful plaintiff in inverse condemnation recovery of reasonable expenses necessary to proceeding) to the defendant property owner in a direct condemnation action that was filed in response to an inverse suit on the same property. See Supp §13.30.

Code of Civil Procedure §1036 (former CCP §1246.3) does not apply to precondemnation delay damages, because it allows fees only for the taking of an interest in property, not for simple damage. *People ex rel Dep't of Pub. Works v Peninsula Enters.* (1979) 91 CA3d 332, 360, 153 CR 895, 910; *Stone v City of Los Angeles* (1975) 51 CA3d 987, 997, 124 CR 822, 828.

The court in *Holtz v San Francisco BART Dist.* (1976) 17 C3d 648, 131 CR 646, agreed that attorney's fees are not recoverable in an inverse condemnation action for damages, because the statute applies only to a taking of property. But the court concluded that withdrawal of lateral support (see §13.19) was a taking rather than a damaging; thus, former CCP §1246.3 did apply. The court commented that the statutory phrase "taking of any interest in real property" encompasses lesser interferences with property rights than the concept of "taking" within the meaning of Cal Const art I, §19. See also *Jones v People ex rel Dep't of Transp.* (1978) 22 C3d 144, 148 CR 640 (temporary loss of access); *City of Los Angeles v Tilem* (1983) 142 CA3d 694, 191 CR 229 (temporary economic damage caused by a pending condemnation action that was abandoned); *Orme v State ex rel Dep't of Water Resources* (1978) 83 CA3d 178, 147 CR 735 (temporary flooding).

The words "in the opinion of the court" in CCP §1036 allow the trial court considerable discretion in determining the amount of fees. *City of Los Angeles v Waller* (1979) 90 CA3d 766, 780, 154 CR 12, 20.

When there is no de facto taking and no entitlement to precondemnation damages under *Klopping v City of Whittier* (1972) 8 C3d 39, 104 CR 1 (see §§4.7–4.7A), there can be no recovery of litigation expenses under CCP §§1036 and 1250.410. *City of Los Angeles v Property Owners* (1982) 138 CA3d 114, 187 CR 667.

When property that is the subject of a real estate sale agreement providing for a broker's commission is taken by eminent domain before close of escrow, the broker is not entitled to a commission. The broker's right to compensation depends on performance of the sales contract. *City of Turlock v Zagaris* (1989) 209 CA3d 189, 256 CR 902.

For discussion of *City of Los Angeles v Ortiz,* cited in Book §1.9, see Comment, *Sympathy But No Tea,* 2 U San Fern L Rev 49 (Winter 1972–1973).

See Supp §8.33 for discussion of attorneys' contingency fees on abandonment.

[§1.10] Other Expenses

A condemnor entering property to make a preliminary survey and studies must compensate the owner for any damages caused by the entry and by any tests made and is liable for the owner's court costs and reasonable attorneys' fees expended to obtain this compensation. See Book §4.71.

Code of Civil Procedure §1246.3 has been repealed and replaced by CCP §1036. Code of Civil Procedure §1246.4 has been repealed and replaced by CCP §§1268.610–1268.620.

[§1.11] Delay

Code of Civil Procedure §1260.010 has replaced former CCP §1264. Condemnation cases continue to have priority at trial.

ACCEPTING CASE

Attorney's Fee Agreements

[§1.15] Express Fee Contracts

Since publication of the Book, bar association fee schedules have been invalidated as price-fixing devices. *Goldfarb v Virginia State Bar* (1975) 421 US 773.

There are various fee arrangements for condemnation cases, including an hourly rate; an hourly charge for initial investigation to be converted to a contingency fee if the case warrants pursuit; a contingency fee arrangement based on a percentage of the award or settlement in excess of the condemning agency's offer before the attorney's involvement; a fixed percentage of the total recovery; and combinations of these arrangements. The most common arrangement is a contingency based on the percentage of increase over the condemnor's offer.

Beginning January 1, 1987, matters that do not involve contingency fees are subject to Bus & P C §6148, which requires a written contract for attorneys' services if it is reasonably foreseeable that the expense to the client will exceed $1000. The statute is framed in terms of "expense to a client," not in terms of attorneys' fees. Therefore other fees or costs such as deposition expenses must be considered. Failure to provide a written contract when required permits the client to void the agreement with the attorney, who may then recover reasonable fees only, not the amount provided for in the agreement.

There are four exceptions to the requirement for a written contract: (1) services rendered in an emergency to avoid foreseeable prejudice to the client's rights or when a writing is impractical; (2) services rendered that are of the same general kind as those previously paid for by the client; (3) when a client knowingly waives the Bus & P C §6148 provisions for providing a written contract; and (4) when the client is a corporation.

The contract must show the hourly rate or the standard rates, fees, and charges applicable to the matter. The general nature of the legal services and the respective responsibilities of the attorney and the client in pursuing the matter must also be set out. The State Bar of California has prepared sample contracts. They are available for $3.50 by writing the State Bar of California, Fee Agreements, P.O. Box 24527, San Francisco, CA 94124–9959.

Contingency fee contracts must be in writing and are governed by Bus & P C §6147. They must include a statement disclosing the contingency fee rate and a statement on how disbursements and costs will affect the fee and the client's recovery. Bus & P C §6147. The client must be given a signed copy of the contract. Bus & P C §6147. Unless the claim is subject to Bus & P C §6146 governing actions for medical malpractice, or is a workers' compensation claim, the contract must state that the fee is not set by law but is negotiable between attorney and client. Failure to comply with §6147 renders the agreement voidable at the client's option, and the attorney is then entitled to collect a reasonable fee. See sample form in Supp §1.17.

In *Charlie Sturgill Motor Co.*, TC Memo 1973–281, the Tax Court allowed a landowner to deduct as a business expense attorney's fees paid in an unsuccessful defense of a condemnation action. Although the land had been rented to another, renting property was not the landowner's primary business. In reaching its decision, however, the Tax Court relied on an earlier decision that was subsequently reversed in *Madden v Commissioner* (9th Cir 1975) 514 F2d 1149. See Supp §12.2.

For cases discussing the tax treatment of attorneys' fees awarded in condemnation cases, see Supp §12.2.

[§1.16] Fees in Event of Abandonment

Code of Civil Procedure §1255a has been repealed. The new sections covering abandonment and recovery of costs and disbursements are CCP §§1268.510 and 1268.610. For discussion of abandonment under the Eminent Domain Law (CCP §§1230.010–1273.050), see Supp §§8.31–8.33.

Under CCP §1268.610 (former CCP §1255a(c)), plaintiff generally re-imburses defendant for litigation expenses whenever (1) the proceeding is wholly or partially dismissed for any reason (the new section sets aside the rule of *City of Industry v Gordon* (1972) 29 CA3d 90, 105 CR 206, denying reimbursement on dismissal for failure to prosecute); or (2) defendant defeats plaintiff's right to take in whole or in part. CCP §1268.610.

In the case of a partial dismissal or defeat of part of the take, defendant cannot include in its expenses costs that would have been incurred in defending the remaining action. CCP §1268.610(b).

Reimbursement of defendant's litigation expenses when the complaint is amended to add to the property sought to be taken, rather than to reduce the take, is covered by CCP §1250.340.

The determination of the amount of attorneys' fees is within the discretion of the court. The court may consider a contingency fee contract in setting the amount, but it must give primary consideration to factors such as number of hours spent on the case, reasonable hourly rate of the attorney, difficulty of the issues involved, skill in presenting the issues, and the extent to which the litigation precluded other employment by the attorney. See *City of Oakland v Oakland Raiders* (1988) 203 CA3d 78, 249 CR 606, involving a successful challenge of the right to take (see Supp §6.6), in which the court set attorneys' fees by multiplying the number of hours devoted to the case by an hourly rate similar to those charged by top law firms in the geographic area and then raising the fees to account for factors such as complexity of the issues, the need for counsel to act quickly throughout the litigation, and deferral of fees, as well as the results obtained. See also *State v Meyer* (1985) 174 CA3d 1061, 1073, 220 CR 884, 891, and §8.33 for discussion of award of litigation expenses on abandonment.

[§1.17] Form: Letter Agreement

The following contract provisions are generally applicable to a contingency fee arrangement (see Supp §1.15) in a direct condemnation case, and they replace the form in Book §1.17. They may be used in a letter agreement form or in a formal contract.

This agreement is by and between _ _[name] _ _ (hereafter called "Client") and _ _[name] _ _, attorney at law (hereafter called "Attorney").

1. Client is the owner of real property (hereafter called "subject property"), described in Exhibit A attached and incorporated by reference in this agreement. This property is the subject of a condemnation action by _ _[name of condemnor] _ _ in _ _ _ _ _ _ _ County Superior Court, Case No. _ _ _ _, for a public project known as _ _ _ _ _ _ _ _.

Comment: If the condemnation action has not been filed before an attorney is retained, the language regarding the name of the case can be replaced by "This property is the subject of a declaration of necessity by _ _[*name of condemnor*]_ _" or other language generally describing the anticipated condemnation action.

2. Attorney agrees to represent Client in connection with this condemnation action for a contingency fee of _ _% of the difference between the total ultimate award that is obtained whether by trial or by settlement out of court and the highest offer in writing already made to Client by the condemning authority, which offer is in the amount of $_ _ _ _ _ _. However, if the case is settled before the 30-day period before the time first set for trial, the fee will be calculated at _ _% of the difference between the settlement figure and the aforesaid highest offer in writing made by the condemning authority. If no increase in value is obtained, Attorney is not entitled to any fee.

Comment: When the attorney is retained before an offer is made to the client by the condemnor, several options are available, depending on the amount of work anticipated by the attorney before the offer is made. Among those options are (1) an hourly rate for designated preliminary work to be converted to a prearranged contingency fee as soon as an offer is made, (2) a smaller contingency fee based on overall compensation, not the offer, or (3) if the offer is anticipated soon and there will be minimal involvement by the attorney, the contingency rate can be negotiated between the attorney and the client to be applied to a subsequent designated offer. A key factor in deciding how to handle this situation is whether the attorney's efforts can positively affect the pending offer from the condemnor.

The percentage amount for calculating a contingency fee depends on several factors: complexity of the case, anticipated dollar difference between condemnor and condemnee, number of issues or claims regarding compensation, and number of witnesses anticipated for trial.

There is no general rule of practice that calls for a two-step contingency rate as set forth in the form above. Many attorneys simply have one contingency rate. The suggested difference in percentage of contingency fee, depending on whether settlement occurs 30 days or more before the date first set for trial, is based on the following considerations: First, the law encourages parties to settle at least 30 days before trial. CCP §1250.410. See Supp §7.12A. Second, the law provides for an exchange of valuation data 40 days before trial. CCP §1258.220. See Supp §9.6. Third, the last 30 days before trial require intensive preparation for trial.

3. "Total ultimate award" is defined to include all compensation recovered, whether by judgment, settlement, or otherwise, by Client or any transferee, lienholder, lessee, or other person having or claiming an interest in the subject property, including any other asset or performance of work in lieu of monetary compensation for the taking or damaging of subject property by the condemning agency.

Comment: In a partial taking of the client's property, negotiations may result in construction of improvements, access openings, or other property rights to serve the remaining property instead of monetary compensation. Although a beneficiary of a deed of trust or lessee may share a portion of the compensation otherwise awarded to the owner, such subsequent apportionments of the award should not be deducted before calculating the attorney's fee. But a lessee's recovery of loss of goodwill for its business or compensation for equipment and machinery are not to be considered a part of the total ultimate award; such payments do not relate to compensation for the owner's property interest.

For discussion of CCP §1250.410 (formerly CCP §1249.3) on recovering litigation expenses, see Supp §1.9.

4. A lien is hereby granted and it is expressly agreed that this contract creates a lien to the extent of the percentage of attorneys' fees set out above against any claim, case, or cause of action and proceeds from any settlement or judgment, however obtained; Client hereby expressly assigns to Attorney said percentages of such money that may become due and payable in settlement of this matter or through judgment or otherwise. In order that Attorney may account fully and expediently, Client expressly gives Attorney the power of attorney to execute all complaints, claims, contracts, checks, settlements, compromises, releases, verifications, dismissal, drafts, orders, and deposits, or other similar documents, and hereby authorizes Attorney to pay all litigation expenses, legal and nonlegal costs, whether advanced or incurred, by them in handling this matter. No settlement shall be binding without Client's prior approval.

5. Payment of attorneys' fees set forth shall be made immediately on payment by the condemning authority of the proceeds of the judgment or settlement.

6. No retainer will be paid to Attorney.

Comment: A retainer may be appropriate in some complex cases, when, for example, an hourly rate is combined with a contingency fee.

7. The attorneys' fees set forth in this agreement relate only to obtaining additional compensation in this condemnation action. Any

other work done on behalf of Client involving subject property that does not relate to increasing the compensation will be charged separately.

8. If the court permits recovery of litigation expenses under CCP §1250.410, including attorneys' fees, it may not award all litigation expenses. If it does not award all litigation expenses, Attorney shall be entitled to the fee agreed to in this document, despite any amount awarded by the court as attorneys' fees.

9. Attorney may advance necessary court costs, such as filing fees, deposition costs, and court reporter's fees, which will then be billed to Client for reimbursement. These costs are reimbursable to Client by the condemning agency if the case goes to trial, and any reimbursement of such costs shall not be included in the total ultimate award.

10. Client is to pay all costs of appraisers, engineers, and other experts as well as related costs incurred in preparing the case and taking it through trial. These expenses shall not be deducted from the total ultimate award for the purpose of calculating a contingency fee. No appraiser or other expert will be hired without Client's consent, and no nonlegal costs in excess of $250 will be incurred without Client's prior approval.

11. This agreement covers Attorney's services through trial and judgment, but it does not relate to any appeal or retrial, if necessary. Thus, if there is an appeal, a further fee arrangement will be made for additional services.

Comment: See clause VII of the form in Supp §1.17A for an alternative treatment of services for a retrial or an appeal.

12. If there is an abandonment in whole or in part of the subject property, Client will be responsible for a reasonable fee (based on considerations of time spent and complexity of the case, although this is otherwise a contingency contract) for all legal services in regard to the condemnation. Attorney will seek to recover that fee and other expenses on Client's behalf from the condemning agency in accord with the provisions of CCP §1268.610 regarding recovery of fees and costs on abandonment.

Comment: This paragraph may specify either an hourly rate or a contingency fee. If a contingency fee is negotiated for abandonment, it should specify the owner's desire to retain the property. See *Glendora Community Redev. Agency v Demeter* (1984) 155 CA3d 465, 202 CR 389, which allowed an award of attorneys' fees based on a contingency fee contract specifically relating those fees to abandonment, when the trial court had considered other factors necessary to determine the reasonableness of the fees. However, the court noted that it was not bound by the fee agreement.

If Client chooses to discharge the Attorney before the conclusion of the case by settlement or judgment, Client immediately will pay attorney reasonable attorneys' fees for services rendered and costs incurred to date.

13. The fees recited in this agreement are not set by law but have been negotiated between Client and Attorney.

Comment: On contingency fees generally, see Bus & P C §6147. Although §6147 specifically states that it applies to fee contracts for the representation of a plaintiff on a contingency basis, the attorney representing a defendant in a direct condemnation action should include in the contingency fee contract (which must be in writing) a specific statement that the fee has been negotiated between the attorney and the client and is not set by law, as required by Bus & P C §6147(a)(4). See other required statements set out in Bus & P C §6147(a)(1)–(5).

Dated: _ _ _ _ _ _   _____
                                                 Client

Dated: _ _ _ _ _ _   _____
                                                 Attorney

Comment: Other provisions may be appropriate for this contract, depending on the circumstances of the case presented. For example, the attorney may elect to receive an hourly rate instead of a contingency fee if the attorney recommends a settlement but the client will not agree to it. When there are several property owners, they may be unable to agree on the settlement of the case or on hiring an expert. Thus, the contract may provide a manner in which to decide such questions by a majority vote.

If it is the client's desire to contest the public agency's right to take, an hourly rate contract for the efforts involved in that part of the litigation is appropriate and may be combined with the contingency fee contract relating to pursuing any increase in compensation for the property taken or damaged, or both.

In urban developed areas, or in areas where there is a history or suspicion of soil or groundwater contamination from the storage of petroleum products or hazardous materials, condemnors, either before filing the complaint or while litigation is pending, may undertake investigations to determine the existence of hazardous material within properties to be acquired. If hazardous materials are discovered in the subsurface, the condemnor may then seek an offset against the appraised value of the land to the extent of the required cleanup under federal and state laws, as well as local ordinances. See, *e.g.,* the Clean Water Act (33 USC §§1251–1387); Comprehensive Environmental Response Compensation and Liability Act (CERCLA) (42 USC §§9601–9675); Wat C §§13000–13999.16.

Becausee this type of investigation is not always undertaken before the initial offer of compensation to the property owner, if the issue is anticipated, it is advisable to provide, in the fee contract, a statement such as:

If the subject property is discovered to contain soil or groundwater contamination, the condemning authority may allege an offset to the fair market value of the property for the necessary cost of cleanup or restoration of the soil or groundwater condition. The current offer by the condemning agency does not reflect any such offset. Such contamination of the property would be a preexisting condition of the property and, accordingly, the base amount for calculating the contingency fee shall be adjusted downward to reflect any alleged offset. To defend against this claim within the context of the condemnation litigation, it will probably be necessary to hire experts in soils, geotechnical, and water resource engineering to investigate the site and review any study and recommended remedial program of the condemning authority.

This fee agreement does not cover any separate claim or action that may be commenced against a third party, such as an insurance carrier, neighboring property owner, tenant, or prior owner, who may be responsible for the contamination, nor does it cover the defense of any claim or action commenced by a third party against client.

Comment: When the condemnor has already deducted its estimated cost of cleanup from the offer of value, but will allow the owner to clean up any contamination and the owner is willing to do so, the fee contract can provide for upward adjustment of the base amount to calculate the contingency fee to the extent the agency lessens its claim of offset for work performed at the owner's expense. In this situation, the attorney may provide for an hourly rate separate from the contingency fee for overall compensation of the property taken to cover efforts to negotiate restoration of the property. Because the owner is expending money to remedy the contamination and thus reinstate the full measure of the condemnor's appraisal value for the property, the attorney should not calculate a contingency fee without recognizing the owner's efforts to reinstate the appraisal value.

Contamination of the condemned property presents the possibility of other issues, *i.e.,* insurance coverage, third party liability from either a predecessor in interest or a neighboring property, and deciding whether the remedial action relates to the ultimate development of the property that would occur in the open market, or the project itself. The condemnation attorney may wish to consult an environmental liability attorney for assistance. In some cases, it may be beneficial to separate the contamination issue from the compensation issue, if possibly, by a motion for bifurcation.

Although the agency may have estimated the cost of clean-up at the beginning of the lawsuit and made a corresponding deduction from its appraisal for determining probable compensation, these estimates can change during the preparation of the case for trial based on further site investigation and evaluation. Thus, in a fee contract that uses the initial deduction of the remedial work as a base for calculating the contingent fee, there should be language (as suggested in the above form) to change the base, if necessary. But, changing the base for computing the fee can work against the attorney if the attorney's efforts contribute to a downward adjustment. Some practitioners have taken the position that the most appropriate way to handle the fee issue in a condemnation case with contamination is to treat the cost of clean-up as a lien against the property. Accordingly, the fee contract is drawn to the final determination of the cost of clean-up as a required expense against the property's value, but this cost is not deducted from what is otherwise the property's fair market value for the purpose of calculating fees. In order to make this adjustment at trial, a special verdict identifying the value of the property with and without the remedial costs should be requested of the jury.

[§1.17A] Form: Attorney-Client Agreement for Inverse Condemnation

This agreement is by and between _ _ _ _ _ _ (here called "Client") and _ _ _ _ _ _, Attorney at Law (here called "Attorney").

1. Client is the owner of the real property (here called "subject property"), described in Exhibit A attached and incorporated by reference in this agreement;

2. The parties by means of this agreement desire to set forth the terms and conditions under which Attorney shall render legal services and Client shall pay Attorney's fees, costs, and expenses for legal services to recover for the taking of, damages to, or detriment to the economic value and marketability of the subject property by appropriate legal remedies, including inverse condemnation, resulting from actions by

_ _

_ _

and certain officials of these public entities, acting separately or in concert.

NOW, THEREFORE, Client and Attorney agree as follows:

I.   DEFINITIONS:

1. "Legal services" shall mean all work that, in the opinion of Attorney, is reasonable or necessary to represent Client's interests in this matter, including, but not limited to, preparation, negotiations, and trial.

2. "Total just compensation" shall mean the sum of all of the following items however obtained:

(1) The value of the interest in the subject property taken or damaged, including improvements;

(2) Severance damages, if any;

(3) Interest, if any;

(4) The fair market value of any property or other asset that Client may receive in lieu of or in addition to monetary compensation.

II.   ATTORNEY'S FEE:

Attorney shall receive as a fee _ _% of the total just compensation. The fees recited in this agreement are not set by law, but have been negotiated between Client and Attorney.

Comment: Inverse condemnation cases often involve difficult challenges to a government agency's activities. Particularly in cases challenging municipal land use regulation (see Supp §§13.22–13.22O), attorneys may choose to negotiate fees based on a combined hourly rate and a smaller contingency fee or only on an hourly rate.

See Bus & P C §6147 on the requirements for contingency fee contracts. Except in certain medical malpractice cases or workers' compensation cases, Bus & P C §6147 requires that the contingency fee contract with a plaintiff contain a statement that the fees have been negotiated. See Supp §1.15 for additional information on contingency fee contracts.

III.   PAYMENT OF COSTS:

Client shall pay all reasonable and necessary appraisal, engineering, and other related fees and costs incurred by Attorney in connection with the performance of this agreement. Attorney will advance legal costs as they are incurred in connection with this matter. Client will advance all nonlegal costs related to this matter. No appraiser, engineer, or other person shall be hired without Client's prior approval and no nonlegal costs in excess of $250 will be incurred without Client's prior approval.

IV. TIME OF PAYMENTS:

Payment of the Attorney's fee set forth in Paragraph II above will be made immediately on payment by the condemning authority of the proceeds of the judgment or settlement.

V. LIEN AND POWER OF ATTORNEY:

A lien is hereby granted, and it is expressly agreed and understood that this contract creates a lien to the extent of the percentage of Attorney's fees set out above against any claim, case, or cause of action and proceeds thereof and against any judgment or settlement, however obtained; and Client hereby expressly assigns to Attorney said percentages of any such money that may become due and payable in settlement of this matter or through judgment or otherwise. In order that Attorney may account fully and expediently, Client expressly gives to Attorney the power of attorney to execute all complaints, claims, contracts, checks, settlements, compromises, releases, verification, dismissals, drafts, orders, and deposits, or other similar documents, and hereby authorizes Attorney to pay all costs, both legal and nonlegal, advanced or incurred by them in the handling of this matter. No settlement shall be binding without Client's prior approval.

VI. REIMBURSEMENT OF COSTS:

Any reimbursement of costs, disbursements, and expenses made by the court pursuant to CCP Section 1036, if the action and inverse condemnation is successful, shall be paid to Client, after payment of Attorney's fees and reimbursement of any costs incurred by Attorney.

VII. RETRIAL OR APPEAL:

If it should become necessary to undertake or defend against an appeal the Attorney shall be paid, in addition to the contingent fees provided for above, an hourly rate of $_ _ _ _ _ _ per hour for time spent on any such appellate work. If there is a retrial, the contingent fee as set forth above in Paragraph II of this Agreement, shall continue to apply.

Comment: See clause 11 of the form in Supp §1.17 for an alternative treatment of services for a retrial or an appeal.

VIII. CLIENT COOPERATION:

Client agrees to provide Attorney with all information, data, and other forms of cooperation necessary for or convenient to the handling of this matter, including any and all other information that in the opinion of the Attorney is material or relevant. Client further agrees to appear as a witness on his own behalf as necessary and to employ such other witnesses as are, in Attorney's opinion, necessary to a successful resolution for Client.

IX. RETAINER:

No retainer will be paid to Attorney.

Comment: A retainer is appropriate when an hourly rate is combined with a contingency fee or when only an hourly rate is charged.

X. ASSOCIATION OF ATTORNEYS:

Attorney shall retain the right to associate other counsel for the purpose of preparing, negotiating, or trying this matter, provided, however, that other than as provided in this agreement there shall be no additional attorneys' fees paid by Client as a result of such association.

XI. AGREEMENT BENEFITS AND BINDS SUCCESSORS:

The provisions of this agreement shall inure to the benefit of and shall bind the heirs, administrators, executors, successors in interest, and assigns of Client.

XII. PRIOR SALE OF SUBJECT PROPERTY:

If the subject property is sold or transferred before completion of Attorney's representation of Client, Client agrees to pay Attorney a reasonable fee related to either the sale price of the subject property or the Attorney's efforts and results obtained for Client by Attorney as of the date of sale or transfer. Alternatively, Client agrees to arrange for the transferee to assume the obligations of Client herein.

XIII. DISCHARGE OF ATTORNEY

Client retains the right to discharge Attorney at any time and to discontinue any efforts toward pursuing this matter. But, if Client decides to discharge Attorney or discontinue pursuit of the matter before Attorney and Client have reached what they mutually agree is a final conclusion, Client will immediately pay Attorney reasonable attorney's fees and costs for services rendered and costs incurred to date. In no event shall a reasonable fee for services rendered be less than $_ _ _ _ _ _ per hour for all Attorney's time spent on the matter.

Dated: _ _ _ _ _ _

_____
Client

Dated: _ _ _ _ _ _

_____
Attorney

2

Attorney's Role in Determining Facts

OBTAINING INFORMATION FROM CLIENT

[§2.7] Conversations With Condemnor's Agents

Code of Civil Procedure §1242(b), which authorized condemning agencies to enter on property to make surveys, studies, and other investigations, has been repealed and replaced by CCP §1245.010.

[§2.9] Title

On implied dedication, see *County of Orange v Chandler-Sherman*

Corp. (1976) 54 CA3d 561, 126 CR 765, and *Richmond Ramblers Motorcycle Club v Western Title Guar. Co.* (1975) 47 CA3d 747, 121 CR 308. Both opinions limit *Gion v City of Santa Cruz* (cited in Book §2.9). The supreme court in *County of Los Angeles v Berk* (1980) 26 C3d 201, 212, 161 CR 742, 749, held that its decision in *Gion* merely restated and clarified well-established former law and could be retroactively applied to events giving rise to an implied dedication that occurred before the decision.

[§2.10] Mortgages; Deeds of Trust

For discussion of trust deeds and mortgages, see California Mortgage and Deed of Trust Practice (2d ed Cal CEB 1990). See also *Carson Redev. Agency v Adam* (1982) 136 CA3d 608, 186 CR 615, holding that the beneficiary under a deed of trust has a compensable interest in property under condemnation even though the underlying obligation has become barred by the statute of limitations.

The seller under a land-sales contract retains legal title to the property until the buyer completes the purchase and therefore executes a deed of trust secured by the seller's interest in the property. In distributing condemnation proceeds, if the beneficiary of a trust deed executed by the seller following a land-sales contract has notice of the land sale contract, the beneficiary is entitled only to an amount representing the seller's interest in the contract, not to the beneficiary's entire lien. *Alhambra Redev. Agency v Transamerica Fin. Serv.* (1989) 212 CA3d 1370, 261 CR 248.

[§2.11] Other Encumbrances

A building restriction favoring a landowner constitutes "property" within the meaning of Cal Const art I, §19 (former Cal Const art I, §14, was repealed on November 5, 1974); thus, whenever damage to that landowner from a violation of such a restriction results, compensation must be paid. *Southern Cal. Edison Co. v Bourgerie* (1973) 9 C3d 169, 107 CR 76. The court stated that its ruling applies whether the condemnor is a public or a private entity.

In condemnation cases, the courts use the same method of valuation for restrictive covenants and equitable servitudes as for appurtenant easements, *i.e.,* an analysis of the decrease in value of the dominant estate resulting from the taking of the easement. *Redevelopment Agency v Tobriner* (1984) 153 CA3d 367, 200 CR 364.

[§2.12A] Options

An option to purchase the condemned parcel is significant for two reasons. It can be introduced as an admission against interest with respect to the value of the property, but not as direct evidence. Evid C §§813(a)(2), 822(a)(2). It can also give rise to an apportionment of the judgment between the option holder and the defendant owner. *County of San Diego v Miller* (1975) 13 C3d 684, 693, 119 CR 491, 496. This decision was interpreted in a subsequent appeal of the same case after retrial. *County of San Diego v Miller* (1980) 102 CA3d 424, 162 CR 480; see Supp §10.12. Generally, if an unexercised option has expired and has not been renewed before a condemnation action is filed, the holder has no compensable property right, even if he maintained his interest through a lengthy planning process and a preacquisition bond election. *City of Walnut Creek v Leadership Hous. Sys.* (1977) 73 CA3d 611, 140 CR 690. However, the rule of that case does not preclude an option holder from seeking damages for abandonment of the option because of unreasonable precondemnation conduct; he or she must show a de facto taking during the option period. *Toso v City of Santa Barbara* (1980) 101 CA3d 934, 949, 162 CR 210, 218.

Note that when property that is the subject of a real estate sales agreement providing for a broker's commission is taken by eminent domain before close of escrow, the broker is not entitled to a commission. The broker's right to compensation depends on performance of the sales contract. *City of Turlock v Zagaris* (1989) 209 CA3d 189, 256 CR 902.

[§2.14] Improvements; Proximity to Service of Summons

The property taken must be valued as improved. CCP §1263.210 (former CCP §1249.1, repealed operative July 1, 1976). Under former CCP §1249, improvements made after service of summons could not be taken into account in determining compensation. Code of Civil Procedure §1263.240 continues this general rule but allows exceptions when the improvement was made (a) by a public utility for its service, (b) with the written consent of the condemnor, or (c) under a court order after a noticed hearing balancing the respective hardships of defendant and plaintiff. But see *City of Santa Barbara v Petras* (1971) 21 CA3d 506, 98 CR 635, in which the court ruled that former CCP §1249 did not preclude compensation for improvements made in good faith after service of summons when they were made under a preexisting contractual obligation (a lease in this case).

[§2.15] Property Taxes

Under the recommendation of the California Law Revision Commission, the provisions of the Code of Civil Procedure and the Revenue and Taxation Code governing the apportionment, payment, and cancellation of ad valorem property taxes in condemnation proceedings have been revised, effective January 1, 1980. See Supp §10.15 for discussion of key provisions.

In June 1982 the voters adopted a proposition amending Cal Const art XIIIA to provide that purchase of replacement "comparable property" for land taken by eminent domain proceedings, by acquisition of a public agency, or by governmental action that has resulted in a judgment of inverse condemnation is not a "change in ownership" for the purpose of readjusting the base for property tax valuation. This measure applies to affected properties only for property tax rolls established on or after March 1, 1983. Revenue and Taxation Code §68 further implements the rule.

On property taxes generally, see 1 California Taxes, chap 1 (2d ed Cal CEB 1988).

[§2.16] Relocation of Home or Business

The courts have shown a willingness to liberally construe the displaced person language of the Relocation Assistance Act (Govt C §§7260–7276) discussed in Supp §4.53. For example, a business tenant displaced by a 30-day notice of termination after the public agency has purchased real property for public use is entitled to the same relocation benefits as a tenant displaced as a result of acquisition under a condemnation action. *Superior Strut & Hanger Co. v Port of Oakland* (1977) 72 CA3d 987, 140 CR 515. An owner of a business qualified as "displaced," for purposes of entitlement to relocation benefits, when he purchased replacement rental property after initiation of the condemnation action but before the proceedings were completed. *Mitakis v Department of Gen. Servs.* (1983) 149 CA3d 684, 197 CR 142.

Under Govt C §7260(c), displaced persons include those persons displaced as a result of an owner participation agreement, or acquisition carried out by a private person for, or in connection with, a public use, *i.e.,* redevelopment.

[§2.20] Vegetation, Soil, Mineral Deposits, and Geologic Considerations

Code of Civil Procedure §1249.2 has been repealed. The defendant has the right to grow and harvest crops and retain the profit up to the time the property is actually taken. CCP §1263.250.

The Alquist-Priolo Special Studies Zones Act (Pub Res C §§2621–2630; formerly called the Alquist-Priolo Geologic Hazard Zones Act) requires the state geologist to map "appropriately wide special studies zones to encompass all potentially and recently active traces of the San Andreas, Calaveras, Hayward, and San Jacinto Faults" and other active faults. Pub Res C §2622. These maps not only provide geologic information but are also the basis for regulation of new real estate development in accord with policies established by the State Mining and Geology Board. Pub Res C §2623.

Defects in the subsurface of the property may exist because of soil or groundwater contamination from the on-site storage of hazardous materials. Federal and state laws require curative work for such a problem, and the condemning agency, if hazardous materials are discovered in the soil or groundwater, may contend that the cost of cleanup should be offset against value. See generally the Clean Water Act (33 USC §§1251–1387); Porter-Cologne Water Quality Control Act (Wat C §§13000–13999.16); Real Property Hazardous Substance Release Disclosure Requirements (Health & S C §25359.7).

[§2.20A] Environmental Factors

The California Environmental Quality Act of 1970 (CEQA) (Pub Res C §§21000–21176) re-established a broad policy to regulate both public and private activities found to affect the quality of the environment. *Friends of Mammoth v Board of Supervisors* (1972) 8 C3d 247, 104 CR 761. The environment is defined as "the physical conditions which exist within the area which will be affected by a proposed project, including land, air, water, minerals, flora, fauna, noise, objects of historic or aesthetic significance." Pub Res C §21060.5. An environmental impact report is required on any project that public agencies, boards, or commissions propose to carry out or approve, when that project may have a significant effect on the environment. Pub Res C §21100; see Guidelines for Implementation of the California Environmental Quality Act of 1970 (14 Cal Code Regs §§15000–15387).

Environmental impact reports for the subject property regarding any prior development proposal, neighboring properties, or the project giving rise to the condemnation action may provide valuable information about the character and potential of the land. For discussion of the physical nature of a parcel and the question of highest and best use, see Book §4.8.

For further discussion of CEQA, see California Zoning Practice Supp §§3.81–3.87 (Cal CEB).

OTHER MEANS OF OBTAINING FACTS

[§2.25] Condemnor

See §7.4 on the condemnor's dual responsibilities in negotiating the price of the property.

[§2.26] Discovery Procedures

The procedure for exchange of valuation data remains substantially the same under CCP §§1258.210–1258.300, but is stated more simply than in former CCP §§1272.01–1272.09.

The discovery procedures applicable to actions filed after July 1, 1987, may be restricted by the court, and abuses of the procedures are subject to sanctions. CCP §2019. The new civil discovery rules also place new limits on when discovery must be completed (CCP §2024) and the allowable number of specially prepared interrogatories (CCP §2030(c)). Furthermore, a party may demand that the other party allow for entry on the land for the inspection, measurement, surveying, photographing, testing, or sampling of that land. CCP §2031(a)(3).

The complete discovery rules, as revised, are contained in CCP §§2016–2036 and Cal Rules of Ct 331–337. Former CCP §§2002–2036, which controlled discovery when the Book was written, have been repealed.

For further information, see Civil Discovery Practice in California (Cal CEB 1988).

3

Selection of Valuation Experts

[§3.1] NEED FOR EXPERT TESTIMONY

Former CCP §1267, limiting the number of appraisal witnesses, was not reenacted in the Eminent Domain Law (CCP §§1230.010–1273.050). But the court, under Evid C §723, retains the general right to control the number of experts called to testify.

FACTORS TO CONSIDER IN SELECTING PROFESSIONAL APPRAISER

[§3.6] Professional Appraisal Societies

Several appraisal associations mentioned in Book §3.6 have new addresses:

American Institute of Real Estate Appraisers
430 N. Michigan Ave.
Chicago, IL 60611–4088

American Society of Appraisers
P.O. Box 17265
Washington, DC 20041

American Society of Farm Managers and Rural Appraisers
950 S. Cherry St.
Suite 106
Denver, CO 80222

American Society of Real Estate Counselors
430 N. Michigan Ave.
Chicago, IL 60611

International Right of Way Association
(formerly American Right of Way Association)
(Address and telephone number unavailable to CEB as of September 24, 1990.)

Society of Real Estate Appraisers
225 N. Michigan Ave.
Suite 724
Chicago, IL 60601

In 1986 California adopted CC §§1922–1922.14, operative January 1, 1988, providing for the certification of appraisals, setting standards for the appraisals, and imposing certain duties on appraisers. Under the new law an appraiser accepting an assignment for a certified appraisal is prohibited from accepting a contingency fee on reporting a pre-established conclusion. The legislation generally protects investors in mortgages, trust deeds, and other interests in real property from deceptive and misleading appraisals. As special legislation, the Eminent Domain Law (CCP §§1230.010–1273.050) does not require that an appraiser testifying in a condemnation case prepare a certified appraisal.

HIRING APPRAISER

[§3.8] Fee Arrangements

Code of Civil Procedure §1249.3 has been repealed and replaced by CCP §1250.410, which provides that defendant's litigation expenses, including reasonable appraisal fees, are reimbursable in a direct condemnation action when necessarily incurred to protect defendant's interest, provided plaintiff's final offer was unreasonable and defendant's final demand was reasonable. CCP §1250.410; see *Community Redev. Agency v Friedman* (1977) 76 CA3d 188, 143 CR 160. Regarding posttrial motion for recovery of cost and litigation fees, see Supp §10.23A.

Reasonable legal, appraisal, and engineering fees are recoverable as part of costs, disbursements, and expenses in inverse condemnation actions when the property owner obtains an award or settlement. CCP §1036 (former CCP §1246.3); see discussion in Supp §13.30.

The court in *Holtz v San Francisco BART Dist.* (1976) 17 C3d 648, 131 CR 646, held that CCP §1036 (former CCP §1246.3) allows recovery of attorney's and expert's fees in a successful inverse condemnation action only when there is a taking of the property or a property interest. The statute does not apply to damage cases, but the court decided in *Holtz* that loss of lateral support was a taking and not a damaging of property. The statutory phrase "taking of any interest in real property" encompasses lesser interferences with property rights than the concept of "taking" within the meaning of Cal Const art I, §19. See also *Jones v People ex rel Dep't of Transp.* (1978) 22 C3d 144, 148 CR 640.

Appellate courts recognize that the trial judge has considerable discretion in determining the amount of fees under CCP §1036. See *City of Los Angeles v Waller* (1979) 90 CA3d 766, 154 CR 12.

Litigation expenses are allowed on abandonment. CCP §§1268.510, 1268.610 (former CCP §1255a).

[§3.9] Form: Appraisal Agreement

Renumber paragraph 6 in the Book §3.9 as paragraph 7 and insert the following:

6. Any award of appraisal fees pursuant to CCP Section 1250.410 shall be paid directly to _ _[name of client]_ _. _ _[Name of appraiser]_ _ shall be entitled to the fee stated in paragraph 4 of this agreement notwithstanding any such award.

Comment: For discussion of CCP §1250.410 (former CCP §1249.3), see Supp §1.9.

[§3.10] Court-Appointed Appraisers

Code of Civil Procedure §1266.2 was repealed. The former statute required that fees be established according to a community standard, which limited the court in obtaining a qualified expert if there was no expert available in the community. See 12 Cal L Rev'n Comm'n Reports 2100 (1974).

4

Just Compensation

PART ONE: BASIC CONSIDERATIONS AND APPROACHES TO VALUATION

[§4.1] JUST COMPENSATION STANDARD: FAIR MARKET VALUE

Code of Civil Procedure §1263.320(a) codified existing case law relating to fair market value but omitted any reference to "the open market" (see *Sacramento S. R.R. v Heilbron,* cited in Book §4.1). This change is intended to assure that the standard applies to special purpose properties. Comment to CCP §1263.320. Code of Civil Procedure §1263.320(b) allows any just and equitable method of valuation in cases in which there is no relevant market. See *Redevelopment Agency v First Christian Church* (1983) 140 CA3d 690, 189 CR 749; *City of Commerce v National Starch & Chem. Corp.* (1981) 118 CA3d 1, 173 CR 176; *City of Pleasant Hill v First Baptist Church* (1969) 1 CA3d 384, 82 CR 1, regarding valuation of special purpose properties.

For the purpose of valuation, neither the court nor the appraiser may consider the tax benefits of a particular transaction. *City of Los Angeles v Tilem* (1983) 142 CA3d 694, 191 CR 229. The court stated that fair market value cannot be based on specific arrangements, such as a lease-option agreement, between private parties and on benefits that may incidentally result from such arrangements, reasoning that market value does not depend on the personal worth of the property's owner or his personal relationship to the property taken.

To determine market values, a party need not show the existence of an actual seller and buyer or market, only of potential sellers and buyers in a potential market. *South Bay Irrig. Dist. v California-American Water Co.* (1976) 61 CA3d 944, 970, 133 CR 166, 184 (valuation of property of privately owned waterworks systems operating in public utility).

Compensation cannot be based on a speculative projected use for the property. *PG&E v Zuckerman* (1987) 189 CA3d 1113, 1146, 234 CR 630, 651. It is not proper to value property based on capitalizing a hypothetical business. But when a particular use can be shown to be reasonable, the property can be valued on the basis of rental value for that use and the use does not yet have to be established on the property. *People ex rel Dep't of Water Resources v Andresen* (1987) 193 CA3d 1144, 238 CR 826.

DETERMINATION OF FAIR MARKET VALUE AND HIGHEST AND BEST USE

Enhancement and Blight Due to Project Impact

[§4.5] "Probability of Inclusion" Test for Enhancement

In *Merced Irrig. Dist. v Woolstenhulme,* cited in Book §4.5, the court advised that the trial judge should conduct an inquiry in chambers into the date of "probable inclusion" and make an early determination on the issue. Without this determination, the trial court cannot properly determine the admissibility of sales offered as comparable to the condemned property and will find it impossible to devise comprehensible instructions to "explain to the jury which 'enhanced value' is to be included in just compensation and which is to be excluded."

Following that direction, BAJI No. 11.77 (rev 1986) offers the following jury instructions when the court finds that at the time the plans for the proposed project first became public, it was not probable that the subject property would be taken for the public improvement:

In determining the fair market value of the property, you may not include any change caused by the proposed improvement [that is, the use which the plaintiff is to make of the property]. [However, you must include any increase in the market value of said property caused by the proposed improvement that occurred before _ _[date]_ _.]

[You may not include any change in value because the property is being taken by eminent domain proceedings, that is, any change based on speculation as to what the plaintiff ultimately may be required to pay in this proceeding.]

[You may not include any change in value because of any preliminary action of the plaintiff relating to the taking of the property, such as _ _ _ _ _ _ _.]

The Use Note for this instruction indicates that only the portion germane to the case should be used at trial.

Whenever a public project has separate units (see Book §4.6), the court must clearly describe the project that may produce enhancement.

Following *Woolstenhulme,* the court in *City of Los Angeles v Retlaw Enters.* (1976) 16 C3d 473, 128 CR 436, ruled that a trial court could properly admit a sale of the property occurring six months after the property's probable inclusion in the project if the court also instructed the jury to disregard the sale price to the extent that it reflected noncompensable project enhancement. The inadmissibility of a sale of property after the filing of lis pendens (Evid C §815) was distinguished from the determination of the date of probable inclusion; the court held that the latter does not rise "to the level of *record* notice." 16 C3d at 484, 128 CR at 443.

Code of Civil Procedure §1263.330 provides that fair market value is determined as if the property's value had not been enhanced or reduced by:

(a) The project for which the property is taken,

(b) The eminent domain proceeding in which the property is taken, and

(c) Any preliminary actions of the plaintiff relating to the taking of the property.

Further expanding on *Woolstenhulme* and CCP §1263.330, in *City of Los Angeles v Decker* (1977) 18 C3d 860, 869, 135 CR 647, 652, the court ruled that if airport parking is the highest and best use of the property *"in the hands of defendant and not as a part of the project,"* defendant owner is entitled to present evidence to that effect (emphasis in original). Although the property was being condemned for airport expansion, the property owner was not precluded from showing that the highest and best use of the property was the same as proposed by the project.

The court cited the traditional rule that the defendant has the burden of establishing the reasonable probability under the zoning restrictions that private developers would put the property to such use. However, the court also advised the trial court that under then-new CCP §1260.210 it was no longer appropriate to instruct the jury that the defendant has the burden of proof on compensation. See §9.19 regarding burden of proof.

A disused quarry with mineral resources being taken by the state for use of the rock in the quarry to repair two dams could be valued on the basis of its highest and best use as a quarry rather than as grazing land. Although the *Woolstenhulme* rule of project enhancement applies to the prospects of condemnation, it does not preclude the expectation that the state would use the quarry from time to time on a temporary basis for dam repairs. The quarry was used in this fashion previously by the state, the quarry was in close proximity to the dams, and repairs were likely. But it was not proper to present evidence of the value of the rock to be used by the state in its dam repair. Here, the value could be determined by looking at market demand and average market price for the rock. *People ex rel Dep't of Water Resources v Andresen* (1987) 193 CA3d 1144, 238 CR 826.

[§4.6] Separate Public Project

In *Parker v City of Los Angeles* (1974) 44 CA3d 556, 118 CR 687, it was not necessary to allocate damages between the units and phases of a taking (airport runways), because the difference in the effects was minimal.

[§4.7] Effect of Blight on Value

In *Klopping v City of Whittier* (1972) 8 C3d 39, 104 CR 1, cited in Book §4.7, the court held that "a condemnee must be provided with an opportunity to demonstrate that: (1) the public authority acted improperly either by unreasonably delaying eminent domain action following an announcement of intent to condemn or by other unreasonable conduct prior to condemnation; and (2) as a result of such action the property in question suffered a diminution in market value." 8 C3d at 52, 104 CR at 11.

But in determining market value, the trier of fact should disregard not only the fact of filing of the condemnation action but also the value-depressing effect of the condemnor's actions, even in the absence of unreasonable activity. "*Klopping* made unreasonable or oppressive conduct a condition to the recovery of damage caused by precondemnation activity" in an inverse condemnation action in order not to jeopardize proper planning for a project. *Orange County Flood Control Dist. v Sunny Crest Dairy, Inc.* (1978) 77 CA3d 742, 755, 143 CR 803, 810.

In *Orange County,* the court traced *Klopping* back to one of its predecessors, *Buena Park School Dist. v Metrim Corp.* (1959) 176 CA2d 255, 1 CR 250, to reaffirm that value should be determined without regard to the filing of the action and the steps leading toward it, whether reasonable or not. Here, the condemnation action taking part of the land made it uneconomical to continue a cash-and-carry dairy business on the property. The property owner was allowed to base the property's value on this prior use as the highest and best use, even though the use no longer existed on the date of value. Similarly, in *Metrim,* the condemnation action precluded the recording of a final subdivision map, but the owner was allowed to show the value of the land as lots in the process of subdivision and near completion.

The court in *Redevelopment Agency v Del-Camp Invs.* (1974) 38 CA3d 836, 842, 113 CR 762, 767, held that the trial court did not prejudicially prevent the property owner from showing that the redevelopment project had a depressing effect on values when (1) the appraisers for both sides agreed on the principal comparable sale, (2) no testimony was offered to show that the sale was tainted by the project, (3) there was no indication that any appraiser used depressed or enhanced values in applying the income approach (see Book §4.44), and (4) there was no showing that any appraiser had based his opinion on actual rentals.

Code of Civil Procedure §1263.330 provides that the project, the condemnation action, or any preliminary steps of the condemnor relating to taking the property shall not affect compensation. See BAJI No. 11.77, quoted in Supp §4.5.

[§4.7A] Precondemnation Damages

Klopping v City of Whittier (1972) 8 C3d 39, 104 CR 1, was an inverse condemnation action permitting recovery of precondemnation damages (loss of rental income), when the owner showed that the condemnor excessively delayed bringing its condemnation action. See generally Supp §13.21. Such damages may be asserted in a direct condemnation action as well.

On the basis of *Klopping,* BAJI No. 11.79 (rev 1986) provides the following instruction:

In determining fair market value, you must disregard any decrease in market value caused by the likelihood that it would be acquired for the public improvement.

[However, because the plaintiff excessively delayed the commencement of this action following an announcement of intent to condemn subject property, you shall include in your verdict [the amount of defendant's loss of rental income from the subject property, if any, due to such delay] [the additional amount, if any, the subject property would have been worth on the date of valuation but for such delay].]

The Use Note for this instruction states that it will require revision to spell out unreasonable conduct of the condemnor within the *Klopping* rule other than excessive delay in commencing the action following the public announcement of intent to condemn. In *Redevelopment Agency v Contra Costa Theatre, Inc.* (1982) 135 CA3d 73, 79, 185 CR 159, 163, the court held that whether there has been unreasonable delay by the condemnor is a question for the court and not the jury.

Note that BAJI No. 11.79 (rev 1986) refers only to loss of rental income and would thus need revision when specifying other losses.

For discussion of *Klopping* and condemnation blight, see Kanner, *Condemnation Blight: Just How Just Is Just Compensation?* 48 Notre Dame Law 765 (1973).

When precondemnation liability is demonstrated, the measure of damages can include cost of repairs, loss of use, lost rents, lost profits, or increased operating expenses pending repairs. *City of Los Angeles v Tilem* (1983) 142 CA3d 694, 191 CR 229.

To seek *Klopping* precondemnation damages, the owner must plead special damage (*Richmond Redev. Agency v Western Title Guar. Co.* (1975) 48 CA3d 343, 122 CR 434; see Supp §8.18A) caused by the delay in effecting condemnation and present proof of its depressing effect on the property (*City of Los Angeles v Lowensohn* (1976) 54 CA3d 625, 127 CR 417; *Redevelopment Agency v Del-Camp Invs.* (1974) 38 CA3d 836, 113 CR 762). Precondemnation damages for the difference between the rental value of homes unaffected by the airport project and their rental value affected by that project may not be awarded when there is no evidence that any of the homeowners in the lawsuit intended or attempted to rent their homes either before or after the adoption of the project. *City of Fresno v Shewmake* (1982) 129 CA3d 907, 181 CR 451. Likewise, when property is held for investment until the time its value increases, there is no de facto taking absent proof by the landowners that the condemnor's conduct affected the properties' market value. *City of Los Angeles v Property Owners* (1982) 138 CA3d 114, 187 CR 667.

In *Lowensohn*, precondemnation damages in the form of holding costs of taxes and insurance were disallowed when the proof failed to show that the delay interfered with any use of the subject property.

However, in *Stone v City of Los Angeles* (1975) 51 CA3d 987, 124 CR 822 (an inverse condemnation action that was consolidated with a subsequent direct action), carrying expenses were allowed. The award of full market value in the direct condemnation award did not preclude damages for loss of use caused by the delay.

In *City of Los Angeles v Monahan* (1976) 55 CA3d 846, 127 CR 763, the property owners instituted an inverse condemnation case for damages resulting from airport operations. Later, the public agency filed a direct action and the property owners stipulated to proceed under the direct action and waive all claims in inverse condemnation. The court of appeal said that this stipulation might waive any precondemnation damages, but it recognized that the stipulation preceded the judicial recognition in *Klopping* of precondemnation damages. Consequently, the owners could not have intentionally relinquished a known right. Nonetheless, factually the case did not concern precondemnation damages, but a de facto taking. The loss of value to the properties "was due entirely to the adverse effect of jet operations at the Los Angeles International Airport and such damages in inverse condemnation" had been waived in converting the case to a direct taking. 55 CA3d at 853, 127 CR at 767.

The precondemnation actions of a redevelopment agency in declaring the area blighted and subject to condemnation, acquiring and demolishing buildings near the subject property, boarding up other nearby buildings, and closing streets in the vicinity gave rise to an inverse condemnation cause of action in federal court based on a de facto taking. *Eleopoulos v Richmond Redev. Agency* (ND Cal 1972) 351 F Supp 63; see §13.21. See also *Garland v City of St. Louis* (8th Cir 1979) 596 F2d 784; *Richmond Elks Hall Ass'n v Richmond Redev. Agency* (9th Cir 1977) 561 F2d 1327. But see *Sayre v City of Cleveland* (6th Cir 1974) 493 F2d 64, in which the court held that mere inclusion of property in a general neighborhood renewal plan does not constitute a taking even though it results in a decrease in property value; and *Smith v State* (1975) 50 CA3d 529, 123 CR 745, in which the court found the delay caused by public hearings and ongoing environmental studies for a proposed freeway reasonable. See also *Elgin Capital Corp. v County of Santa Clara* (1975) 57 CA3d 687, 129 CR 376.

The court in *Selby Realty Co. v City of San Buenaventura* (1973) 10 C3d 110, 109 CR 799, held that mere enactment of a general plan for future development of an area, indicating potential public streets through plaintiff's land, does not amount to inverse condemnation. In *Selby,* the county and city adopted a joint area general plan under Govt C §§65300–65651 (see §4.12). The plan contained a traffic circulation element showing an extension of a city street through the property owner's land, which was zoned multiple residential. When the owner applied to the city for a building permit to construct an apartment complex on its property, the city denied the permit because the owner refused to dedicate the extension of the street shown on the general plan.

In *Selby* the supreme court did not find the *Klopping* rule of unreasonable conduct to apply. A general plan is necessary for orderly community progress and growth, and it is subject to alteration or abandonment. Nonetheless, although a cause of action in inverse condemnation was not stated, the court allowed the plaintiff to proceed under administrative mandamus (CCP §1094.5) to reach plaintiff's claim that the city refused to issue the permit unless plaintiff complied with an assertedly invalid condition. See §4.64 regarding public power to require dedication.

The *Selby* rule was followed in *Dale v City of Mountain View* (1976) 55 CA3d 101, 127 CR 520, in which a golf course under lease until the year 2011 was found not to be inversely condemned by land use designation as open space on a general plan map. The mandate that zoning be consistent with the general plan (Govt C §65860) may now require courts to examine evidence of the precision of the general plan, its implementation, and the probability of amendment to answer whether the plan is exacting enough to constitute a taking. See Supp §4.12. At the time *Dale* was decided, a charter city was exempt from the requirements of Govt C §65860 under Govt C §65803. See 55 CA3d at 108 n5, 127 CR at 524 n5. Now §65860 has been amended to require that charter cities with a population of two million or more, *i.e.,* Los Angeles, make their pre-1979 ordinances consistent with the general plan of the city by July 1, 1982.

Relying on *Selby,* the court in *Smith v State, supra,* held that a freeway plan did not constitute a compensable taking, because it was still subject to modifications. Likewise, under Selby there is no compensable taking when property included in a city's open space plan is neither condemned nor committed to development, pending results of a bond election to acquire the property. *City of Walnut Creek v Leadership Hous. Sys.* (1977) 73 CA3d 611, 140 CR 690. See also *Toso v City of Santa Barbara* (1980) 101 CA3d 934, 162 CR 210, which held, relying on *Agins v City of Tiburon* (1979) 24 C3d 266, 157 CR 372 (see discussion of *Agins* and subsequent developments in case law in Supp §13.22B), that a public hearing concerning possible acquisition, the placing on the ballot of an advisory measure concerning the purchase of the property, and the failure to rezone the property did not amount to unreasonable precondemnation activities. Nor was the denial of a use permit, at the same time that general and redevelopment plans had been drafted and negotiations were initiated for acquisition, sufficient to prove precondemnation damages. *Redevelopment Agency v Contra Costa Theatre, Inc.* (1982) 135 CA3d 73, 185 CR 159.

A showing that the agency's conduct went beyond mere general planning is not enough to state a cause of action. The claimant must also show that obstacles were placed in plaintiff's path regarding the use of the land. *Jones v City of Los Angeles* (1979) 88 CA3d 965, 972, 152 CR 256, 261. In *Briggs v State ex rel Dep't of Parks & Recreation* (1979) 98 CA3d 190, 159 CR 390, the denial of a development permit by the State Coastal Commission was held to comply with that agency's statutory mandate, and correspondence to the commission from the State Director of Parks stating his department's interest in the property was only an assignment of priority. See also *Mira Dev. Corp. v City of San Diego* (1988) 205 CA3d 1201, 252 CR 825 (writ of mandate case regarding refusal to rezone, discussing inverse condemnation cases), holding there was no abuse of discretion by a municipality that denied a zoning application to change the designation from single family to multifamily residential for property under consideration for acquisition as a city park.

When the state went beyond the announcement of a freeway plan and denied the property owners the right to subdivide the property by depriving them of the necessary access to local streets, the court found a taking in *Jones v People ex rel Dep't of Transp.* (1978) 22 C3d 144, 148 CR 640.

Acting under Str & H C §100.2, which forbids any road from opening into a freeway without approval of the California Highway Commission, the local legislative body refused to approve a subdivision map that provided for access through the proposed freeway route. Although the route was later abandoned (after trial court judgment in favor of plaintiffs), the property owners were entitled to precondemnation damages because of the showing that the lack of access prevented development of the land. The court based its ruling on the denial of access and declined to decide whether the application of *Klopping* required that the legislative body first adopt a resolution of condemnation. 22 C3d at 151, 148 CR at 644. In *People ex rel Dep't of Pub. Works v Peninsula Enters.* (1979) 91 CA3d 332, 356, 153 CR 895, 908, the court held that direct and special interference creating precondemnation damages can occur even without a formal resolution of condemnation.

In *County of Los Angeles v Smith* (1976) 55 CA3d 749, 127 CR 666, the court refused to extend *Klopping* to a claimed threat of future temporary interruption of access from the remainder property to an adjoining street during construction of the improvement. This threat differed from the future condemnation cloud of *Klopping,* in which total destruction of any intervening use was threatened. See chap 5 on severance damages.

Even when unreasonable conduct is shown, unless there is a definitive interference with the use of land, damages cannot be awarded. In *City of Los Angeles v Waller* (1979) 90 CA3d 766, 778, 154 CR 12, 19, the appellate court refused to overturn a jury determination that appellants did not sustain damages when vacant land remained so and there was no showing of interference with the highest and best use of that land pending condemnation. To show inverse condemnation, it must be shown that obstacles were placed in the path of the development of the land.

When there is no assurance that property will in fact be taken, there cannot be unreasonable delay. *Johnson v State* (1979) 90 CA3d 195, 153 CR 185; *Jones v City of Los Angeles* (1979) 88 CA3d 965, 971, 152 CR 256, 262.

In *Taper v City of Long Beach* (1982) 129 CA3d 590, 181 CR 169, the city unreasonably dragged out the negotiations, progressively reduced its offers, and unreasonably delayed starting an eminent domain action, while at the same time the city manager stated on several occasions that the city intended to acquire the land and would not permit the property owner to develop and use the property, even though there was a 1963 agreement between the city and the owner that would have permitted development. The court held that the city's conduct was more than general land use planning and gave rise to a claim of precondemnation damages. However, the court held that the period of time during which the property owner was deprived of the right to use the property was not so protracted as to be considered permanent and result in a de facto taking. For discussions of de facto taking, see Book §4.7 and Supp §13.21.

Former CCP §1243.1, discussed in Book §4.7, concerning precondemnation activities, has been modified and replaced by CCP §1245.260. The new statute specifies that a claim is not required, but provides for a statute of limitations of one year after the six months given the public entity to implement its resolution of necessity by condemnation. Although the statute restricts the period for which damages may be claimed, it does not preclude introducing all of the agency's acts (including those before the beginning of that period) into evidence to show unreasonable conduct. *Jones v City of Los Angeles* (1979) 88 CA3d 965, 970, 152 CR 256, 260.

Precondemnation delay damages generally do not continue to accrue after the time the condemnor files the action. The period of delay ends with the filing of the action, at which time the agency is no longer engaged in the type of unreasonable behavior that produces damages under *Klopping*. Further damages for litigation delay may be awarded in those rare instances when the condemning agency has purposely and in bad faith pursued an unconscionably dilatory course of action in its conduct of the litigation. *People ex rel Dep't of Pub. Works v Peninsula Enters.* (1979) 91 CA3d 332, 359, 153 CR 895, 910.

A condemnee may not allege delay damages for the first time in a memorandum of costs after the condemnor has filed an abandonment of its condemnation action. *State v Meyer* (1985) 174 CA3d 1061, 220 CR 884.

Highest and Best Use

[§4.8] Physical Nature of Parcel

The California Environmental Quality Act (CEQA, Pub Res C

§§21000–21176) requires an environmental impact report (EIR) for any proposed development that might have a significant impact on the environment when the proposed project requires a permit or similar entitlement for use by a public agency. See Pub Res C §§21065(c), 21100–21161; *Friends of Mammoth v Board of Supervisors* (1972) 8 C3d 247, 104 CR 761. CEQA, if applicable to the project, may raise new questions concerning the physical nature of subject property when considered for its highest and best use.

The requirements of an EIR subject the project to a searching inquiry of its own physical nature and its interrelationship to the surrounding environment. Public Resources Code §21100 states that an EIR must set forth detailed information on the following:

(a) The significant environmental effects of the proposed project.

(b) Any significant environmental effects that cannot be avoided if the project is implemented.

(c) Mitigation measures proposed to minimize the significant environmental effects, including, but not limited to, measures to reduce wasteful, inefficient, and unnecessary consumption of energy.

(d) Alternatives to the proposed project.

(e) The relationship between local short-term uses of man's environment and the maintenance and enhancement of long-term productivity.

(f) Any significant irreversible environmental changes that would be involved in the proposed project should it be implemented.

(g) The growth-inducing impact of the proposed project.

The report must also contain a statement briefly indicating the reasons for determining that various effects of a project are not significant and consequently have not been discussed in detail in the EIR. For purposes of this section, any significant effect on the environment must be limited to substantial, or potentially substantial, adverse changes in physical conditions that exist within the area as defined in Pub Res C §21060.5.
See also Guidelines for Implementation of the California Environmental Quality Act of 1970 (14 Cal Code Regs §§15000–15387); Supp §2.20A. For a more complete discussion of EIRs, see California Zoning Practice Supp §§3.81–3.86 (Cal CEB).

The court in *Smith v State* (1975) 50 CA3d 529, 123 CR 745, found that delay in implementing a public project caused in part by ongoing studies of environmental impact was neither unreasonable nor evidence of a de facto taking. See Supp §§4.7, 13.21.

[§4.9] Future Adaptability

When Caltrans condemned a strip of land that was part of a railroad's right-of-way, and the act, under which the railroad had acquired the property, allowed it to use the land for any beneficial use, the property was to be valued on the basis of its potential use as a comprehensive transportation corridor and not just as the existing double track operation. *People ex rel Dep't of Transp. v Southern Pac. Transp. Co.* (1978) 84 CA3d 315, 148 CR 535.

[§4.11] Zoning Changes

Although it may not be possible to prove unlawful precondemnation conduct (see Supp §4.7A) in the denial of a use permit, an alternative approach is to submit evidence of the reasonable probability of a change in use in the near future for consideration of the highest and best use of the property. In *Redevelopment Agency v Contra Costa Theatre, Inc.* (1982) 135 CA3d 73, 185 CR 159, the court allowed the jury to hear the condemnee-tenant's expert's opinion on the probability that a drive-in theater would be expanded from a single screen to a multiscreen operation, although an application for a use permit to do so was denied six months before the filing of the condemnation action. The tenant also attempted to show that it might be changed over to a flea market operation, but that evidence was properly excluded because the lease for the property did not permit that type of use.

Following *City of Fresno v Cloud,* cited in Book §4.11, *City of Porterville v Young* (1987) 195 CA3d 1260, 241 CR 349, ruled that in condemning undeveloped but commercially zoned land for street widening, the land should be valued at its prior precommercial use as agricultural land because dedication of the condemned land would be required in order to obtain the necessary permits for commercial development.

[§4.12] Sources of Zoning Information

The 1973 amendment to Govt C §65860 made January 1, 1974, the deadline by which county or city zoning ordinances must conform to the general plan of the county or city. If the ordinances are found to be inconsistent with the general plan, they must be amended within a reasonable time to conform. Charter cities other than Los Angeles are exempt from these requirements. Govt C §§65803, 65860(d). For Los Angeles the deadline was July 1, 1982. Govt C §65860. See also *City of Los Angeles v State* (1982) 138 CA3d 526, 187 CR 893. At the same time, Govt C §65361 allows no more than four amendments to mandatory elements of the general plan during the calendar year, with certain exceptions. See California Zoning Practice §2.29 (Cal CEB 1969).

Relying on opinions admitting evidence of zoning and other legislative and administrative restrictions that a buyer would take into consideration in arriving at the fair market value of the property, the court held that the California Coastal Zone Conservation Act of 1972, Pub Res C §§27000–27650 (repealed by Pub Res C §27650, January 1, 1977, and superseded by the California Coastal Act of 1976, Pub Res C §§30000–30900), must be considered in valuing coastal property being sought in eminent domain proceedings. The Act was not unconstitutionally intended to depress property values to facilitate public acquisition, but rather was similar to various valid interim zoning measures aimed at preserving the status quo while a comprehensive plan is being developed. *People ex rel State Pub. Works Bd. v Talleur* (1978) 79 CA3d 690, 145 CR 150.

However, "evidence of legislative and administrative restrictions is inadmissible if it limits the scope of the taking as defined in the resolution of necessity." *County of San Diego v Bressi* (1986) 184 CA3d 112, 124, 229 CR 44, 50. See Supp §6.18 regarding resolution of necessity.

Lands under either the Land Conservation Act of 1965 (Govt C §§51200–51295; see §51295), often referred to as the Williamson Act, or the Timberland Preserve Zoning Act (Govt C §§51100–51155; see §51155) are valued for eminent domain purposes as if the lands were not under such restrictions.

[§4.13] Rezoning or Development Due to Project

In *City of Los Angeles v Decker* (1977) 18 C3d 860, 135 CR 647, although the city's intended use of the property for airport parking could not be considered on the question of value, the court held that it was proper to introduce other city evidence of the need for airport parking, in light of the landowner's position that private airport-related facilities (rent-a-car lots and parking) constituted the highest and best use. The city had withheld information in the final version of an environmental impact report showing an acute need for airport parking; the court granted a new trial because the information was known in advance of trial and concealed.

It was proper for a property owner to show that it was reasonably probable that grazing land that had formerly been quarried and that still contained a remaining reserve of mineral deposits should be valued as a quarry. The state had condemned the property to obtain rock from the quarry to repair dams in the area. *People ex rel Dep't of Water Resources v Andresen* (1987) 193 CA3d 1144, 238 CR 826.

The jury should determine whether any potential buyer for the property would know that development was contingent on conditions equivalent to the condemning agency's final plans for the project. In *Coachella Valley Water Dist. v Western Allied Props.* (1987) 190 CA3d 969, 235 CR 725, the property owner was erroneously precluded by the trial court from introducing evidence of a less expensive means than the project to drain the property.

[§4.13A] Evidence of Improper Zoning

If zoning is imposed on subject property to depress its value, the condemnee may collaterally attack the validity of the zoning ordinance and, if successful, may require that the property be valued free of the restrictions of the invalid ordinance. See *Klopping v City of Whittier* (1972) 8 C3d 39, 46, 104 CR 1, 7 (discussed in Supp §4.7A); *Peacock v County of Sacramento* (1969) 271 CA2d 845, 77 CR 391 (discussed in Book §13.20 and Supp §13.22F). However, for the property owner to be able to attack the suspect ordinance, the agency condemning the property must be the same governing body that adopted the ordinance. *People ex rel Dep't of Pub. Works v Southern Pac. Transp. Co.* (1973) 33 CA3d 960, 966, 109 CR 525, 528. In the latter case, the City of Los Angeles had rezoned abandoned railroad rights-of-way to frustrate their use for anything other than street purposes. The defendant's abandoned right-of-way was acquired by a different public agency, the State Department of Public Works. The court held that to exclude evidence of the city's zoning restrictions shifts the "financial burden of the disguised taking from the city to the state. It permits a condemnee which failed to pursue its remedies for inverse condemnation against the city to recover compensation from an entity not directly responsible for the damage compensated." 33 CA3d at 966, 109 CR at 529.

Compare this approach with the rule stated in a number of inverse condemnation cases concerning precondemnation damages (see Supp §4.7A) that a writ of mandate, not inverse condemnation, is the appropriate remedy to attack an abuse of discretion in refusing a request to develop. See, *e.g., Agins v City of Tiburon* (1979) 24 C3d 266, 157 CR 372, aff'd 447 US 255, which was generally disapproved in *First English Evangelical Lutheran Church v County of Los Angeles* (1987) 482 US 304, both of which are discussed in Supp §13.22B. See also *Mira Dev. Corp. v City of San Diego* (1988) 205 CA3d 1201, 252 CR 825, a writ of mandate case discussing inverse condemnation cases regarding a municipality's refusal to rezone land.

[§4.14] Witness Qualifications

Insufficient knowledge concerning the source of a plan indicating proposed industrial land uses is a foundational deficiency justifying exclusion of evidence to that effect. *City of Los Angeles v Lowensohn* (1976) 54 CA3d 625, 127 CR 417.

The California Environmental Quality Act, Pub Res C §§21000–21176, may suggest additional considerations to guide a witness in preparing testimony to support an opinion concerning the highest and best use of subject property. See Supp §§2.20A, 4.8.

[§4.14A] Other Land Development Controls

It is not only zoning ordinances that should be considered in determining highest and best use; other land development controls may play an important role in analyzing the issue, *e.g.,* the Subdivision Map Act (Govt C §§66410–66499.37), local subdivision ordinances (*State ex rel Dep't of Water Resources v Clark* (1973) 33 CA3d 463, 109 CR 39), building moratoriums (Govt C §65850), and the California Coastal Act of 1976 (Pub Res C §§30000–30900). See *State v Superior Court* (Veta) (1974) 12 C3d 237, 115 CR 497; *California Cent. Coast Regional Coastal Zone Conserv. Comm'n v McKeon Constr.* (1974) 38 CA3d 154, 112 CR 903. See also California Zoning Practice Supp §§3.88–3.96 (Cal CEB).

Evaluating Existing Zones of Value

[§4.18] Combining Parcels; "Assemblage" Theory

In *U.S. v Fuller* (1973) 409 US 488, the Supreme Court held that, although the condemnee's use of his land for cattle grazing was made more valuable by his additional use of adjoining federal land for the same purpose, this enhanced value could not be considered, because the condemnee's only interest in the adjoining land owned by the condemnor was a revocable permit. See *U.S. v Certain Land Situated in City of Detroit* (ED Mich 1982) 547 F Supp 680, which distinguished *Fuller* by holding that the *Fuller* rule is limited to situations in which use of adjacent federal land is dependent on a federal license or permit. The potential benefit derived from adjacent federal land cannot be excluded as a matter of law in determining the condemned parcel's value.

[§§4.19–4.22] DATE OF VALUATION

Former CCP §1249 has been modified and replaced by CCP §1263.120. The new section makes the date of "commencement of the proceeding" (date the complaint is filed) the valuation date if the case is brought to trial within one year. Under the former statute the date of valuation was the date of issuance of the summons. Code of Civil Procedure §1263.130 continues the rule that, if the case is not brought to trial within one year, the date trial begins will become the valuation date unless the delay beyond the one-year period is caused by the condemnee.

The new law also allows the condemnor to establish the date of value by making a deposit of probable compensation. The date of value is the date the deposit is made. CCP §1263.110. It is an open question whether an increase in the deposit under CCP §1255.030 shifts the date of value to the date the increase is deposited. For procedure in making a deposit of probable compensation, see Supp §§8.7–8.8.

Code of Civil Procedure §1263.210 continues the substance of former CCP §1248(1), providing compensation for improvements placed on the property.

Code of Civil Procedure §1263.240 maintains the rule of former CCP §1249 that improvements made after service of summons are not compensable unless the improvement was made (1) by a public utility for its system, (2) with the written consent of the condemnor, or (3) under court order after a noticed public hearing balancing the respective hardships of the parties.

Code of Civil Procedure §1263.230(a) continues the same dates as former CCP §1249.1 for precluding compensation for removed or destroyed improvements. See Book §4.22. Further, it allows a defendant to move before the effective date of the order of immediate possession and shift the risk of loss to the plaintiff 24 hours after the receipt of a notice that defendant has moved. When improvements are removed or destroyed at any time by defendant, they cannot be considered for compensation. Any damage caused to the remaining property by that removal or destruction is taken into account to the extent it reduces the value of the remaining property. CCP §1263.230(b).

Code of Civil Procedure §1263.120 (former CCP §1249), which requires assessment of damages as of the date of trial when the case has not been brought to trial within one year, is a procedural section designed to prompt condemning authorities to an early trial date. It is concerned with the value of the property after the right to compensation has been established; but the determinations of ownership, larger parcel, severance damages, and special benefits are established as of the time summons is issued and the mandatory lis pendens is filed, *i.e.,* at the beginning of the action. *People ex rel Dep't of Pub. Works v Simon Newman Co.* (1974) 37 CA3d 398, 404, 112 CR 298, 302. *Simon Newman Co.* held that special benefits were offset against severance damages even though the condemnee had agreed with a federal agency, before beginning the action, to dispose of the lands found to be benefited, and even though the condemnee did not own those lands on the date of trial, which was the valuation date. The court reasoned that later transactions affecting the parcels involved are taken with notice of the pendency of the action.

The dates fixed by statute are to be used only absent a binding stipulation fixing the date of value. When the parties have stipulated to a particular date of value, that date controls and evidence of conditions on an earlier date of issuance of summons (now the filing of the complaint) cannot be admitted to determine value. *State v Clark* (1973) 33 CA3d 463, 109 CR 39. In *Clark,* between the date of issuance of summons and the stipulated date of value, the county had imposed more restrictive subdivision policies that diminished the highest and best use of the land. See Supp §4.14A.

The holding in *Clark* is subject to an exception when the condemnation action itself adversely affects conditions before the stipulated valuation date. In *Orange County Flood Control Dist. v Sunny Crest Dairy, Inc.* (1978) 77 CA3d 742, 143 CR 803, a nonconforming use was allowed to lapse because it was economically unfeasible after the condemnor took possession of part of the property being condemned. The property owner was allowed to show that the highest and best use of the land on the date of value was the previous cash-and-carry dairy operation, the loss of which was the direct result of the condemnor's steps in acquiring the property by condemnation. See CCP §1263.330; Supp §4.7. In *Clark,* the use impairment was not caused by the condemnor but by another public agency, and the owner sought to use two dates of value.

[§4.24] Valuation Date on Retrial

The *Murata* rule, discussed in Book §4.24, stating that the date of value remains the same on retrial, was changed by CCP §§1263.140–1263.150. If a retrial is not held within one year of "commencement of the proceeding" (*e.g.,* filing of the complaint; see CCP §1250.110), the date of valuation is the date the new proceedings begin. But if justice requires, the court may set a different date. One factor that may be considered by the court is misconduct of a party. See Comment to CCP §1263.150. Code of Civil Procedure §§1263.140–1263.150 are subject to CCP §1263.110, which permits a condemnor to make a prejudgment deposit of probable compensation to establish the date of valuation. See Supp §§4.19–4.22, 8.8.

The same rule applies whether the retrial is after an appeal (CCP §1263.140) or after a mistrial (CCP §1263.150).

[§4.25] BASIC APPROACHES TO VALUATION

Code of Civil Procedure §1263.320(b) allows use of any just and equitable method of valuation in cases in which no relevant market exists.

In approving use of the cost of reproduction method (see §4.38), the court in *People ex rel Dep't of Transp. v Southern Pac. Transp. Co.* (1978) 84 CA3d 315, 325, 148 CR 535, 541, stated: "The rules for determining value of condemned land are not to be considered inflexible. In each case just compensation is the goal and if rigid application of a rule tends to produce an injustice, the court must deviate from that rule."

Market Data Approach; Comparable Sales

Trial Court's Discretion

[§4.27] Weighing Aspects of Comparability

Evidence Code §822(a) and (b) were redesignated Evid C §822(a)(1) and 822(a)(2), respectively. For actions filed after December 31, 1987, Evid C §822(a)(1) was amended to permit the admission and use of evidence of the price and acquisition of comparable property that is *already* in public use. The statutory wording is confusing because the exception language follows very closely the rule itself. The statute's purpose is to address an acquisition such as a municipality acquiring an existing public utility or service district for the same use as the property could have been taken by condemnation. In such a case, it is proper to use a public agency's contractual acquisition of another public utility as a comparable sale. See 11 CEB Real Prop L Rep 20, 29 (Jan. 1988) for additional discussion.

[§4.28] Effect of Public Improvement on Comparability

The sale price of subject property sold after the date of its probable inclusion within the proposed public project is admissible at the discretion of the trial court to shed light on the unenhanced value of that property, even though the sale reflects enhanced value. *City of Los Angeles v Retlaw Enters.* (1976) 16 C3d 473, 128 CR 436.

Comparability of Sale

[§4.30] Time and Location of Sale

See *PG&E v Zuckerman* (1987) 189 CA3d 1113, 234 CR 630, regarding adjusting sales for time.

[§4.31] Nature of Land and Improvements

Evidence Code §822(d) has been redesignated Evid C §822(a)(4).

A recent sale of subject property before the condemnation action may be considered; but in the absence of an adequate evidentiary basis it cannot be adjusted by a fixed multiplier to account for the extra value added by improvements to the property or for the effect of market forces. *People ex rel Dep't of Pub. Works v Peninsula Enters.* (1979) 91 CA3d 332, 348, 153 CR 895, 903. Sales of other property that includes fixtures, lights, improvements, and personal property not included in the subject property cannot be considered comparable. *PG&E v Zuckerman* (1987) 189 CA3d 1113, 1130, 234 CR 630, 640.

[§4.33] Sale for "Money" or Equivalent

The phrase "in terms of money," which comes from the 1909 *Heilbron* decision, cited in Book §4.33, has been deleted from the definition of fair market value in CCP §1263.320. The official Senate Legislative Committee Comment to that section states that the phrase was omitted because it was confusing.

Glendale Fed. Sav. & Loan Ass'n v Marina View Heights Dev. Co. (1977) 66 CA3d 101, 141, 135 CR 802, 826, although not a condemnation case, discusses condemnation law regarding the definition of fair market value without noting the deletion of the phrase "in terms of money" from CCP §1263.320. The court held that discounting the sale of comparable property on terms to reflect its cash value is proper. Based on *Glendale* and BAJI Nos. 11.81 and 11.82 (rev 1986), regarding the analysis of the evidence of comparable sales, counsel should direct the jury to consider "how much should the sale price on terms be discounted to reflect its equivalent in cash." However, although the terms of a comparable sale are relevant evidence, it does not appear proper to discount a comparable sale. Discounting may be, in effect, an improper opinion under Evid C §822(a)(4) (formerly Evid C §822(d) before renumbering) of the value of a comparable sale. See §9.49. Furthermore, a sales transaction for a given price can reflect varying considerations between buyers and sellers. Sellers are often influenced by tax considerations to refuse a cash transaction. The court in *Buena Park School Dist. v Metrim Corp.* (1959) 176 CA2d 255, 264, 1 CR 250, 256, stressed that the manner of the actual sale is "not involved" in the definition of fair market value. It is thus arguable that BAJI Nos. 11.81 and 11.82 are improper.

In *People ex rel Dep't of Pub. Works v Reardon* (1971) 4 C3d 507, 93 CR 852 (discussed in Book §4.33), a transaction involving an exchange of properties on which the parties to the sale had fixed a monetary value was allowed as a comparable sale under Evid C §816. Distinguishing *Reardon,* the court in *San Diego Gas & Elec. Co. v 3250 Corp.* (1988) 205 CA3d 1075, 252 CR 853, ruled that an exchange of property between the condemnee and the state of California was an integrated transaction and thus inadmissible under Evid C §822(a)(1), which prohibits introducing evidence of value from sales to condemning agencies.

Cost Approach

[§4.38] Definition

In the appraisal of a seven-story hotel building approximately 60 years old that was being acquired for a redevelopment project, the agency's appraisals were not to be disregarded because they made no effort to use the replacement or reproduction cost method. See Book §4.43. The agency's expert witnesses stated that the cost approach did not apply because of the building's age and the impossibility of replacement, and the property owner's appraisers conceded that the cost approach was not reliable for the property because of the difficulty in evaluating the depreciation factor and changing building requirements. *Redevelopment Agency v Del-Camp Invs.* (1974) 38 CA3d 836, 113 CR 762, also discussed in Supp §4.47. See also *People v Ocean Shore R.R.* (1948) 32 C2d 406, 428, 196 P2d 570, 584; *State v Stevenson* (1970) 5 CA3d 60, 63, 84 CR 742, 744.

The cost approach was an acceptable basis for an opinion of value of a waterworks company, but it did not itself establish market value. The approach was relevant only to the extent that it developed factors that hypothetical buyers and sellers would consider. *South Bay Irrig. Dist. v California-American Water Co.* (1976) 61 CA3d 944, 975, 133 CR 166, 188. See also *San Gabriel Valley Water Co. v City of Montebello* (1978) 84 CA3d 757, 148 CR 830. Because the cost approach separately values each intangible asset and each physical asset, it may result in an inflated market value.

Appraiser's Role

[§4.43] Replacement and Reproduction

For a special use building such as a church, replacement cost less depreciation or obsolescence is a more just and equitable method of valuation than fair market value. *Redevelopment Agency v First Christian Church* (1983) 140 CA3d 690, 189 CR 749.

American Institute of Real Estate Appraisers, The Appraisal of Real Estate (5th ed 1967), has been superseded by a ninth edition published in 1987.

Income Approach

[§4.47] Land Residual and Overall Capitalization Processes

The court in *Redevelopment Agency v Del-Camp Invs., Inc.* (1974) 38 CA3d 836, 113 CR 762, approved use of an overall capitalization process for appraisal of a 60-year-old, seven-story building with ground floor stores and hotel rooms on the upper floors. See Supp §4.38.

In valuing a public utility as a going concern, the court properly relied primarily on the capitalization-of-income method of appraisal. *South Bay Irrig. Dist. v California-American Water Co.* (1976) 61 CA3d 944, 133 CR 166. It is not proper to value property based on capitalizing a hypothetical business. Rather, the property must be valued on the basis of its rental value for a particular use. *People ex rel Dep't of Water Resources v Andresen* (1987) 193 CA3d 1144, 238 CR 826, approved capitalization of future royalties to value a rock quarry.

[§4.48] Gross Rent Multiplier

The court in *Redevelopment Agency v Del-Camp Invs..* (1974) 38 CA3d 836, 842, 113 CR 762, 766, approved use of a gross rent multiplier ("what an owner operator would pay for property producing a total gross rent") for appraisal of a 60-year-old hotel building with ground floor stores.

[§4.49] Legal Tests of Income Approach

In 1978 Evid C §817 was amended to prohibit consideration of a lease of only the property or property interest being taken in determining value if the lease was entered into after the lis pendens was filed. But Evid C §817 does not preclude evaluating a leasehold that is not yet established on the property if that use can be shown to be reasonably probable. In *People ex rel Dep't of Water Resources v Andresen* (1987) 193 CA3d 1144, 238 CR 826, a rock quarry that had been disused for a period of time was valued on the basis of local markets for its rock and its rental value for quarrying.

Evidence Code §818 permits consideration of leases on comparable property as a part of the capitalization method. It does not preclude examination of land leases in the general area of the condemned parcel for the sole purpose of determining the prevailing return on investment for vacant land in that general area leased to a developer. *People ex rel Dep't of Pub. Works v Peninsula Enters.* (1979) 91 CA3d 332, 350, 153 CR 895, 904.

Evidence Code §822(f) has been redesignated as Evid C §822(a)(6).

[§4.51] Economic Approach; Unimproved Lands

An economic analysis approach is a proper method to determine the market value of a tract of land when its highest and best use is for subdivision and sale of lots. *Drakes Bay Land Co. v U.S.* (Ct Cl 1972) 459 F2d 504. See also a companion case, *U.S. v 100 Acres of Land* (9th Cir 1972) 468 F2d 1261, 1266, which refers to this appraisal technique as the "developer's residual approach."

PART TWO: SPECIFIC VALUATION PROBLEMS

[§4.52] FIXTURES AND EQUIPMENT

Former CCP §1248(1), providing that improvements placed on property are compensable, has been replaced by CCP §1263.210 without substantive change. Former CCP §1248(b), defining improvements, has been modified and replaced by CCP §1263.205. This statute states that improvements include "any machinery or equipment installed for use on property taken by eminent domain" that cannot be removed without substantial economic loss or substantial damage to the realty. This differs from the prior statute in not requiring that the equipment be used for manufacturing or other industrial uses. The former statute mentioned only equipment. The purpose of adding "machinery" when enacting the new statute was probably to prevent an excessively narrow definition of "equipment."

If the parties disagree whether particular property is an improvement pertaining to realty, either party, at least 30 days before the effective date of an order of possession, may move the court for a determination. CCP §1260.030. The test for substantial economic loss requires comparing the value of the property in place with its value if removed and sold. CCP §1263.205(b). Code of Civil Procedure §1263.205 codifies the holding in *City of Los Angeles v Sabatasso* (1970) 3 CA3d 973, 83 CR 898, that severance damages may be sought for improvements located on the remainder.

The court, after a noticed hearing and on a finding of hardship, may permit a defendant to make improvements after service of summons; such improvements may be considered in determining compensation. CCP §1263.240(c); see Supp §§4.19–4.22. At the same time, the court may limit the extent to which the improvements may be considered in the award of compensation. The purpose of this section is to allow a defendant making improvements in good faith to be compensated. Such an instance may occur "where an improvement is near completion, the date of the public use of the property is distant, and the additional work will permit profitable use of the property" in the interim. 12 Cal L Rev'n Comm'n Reports 1828–1829 (1974).

When the summons is served during construction of an improvement, the owner may recover for work necessary to protect the public or for partially installed machinery or equipment. CCP §1263.620.

When the owner of the improvements elects to remove any or all the improvements and the condemnor agrees to their removal, the owner can receive compensation for their reasonable removal and relocation cost, unless the cost exceeds the market value of the improvements. To implement this election, the property owner must give written notice of the election within 60 days after service of summons. The condemnor has 30 days thereafter to serve notice of its refusal. The defendant may cause no more damage to any structure than is reasonably necessary to remove the improvements; the structure is valued without regard to such damage. CCP §1263.260.

Code of Civil Procedure §1263.270 authorizes the court, on motion of any party, to acquire the entire improvement located both on and outside the take, together with any easement necessary to effect demolition, removal, or relocation. See Supp §5.12A.

The court in *Community Redev. Agency v Abrams* (1975) 15 C3d 813, 126 CR 473 (discussed in Supp §4.61), refused compensation for inventory of "ethical drugs" in the taking of a pharmacy because it was movable, nonaffixed personal property.

Under CCP §1263.205 (former CCP §1248b), the lessee in a month-to-month tenancy of the condemned property was entitled to valuation of its concrete batch plant as a part of the realty, rather than at its removal value, when the lessor had been compensated for the value of the land without improvements. *Concrete Serv. Co. v State ex rel Dep't of Pub. Works* (1972) 29 CA3d 664, 105 CR 721.

Fixtures on special purpose property can have substantial value in excess of salvage value, which justifies using accelerated depreciation to determine damages to remaining property. *City of Commerce v National Starch & Chem. Corp.* (1981) 118 CA3d 1, 14, 173 CR 176, 183; see discussion in Supp §5.23A.

Distinguishing *Concrete Serv. Co. v State* and *Redevelopment Agency v Diamond Props.*, both cited in Book §4.52, the court in *Pacific Outdoor Advertising Co. v City of Burbank* (1978) 86 CA3d 5, 149 CR 906, held that termination of plaintiff's lease, which allowed the owner to lease the land to a city for parking, did not give rise to damages when the city had not threatened to exercise its power of condemnation. The new lease was negotiated in the open market.

In *Lanning v City of Monterey* (1986) 181 CA3d 352, 226 CR 258, the court held that, because the condemning agency acquired land subject to an existing lease that allowed either party to terminate on six months' notice and provided that the lessee would receive compensation for the taking or destruction of its improvement, the city could not purchase the property and then give notice of termination without paying compensation for the lessee's improvements. In *Peter Kiewit Sons' Co. v Richmond Redev. Agency* (1986) 178 CA3d 435, 223 CR 728, however, the court held that purchase by a public entity of all of the property covered by a lease to plaintiff did not terminate the lease, because the public entity did not engage in a pattern of conduct designed to evict plaintiff from the site or to take the balance of its tenancy without compensation. Plaintiff was allowed to occupy the property until expiration of its lease and received everything it was entitled to under the lease, but no new lease mutually acceptable to both parties was entered into. The court held that CCP §1265.110 (providing that the lease terminates when the entire property is taken) applies only to acquisitions by eminent domain and not to acquisitions by purchase unless the conduct of the acquiring entity is the "substantial equivalent" of condemnation and fairness requires the application of CCP §1265.110.

On recovery of damages for loss of personal property and inventory, see Supp §4.52A.

[§4.52A] INVENTORY; PERSONAL PROPERTY

A property owner can recover damages for loss of personal property, such as inventory, resulting from inverse condemnation. *McMahan's of Santa Monica v City of Santa Monica* (1983) 146 CA3d 683, 194 CR 582. Because the inventory in *McMahan's* was not unique and was readily replaceable, the measure of damages was the inventory's wholesale, rather than retail, value. Otherwise, an award of retail value would have resulted in a windfall. If the owner had been a consumer, the appropriate damages would have been the retail price. For further discussion of *McMahan's*, see Supp §13.4.

The owner of an automobile salvage business was entitled to be compensated for the value of his business inventory minus the amount obtained at a salvage sale because the owner's inability to relocate the business was the result of the nature of the business and the lack of any appropriately zoned property within a reasonably accessible area. The fact that the condemning agency sought to condemn only real property was not determinative on the question of whether the exercise of eminent domain resulted in the taking or damaging of personal property. *Baldwin Park Redev.*

Agency v Irving (1984) 156 CA3d 428, 202 CR 792. See also *City of Oakland v Oakland Raiders* (1982) 32 C3d 60, 67, 183 CR 673, 677, pointing out that neither the federal nor state constitution makes any distinction between real property and personal property with respect to the requirement that just compensation is required when property has been taken or damaged.

[§4.53] MOVING AND RELOCATION COSTS

Rules and regulations governing relocation assistance must now conform to the guidelines adopted by the Department of Housing and Community Development. Govt C §7267.8. See 25 Cal Code Regs §§6000–6198 for regulations. Former 2 Cal Adm C §§880–883 have been repealed. Federally funded projects are subject to federal law. The California Code of Regulations was formerly called the California Administrative Code.

Health and Safety Code §33413 requires that, whenever a redevelopment project causes the destruction or removal of dwelling units from the low- and moderate-income housing market, the community redevelopment agency must rehabilitate, redevelop, or construct an equal number of replacement dwelling units with an equal or greater number of bedrooms at affordable housing cost within the territorial jurisdiction of the agency within four years. Further, specified percentages of new or rehabilitated dwelling units must be made available to persons and families of low or moderate income and to very low-income households.

The community redevelopment agency may provide fewer replacement dwellings only if (1) the total number of bedrooms in the replacement dwelling units equals or exceeds the number of bedrooms in the destroyed or removed dwelling units and (2) the replacement units are affordable to the same income level of households as the destroyed or removed units. Health & S C §33413(f).

Any city, county, or city and county may establish a central relocation office to coordinate all relocation activities within its jurisdiction. Among the office's duties would be the approval of relocation plans submitted by public entities within its jurisdiction and coordination of the execution of these plans. Govt C §7261.6.

For discussion of the legislative history of California relocation assistance, see *Parking Auth. v Nicovich* (1973) 32 CA3d 420, 108 CR 137.

Benefits recoverable under the Relocation Assistance Act (Govt C §§7260–7277) cannot be asserted in the condemnation trial; the party must make a claim under Govt C §7266. *Orange County Flood Control Dist. v Sunny Crest Dairy, Inc.* (1978) 77 CA3d 742, 766, 143 CR 803, 817. A party seeking relocation benefits by mandamus action must first exhaust administrative remedies by making a written request for the assistance. *Baiza v Southgate Recreation & Park Dist.* (1976) 59 CA3d 669, 130 CR 836. If the claim under Govt C §7266 is denied, action for relocation relief in a condemnation action should be sought by cross-complaint for administrative mandamus, rather than answer, and severed during the trial of the condemnation action. *City of Mountain View v Superior Court* (1975) 54 CA3d 72, 126 CR 358. But see *McKeon v Hastings College of the Law* (1986) 185 CA3d 877, 230 CR 176, which permitted a claimant to seek relocation assistance in an action for declaratory and injunctive relief.

The Eminent Domain Law (CCP §§1230.010–1273.050) does not change the rules for relocation assistance, but it does provide that, if two or more statutes provide compensation for the same loss, compensation may be paid only once. CCP §1263.010(b). See *Baldwin Park Redev. Agency v Irving* (1984) 156 CA3d 428, 202 CR 792, which held that the Relocation Assistance Act (Govt C §§7260–7277) is not an adequate substitute for the constitutional requirement of just compensation. The Act is a legislative recognition of a need to compensate certain business losses that occur as a result of condemnation, but it contemplates that the relocation compensation is independent of the condemnation proceedings. Government Code §7275 was added in 1975 to the relocation assistance law, making the purchase price and other consideration paid by a condemning agency public information.

When a "displaced person" under the relocation assistance laws failed to take appropriate action to claim benefits or cooperate with the public agency to enable it to determine benefits, that person could not quash a writ of execution otherwise properly issued to obtain possession of the property. *City of Los Angeles v Decker* (1976) 61 CA3d 444, 132 CR 188.

A government entity cannot avoid the provisions of the relocation assistance laws by converting the status of a person entitled to relocation assistance to that of its tenant, terminating the tenancy, and denying that the person was displaced by government action. An actual exercise of the power of eminent domain is not a prerequisite to relocation benefits. The acquisition of real property for public use, whether by condemnation or otherwise, triggers the provisions of relocation assistance laws. *Superior Strut & Hanger Co. v Port of Oakland* (1977) 72 CA3d 987, 140 CR 515. In that case, the agency entered into two agreements with the tenant after it acquired the property; then, when the tenant refused to move after a notice to quit, the agency continued to accept rent. Because the tenant was in lawful possession, it qualified for relocation benefits. However, a lessee who was in possession with six months left on its lease at the time of acquisition and held over after expiration of the lease without the agency's consent became a tenant at sufferance and did not qualify for relocation benefits as a displaced person. *Peter Kiewit Sons' Co. v Richmond Redev. Agency* (1986) 178 CA3d 435, 223 CR 728. In *Peter Kiewit Sons'* the tenant tendered rent after expiration of the lease but it was refused by the agency. There was no evidence that the conduct of the acquiring public agency was the substantial equivalent of condemnation; the tenant received all it was entitled to under its lease.

In *McKeon v Hastings College of the Law, supra,* the court determined that the burden of proof to demonstrate what caused residents to move from a low-rent hotel being taken was on the displaced persons when there was normally a great deal of turnover at the hotel.

Postacquisition tenants can qualify as "displaced persons" entitled to relocation benefits if they entered their tenancies without knowledge of the acquisition. But, in such cases, the condemnor would not be required to continue to maintain the structures in habitable condition or to do further environmental analysis. *Cavanaugh v State* (1978) 85 CA3d 354, 149 CR 453.

Tenant occupants who own their own houses located on land under long term leases are entitled to the same replacement housing benefits as owner occupants. *Albright v State* (1979) 101 CA3d 14, 161 CR 317.

Tenants of a mobilehome park, which was under lease from an airport district to a mobilehome park operator, did not qualify as displaced persons under Govt C §7260(c) when the master lease had expired by its own terms. The reversion of the right of possession of the land to the airport district did not constitute an acquisition under the relocation guidelines. *Stephens v Perry* (1982) 134 CA3d 748, 184 CR 701.

When a property owner vacated his home after the condemnor's offer to purchase but before the purchase or taking of possession, the owner was not entitled to last resort housing benefits when the condemnor concluded that the property would not be needed for the project because the owner was not required to move. *Osburn v Department of Transp.* (1990) 221 CA3d 1339, 270 CR 761.

A telephone company is not entitled to relocation assistance benefits for the cost of relocating its telephone cables from a public street that is vacated to make way for a redevelopment project. Legislation for such benefits must be specific and cannot be inferred from the general definitions in the relocation assistance law. *Pacific Tel. & Tel. Co. v Redevelopment Agency* (1978) 87 CA3d 296, 151 CR 68. See also *East Bay Mun. Util. Dist. v Richmond Redev. Agency* (1979) 93 CA3d 346, 155 CR 636, which decided the same question under the Community Redevelopment Law (Health & S C §§33000–33738). Note, however, that a land developer whose building project creates the need for a public improvement that requires the relocation of utility poles must pay for those poles rather than the utility. *PG&E v Dame Constr. Co.* (1987) 191 CA3d 233, 236 CR 351.

A water district that maintains a pipeline in a city street must bear its own pipeline relocation costs to make way for a storm drain extension to be built within the right of way, even if the city installing the storm drain is exercising its authority beyond the city limits. California follows the common-law rule that "a privately owned public utility's franchise rights in a public street are subject to an implied obligation to relocate its facilities at its own expense when such relocation is necessary to make way for a proper governmental use of the street." *City of Anaheim v Metropolitan Water Dist.* (1982) 133 CA3d 247, 250, 184 CR 16, 18.

An owner purchasing replacement rental property, after a public agency had initiated condemnation proceedings but before those proceedings were completed, qualifies for relocation assistance. Government Code §7262(c) does not require a business owner to discontinue his or her business before purchasing property to replace that which is being acquired; nor does the statute require that a person being displaced obtain replacement property only after title of the acquired property has passed to the condemning agency. See *Mitakis v Department of Gen. Servs.* (1983) 149 CA3d 684, 197 CR 142.

Government Code §§7263 and 7264 have been amended to give the public agency discretion to shorten the owner's or renter's occupancy requirement from 180 days or 90 days, respectively.

A 90-day residency before negotiations for acquisition commence is a requirement for financial assistance under Govt C §7264 (cash payments to assist displaced persons in obtaining comparable replacement housing), but is not a condition of eligibility for "last resort housing" under Govt C §7264.5 (public entity provides comparable replacement housing when it is otherwise unavailable). *Garcia v Anthony* (1989) 211 CA3d 467, 259 CR 393.

In *Beaty v Imperial Irrig. Dist.* (1986) 186 CA3d 897, 231 CR 128, the court held that property owners who have successfully prosecuted an inverse condemnation action that is a substitute for a direct condemnation action and who have been displaced from their property by a public entity's appropriation or acquisition of their property are entitled to relocation benefits under Govt C §§7260–7277.

[§4.54] LEASEHOLDS

Code of Civil Procedure §1248 has been repealed. Code of Civil Procedure §1235.125 defines the term "interest in property" to include all interests of whatever character and extent. Code of Civil Procedure §1260.220 provides that each individual interest is compensable, and retains the condemnor's option to have the interests in property valued separately or as a whole.

[§4.55] Theories of Valuation

Code of Civil Procedure §1260.220 continues the procedure of former CCP §1246.1, allowing plaintiff to require that compensation be first determined as between plaintiff and all defendants claiming an interest in the taking. The section is only procedural; it does not affect the rule of *People v Lynbar, Inc.*, cited in Book §4.55, allowing enhanced value created by the existence of a favorable lease. See Comment to CCP §1260.220.

See *People ex rel Dep't of Pub. Works v Amsden Corp.* (1973) 33 CA3d 83, 109 CR 1 (discussed in Supp §4.56), in which the courts, following *People v Lynbar, Inc.*, held that the condemnor pays for the property in its condition on the date of valuation. The *Amsden* court allowed the jury to have evidence of a master lease on the property, but not of a sublease that was not in existence on the date of valuation.

[§4.56] Elements of Valuation

The opinion in *People ex rel Dep't of Pub. Works v Amsden Corp.* (1973) 33 CA3d 83, 109 CR 1, sets forth several points regarding valuation of property under lease. The case concerned an unimproved parcel encumbered by a 50-year master ground lease. That lease provided that the "true value" of the property as of May 1968 was $270,000, and that if the property was condemned the lessor would receive that amount and any excess would go to the lessee. The lessee subsequently entered into a sublease for a portion of the property with a 48-year term; the sublease was subject to the sublessee's success in obtaining financing within 150 days, which did not occur. The condemnor and owner-lessor stipulated to value in the amount of $274,350 as of April 1970, the valuation date. The case proceeded to trial with only the lessee and the sublessee contesting the issue of value. See Supp §4.49 on amendment of Evid C §817.

The following points were established by the appellate court:

(1) Stipulation as to value between the owner-lessor and the condemnor was admissible and did not remove the issue of fair market value from the jury. The evidence indicated that there was no dispute between the owner and the condemnor. There was no evidence of compromise or settlement. Because Evid C §813 allows the owner to testify and he was not called on to do so, there was an admission by implication that he would have testified in accordance with the stipulation.

(2) The statement of "true value" in the master lease apparently was admissible on the issue of value, although the opinion generally discusses that amount in regard to apportionment. See §§4.57, 10.7.

(3) The sublease was not admissible because the master lease was the only lease in existence on the valuation date. The trial court followed this rule by the practical compromise, which seems to have been approved by the appellate court, of allowing evidence of the sublease's capitalization value (see Book §4.44) but excluding the document and its precise terms as not relevant until the apportionment proceedings.

The possibility that the current lease on the condemned property may be renewed is a proper factor in measuring just compensation for improvements on the property taken. *Almota Farmers Elevator & Warehouse Co. v U.S.* (1973) 409 US 470.

[§4.57] Apportionment of Award Between Lessor and Lessee

Code of Civil Procedure §1260.220 continues the rule of apportionment of former CCP §1246.1.

A tenant may contractually waive the right to compensation by a provision in the lease. *People ex rel Dep't of Pub. Works v Amsden Corp.* (1973) 33 CA3d 83, 88, 109 CR 1, 4.

See Goldberg, Merrill & Unumb: *Bargaining in the Shadow of Eminent Domain: Valuing and Apportioning Condemnation Awards Between Landlord and Tenant,* 34 UCLA L Rev 1083 (1987).

[§4.58] Total Take

Code of Civil Procedure §1265.110 provides that when the entire property is taken, the lease terminates. But the lessee retains the right to seek compensation for loss of the lease. See CCP §1265.150. Valid provisions in the lease contract supersede the statutory rules. CCP §1265.160. Code of Civil Procedure §1265.110 codifies the rule of *City of Pasadena v Porter* and *Carlstrom v Lyon Van & Storage Co.,* cited in Book §4.58, that the taking of the entire demised premises for public use by eminent domain or agreement operates to release the tenant from liability for subsequently accruing rent.

In *Lanning v City of Monterey* (1986) 181 CA3d 352, 226 CR 258, the court held that, when a lease has a termination clause and a provision for compensating the lessee for its improvements, a condemning agency may not purchase property and take title subject to the lease without paying compensation for those improvements. Such a purchase is the substantial equivalent of the exercise of eminent domain. In *Peter Kiewit Sons' Co. v Richmond Redev. Agency* (1986) 178 CA3d 435, 223 CR 728, however, the court held that purchase by a public entity of all of the property covered by a lease to plaintiff did not terminate the lease, because the public entity did not engage in a pattern of conduct designed to evict plaintiff from the site or to take the balance of its tenancy without compensation. Plaintiff was allowed to occupy the property until expiration of its lease and received everything it was entitled to under the lease, but the parties did not enter into a new mutually acceptable lease. The court held that CCP §1265.110 (providing that the lease terminates when the entire property is taken) applies only to acquisitions by eminent domain and not to acquisitions by purchase unless the conduct of the acquiring entity is the "substantial equivalent" of condemnation and fairness requires the application of CCP §1265.110.

[§4.59] Partial Take

Code of Civil Procedure §1265.120 abolishes the rule of *City of Pasadena v Porter,* discussed in Book §4.59, which required continuation of the lessee's full rental obligation for the duration of the lease in cases of partial taking, with compensation to the lessee for the present equivalent of the future rents attributable to the portion taken. Now, the lease terminates on the part taken and the rent obligation is abated proportionately.

If, however, the taking is sufficient to frustrate the entire lease, the court, on the petition of any party to the lease, has authority to terminate the entire lease. CCP §1265.130. At the same time, the lessee may pursue its right to compensation. CCP §1265.150.

Termination or partial termination of the lease occurs when title passes or on the effective date of immediate possession, whichever occurs first. CCP §1265.140.

[§4.60] Improvements

Under CCP §1263.205 (former CCP §1248b), the lessee in a month-to-month tenancy of condemned property for which the lessor had been compensated for the value of the land without improvements was entitled to valuation of its concrete batch plant as part of the realty, rather than only its removal value. *Concrete Serv. Co. v State ex rel Dep't of Pub. Works* (1972) 29 CA3d 664, 105 CR 721.

The value of improvements made during a lease term that have useful life values beyond the remaining lease must be considered in the valuation of a leasehold interest because of the possibility of lease renewal. *Almota Farmers Elevator & Warehouse Co. v U.S.* (1973) 409 US 470.

[§4.61] BUSINESS LOSSES; GOODWILL

In *Community Redev. Agency v Abrams* (1975) 15 C3d 813, 126 CR 473, the owner of a drugstore acquired by a redevelopment agency was found by the trial court to be incapable of relocating his business in a new area because of his age and poor health. The lower court concluded that his goodwill had been taken and that his stock of "ethical drugs" (*i.e.,* drugs in open containers that could not economically be resold to another pharmacist) had been rendered valueless, but it awarded compensation only for the drug inventory. The supreme court refused to find a constitutional basis for compensation for loss of goodwill and reversed the award for loss in the value of the ethical drugs, holding that the drugs were personal property and their loss was not a direct result of the condemnation action. The loss occurred because of the practical effect of the condemnation on the defendant's particular circumstances. See also *County of San Diego v Morrison* (1984) 153 CA3d 234, 200 CR 187.

Abrams was distinguished in *Baldwin Park Redev. Agency v Irving*

(1984) 156 CA3d 428, 202 CR 792, which allowed the owner of an automobile salvage business compensation for the value of business inventory less the salvage value that had been obtained in selling the inventory, when the owner was unable to relocate the business because of the lack of any appropriately zoned property within a reasonably accessible area. The court found that the owner's loss was a direct result of the condemnation action.

Code of Civil Procedure §1263.510 allows compensation for loss of goodwill in both total and partial takings. The owner has the burden of proving that:

(1) The loss is caused by the taking or injury to the remainder;

(2) The loss cannot reasonably be prevented by relocation or other prudent steps;

(3) There will be no compensation by way of relocation assistance (see Govt C §7262; Supp §4.53); and

(4) The loss of goodwill is not compensated from other sources. Goodwill is defined as the "benefits that accrue to a business as a result of its location, reputation for dependability, skill or quality, and any other circumstances resulting in probable retention of old or acquisition of new patronage." CCP §1263.510(b).

Any excess special benefits remaining after being offset against severance damages (see generally chap 5) must be offset against any award for goodwill. CCP §1263.410. It would appear, however, that when the tenant-owner of the business seeks loss of goodwill and the landlord receives the benefits, the effect should not apply to the tenant.

The owner of a business who claims compensation for goodwill must make his or her state tax returns available to plaintiff on conditions determined by the court. CCP §1263.520. The provision for this compensation is not intended to apply to inverse condemnation claims for temporary interference with or interruption of business. CCP §1263.530. Code of Civil Procedure §1250.320(b) declares that a defendant who seeks compensation for goodwill must include the claim in the answer to the complaint, but the amount of compensation need not be specified. See Supp §§8.17–8.18.

Comment to CCP §1263.510 states:

The determination of loss of goodwill is governed by the rules of evidence generally applicable to such a determination and not by the special rules relating to valuation in eminent domain. . . . Thus, the provisions of Evidence Code Sections 817 and 819 that restrict admissibility of income from a business for the determination of value, damage, and benefit in no way limit admissibility of income from a business for the determination of loss of goodwill.

A claim for loss of business goodwill may not be pursued on a complaint filed before January 1, 1976, the effective date of CCP §1263.510. *Carson Redev. Agency v Wolf* (1979) 99 CA3d 239, 160 CR 213. When the original proceeding was initiated before the effective date of the new law, the retrial of the case subsequent to the operative date did not allow a defendant to seek loss of business goodwill. *County of San Diego v Morrison* (1984) 153 CA3d 234, 200 CR 187.

A city's payment of business goodwill in a condemnation proceeding it pursued at its own discretion did not constitute the payment of state-mandated costs under former Rev & T C §2231(a) or §2207 for the purpose of cost reimbursement of the city by the state. *City of Merced v State* (1984) 153 CA3d 777, 200 CR 642.

Under CCP §1263.510, the value of goodwill is not limited to patronage but includes the decrease in market value of a business caused by a forced relocation to more expensive premises. *People ex rel Dep't of Transp. v Muller* (1984) 36 C3d 263, 203 CR 772. The court held that patronage and low rents are some of the many "benefits" under the statute that accrue to a business because of its location.

The attorney and the goodwill expert should consider the following factors and document them to the extent possible when a business property is forced to relocate because of the condemnation action:

1. Is a new location available or are potential sites unsuitable or too costly?

2. How well does the new location retain existing customers?

3. Are there increased costs of rent and operation at the new location?

4. What is the effect on customers of a pending announcement of taking of property or of filing a condemnation action when a new location has not been found or secured? Production or fabrication businesses, such as a machine shop, may lose customers who fear that discontinuation and relocation will affect quality or disrupt delivery schedules.

5. Is there temporary loss of goodwill during period of transition from old to new location?

    (a) Cost of retaining key employees although business is decreased;

    (b) Slowdown at old location pending move;

    (c) Duplication of costs on phased move to avoid loss in production;

    (d) Extra efforts to maintain customers;

    (e) Effect on delivery of product or services during move;

    (f) Start-up time at new location.

Neither CCP §1263.010 (compensation for property taken by condemnation) nor CCP §1263.510 (right to compensation for loss of goodwill) indicates the methods for valuing goodwill. To determine the value of loss of goodwill applicable to a leasehold interest, the capitalization of excess income approach may be used with a fair market value analysis to determine the proper rate of capitalization. *Community Dev. Comm'n v Asaro* (1989) 212 CA3d 1297, 1302, 261 CR 231, 233.

On the issue of compensation for goodwill, neither party had the burden of proof when both sides acknowledged that there was a loss and the only question was the amount of compensation. *Redevelopment Agency v Metropolitan Theaters Corp.* (1989) 215 CA3d 808, 263 CR 637.

EASEMENTS

[§4.62] Valuation When Condemned Property Already Burdened With Easement

Just as an easement is compensable "property," a taking that violates a building restriction on the property (such as an equitable servitude or a restrictive covenant) requires payment of just compensation. *Southern Cal. Edison Co. v Bourgerie* (1973) 9 C3d 169, 107 CR 76.

The standard for valuation of an appurtenant easement requires an analysis of the diminution in value of the dominant tenement resulting from the taking of the easement. This same method of valuation applies to restrictive covenants and equitable servitudes. *Redevelopment Agency v Tobriner* (1984) 153 CA3d 367, 200 CR 364.

When the interest being condemned is an easement appurtenant to a dominant estate and that easement is not needed by the dominant estate, the damages will be small or nonexistent. In *Redevelopment Agency v Tobriner* (1989) 215 CA3d 1087, 264 CR 481, the easement in question was for parking and ingress and egress over an area, in the rear of a shopping center, owned in common by the shopping center tenants and subject to their unanimous agreement on any alternative use. Analyzing the circumstances the trial court determined that a nonexclusive appurtenant easement was of no value.

[§4.63] Valuation When Public Agency Imposes Easement

In condemnation of an easement for construction of a tunnel, the landowner is not entitled to recover for the value of the material removed by excavation if the value of the material is less than the cost of removal. The measure of value is the detriment to the estate and not the benefit to the condemnor. If the value of the removed minerals exceeded removal costs, the estate would have been reduced in value and the owner entitled to compensation. *Yuba County Water Agency v Ingersoll* (1975) 45 CA3d 452, 119 CR 444.

DEDICATION PROBLEMS

[§4.64] Power To Dedicate

In *City of Torrance v Superior Court* (1976) 16 C3d 195, 127 CR 609, a developer had acquired and developed land, relying on the city's representations that it would acquire a portion of the land through a pending condemnation suit. After continued delays the city determined to acquire the land by forced dedication and attempted to abandon the condemnation action. The supreme court held that the trial court acted properly in setting aside the abandonment under former CCP §1255a(b) (now CCP §1268.510(b)). There was ample evidence to support the findings that the developer had relied to its detriment on the pending proceeding and could not be restored to its prior position.

[§4.65] Effect on Valuation of Property Subject to Dedication

Code of Civil Procedure §748.5 has been repealed. In its place CCP §771.010 was enacted, adding greater restrictions to the creation of the presumption that a dedication has lapsed.

Following *City of Fresno v Cloud,* cited in Book §4.65, the court in *City of Porterville v Young* (1987) 195 CA3d 1260, 241 CR 349, held that an undeveloped but commercially zoned strip of land that was condemned for a street widening should be valued at its prior precommercial use as agricultural land because dedication of the condemned land was necessary in order to obtain the permits required for commercial development.

[§4.66] Implied Dedication of Public Recreational Easements: *Gion* Doctrine

The court in *Richmond Ramblers Motorcycle Club v Western Title Guar. Co.* (1975) 47 CA3d 747, 121 CR 308, refused to extend the application of the *Gion/Dietz* doctrine from roads, beaches, and shoreline areas to open fields and hillsides of inland areas. In *County of Los Angeles v Berk* (1980) 26 C3d 201, 213, 161 CR 742, 751, however, the supreme court held that its decision in *Gion* merely restated and clarified well-established former law and could be retroactively applied to events giving rise to an implied dedication that occurred before that decision.

In *Taper v City of Long Beach* (1982) 129 CA3d 590, 181 CR 169, agreements made in 1963 between the city and owner regarding an exchange of quitclaim deeds, and in 1968 between the state and owner regarding the fixing of the boundary between the property and state tidelands, each of which were entered into before the 1970 *Gion* decision and did not involve the easements at issue, did not give rise to equitable estoppel against the city or the state, which asserted public recreational and pathway easements in the land condemned.

See also *Cherokee Valley Farms, Inc. v Summerville Elementary School Dist.* (1973) 30 CA3d 579, 106 CR 467, in which the court permitted a school district to quiet title by implied dedication of property that had been occupied and used as a school or for school purposes for 78 years. The former owner of a larger tract encompassing the school property and his successors had acquiesced in the school use, and the district had spent substantial public funds to build and rebuild a structure on the land. See also *County of Orange v Chandler-Sherman Corp.* (1976) 54 CA3d 561, 126 CR 765 (public use of beach area had been casual rather than substantial; no implied dedication found).

In *Aptos Seascape Corp. v County of Santa Cruz* (1982) 138 CA3d 484, 188 CR 191, the court refused to apply the *Gion* doctrine when the path to the beach was blocked by two wooden fences, the ranch owner saw only occasional people using the path, the beach was generally desolate, cars that were parked on roads leading to the beach were towed away, there was no governmental maintenance of the area, and the owners occasionally gave groups specific permission to use the beach.

For further discussion of the *Gion/Dietz* decision, see Shavelson, *Gion v City of Santa Cruz: Where Do We Go From Here?* 47 Cal SBJ 415 (1972) and the response to that article by Berger, *Gion v City of Santa Cruz: A License to Steal?* 49 Cal SBJ 24 (1974).

[§4.67] TREES AND SHRUBS

Although asparagus plants on condemned lands are not within the scope of CCP §1263.205 (former CCP §1248b), under which certain equipment is deemed part of the realty, the plants qualify as part of the realty under CC §§658 and 660, which define a thing as part of the realty "when it is attached to it by roots, as in the case of trees, vines, or shrubs." *People ex rel Dep't of Water Resources v Gianni* (1972) 29 CA3d 151, 156, 105 CR 248, 251.

[§4.68] HARVESTING CROPS

Code of Civil Procedure §1263.250, which replaces former CCP §1249.2, makes clear that after service of the summons the defendant has the right to grow and harvest crops and retain the profit up to the time the property is actually taken. If the taking of possession prevents defendent from harvesting and marketing the crops, compensation is awarded for the fair market value of the crops at the date of change of possession. Plaintiff can obtain a court order precluding the planting of crops after service of summons, but must pay for the loss of the use of the property. CCP §1263.250(b). See CCP §1263.240 and Supp §§4.19–4.22 for general rule on improvements after service of summons.

[§4.68A] MINERAL RESOURCES

The valuation of property for gas storage is addressed in *PG&E v Zuckerman* (1987) 189 CA3d 1113, 234 CR 630. The court in that case made numerous rulings regarding valuation as follows:

(1) Greater latitude is given to an expert in valuing a property if there are no true comparables.

(2) In adjusting comparables to the date of value, the rate of inflation for the gross national product and State Board of Equalization factors for petroleum-producing properties could be used, but not wellhead prices, which relate to evidence of profits derived from a business.

(3) An expert could not base an increase in value for storage property on an increase in the value of a producing property.

(4) When there is no evidence that storage property is suited for further oil and gas exploration at a depth below the storage facility, the increased cost of slant drilling to that depth from other property is too speculative to give rise to severance damages for the inability to drill from the storage property. See Supp §5.8 regarding severance damages.

See also *U.S. v 22.80 Acres of Land* (9th Cir 1988) 839 F2d 1362 on the valuation of mineral deposits.

[§4.70] URBAN RENEWAL VALUATION PROBLEMS

Condemnation blight (see §4.7 and Supp §4.7A) caused by urban renewal takings or planning is frequently asserted by property owners because of the long delays that usually occur between announcement of a project and acquisition of all lands necessary to the project. Compare *Eleopoulos v Richmond Redev. Agency* (ND Cal 1972) 351 F Supp 63 (cause of action for de facto taking was stated when owner's property was designated as part of project, neighboring properties were acquired, and buildings were demolished and boarded up, but no action was instituted against subject property) with *Sayre v City of Cleveland* (6th Cir 1974) 493 F2d 64 (mere inclusion of real estate in general neighborhood renewal plan does not constitute taking, even though the action caused decrease in property value).

The 60-day statute of limitations in Health & S C §33500, regarding an attack on the redevelopment plan as adopted, does not apply to actions alleging illegal implementation of the plan. *Redevelopment Agency v Herrold* (1978) 86 CA3d 1024, 150 CR 621.

Under Health & S C §33399, when a public agency has adopted a redevelopment plan but has not instituted a condemnation action to acquire any property under the plan within three years of its adoption, the owner of any affected parcel may offer in writing to sell the property to the agency at its fair market value. If the agency then does not acquire or commence proceedings within 18 months, the owner may file an inverse action for damages for any interference with possession and use of the property caused by the plan.

Code of Civil Procedure §1243.1, replaced and clarified by CCP §1245.260, permits an action for inverse condemnation if a condemnation suit is not filed within six months after the resolution to condemn, or if a condemnation suit is filed but the summons and complaint are not served within six months after filing.

[§4.71] ENTRY FOR PRELIMINARY SURVEY AND STUDIES

Code of Civil Procedure §1245.010 continues the provisions of former CCP §1242(b), permitting entry for preliminary surveys and studies. Code of Civil Procedure §§1245.020 and 1245.030, concerning court orders and deposits, replace former CCP §1242(a)–(b); CCP §§1245.040–1245.050 replace former CCP §1242.5(c)–(d).

Code of Civil Procedure §1245.060 replaces former Govt C §816 and sets forth the same standard for a condemnor's liability for damages caused by entry for suitability studies. An owner need not file a prior claim (see Book §13.7); recovery may be by an independent civil action or by application to the court if the condemnor has made a deposit before trial, but not by a claim for just compensation in an eminent domain proceeding.

A broad right of entry given by the property owner to the condemnor, not merely to survey, but to construct a public highway, was equivalent to an order for immediate possession (see Book §§8.7–8.10), and the owner was entitled to prejudgment interest from the date of taking possession. *People ex rel Dep't of Pub. Works v Williams* (1973) 30 CA3d 980, 106 CR 795.

5

Severance Damages

[§5.1] INTRODUCTION

Severance damage is compensation for injury to the remainder in a partial taking. CCP §1263.410(a) (former CCP §1248(2)). That compensation is measured by the damage to the remainder reduced by any benefit to the remainder. CCP §1263.410(b) (former CCP §1248(3)). Damage can be caused by severance of the remainder from the part taken and/or construction and use of the project as proposed, whether or not that project is located on the part taken. CCP §1263.420. The latter statutory provision abrogates the rule of *People ex rel Dep't of Pub. Works v Symons* (1960) 54 C2d 855, 9 CR 363; see Supp §5.6.

Special benefits are now defined in CCP §1263.430 (former CCP §1248(3)).

REQUIREMENTS OF SEVERANCE DAMAGES

[§5.2] Existence of Larger Parcel

"Larger parcel" remains undefined in the Eminent Domain Law (CCP §§1230.010–1273.050), as it was under the former law. The deliberate omission "permits continued judicial development of the concept." 12 Cal L Rev'n Comm'n Reports 1835 (1974).

[§5.6] Improvement Need Not Be Located on Property Taken; *Symons* Rule Abrogated

The rule of *People ex rel Dep't of Pub. Works v Symons* (1960) 54 C2d 855, 9 CR 363, which required that the improvement alleged to have caused the damage be located on the property taken from the defendant, has been abrogated by CCP §1263.420(b). Now damages may be awarded whether or not it "is caused by a portion of the project located on the part taken." See Supp §5.22 regarding severance damages due to noise, dust, fumes, and vibrations.

Likewise, benefits (see §5.25) need not be derived from the portion of the project located on the property taken. CCP §1263.430 (codifying *People ex rel Dep't of Pub. Works v Hurd* (1962) 205 CA2d 16, 23 CR 67).

[§5.8] MEASURING SEVERANCE DAMAGES

Code of Civil Procedure §1263.410(a), defining severance damage as compensation for the injury to the remainder when only part of the property is taken, replaces former CCP §1248(2) without substantive change.

The owners of a cattle ranch were not entitled to severance damages from the taking of a right-of-way through their property for the construction of power lines when the evidence showed that the highest and best use of the property would continue to be a cattle ranch and that power lines do not affect the remainder under that use. *PG&E v Parachini* (1972) 29 CA3d 159, 105 CR 477.

In a case involving property to be used in the recovery of injected gas, a landowner's expert's testimony about the cost of slant drilling to explore the earth beneath the condemned storage reservoir was not sufficient to support severance damages. A showing that the property was suited for further gas exploration and that any potential deposit could not be produced from wells outside the condemned area was also required. The condemnation award given by the trial court and denied by the appellate court was based on a speculative projected use for the property claimed by the owner. *PG&E v Zuckerman* (1987) 189 CA3d 1113, 1195, 234 CR 630, 650.

[§5.11] Cost To Cure

In *Ventura County Flood Control Dist. v Security First Nat'l Bank* (1971) 15 CA3d 996, 93 CR 653, the condemned portion of a lemon ranch was a row of large trees serving as a windbreak. Severance damages were allowed for both the cost of replacing the windbreak and the decreased productivity of the ranch during the ten years required to grow a new windbreak. The reduction in probable income from operating the lemon ranch without a windbreak would be a factor considered in determining the fair market value of the ranch.

[§5.11A] Development Potential of Property in Before Condition

When property is located in a flood plain affected by the project to construct a flood control channel, there is a question whether the property could be developed in its before condition without the benefits of the project. In this case, it was error for a trial court to exclude evidence from the property owner concerning historic conditions that caused water flows to be directed elsewhere and showing that a lesser improvement of flood control was adequate for flood control of the property. *Coachella Valley Water Dist. v Western Allied Props.* (1987) 190 CA3d 969, 235 CR 725.

[§5.12] Measurement When Project Not Completed

Rather than assessing damages and benefits on the assumption that the improvement is completed (see *People ex rel Dep't of Pub. Works v Schultz Co.* (1954) 123 CA2d 925, 268 P2d 117, and cases cited in Book §5.12), CCP §1263.440(a) provides that compensation for damages and offset for benefits be computed in a manner that takes into account any delay in the schedule for completing the improvement. Thus it provides for "discounting" of both damages and benefits, and there are at least three possible dates to consider: the date of judgment or possession, the date of construction, and the date of use.

Code of Civil Procedure §1263.440(b) provides that the value of the remainder in the original condition, unaffected by any enhancement or blight, be used as the basis to compute both damages and benefits. See also CCP §1263.330.

Compensation for injury to the remainder must reflect the project as proposed. CCP §1263.450. This statute does not modify the rule of *People ex rel Dep't of Pub. Works v Schultz Co., supra,* that damages be assessed on the basis of the most injurious lawful use reasonably possible when the condemnor has no specific proposal for the manner of construction and use of the project. The section goes on to direct the decisionmaker to consider any physical features, *e.g.,* access roads, fencing, and drainage facilities (see former CCP §1248(5), which was replaced by CCP §1263.450) provided by plaintiff to mitigate the damage or provide benefit to the remainder.

It is not proper for the condemnor to introduce evidence that purports to limit the scope of the taking by contradicting the resolution of necessity. See §6.18. In *County of San Diego v Bressi* (1986) 184 CA3d 112, 229 CR 44, the resolution described a navigation easement for overflight by any aircraft, including jumbo jets, for both commercial and noncommercial flights, but the county sought to introduce evidence that its airport would remain a satellite facility and not be expanded to serve commercial aircraft. The court held that only evidence coextensive with the scope of the easement may be introduced.

The importance of the existence of construction plans for the project at the time of the condemnation action to determine the scope of foreseeable damage from that project is illustrated by the following two inverse condemnation cases. First, the court in *Ellena v State* (1977) 69 CA3d 245, 138 CR 110, denied inverse liability on the doctrines of res judicata and collateral estoppel when the project allegedly caused extensive flooding damage over a year after the condemnation action was settled by stipulated judgment. The court determined that the property owner had actual and constructive knowledge of the plans for the project before entering the stipulated judgment. In *Mehl v People ex rel Dep't of Pub. Works* (1975) 13 C3d 710, 119 CR 625, however, the court held that the property owners were not estopped in a later action for damage from similar flooding problems, because the plans for the drainage facility were nonexistent when the owners conveyed the property to the state for freeway purposes. See §13.23 for discussion of the defense of collateral estoppel in inverse condemnation cases.

In a partial taking of residential property for the widening of a street, including a four-foot strip of property intended for underground utilities, the condemnor in *City of Salinas v Homer* (1980) 106 CA3d 307, 165 CR 65, reserved the right to use the strip for any other purposes. Though the condemnor had no plans at the time to use it for any other purpose, it was proper for the court to award damages for the cloud on the property caused by the reservation of rights. The reservation required the property owner to warn all potential buyers of its existence, thus reducing the present value of the property. The court rejected the argument that the damages were speculative and depended on an actual change of use by the condemnor.

[§5.12A] Improvements Straddling the Take Line

When an improvement is located partially on the land taken and partially on the remainder, the court can determine on the motion of any party that the condemnor must take the entire improvement, together with any necessary easement for the demolition or removal of the improvement. CCP §1263.270; see *County of Los Angeles v Smith* (1976) 55 CA3d 749, 127 CR 666 (condemnor condemned entire structure straddling take line and took a temporary easement over the remainder to effect the removal).

See also CCP §§1240.150 (granting condemnor broad authority to acquire all or a portion of remainder by agreement or by a condemnation proceeding initiated with owner's consent), and 1240.410 (excess condemnation, discussed in Supp §6.10).

[§5.13] Condemnee's Duty To Mitigate Damages

Expenses incurred to bring about a different use on the remaining property were not justified as mitigation of severance damages when the entire property's former use had been terminated by the taking. The court found no evidence to show that, absent the expenditures for title fees, attorney's fees, and broker's commissions in negotiating a mobilehome park lease, the highest and best use after the taking might have been different. The property owner did recover severance damage to the value of the remainder, however, because the new use was not as valuable as the former. *Orange County Flood Control Dist. v Sunny Crest Dairy, Inc.* (1978) 77 CA3d 742, 764, 143 CR 803, 815.

Litigation and engineering expenses incurred by landowners in a separate lawsuit to the condemnation action to compel the agency to comply with the project plans and to comply with the environmental impact report did not constitute mitigation costs for which the owners were entitled to severance damages under CCP §1263.420. The statutory rule authorizing award of severance damages applies only to mitigation damages caused by the taking, not to expenses incurred in preventing or modifying the taking. *Placer County Water Agency v Hofman* (1985) 165 CA3d 890, 211 CR 894.

EXAMPLES OF COMPENSABLE SEVERANCE DAMAGES

Interference With Access

[§5.16] Immediate Access to Adjacent Street

In *Ratchford v County of Sonoma* (1972) 22 CA3d 1056, 99 CR 887, a county board of supervisors exceeded its authority in abandoning a portion of a mapped but undeveloped street of a recorded subdivision, although dedication had never been accepted. The record showed no public benefit from abandonment, and no evidence that the portion would not be necessary for prospective use. The court held that the board had no right to surrender the inchoate rights of abutting owners.

"Property which requires substantial expenditure to establish access thereto is obviously worth less to a potential buyer than the identical property with access already provided." *City of Los Angeles v Ricards* (1973) 10 C3d 385, 388, 110 CR 489, 491. This principle is equally applicable to weighing aspects of comparability in the market data approach to value. See Book §4.27.

Loss of Use

[§5.20] Interference With Remainder During Construction Period

In *City of Los Angeles v Ricards* (1973) 10 C3d 385, 110 CR 489, an inverse condemnation case, there was substantial temporary impairment of access without recovery by the property owner. City construction upstream had caused a diversion of waters that destroyed a private bridge that provided the sole means of access to plaintiff's property. The bridge was reconstructed by the city two years later; during the interim there was no access to the property. The court held that there was a taking but that the owner was entitled only to nominal damages because she had no intention of putting the subject property to any use during that time, and thus lost nothing by the taking. Compensation was made by replacement of the bridge.

City of Los Angeles v Ricards, supra, was distinguished in *Jones v People ex rel Dep't of Transp.* (1978) 22 C3d 144, 148 CR 640, in which the temporary (1967 to 1975) loss of access prevented subdivision of plaintiffs' property and made it unsalable. The local legislative body would not allow a street connection to plaintiffs' property because that property lay within a proposed freeway route that was the subject of a freeway agreement (see Str & H C §100.2) between the local agency and the state. The state informed the property owners that access to the remaining lands would be restored by construction of a frontage road. The freeway, however, was never built; it was abandoned in 1975 after trial court judgment in favor of plaintiff. Unlike *Ricards,* the property owners made several unsuccessful efforts to sell the property in the interim.

See also *Clay v City of Los Angeles* (1971) 21 CA3d 577, 98 CR 582 (when city street was washed out by flood, destroying access to private property, city was obligated, within reasonable time after receiving notice of the destruction of street, either to restore street or to pay just compensation to owners for loss of access).

There was no compensable loss of use of the remainder of defendant's property in a case in which the condemnor took title to a commercial building straddling the take line and a temporary easement over the remainder to remove the building. The property owner did not show that the easement restriction constituted any limitation after removal of the structure, and there was no continued interruption of access to the remainder. *County of Los Angeles v Smith* (1976) 55 CA3d 749, 127 CR 666.

"Temporary severance damage" is sometimes used to describe damages for a temporary taking. In *Orange County Flood Control Dist. v Sunny Crest Dairy, Inc.* (1978) 77 CA3d 742, 143 CR 803, the owner terminated the entire property's existing use as a cash-and-carry dairy operation at the time of the take and began to develop a mobilehome park. The owner sought to recover the fair rental value of the remainder as a cash-and-carry dairy for two years during which the mobilehome park was developed on the theory of a temporary taking of the remainder. Recovery for a temporary taking of the remainder was denied because the evidence showed that the condemnor did not physically take the remainder or impair its use for mobilehome park development. The attempt to recover for a temporary taking was in the nature of a business loss and, as such, was not compensable.

[§5.22] Noise, Dust, Fumes, and Vibrations

In *Varjabedian v City of Madera* (1977) 20 C3d 285, 142 CR 429, the supreme court allowed recovery of nuisance damages caused by noxious odors emanating from a city's sewage treatment plant. The court also held that a plaintiff can state a claim for inverse condemnation if he or she can establish that his or her property has suffered a direct, peculiar, and substantial burden as a result of recurring sewage odors from a sewage facility. That type of damage apparently would be more difficult to prove as severance damages in a direct condemnation action before construction of the city's sewage treatment plant. The *Varjabedian* complaint was based on allegations that the property could not be used for residential purposes because the path of prevailing winds led directly from the plant to the property and the gaseous invasions were recurrent. An environmental impact report for the project might provide evidence for a claim of reasonable anticipation of the damage in a direct condemnation suit.

In *Harding v State ex rel Dep't of Transp.* (1984) 159 CA3d 359, 205 CR 561, property owners were allowed to pursue a cause of action in inverse condemnation for damages due to noise, loss of air and light, dust, dirt, and highway debris from construction of a freeway embankment directly in front of the owners' house, even though no portion of the owners' lot was taken for the freeway. The court held that the owner should be allowed to establish that the property suffered a peculiar and substantial burden as a result of proximity to the highway. The court did not allow a recovery under these same facts for nuisance, because CC §3482 provides "that nothing which is done or maintained under express authority of a statute can be deemed a nuisance," and the Streets and Highways Code gives the state the authority to construct and maintain highways and to construct noise attenuation barriers. The court distinguished *Varjabedian v City of Madera, supra,* in which nuisance damages were allowed for noxious sewer odors, by noting that when a public entity is authorized by statute to construct and maintain a facility and it is not done in an unreasonable manner or is unreasonably dirty, no cause of action exists. In *Varjabedian,* the court held that the statute authorizing the construction and maintenance of a sewage facility did not authorize the emanation of noxious odors from the plant. *Varjabedian v City of Madera* (1977) 20 C3d 285, 292, 142 CR 429, 434.

In *County of San Diego v Bressi* (1986) 184 CA3d 112, 229 CR 44, damages from the taking of an avigation easement were based on the fact that the underlying property would be usable only for low-density uses, because of noise vibrations, fumes, and crash hazards from low-flying aircraft. See §13.20 for discussion of public entity liability for damages from overflying aircraft in the vicinity of an airport.

See Comment, *The Highway Case: Noise as a Taking or Damaging of Property in California,* 20 Santa Clara L Rev 425 (1980).

[§5.22A] Health Hazards From Project

In 1988, two appellate court cases were decided in which the possibility of a health hazard from electromagnetic radiation from the operation of a power line was held to diminish the value of the remaining property. In *San Diego Gas & Elec. Co. v 3250 Corp.* (1988) 205 CA3d 1075, 252 CR 853, testimony about potential adverse biological effects resulting from the electromagnetic field produced by a transmission line was allowed on the basis that these potential effects were widely known and would thus reduce the market value of the remaining property in its after condition. In *San Diego Gas & Elec. Co. v Daley* (1988) 205 CA3d 1334, 253 CR 144, the trial court properly refused a mini-trial on the merits of the controversy of health hazards caused by electromagnetic radiation from power lines, but it did permit evidence about the controversy because, to ascertain severance damages, the court would have to determine whether a fear of the danger existed that affected market value. Incidentally, one of the sources of information supporting the property owner's claim was the project's Environmental Impact Report (see Supp §2.20A), which contained information that there were several studies suggesting that electromagnetic radiation has a detrimental effect on humans and animals, and further investigation was advised. The *Daley* decision also discusses other recent cases throughout the nation regarding buyer fear of electromagnetic radiation.

[§5.23] Agricultural Land

The need to examine severance damages to agricultural land was demonstrated in an inverse condemnation case. When a property owner settled a condemnation action by stipulated judgment and the public project concerned construction of an elevated freeway and drainage system over the owner's vineyard, the doctrines of res judicata and collateral estoppel precluded a later inverse condemnation claim for damage caused by heavy rains when the drainage system allegedly failed and caused considerable erosion to the remaining land more than a year after the settlement. One of the key considerations in the court's determination was that the plans for the project were known at the time of the stipulation, giving support to the trial court's finding that the damage was reasonably foreseeable as a result of the construction of the improvements proposed in the original plan. *Ellena v State* (1977) 69 CA3d 245, 138 CR 110. Compare *Mehl v People ex rel Dep't of Pub. Works* (1975) 13 C3d 710, 119 CR 625, discussed in Supp §5.12.

[§5.23A] Special Purpose Property

The partial taking of special purpose property that has extensive fixtures (machinery and equipment) may substantially impair the use of the remainder. In *City of Commerce v National Starch & Chem. Corp.* (1981) 118 CA3d 1, 14, 173 CR 176, 183, the court admitted evidence of accelerated depreciation of the fixtures for the purpose of determining severance damages, because the market was limited for an adhesives manufacturing plant and the loss of expansion capability caused by the taking required that the operation be discontinued in three to five years.

[§5.24] Other Types of Severance Damages

(4) See *County of San Diego v Bressi* (1986) 184 CA3d 112, 229 CR 44 (downgrading of use from commercial to storage and warehousing because of avigation easement for overflights to serve an airport).

(7) The rule of *City of Los Angeles v Sabatasso* (discussed in Book §5.24(7)) that severance damages may be sought for improvements located on the remainder, is codified in CCP §1263.205(a). Moreover, that section makes it clear that "improvements" includes machinery and equipment installed on the property, eliminating the requirement of former CCP

§1248b that the equipment be designed for manufacturing or industrial purposes.

(8) In *City of Baldwin Park v Stoskus* (1972) 8 C3d 563, 105 CR 325, the supreme court reversed the lower court opinion discussed in Book §5.24(8). The court held that if imposition of a special assessment is not a direct result of the taking, the assessment lien is not recoverable as severance damages. The court also rejected the property owner's proposed rule that the amount of severance should include the special assessment, less any benefits that will accrue. Such a proposal, the court held, permits a collateral attack on the amount of the assessment and unduly complicates eminent domain proceedings.

(9) Competition by a public utility with a private water company. See Pub Util C §1503; *San Gabriel Valley Water Co. v City of Montebello* (1978) 84 CA3d 757, 766, 148 CR 830, 835.

SPECIAL BENEFITS

[§5.25] Nature of Special Benefits

The Eminent Domain Law (CCP §§1230.010–1273.050) continues court-developed rules concerning the offset of benefits against severance damages (CCP §1263.430, superseding former CCP §1248(3)), and allows the courts to continue to develop the law in this area. 12 Cal L Rev'n Comm'n Reports 1837 (1974). Code of Civil Procedure §1263.430 defines benefit to the remainder as that benefit caused by the construction and use of the project in the manner proposed, whether or not it is generated from a portion of the project located on the land taken.

Code of Civil Procedure §1263.440 directs that (1) damage and benefit be computed to reflect any delay in the construction and use of the project as proposed (see Supp §5.12)) and (2) the value in the "before" condition be considered apart from any enhancement and blight.

There is an important exception to the rule that benefits can only be offset against damages and cannot be used to reduce compensation for the take: Excess benefits are deducted from any compensation for goodwill. CCP §1263.410(b). See CCP §1263.510; Supp §4.61.

Benefits accruing from actual construction activity of a project, *e.g.,* development of a gravel pit on the remainder, do not qualify as special. "Special benefits have traditionally been limited to increases in value that occur after the construction and incident to the public use of the improvement." *People ex rel Dep't of Pub. Works v Simon Newman Co.* (1974) 37 CA3d 398, 409, 112 CR 298, 305.

[§5.28] Examples of General Benefits

(f) Development of a gravel pit on condemnee's land and purchase of that gravel for use in the construction of the project when evidence showed that the gravel could have been obtained from any number of sources in the immediate vicinity. *People ex rel Dep't of Pub. Works v Simon Newman Co.* (1974) 37 CA3d 398, 112 CR 298.

Other Special Benefits Problems

[§5.30] Benefits From Concurrent But Separate Public Project

Although the state joined acquisitions by the Department of Water Resources for an aqueduct and by the Department of Public Works for a freeway in the same action, special benefits occasioned by the freeway construction could not be offset against the severance damage caused by the aqueduct construction. Code of Civil Procedure §1248(3), which authorized damages and benefits to be assessed for the "construction of the improvement," did not allow offsetting of damages and benefits between distinct and separate projects simply because they were joined in one action. *People ex rel Dep't of Pub. Works v Simon Newman Co.* (1974) 37 CA3d 398, 112 CR 298.

Code of Civil Procedure §1248(3) has been repealed and superseded by CCP §§1260.230, 1263.410, 1263.430.

[§5.31] Special Assessment Proceedings

The supreme court in *City of Baldwin Park v Stoskus* (1972) 8 C3d 563, 105 CR 325, overruled the court of appeal decision cited in Book §5.31 and held that an assessment lien cannot be considered for valuation of severance damages. See Supp §5.24.

The supreme court in *White v County of San Diego* (1980) 26 C3d 897, 163 CR 640, upheld an assessment against commercial property for widening of a major thoroughfare when the right-of-way assessment was measured by the compensation paid for the strip of land taken. Compare *White* with *Spring Street Co. v City of Los Angeles,* cited in Book §5.31.

The Improvement Act of 1911 (Str & H C §§5000–6794) has been amended to transfer some of its provisions to the Public Contract Code. Streets and Highways Code §§6765–6771 and 6786–6793 have been repealed and replaced by Pub Cont C §§20853–20859 and 20867–20874, respectively, without substantial change. Part of Str & H C §6764 has been transferred to Pub Cont C §20852.

The Improvement Bond Act of 1915, cited in Book §5.31, is supplemented by provisions relating to refunding of bonds at Str & H C §§9000–9481, 9500–9707.

[§5.32] Special Verdict To Ascertain Specific Amounts on Claims of Severance Damage

It is not necessary that an expert assign separate sums for each element of market value and severance damage that he or she considers. *PG&E*

v Hufford (1957) 49 C2d 545, 561, 319 P2d 1033, 1042. But it is the responsibility of the party who seeks appellate review challenging the admissibility of some element of severance damage to submit special verdict forms to the trial court to establish the extent to which the jury relied on the alleged erroneously admitted evidence. *San Diego Gas & Elec. Co. v Daley* (1988) 205 CA3d 1334, 1351, 253 CR 144, 154.

6

Public Use and Necessity Defenses

INTRODUCTION

[§6.1] Constitutional and Statutory Limitations on Eminent Domain

By approval of the voters in the 1974 general election, Cal Const art I, §14 was replaced by art I, §19, which reads in part:

Private property may be taken or damaged for public use only when just compensation, ascertained by a jury unless waived, has first been paid to, or into court for, the owner.

Code of Civil Procedure §1240.010 restates the constitutional limitation that the power of eminent domain may be exercised only for a public use. The Eminent Domain Law (CCP §§1230.010–1273.050) does not continue the former CCP §1238 listings of public uses on behalf of which condemnation may be undertaken.

Code of Civil Procedure §§1240.010 (public use limitation) and 1240.020 (statutory delegation for condemnation authority required) replace CCP §1241(1); CCP §§1240.030 (public necessity required), 1240.040 (resolution of necessity required), and 1245.210–1245.390 (requirements of resolution of necessity) replace CCP §1241(2); CCP §§1240.610–1240.700 (condemnation for a more necessary public use) replace CCP §1241(3).

Code of Civil Procedure §1240.110 (former CCP §1239) permits any person authorized to condemn to acquire any interest in the property that is necessary for that use. Former law distinguished between taking a fee and an easement. See Taylor, *The Right To Take—The Right To Take the Fee or Any Lesser Interest*, 1 Pac LJ 555 (1970). The statute does not, however, abrogate other statutes limiting the interest that may be taken in particular circumstances. CCP §1240.110(b). See Supp §6.6.

The supreme court held that the term "blighted area" in the Community Redevelopment Law (Health & S C §33030) could not include a commercially prosperous golf course. *Sweetwater Valley Civic Ass'n v City of National City* (1976) 18 C3d 270, 133 CR 859. See *Regus v City of*

Baldwin Park (1977) 70 CA3d 968, 139 CR 196. Lacking any evidence of blight in a particular noncontiguous site within a project, the court held it was improper to include that site in a redevelopment area in order to provide enough money for the entire project. See also *Emmington v Solano County Redev. Agency* (1987) 195 CA3d 491, 237 CR 636.

A cable television company could not take property by eminent domain, because it was not granted statutory authority to condemn property and was not a quasi-municipal or quasi-public entity. *Cox Cable of San Diego, Inc. v Bookspan* (1987) 195 CA3d 22, 240 CR 407.

[§6.2] Significance of Public Use and Necessity

Code of Civil Procedure §1268.610 continues the rule of former CCP §1246.4 that plaintiffs must reimburse defendant's litigation expenses if the right to take is defeated.

[§6.3] Public Use and Necessity Distinguished

The judgment determines the right to take and fixes the compensation the plaintiff must pay. CCP §1235.130 (former CCP §1264.7).

PUBLIC USE

[§6.4] Definition

See *National City Business Ass'n v City of National City* (1983) 146 CA3d 1060, 194 CR 707, which found sufficient evidence to substantiate an agency's determination of blight, and *Redevelopment Agency v Del-Camp Invs.* (1974) 38 CA3d 836, 113 CR 762, which recognized community redevelopment as a proper public use. But see *Sweetwater Valley Civic Ass'n v City of National City* (1976) 18 C3d 270, 133 CR 859, in which the court held that a redevelopment agency's determination of blight is not conclusive.

See also *Huntington Park Redev. Agency v Duncan* (1983) 142 CA3d 17, 190 CR 744, in which the agency was allowed to condemn a parking lot of one property owner in a redevelopment area for the benefit of another property owner who had entered into a participation agreement with the agency to expand its business. Although the condemnee had also submitted a proposal for development, the court ruled that the agency's selection of the adjoining owner's competing proposal was within the bounds of discretion when there was evidence of advantages in that proposal. An owner who participates in a redevelopment plan does not have an absolute right to develop his own parcel.

California Constitution art I, §14, cited in Book §6.4, has been renumbered art I, §19.

Running an electrical line extension to homeowners' residences is not a public or quasi-public activity constituting a public use. The line extension resulted from a contract between the developer of the subdivision and the utility without the exercise of eminent domain rights. *Cantu v PG&E* (1987) 189 CA3d 160, 234 CR 365.

[§6.5] Determination of Public Use

Code of Civil Procedure §§1238–1238.7, enumerating permissible public uses of the condemnation power, has been repealed. Now see CCP §§1230.010–1273.050. The new legislation no longer enumerates specific public uses. Condemnation may be exercised only by a person expressly authorized by statute to exercise the power for a particular use. CCP §1240.020. Whenever the legislature provides statutory authorization to condemn property for a particular use, that authorization establishes a public use. CCP §1240.010. However, CCP §1240.020 does not preclude judicial scrutiny of the allegation that the proposed use in a particular case is a public use. See generally 12 Cal L Rev'n Comm'n Reports 1696–1697 (1974). These statutory declarations do not purport to be exclusive. For example, Govt C §37350.5 authorizes a city to acquire, under condemnation, any property necessary to carry out any of its powers or functions.

A program of land reform condemning property of large estates was upheld in *Hawaii Hous. Auth. v Midkiff* (1984) 467 US 229. Hawaii created a land condemnation scheme by which the state purchased land owned by lessors and transferred title to lessees in order to reduce the concentration of landownership among relatively few individuals. The Supreme Court upheld the scheme, ruling that it had to abide by the state's determination of public use as long as the exercise of eminent domain was rationally related to a conceivable public purpose. In this case, the condemnation scheme was enacted to rectify the oligopoly of landownership that originated with Hawaii's monarchs. The fact that the land remained in the possession of private parties throughout the condemnation had no effect on the validity of its rationale. But see *Gregory v City of San Juan Capistrano* (1983) 142 CA3d 72, 191 CR 47, which held unconstitutional a rent control law requiring a mobilehome park owner who desires to sell to first offer it to park residents.

Running an electrical line extension to homeowners' residences is not a public or quasi-public activity constituting a public use. The line extension resulted from a contract between the developer of the subdivision and the utility without the exercise of eminent domain rights. *Cantu v PG&E* (1987) 189 CA3d 160, 234 CR 365.

Defenses

[§6.6] Lack of Authority To Condemn

Code of Civil Procedure §1240.110(a), authorizing acquisition of a necessary interest "[e]xcept to the extent limited by statute," recognizes that other statutes may preclude condemnation of certain property. See, e.g., Supp §6.12 (prior public use); Pub Res C §8030 (former CCP §1240(2), regarding certain lands within the public domain of the state or United States); Govt C §37353(c) (existing golf course may not be acquired by a city for the same purpose); Health & S C §§8134, 8560, 8560.5 (cemetery land).

Moreover, CCP §1240.110(b) provides that the section does not expand the scope of authority granted beyond specific statutes and certain "interest in or types of property."

It should be noted that the listing of examples of property or property interests in CCP §1240.110(a) is for illustration only.

A local public entity may condemn only within its boundaries, but extraterritorial condemnation may occur by express statutory authority (e.g., Govt C §61610 regarding community service districts) or when the power is implied as an incident to the existence of other expressed powers. CCP §1240.050.

Code of Civil Procedure §1240.140 authorizes two or more public entities to aquire a particular parcel under a joint exercise of powers agreement both when the parcel is needed for a joint project and when each agency requires a portion for its own use.

The power to condemn implicitly includes the power to condemn for mitigation of environmental effects caused by the authorized activity. It does not include the power to condemn for general environmental purposes unrelated to the agency's powers. *Golden Gate Bridge, Highway & Transp. Dist. v Muzzi* (1978) 83 CA3d 707, 148 CR 197.

In reviewing a dismissal of a condemnation action on a motion for summary judgment, the supreme court, in *City of Oakland v Oakland Raiders* (1982) 32 C3d 60, 183 CR 673, considered the question of whether a city could prove that its proposed acquisition and operation of a professional football franchise was for a valid public use. The court relied on prior decisions that intangible property could be condemned (*Kimball Laundry Co. v U.S.* (1949) 338 US 1; *West River Bridge Co. v Dix* (1848) 47 US (6 How.) 507), California decisions concerning a city's acquisition of a baseball field (*City of Los Angeles v Superior Court* (1959) 51 C2d 423, 333 P2d 745), and a county's acquisition of lands for a county fair (*County of Alameda v Meadowlark Dairy Corp.* (1964) 227 CA2d 80, 38 CR 474), to conclude that the City of Oakland had properly proceeded under law and was entitled to prove to the trial court that its proposed action was an appropriate municipal function.

In answer to the defense that even if a city could own a sports franchise, it cannot condemn an established team, the court relied on *Citizens Util. Co. v Superior Court* (1963) 59 C2d 805, 31 CR 316, which approved condemnation of an operating utility, and on the absence of any legislative prohibition against acquiring an existing business. Government Code §37353(c), which allows a municipality to condemn land for a golf course but prohibits condemnation of an existing golf course, was cited to show that, when the legislature intends to have prohibitions apply, it states these explicitly.

There was no infirmity in the City of Oakland's action to condemn merely because the city intended to promptly transfer to private parties the property interests acquired. Citing CCP §1240.120(b), which states that a person may acquire property with the intent to sell, lease, or exchange it if the transfer is made subject to reservations necessary to protect or preserve the attractiveness, safety, and usefulness of the project, the court stated that it was for the trial court to determine whether the controls set forth in the specific transfer agreement were adequate.

On retrial after the supreme court's decision, the trial court sustained the Oakland Raiders' objections to the taking. On appeal of that decision, however, the appellate court in *City of Oakland v Superior Court* (1983) 150 CA3d 267, 197 CR 729, again returned the matter to the trial court, ruling that the trial court had improperly applied the supreme court's decision to the facts presented.

Finally, in *City of Oakland v Oakland Raiders* (1985) 174 CA3d 414, 220 CR 153, the court held that a city does not have the same inherent power of condemnation that resides in the state. Moreover, although a state may exercise its power of eminent domain even though it indirectly or incidentally burdens interstate commerce, in this case it would have unreasonably burdened professional football, a nationwide business. The California Supreme Court denied review and Oakland's attempt to acquire the Raiders by eminent domain ended. See *City of Oakland v Oakland Raiders* (1988) 203 CA3d 78, 249 CR 606, concerning award of attorneys' fees for successfully challenging the right to take.

[§6.6A] Public Utilities

Various privately owned public utilities are given the power of eminent domain by the Public Utilities Code: railroad corporations (§611), electrical corporations (§612), gas corporations (§613), heat corporations (§614), pipeline corporations (§615), telephone corporations (§616), telegraph corporations (§617), water corporations (§618), wharfingers (§619), common carriers (§620), street railroad corporations (§621), motor or water carriers (§622), warehouses (§623), and sewer system corporations (§624).

[§6.6B] Authority of Private Persons

Code of Civil Procedure §1240.020 states that no person may condemn property for a particular public use unless the legislature has delegated that authority to that person. The Eminent Domain Law (CCP §§1230.010–1273.050) repealed former CC §1001's broad delegation to private persons.

Specific statutes grant condemnation power to certain private persons: nonprofit educational institutions of collegiate grade (Ed C §94500); nonprofit hospitals (Health & S C §1260); mutual water companies (Pub Util C §2729); land chest corporations for low-income housing (Health & S C §35167); and limited dividend housing corporations (Health & S C §34874). These private persons are classifed as "quasi-public entities" (CCP §1245.320), and to condemn they must obtain a resolution of consent from the city or county within whose boundaries the property sought to be condemned is located (CCP §1245.330). See Supp §6.19.

The necessity of a demolition permit for a hospital classified as a quasi-public entity under CCP §1245.320 was discussed in *St. John's Hosp. & Health Center v City of Santa Monica* (1983) 141 CA3d 47, 190 CR 74. A hospital negotiated the purchase of property under threat of eminent domain, intending to demolish the existing structures for parking spaces. Because the property was acquired by negotiation, the special procedures for a quasi-public entity condemnation were not followed. As a result, a demolition permit was required. The hospital did not have the right to proceed with its property as if it had condemned the land.

A private property owner can request any public entity authorized to acquire, construct, own, or operate a sewer system to undertake a condemnation action on behalf of that person for sewer purposes. Health & S C §4967.

The California Law Revision Commission recommended that the power of condemnation not be given to private persons (with a few enumerated exceptions for nonprofit organizations and mutual water companies). 12 Cal L Rev'n Comm'n Reports 1635 (1974).

Effective January 1, 1983, the legislature expanded the authority of a private property owner to exercise the power of eminent domain to acquire a temporary right of entry on adjacent or nearby lands to repair or reconstruct land or improvements. New CC §1002 authorizes that power of condemnation by a private property owner, subject to specific conditions, that (1) there is a necessity to do the repair work and great necessity to enter the adjacent land to carry out the works, (2) the right to enter the adjacent land will be exercised in a manner that provides the least damage to the property and inconvenience to the occupants or owners thereof, and (3) the hardship to the person seeking the exercise of the power of eminent domain outweighs any hardship to the owner or occupant of the adjacent property.

Entry may not be made until after an appropriate court order permitting entry is issued or judgment for the plaintiff is entered. The court may order the payment of compensation in the form of rent for the temporary use of the land. The new law does not allow temporary entry on lands used for commercial production of agricultural commodities and forest products. To implement the authority to temporarily enter neighboring lands for repair, CCP §1245.326 has been added to the Eminent Domain Law (CCP §§1230.010–1273.050), categorizing the private person seeking to exercise this power as a "quasi-public entity" and requiring the legislative body, by resolution, to determine that the conditions required by CC §1002 exist.

In 1976 the legislature enacted a new CC §1001 and CCP §1245.325 to permit a private property owner to condemn appurtenant easements for utility service purposes. The constitutionality of CC §1001 and CCP §1245.325 were upheld in *L & M Prof. Consultants v Ferreira* (1983) 146 CA3d 1038, 194 CR 695. See also Health & S C §4967, which allows a sewer maintenance district to contract to undertake condemnation action on behalf of a property owner in order to provide sanitary sewer service.

Legislative authorization of CC §1001 providing a private right of condemnation to acquire an easement to provide utility service, including electrical service, is the equivalent of a legislative declaration that such use is a public use. *Cantu v PG&E* (1987) 189 CA3d 160, 234 CR 365.

[§6.6C] Failure To Follow California Environmental Quality Act

A municipality's adoption of a resolution of necessity declaring that it was in the public interest to acquire by eminent domain a water company was defeated by a prior environmental impact report that assumed the water company would provide water to a new development approved by the city. Before the city could proceed with condemnation, it should have reviewed the environmental impact report to determine whether the new plan required a supplemental EIR. The EIR was not adequate to support the project for which the water company's facilities were condemned, and it was proper to raise the issue of inadequacy of the prior EIR at the hearing for adoption of the resolution of necessity. *City of San Jose v Great Oaks Water Co.* (1987) 192 CA3d 1005, 237 CR 845.

[§6.9] No Intent To Use Property Within Reasonable Time

The Eminent Domain Law (CCP §§1230.010–1273.050) continues the power to condemn property in anticipation of the condemnor's future needs, but there must be a reasonable probability that the property will be used within seven years after the date of the complaint or after a longer time if the time is shown to be reasonable. CCP §1240.220(a). The date of use is the date when the property is actually devoted to the use for which it was taken or when the construction of the project is started, but delays from extraordinary litigation or from failure to obtain an agreement or permit for construction from a public entity are excluded. CCP §1240.210. If the condemnor does not intend to put the property to use within seven years, the complaint (see Supp §§6.24, 8.1) and resolution of necessity (see Supp §6.18) must state the estimated date of use to put the defendant on notice. CCP §1240.220(b).

The burden is on defendant to prove the lack of reasonable probability that the date of use will be within seven years. CCP §1240.230(b). If dcfcndant proves this, or if the complaint itself states that the date of use is beyond seven years, plaintiff has the burden of showing that the future time of use is reasonable. CCP §1240.230(c). The resolution of necessity is no longer conclusive on this point.

Whether a use can be fairly anticipated is a factual issue and depends on a variety of circumstances. In *PG&E v Parachini* (1972) 29 CA3d 159, 105 CR 477, a 350-foot-wide easement was sought for construction of two electric power transmission lines. Defendants objected to the taking for the second line on the ground that the nuclear generating facility proposed for use in conjunction with the line had not yet been approved by the Public Utilities Commission or the Atomic Energy Commission. The appellate court held that the trial court properly considered that the easement being condemned was to be used for one segment of a complex system for generating and transmitting electricity, arrangements for which must be made further ahead than for a simpler type of use. The evidence showed that the second line would be used when additional nuclear-generating facilities began operating in four to five years, that there was a projected need for additional power plants over the next decade, and that the PUC had approved the projected construction in principle. See also *PG&E v Hay* (1977) 68 CA3d 905, 137 CR 613, in which the court reached the same conclusion under similar facts.

The date of use for property taken under the Federal Aid Highway Act of 1973 (23 USC §§101–407, 49 USC §1602a) must be within ten years, or if it is to take longer, be shown to be reasonable, subject to the same rules on burden of proof as those condemnations subject to the seven-year limitation. CCP §1240.250.

When the state condemned a strip of land adjoining a state highway in an area subject to earth slides for the specific purposes of providing a relatively secure slope adjoining that section of the highway and providing access for any future repair work, the property was being used to maintain the highway and was not being held for future use. *People ex rel Dep't of Transp. v Sullivan* (1978) 78 CA3d 120, 144 CR 100.

East Bay Mun. Util. Dist. v City of Lodi is incorrectly described in Book §6.9. The case is not relevant to the discussion in this section and should be disregarded. It remains true that most challenges based on uncertainty of future use are unsuccessful.

[§6.10] Excess Property Taken

Condemnation of remnants is allowed under CCP §1240.410(b). See also CCP §1240.150. A remnant is defined as "a remainder or portion thereof that will be left in such size, shape, or condition as to be of little market value." CCP §1240.410(a). This definition incorporates the financial remnant theory of *People ex rel Dep't of Pub. Works v Superior Court* (1968) 68 C2d 206, 212, 65 CR 342, 346, discussed in Book §6.10, except that the concept of "excessive damages" is not set forth. Examples of remnants are totally landlocked parcels and parcels reduced below the minimum lot size under zoning standards. Defendant can defeat an excess taking by showing that the condemnor has a reasonable and economically feasible way to avoid creating a remnant. CCP §1240.410(c).

Both the resolution of necessity (see Supp §6.18) and the complaint (see Supp §§6.24, 8.1) must cite CCP §1240.410 in cases concerning excess takings. There is no requirement to plead facts showing that the remnant can be taken; the resolution of necessity creates a presumption that the property may be taken as a remnant. This presumption affects only the burden of producing evidence. Absent any dispute on the issue, the court may find the taking necessary. If the issue is contested, the condemnor has the burden of proof. See CCP §1240.420 and Comment.

[§6.10A] Condemnation for Exchange Purposes

In substitute condemnation, the condemnor agrees with the owner of the land it needs for its project to compensate that owner with other property. The condemnor then condemns the property of a third party to complete the exchange. See CCP §1240.310. The law gives this authority to all public entities with the power of condemnation, but restricts its use as follows:

(1) To cases in which the property required for the project is devoted to or held for some public use and the property owner is authorized to condemn property. The property owner must have agreed in writing to make the exchange, and to devote the substitute property to the same public use. CCP §1240.320.

(2) To cases in which the necessary property is devoted to public use and the condemning agency is required by a court order or judgment, or by agreement with the property owner, to relocate the displaced public use. CCP §1240.330. This situation differs from (1) in that the public entity seeking the substitute property is obligated to relocate the public use of the necessary property itself and then convey the improved new property to the owner of the necessary property.

(3) To cases in which land deprived of utility service or road access by the taking is to have service or access restored. CCP §1240.350.

In all cases, the resolution of necessity (see Supp §6.18) and the complaint (see Supp §§6.24, 8.1) must refer to the statutory authority for the substitute taking.

[§6.11] DEFENSE THAT LAND IS ALREADY APPROPRIATED TO PUBLIC USE; MORE NECESSARY PUBLIC USE

Code of Civil Procedure §1247(3) has been repealed and replaced by CCP §1260.020.

[§6.12] Prior Public Use

The reference to *East Bay Mun. Util. Dist. v City of Lodi,* cited in Book §6.12, is misleading. In *Lodi,* the court held that the anticipated use was contingent and indefinite, and therefore not protected from further appropriation.

[§6.13] Multiple Use

Code of Civil Procedure §1240.510 provides that any person authorized to condemn for a particular use may also condemn property appropriated to a public use for a compatible joint use. If defendant objects and proves that its property is appropriated to a public use, plaintiff then has the burden of proving that the proposed use will not interfere with or impair the existing or planned public use by defendant. CCP §1240.520. The court may regulate the terms and conditions of the joint use. CCP §1240.530.

The complaint (see Supp §§6.24, 8.1) and resolution of necessity (see Supp §6.18) must specifically invoke the authority of CCP §1240.510.

More Necessary Public Use

[§6.14] Determination of More Necessary Public Use

The authority to take for a more necessary public use granted by former CCP §§1240(3), 1240(5), and 1241(3) is continued in CCP §1240.610. Plaintiff, seeking to invoke this authority, must refer specifically to the statute in its complaint (see Supp §§6.24, 8.1) and resolution of necessity (see Supp §6.18). If defendant objects to such a taking and establishes that its property is appropriated to a public use, plaintiff has the burden of proving that its use is more necessary. CCP §1240.620. Defendant also has the right to continue its use as a joint use if the continuance will not interfere with, impair, or require significant alteration of the more necessary use. CCP §1240.630.

In *Southern Cal. Edison Co. v Rice* (9th Cir 1982) 685 F2d 354, land alloted to Native Americans and held in trust by the United States was not property appropriated to a public use, and therefore the condemnation action for a right-of-way to install electrical transmission lines was not subject to dismissal for failure to allege a compatible or more necessary public use.

[§6.15] Statutory Provisions

The law now establishes a general rule of priority that any public use for which the state appropriates property is a more necessary use than the use to which that property has already been appropriated by another person. CCP §1240.640. A public entity is given similar priority over any other person. CCP §1240.650; see former CCP §1240(3). Furthermore, there is a rebuttable presumption that the public use of property appropriated by one local public entity is a more necessary use than any use to which the property may be put by any other local public entity. CCP §1240.660.

There is a rebuttable presumption, however, that property (1) owned by a nonprofit organization whose primary purpose is to preserve the property in its natural condition, (2) open to the public with reasonable restrictions, and (3) irrevocably dedicated to the preservation of native plants and animals is appropriated to the best and most necessary use. CCP §1240.670; see former CCP §1241.9. The same presumption applies to (1) state, regional, county, or city park, open space, or recreational areas; (2) wildlife or water fowl management areas established by the Department of Fish and Game; (3) nationally or state registered historic sites; and (4) ecological reserves. CCP §1240.680 (former CCP §1241.7).

If any of these types of property is sought for state highway purposes, the owner may bring an action for declaratory relief to determine which public use is best and most necessary. CCP §1240.690. Although former CCP §1241.7 allowed public utilities to use this procedure, the provision was not continued, because under CCP §1240.650 a use by a public entity is more necessary than a use by a public utility. The condemnor must give notice to the affected property owner in writing and by newspaper publication. Thereafter the owner has 120 days to file and serve an action in declaratory relief. If the action is not brought within that time period, the presumptions of CCP §§1240.670 and 1240.680 do not apply. CCP §1240.690(d)(1).

Code of Civil Procedure §1260.020 (former CCP §1247(3)) allows the court to determine the respective rights of two public entities condemning the same property.

[§6.16] Restriction on Location of Highway Projects

A state highway project initiated before the effective date of the California Environmental Quality Act of 1970 (Pub Res C §§21000–21176) is not exempt from the provisions of the Act requiring the filing of an environmental impact report, unless the project was fully funded before the Act's effective date. *People ex rel Dep't of Pub. Works v Bosio* (1975) 47 CA3d 495, 516, 121 CR 375, 386.

See *Stop H–3 Ass'n v Dole* (9th Cir 1984) 740 F2d 1442, which explains and applies *Citizens To Preserve Overton Park v Volpe* (1971) 401 US 402, discussed in Book §6.16, to a case concerning the Secretary of the Department of Transportation's authority to approve use of park land for a proposed highway.

[§6.16A] Restriction on Acquisition of State Park Land

In 1982, Pub Res C §5006 was amended and §5006.1 was added to provide that the Department of Parks and Recreation may not spend more than $500,000 for acquisition of land for the park system without first holding a public hearing in the county where the property is located.

NECESSITY

[§6.18] Introduction

Public necessity embraces three elements that must be established before the exercise of the power of eminent domain (CCP §1240.030):

(a) The public interest and necessity require the project.
(b) The project is planned or located in the manner that will be most compatible with the greatest public good and the least private injury.
(c) The property sought to be acquired is necessary for the project.

These elements are established by a proper resolution of necessity. CCP §1245.250. The resolution is a prerequisite to beginning a condemnation action. CCP §§1240.040, 1245.220.

The governing body of the public entity may not adopt a resolution of necessity until it has given each person whose property is to be taken and each person whose name appears on the last equalized county assessment roll written notice and an opportunity to be heard on the elements of necessity. Those persons notified may file a written request to appear and be heard within 15 days after the notice was mailed. Failure to do so results in a waiver of the right to appear and be heard. CCP §1245.235.

In *Conejo Recreation & Park Dist. v Armstrong* (1981) 114 CA3d 1016, 170 CR 891, the court dismissed an eminent domain proceeding because the condemnor park district had failed to give the condemnee notice of a hearing before the board of supervisors at which the condemnor sought approval for condemnation. Due process as well as Pub Res C §5782.5 were held to require the notice, because the condemnees were entitled to an opportunity to make a presentation to the board.

The resolution must contain a finding of the elements of public necessity stated above and a determination that a prelitigation offer (see Supp §7.4) under Govt C §7267.2 has been made to the owner or owners of record, or that the offer was not made because the owner could not be located after a reasonably diligent search. In addition, the resolution must contain a general statement of the public use for which the property is being taken, the statutory authorization, and a description of the general location and extent of the property being taken. CCP §1245.230.

The resolution conclusively establishes the extent of the taking. Evidence may not be introduced to reduce the scope of the taking, and the judgment must conform to the wording of the resolution. If the condemnor wants to change the scope of the taking, it must amend the resolution to describe the limits of its intended use. *County of San Diego v Bressi* (1986) 184 CA3d 112, 229 CR 44. See also *Coachella Valley Water Dist. v Western Allied Props.* (1987) 190 CA3d 969, 235 CR 725.

In *Kachadoorian v Calwa County Water Dist.* (1979) 96 CA3d 741, 158 CR 223, the court held that abandonment of a public alley (under which a public utility maintained a water pipeline) terminated the right-of-way easement for use of the alley, but 50 years of use of that water pipeline as a part of a community system was sufficient to establish the necessity of maintaining the pipeline use and thus to prevent the property owner from quieting title or seeking injunctive relief. The owner could only seek damages on the theory of inverse condemnation.

See generally, Note, *The Justiciability of Necessity in California Eminent Domain Proceedings,* 5 UCD L Rev 330 (1972).

[§6.19] Conclusive Evidence Statutes

Unless a greater vote is required by statute, charter, or ordinance, the resolution must be adopted by a vote of two thirds of all members of the governing board of the public entity, not just the majority of the members present. CCP §1245.240. The resolution is conclusive on necessity, except that it establishes only a rebuttable presumption if (1) acquisition is outside the territorial limits of the public entity (CCP §1245.250(b)) or (2) adoption or contents of the resolution were affected by a gross abuse of discretion by the governing body (CCP §1245.255).

In *Redevelopment Agency v Norm's Slauson* (1985) 173 CA3d 1121, 219 CR 365, a redevelopment agency contracted to sell defendant's property and issue bonds to finance the project without notice to the landowner and before taking any steps to condemn the property. The court concluded that the adoption of the resolution of necessity was a sham and that the agency thus had no right to take the property.

The resolution authorizing condemnation and making the findings of necessity is exclusively a legislative function, not judicial. Thus, CCP §1085 is the applicable procedure for review. The procedure under §1085 requires no written findings of fact in relation to legislative decisions. *Anaheim Redev. Agency v Dusek* (1987) 193 CA3d 249, 239 CR 319. The court distinguished this case from *Redevelopment Agency v Norm's Slauson, supra,* in that in *Slauson,* before the commencement of any hearings of public necessity, the redevelopment agency had contracted with the developer to build condominiums on the land to be acquired. Thus, there was evidence that the issue was predetermined. In *Dusek* the redevelopment agency made a political decision that the court should not overturn. However, in regard to the issue of public use, *i.e.,* whether the redevelopment to eliminate blight is a sufficient statement of public use, a court can review that issue as a matter of law but the property owner had to challenge the redevelopment plan within 60 days following the adoption of that final plan. The challenge through the resolution of necessity of public use was beyond the 60-day statute of limitation. 193 CA3d at 263, 239 CR at 327. See also *San Bernardino County Flood Control Dist. v Grabowski* (1988) 205 CA3d 885, 252 CR 676, distinguishing *Slauson.*

The resolution is invalid if it was brought about by a bribe. CCP §1245.270. See also Supp §6.20.

Code of Civil Procedure §§1245.310–1245.390 sets forth the procedure for the legislative body of the appropriate city or county to adopt a resolution consenting to acquisition by a quasi-public entity (see CCP §1245.320; Supp §6.6A) through the power of eminent domain. The resolution must be adopted by a two-thirds vote of the entire legislative body, not just of those present (CCP §1245.360); it does not expose the city or county to liability for damages caused by the taking (CCP §1245.390).

[§6.20] *Chevalier* Rule

The *Chevalier* rule that a conclusive resolution of necessity cannot be affected by allegations of fraud, bad faith, and abuse of discretion has been superseded. Under new CCP §1245.255, an interested party can collaterally attack the conclusive effect of the resolution by alleging that the adoption or contents of the resolution were affected "by gross abuse of discretion by the governing body."

The Comment to CCP §1245.255 that accompanied the statute when it was enacted in 1975 indicated that one could directly attack a resolution by administrative mandamus (CCP §1094.5). The Law Revision Commission received serious questions about this Comment, based on the argument that resolutions were legislative determinations by the governing body of the condemnor, not quasi-judicial acts. The distinction is important because administrative mandamus generally raises the question of whether substantial evidence supported the quasi-judicial determination of the administrative body. See generally California Administrative Mandamus (2d ed Cal CEB 1989). But if the determinations in a resolution of necessity are considered legislative, the rule of *Dawson v Town of Los Altos Hills* (1976) 16 C3d 676, 129 CR 97, applies. A court cannot invalidate a special assessment finally confirmed by the legislative body in accordance with applicable law unless the facts shown on the face of the record or judicially known show that the assessment is not proportional to the benefits to be bestowed on the properties or that no benefits will accrue. *Dawson* concerned a town council's formation of a sewer assessment district, and the supreme court relied on several prior decisions in concluding that the establishment of a special assessment district is a legislative process. See *Anaheim Redev. Agency v Dusek* (1987) 193 CA3d 249, 254, 239 CR 319, 321, for an in-depth analysis of the legislative background of CCP §1245.255.

Thus, the Law Revision Commission recommended legislation, adopted in 1978, amending CCP §1245.255 to provide that a writ of mandate, rather than administrative mandamus, is available to review the resolution. Furthermore, such a remedy can be used only before an eminent domain proceeding is filed. Thereafter, any objection to the right to take must be made under CCP §1250.350 in the condemnation action itself. See §6.25.

A resolution may be also directly attacked under the Political Reform Act of 1974 (Govt C §91003(b)) when the vote was affected by a conflict of interest. See *San Bernardino County Flood Control Dist. v Grabowski* (1988) 205 CA3d 885, 252 CR 676, discussed in Supp §6.25, in which the property owner failed to properly raise the issue of conflict of interest in the trial below. Further, CCP §1245.270 specifically provides that a resolution brought about by a bribe is invalid.

[§6.22] Bases for Challenge

See Supp §6.28 for a list of grounds for objecting to the right to take.
Chadbourn, Grossman & Van Alstyne, California Pleading (1961) has been replaced by a second edition published in 1981.

[§6.23] Environmental Compatibility as Basis for Challenge

The citation for *Friends of Mammoth v Board of Supervisors,* cited in Book §6.23, is (1972) 8 C3d 247, 104 CR 761.
See Note, *California Environmental Quality Act and Eminent Domain: Failure To Comply With CEQA as a Defense to Condemnation,* 8 Loy LA L Rev 734 (1975).

PROCEDURE IN ALLEGING AND CHALLENGING PUBLIC USE AND NECESSITY

[§6.24] Complaint

Code of Civil Procedure §1250.310 requires that the complaint contain a statement of the right of condemnor to acquire the property. That statement must include:
(1) A general statement of the public use;

(2) An allegation of necessity, which may be satisfied by incorporation of the resolution containing the required findings (see Supp §6.18); and

(3) A reference to the statute authorizing condemnation.

[§6.25] Answer; Objections to Right To Take

Objections to the right to take may be raised by answer or demurrer, but they must be specifically pleaded. CCP §1250.350. The grounds for objection to the right to take are specified in CCP §§1250.360 and 1250.370. See Supp §6.28. Failure to object to the complaint waives the objection (CCP §1250.345), so the objection must be asserted promptly.

The withdrawal of probable compensation deposited for an order of possession constitutes a waiver by operation of law of defendant's challenge of the right to take. See CCP §1255.260 and *San Diego Gas & Elec. Co. v 3250 Corp.* (1988) 205 CA3d 1075, 252 CR 853.

A challenge to disqualify one of the votes on a resolution of necessity based on the Political Reform Act of 1974 (Govt C §§81000–91015) must be made by way of cross-complaint, not answer. On review of Legislative Committee Comments to the 1975 version of CCP §1245.255, the court in *San Bernardino County Flood Control Dist. v Grabowski* (1988) 205 CA3d 885, 252 CR 676, ruled there was an intent to differentiate between direct Political Reform Act attacks on a resolution and collateral attacks arising under the provisions of Eminent Domain Law. The condemnee's right to object by demurrer or answer is limited to those grounds listed in CCP §§1250.360–1250.370. A challenge based on the Political Reform Act is not within the ambit of those two statutes. Therefore, under CCP §1230.040, the general rules of civil pleading apply to a Political Reform Act challenge to the validity of a resolution of necessity. The general rules of civil pleading require that a related cause of action that the defendant has against the plaintiff at the time the answer to the complaint is served be asserted in a compulsory cross-complaint. CCP §426.30. See generally Supp §8.24 on cross-complaints. Until a condemnation action is filed, a writ of mandate is available to challenge the right to take. CCP §1245.255(a)(1).

[§6.27] Trial; Hearing

Objections to the right to take are heard before determination of the issue of compensation, unless the court orders otherwise on the motion of any party. CCP §1260.110. If the court determines that the plaintiff does not have the right to condemn, it may order immediate or conditional dismissal, subject to compliance with an order for corrective action. CCP §1260.120(c).

[§6.28] CHECKLIST

The grounds for objection to the right to take when the resolution of condemnation is conclusive are specified in CCP §1250.360 as follows:

(1) Plaintiff is not authorized by statute to exercise the power for the purpose stated in the complaint;

(2) The stated purpose is not a public use;

(3) Plaintiff does not intend to apply the property to the proposed use;

(4) There is no reasonable probability of use within the applicable period (usually seven years; see Supp §6.9);

(5) The property sought is exempt;

(6) The acquisition is subject to, but does not satisfy, the requirements of CCP §1240.410 (excess condemnation), §1240.510 (condemnation for compatible use), or §1240.610 (condemnation for more necessary use);

(7) In cases of condemnation for a more necessary use, the defendant has the right to continue its use as a joint use under CCP §1240.630; and

(8) Any other ground provided by law, *e.g.*, federal or constitutional grounds or other California codes that establish prerequisites to condemnation.

Code of Civil Procedure §1250.370 specifies the following additional grounds for objection to the right to take when the resolution is not conclusive:

(a) Plaintiff is a public entity and has not adopted a valid resolution of necessity;

(b) Public interest and necessity do not require the project;

(c) The proposed project is not planned in the manner most compatible with the greatest public good and least private injury;

(d) The property sought is not necessary for the project; and

(e) Plaintiff is a quasi-public entity as defined in CCP §1245.320 and has not obtained a proper resolution of consent (see CCP §1245.330).

The conclusiveness of the resolution of necessity may also be attacked collaterally if there was a gross abuse of discretion in its adoption. CCP §1245.255. See Supp §6.20.

Other grounds for objecting to a resolution of necessity are bribery (CCP §1245.270) and conflicts of interest under the Political Reform Act of 1974 (Govt C §91003(b)).

7

Negotiation and Arbitration

DISPARATE POSITIONS OF PARTIES

[§7.4] Condemnor's Dual Responsibilities

The California Relocation Assistance Act (Govt C §§7260–7276; see Book §4.53), establishes the following guidelines for public agencies to encourage acquisition by negotiation and to avoid litigation (Govt C §7267):

(1) Every effort should be made to acquire the property by negotiation and an appraisal should be made before negotiations are initiated by the agency. Govt C §7267.1.

(2) The agency must offer the full amount of its determination of value. It must provide the owner of the land to be acquired with a written summary of the basis for the amount it has established as just compensa-

tion. Govt C §7267.2(a). This section and CCP §1245.230 have been amended to require the offer to be made before the adoption of a resolution of necessity, except in cases of an emergency project, or when the offer cannot be made because the owner cannot be located after a reasonably diligent search. The offer can be conditioned on the legislative body's ratification of the offer by execution of a contract or adoption of a resolution of necessity or both. An amendment to Govt C §7267.2 effective January 1, 1986, provides that if no federal funds are involved, a public entity may make an offer for real property for less than the amount that it believes to be the just compensation when the real property is offered for sale by the owner at a lower price either to the public entity or to the general public within the past six months. Under these circumstances, the public entity must offer the specified price for which the owner is offering the property. Govt C §7267.2(b). See Supp §8.2 for further discussion. If the owner cannot be found after reasonable diligence and is served by publication, the owner may contest the amount of compensation for good cause within one year of the judgment. CCP §1250.125.

An offer consisting of a one-page written summary, generally describing the property to be acquired and stating the amount of the condemnor's appraisal value was held not to comply with Govt C §7267.2; it did not constitute a written summary of the basis for the appraisal figure. Thus, the requirements for a resolution of necessity were not satisfied and the action was dismissed on the condemnee's motion. *City of San Jose v Great Oaks Water Co.* (1987) 192 CA3d 1005, 237 CR 845.

(3) Construction of the improvement should be scheduled to provide at least 90 days' written notice to the owner of any required move from a dwelling. Govt C §7267.3. See also Book §8.9 regarding orders of immediate possession.

(4) If the agency allows the owner or the tenant to continue to occupy the premises on a short-term rental basis, it is entitled only to fair rental value. Govt C §7267.4.

(5) The agency may not use coercion to compel agreement on price. Govt C §7267.5.

(6) The condemnor should not intentionally make it necessary for the owner to institute an action to prove there has been a taking. Govt C §7267.6.

(7) Uneconomic remnants (see §6.10) should be acquired if the owner desires. Govt C §7267.7.

These guidelines are to be followed to the greatest extent possible. Govt C §7267.

In 1975, Govt C §7267 was amended to state that the requirements of Govt C §§7267.1(b) (that property be appraised before negotiation) and 7267.2 (that offer equal amount of the appraisal) do not apply in the acquisition of easements, rights-of-way, covenants, or other nonpossessory interests in acquiring real property for construction, repair, or modification of subsurface sewers, water lines, drains, septic tanks, or storm water drains.

The condemnor's failure to comply with Govt C §7267 does not itself create a cause of action in inverse condemnation. The law, by its own language, creates only a guide to be followed to the greatest extent practicable. *Toso v City of Santa Barbara* (1980) 101 CA3d 934, 162 CR 210. The court in *Taper v City of Long Beach* (1982) 129 CA3d 590, 181 CR 169, distinguished *Toso* and relied on statutory admonitions of Govt C §§7267.5 and 7267.6 to support a finding of precondemnation damage based on evidence that the city dragged out negotiations, progressively reduced its offers, and delayed the commencement of the condemnation action.

There is a high standard of professional responsibility set for a condemnor attorney; like a public prosecutor, he or she must seek impartial justice. *City of Los Angeles v Decker* (1977) 18 C3d 860, 135 CR 647. See also *People ex rel Clancy v Superior Court* (1985) 39 C3d 740, 747, 218 CR 24, 28, discussing the "heightened ethical requirements of one who performs governmental functions."

[§7.7] Limited Authority of Condemnor's Negotiator

When a landowner accepted in writing the original written offer of a school district's supervisor of building planning to purchase property after institution of a condemnation action, specific performance was not allowed. *Santa Monica Unified School Dist. v Persh* (1970) 5 CA3d 945, 85 CR 463 (contract could not be enforced because requirement of Ed C §1002.5 and former §15961 that district's board ratify or approve contract had not been met). Education Code §15961 has been repealed and superseded by Ed C §§39656 and 81655, which authorize the board to delegate authority to make contracts.

[§7.8] MULTIPLE INTEREST HOLDERS

Code of Civil Procedure §1246.1 has been replaced by CCP §1260.220.

[§7.9] SUBJECTS FOR NEGOTIATION

The Eminent Domain Law (CCP §§1230.010–1273.050) allows the condemnor and property owner to enter into an agreement to perform certain work, such as relocation of structures and the construction of fences and driveways, to reduce the amount of compensation. CCP §1263.610. See also CCP §1263.450, discussed in Supp §5.12.

[§7.10] PREPARATION FOR NEGOTIATION

Exchange of valuation data is now governed by CCP §§1258.210–1258.300 (former CCP §§1272.01–1272.07).

NEGOTIATION TECHNIQUES

[§7.11] Approach to Negotiation

Offers of settlement may not be admitted in evidence at the trial of the issue of compensation. *People ex rel Dep't of Pub. Works v Southern Pac. Transp. Co.* (1973) 33 CA3d 960, 109 CR 525. See Supp §9.49.

[§7.12A] Pretrial Offer

See Supp §§9.14A–9.14B on the mandatory pretrial offer and demand.

For discussion of recovery of attorneys' fees and litigation expenses when the demand is reasonable but the offer is not, see Supp §10.23A.

[§7.13] Exchange of Appraisals

The procedures for exchange of valuation data have been revised and are now governed by CCP §§1258.210–1258.300. The time of demand has been advanced to no later than ten days following the date of selection of the trial date. Thereafter, a party must file a noticed motion and make a showing of good cause. CCP §1258.210(a). There is no need to file a cross-demand to reach the initiating party's valuation data, as suggested by former CCP §1272.01(b). The date of exchange is the time agreed on by the parties; if there is no agreement, the date is either 40 days before trial or the date selected by the court on noticed motion of either party showing good cause. CCP §1258.220.

[§7.15] FORM: SETTLEMENT AGREEMENT

Comment: Former CCP §1246.2 (see Comment to form in Book §7.15, ¶2), which prohibited prepayment penalties when the property acquired for public use is encumbered by a lien, was replaced by CCP §1265.240.

In view of CCP §1268.610, which allows for litigation expenses on dismissal for any reason, it is appropriate to include a waiver of the expenses. See Book §7.15, ¶6.

Revenue and Taxation Code §4986 provisions concerning the date of apportionment of taxes are now found in Rev & T C §5082.

[§§7.16–7.17] ARBITRATION

Code of Civil Procedure §§1273.010–1273.050 continue without substantive change the rules on arbitration of compensation set forth in former CCP §§1273.02–1273.06.

8

Pleadings

COMPLAINT

[§8.1] Statutory Requirements

The Eminent Domain Law (CCP §§1230.010–1273.050) revises the requirements for pleading a condemnation action. Code of Civil Procedure §1250.310 requires a complaint to set forth the following:

(1) The names of all plaintiffs and defendants.

(2) A description of the property. The interest of each defendant in the property may be indicated, but it is not required. The description does not have to indicate that the property taken is a part of a larger parcel.

(3) If plaintiff claims an interest in the property, it must declare the nature and extent of that interest.

(4) A statement of plaintiff's right to take, containing (a) a general statement of the public use for which the property is sought, (b) an allegation of necessity and reference to the resolution of necessity, and (c) a statement of the statutory authorization.

(5) A map showing the property described in the complaint and its relationship to the project for which it is being taken.

The filing of the complaint rather than issuance of the summons begins a condemnation proceeding. CCP §1250.110.

The reference in Book §8.1 to 6 California Forms of Pleading and

Practice 417–443 (1971) should now be to 6 California Forms of Pleading and Practice, *Eminent Domain* 143–157 (1985).

[§8.2] Sample Form: Complaint

The following form of complaint is used by the California Department of Transportation, Legal Division.

[*Title of court*]

[*Title of case*]

No. _ _ _ _
Parcels _ _ _ _

**COMPLAINT IN EMINENT DOMAIN
CCP §1250.310**

Plaintiff complains of defendants and for cause of action alleges that:

I

The Department of Transportation is, and at all times herein mentioned has been, the duly authorized body in charge of State highways and is by law vested with authority to exercise in the name of the People of the State of California the right of eminent domain for the purpose of acquiring property for State highway purposes, a public use.

Comment: The complaint first states, in paragraph I, each person seeking to take the property being condemned. CCP §1250.210. The plaintiff must be a person authorized by statute to exercise the power of eminent domain to acquire the property sought for the purpose stated in the complaint. CCP §1240.020. Here, the condemnor has also included a general statement of the public use ("State highway purposes") to satisfy CCP §1250.310(d)(1).

II

After notice pursuant to Code of Civil Procedure Section 1245.235, at a meeting of the California Transportation Commission duly and regularly convened at _ _ _ _ _ _, California, on _ _ _ _, 19_ _, said California Transportation Commission under Streets and Highways Code Section 102 duly and regularly passed and adopted Resolution of Necessity No._ _ _ _, declaring that public interest and necessity require the acquisition by plaintiff of certain real property in fee

simple absolute unless a lesser estate is described herein for a proposed project for State highway purposes in connection with State highway, Road_ _ _ _ [declared a freeway]. The California Transportation Commission has found and determined and in said resolution declared:

(a) The public interest and necessity require the project.

(b) The project is planned or located in the manner that will be most compatible with the greatest public good and the least private injury.

(c) The property sought to be acquired is necessary for the project.

[*Choose applicable clause*]

(d) The offer required by Government Code Section 7267.2 has been made to the owner or owners of record.

[*or*]

(d) The property is needed for an emergency project to protect the property or the health, safety and welfare of the general public, and therefore, the requirements of Government Code Section 7267.2 are waived at this time.

[*or*]

(d) The offer required by Government Code Section 7267.2 was not made to the owner or owners of record because after a reasonably diligent search, the owner(s) could not be found.

Comment: The condemnor must first adopt a resolution of necessity before it can condemn the property. CCP §§1240.040, 1245.220. The complaint must contain an allegation of the public necessity for the taking. CCP §1250.310(d)(2). See also CCP §1240.030(a). This requirement, however, may be satisfied by incorporation by reference to the resolution containing the appropriate findings and declarations. Some agencies may choose to incorporate the resolution itself into the pleadings. This paragraph also provides a general statement of the public use for which the property is to be taken, and refers to the specific project. The reference to Str & H C §102, which authorizes the Department of Transportation to acquire by eminent domain property necessary for state highway purposes, satisfies the requirement of CCP §1250.310(d)(3).

According to CCP §1245.230, as amended in 1982, the resolution must contain:

(1) A general statement of the public use for which the property is to be taken and a reference to the statute authorizing the condemnation action.

(2) A description of the general location and extent of the property to be taken.

(3) A declaration that the governing body has found and determined the following:

(a) Public interest and necessity require the proposed project,

(b) The proposed project is planned or located in the manner that would be most compatible with the most public good and least private injury,

(c) The property is necessary for the proposed project, and

(d) The offer required under Govt C §7267.2 (see Supp §7.4) has been made to the owner of record. This latter requirement is suspended if the owners of record cannot be found after a diligent search or if the public agency finds that it is involved in an emergency project that does not afford the necessary time for the prelitigation offer. Nonetheless, in those latter cases, Govt C §7267.2 must be implemented within a reasonable time after the adoption of the resolution and never later than 90 days after the adoption of the resolution. This requirement of an offer before the adoption of the resolution of necessity went into effect on January 1, 1983.

The resolution conclusively establishes the extent of the taking and the judgment must conform to the resolution's description of the taking. *County of San Diego v Bressi* (1986) 184 CA3d 112, 229 CR 44.

III

The real property or interests in real property which the Department of Transportation is authorized to acquire by said resolution is situated in the County of _ _ _ _ _ _, State of California, and described as follows:

_ _

_ _

Comment: A description of the property is mandatory. CCP §1250.310(b). The description must be detailed and certain so that the parties know what land is sought. *California Cent. Ry. v Hooper* (1888) 76 C 404, 18 P 599. Unlike former CCP §1244(5), CCP §1250.310 does not require that the complaint state whether the property taken is a part of a larger parcel.

IV

Maps portraying the property described in the complaint and showing its location in relation to the project for which it is to be acquired are attached hereto and marked Exhibits _ _ _ _ and by this reference made a part hereof.

Comment: A map or diagram showing the property described in the complaint is required in all cases. CCP §1250.310(e). Formerly, CCP §1244(4) required the map only if the taking was for right-of-way.

V

All of the herein described property lying within the boundaries of streets, highways, or other public easements is subject to an easement or prescriptive right of the public for use for such purpose.

Comment: When the condemnor itself claims an interest in the property being condemned, the nature and extent of the interest must be alleged. CCP §1250.310(c).

VI

Each defendant named hereinafter appears of record or is known by plaintiff to have or claim an interest in the property described.
For the convenience of the court and parties, and not as allegations to which plaintiff intends to be bound, plaintiff has set out opposite each named defendant a statement of the respective interest of said defendant in said parcel(s):
PARCELS:

[Insert parcels, names, and interests]

Comment: Plaintiff must name as defendants those persons who appear of record or are known to plaintiff to have or claim an interest in the property being condemned. CCP §§1250.220, 1250.310(a). There is no requirement, however, that the nature and extent of defendant's interest in the property being condemned be stated. CCP §1250.310(b). Plaintiff may join in the same complaint all parcels, within the same county, that are sought for the same project. CCP §1250.240. In such cases, the plaintiff should indicate clearly which defendants are connected with the various parcels, although the specific interests need not be stated.

If the only interest of the county or any other taxing agency in the property being condemned is a lien for ad valorem taxes, the county or other taxing agency need not be named as a defendant in the complaint; such a lien is extinguished on acquisition of the property. CCP §1250.250(a); Rev & T C §5083.

However, the holder of a lien securing a special assessment or bond for a special assessment must be named as a defendant. Instead of an answer, the lienholder may certify certain information to the court within 30 days after service of the summons and complaint. CCP §1250.250(b).

The certification must contain a description of the lien and the encumbered property, the amount remaining due on the lien, and the date and amount of installments. A copy of the certification must be sent by first-class mail to all parties to the condemnation proceeding at the same time it is given to the court, and filing or answering is equivalent to a general appearance. CCP §1250.250(c).

VII

Defendants DOE ONE to DOE _ _[e.g., FIFTY]_ _, inclusive, have, or claim to have, an interest in said parcel(s), the exact nature of which is unknown to plaintiff. The true names or capacities, whether individual, corporate, associate, or otherwise, of defendants DOE ONE to DOE _ _[e.g., FIFTY]_ _, are unknown to plaintiff, who therefore sues said defendants by such fictitious names, and will ask leave to amend this complaint to show their true names and capacities and state of incorporation when same have been ascertained.

VIII

The interest of the defendant UNITED STATES OF AMERICA is a tax lien arising under the Internal Revenue laws. The liability of _ _[name and address of taxpayer]_ _ created the tax lien. The _ _ _ _ Office of the Internal Revenue Service filed a notice of said tax lien on _ _ _ _, 19_ _, in the Office of the County Recorder of _ _ _ _ County, California.

[or]

The interest of the defendant UNITED STATES OF AMERICA is as a beneficiary under a Deed of Trust. The Deed of Trust was executed by _ _ _ _ _ _ to _ _ _ _ _ _ _, dated _ _ _ _, 19_ _, and recorded on _ _ _ _, 19_ _, in Book _ _ _ _, page _ _, of Official Records, _ _ _ _ _ _ County.

[Add, if either of above paragraphs is used]

The United States of America is joined herein as a party defendant in accordance with and by virtue of Section 201 of the Federal Tax Lien Act of 1966, Title 28 United States Code Section 2410, subsections (a) and (b).

Comment: The above paragraphs should be included only if the United States government has a tax lien or deed of trust against the property.

IX

Defendant _ _ _ _ _ _ was, at all times herein mentioned, and now is, the duly appointed, qualified, and acting _ _[administrator/executor]_ _ of the estate of _ _ _ _ _ _, deceased, under Probate Case No. _ _ _ _, of the Superior Court of the State of California, in and for the County of _ _ _ _ _ _.

Comment: This paragraph is included if there is an executor or an administrator for a decedent's estate that now holds an interest in the property.

X

Plaintiff is informed and believes, and on such information and belief alleges, that _ _ _ _ _ _ _ is dead, that no executor or administrator of the estate of said _ _ _ _ _ _ _, deceased, has been appointed by any court of the State who is now duly qualified; that no certified copy of an order of the Superior Court of any county of the State of California, appointing an executor or administrator of the estate of _ _ _ _ _ _, deceased, has been recorded in any county of the State of California; that plaintiff, in accordance with Section 1250.220 of the Code of Civil Procedure of the State of California, names as defendants "THE HEIRS AND DEVISEES OF _ _ _ _ _ _, DECEASED, AND ALL PERSONS CLAIMING BY, THROUGH, OR UNDER SAID DECEDENT," and plaintiff also names as defendants "ALL PERSONS UNKNOWN AND CLAIMING INTEREST IN THE PROPERTY."

Comment: This paragraph should be used if plaintiff is informed that the record owner of the property is dead and that there is no known executor or administrator for the estate. In these circumstances, the condemnor can name the heirs and devisees and also unknown defendants if a declaration to this effect is filed with the complaint. CCP §1250.220.

XI

Under Code of Civil Procedure Section 1240.220, the estimated date of use is _ _ _ _ _ _, 19_ _.

Comment: This paragraph is to be included when the property sought is not intended to be used within seven years after the filing of the complaint. CCP §1240.220.

XII

Parcel No. _ _ _ _ is being acquired pursuant to the provisions of _ _[Code of Civil Procedure Section 1240.320 in that it is necessary *to exchange said property with (name owner of "necessary property") to provide for continued public use/Code of Civil Procedure Section 1240.330 in that it is necessary to relocate thereon a public use pursuant to court order, judgment or agreement/Code of Civil Procedure Section 1240.350 in that it is necessary to provide access or utility service to other property]* _ _.

Comment: The above paragraph is to be used if the taking includes lands to be exchanged for property necessary for the project. CCP §§1240.310–1240.350.

XIII

Parcel No. _ _ _ _ **is a remnant and is being acquired under Code of Civil Procedure Section 1240.410.**

Comment: The above paragraph is to be used if the taking includes lands in excess of those necessary for the public project.

XIV

Parcel No. _ _ _ _ **is being acquired for a compatible use under Code of Civil Procedure Section 1240.510.**

Comment: The above paragraph is used if the taking is for a compatible use.

XV

Parcel No. _ _ _ _ **is being acquired for a more necessary public use under Code of Civil Procedure Section 1240.610.**

Comment: The above paragraph is used if the taking is for a more necessary public use than the public use for which it is already appropriated. When a public agency fails to refer specifically to the statutory authority for taking of property already in a public use for more necessary public use in either the complaint or the resolution incorporated by reference, the complaint is fatally defective. *PG&E v Superior Court* (1986) 180 CA3d 770, 225 CR 768.

WHEREFORE, plaintiff prays judgment that:
(1) Said property be condemned to plaintiff's use in fee simple absolute unless a lesser estate is described herein for the purposes set forth in said resolution;
(2) The compensation be ascertained and assessed and the amount

of the award for said property be first determined between plaintiff and all defendants claiming any interest therein;

(3) All liens and encumbrances against said property be deducted from said judgment; and

(4) The court allow such other and further relief as may be deemed proper.

Dated: _ _ _ _ _ _ _   ___[Signature of attorney]___
                                        _ _[Typed name]_ _
                                        Attorney for Plaintiff(s)

Comment: Although the complaint need no longer state that the property taken is part of a larger parcel, in such cases some condemnors still include a statement in the prayer that any severance damages and any special benefits to the remainder be ascertained and assessed. The complaint must be signed by the attorney for plaintiff. CCP §1250.330. Further, under this statute, verification of the complaint does not require verification of the answer if the defendant is represented by an attorney. See generally CCP §446 on verifications.

JURISDICTION AND PROCESS

[§8.2A] Jurisdiction

Except for cases under Public Utilities Commission jurisdiction and arbitration, the superior court has jurisdiction over all eminent domain proceedings. CCP §§1230.060, 1250.010.

See *Washington Water & Light Co. v East Yolo Community Servs. Dist.* (1981) 120 CA3d 388, 396, 174 CR 612, 617, in which a private utility company's complaint for precondemnation damages was dismissed, because it was filed after a direct condemnation action had been brought before the Public Utilities Commission, which had jurisdiction under Pub Util C §1417 to decide whether to grant an increase in compensation for acts or occurrences after the original petition was filed with the PUC.

Filing a petition with the Public Utilities Commission to restrain acquisition of a certain property by a public utility does not deprive the court of jurisdiction in a condemnation action. *PG&E v Parachini* (1972) 29 CA3d 159, 105 CR 477.

[§8.3] Venue

The Eminent Domain Law (CCP §§1230.010–1273.050) simplifies the rules on venue. The proper venue of a condemnation action is the county where the property sought is located; but, if the property is in more than one county, any of those counties may be selected. CCP §1250.020. The rules of CCP §394 permitting change of venue if defendant is a nonresident of, or if plaintiff is not located in, the county where the property is situated are incorporated in CCP §1250.040.

The venue rules for a nonresident were held to apply to an action seeking to condemn property owned by a trust that existed only to facilitate the sale of property without having to obtain signatures from all the beneficiaries and to avoid probate. Because each beneficiary as the equitable owner of the property had the right to appear in the action, the rule requiring venue in a neutral county if a defendant is a nonresident (CCP §394) had to be applied. However, the court observed that the result could have been different if the trustee had had more extensive powers over the trust property. *Anderson v Superior Court* (1983) 142 CA3d 112, 190 CR 646.

Plaintiff has the option of joining an unlimited number of parcels in different ownership in the same action, provided all the property is located in the same county (CCP §1250.240), subject to the court's authority to order separate trials (CCP §1048).

[§8.4] Summons; Service of Process

The contents of the summons are now simplified in accordance with the general requirements of summons in civil actions. Consequently, the summons need no longer contain a description of the property unless served by publication. CCP §1250.120.

When the court orders service by publication, it must also order plaintiff to post a copy of the summons and complaint on the property and record a lis pendens within ten days after the order. CCP §1250.130.

Attorney's Guide to California Jurisdiction and Process §§1.17–1.37 (Cal CEB 1970) have been superseded by 1 California Civil Procedure Before Trial, chaps 13, 24 (3d ed Cal CEB 1990).

[§8.5] Lis Pendens; Statutory Requirements

When service is by publication, the court must also order plaintiff to post a copy of the summons and complaint on the property and record a notice of pendency of action. The order must be posted within ten days after the order of publication. CCP §1250.130. The notice of lis pendens must also be filed within ten days if it was not previously filed when the action was commenced as required by CCP §1250.150.

Code of Civil Procedure §409, the general lis pendens statute, sets forth the requirements for filing a notice of pendency of action while allowing a simpler process in eminent domain actions. Under the general law, the notice must be served by first-class mail, return receipt requested, on all known addresses of the adverse parties and owners of record as shown by the county assessor's office before recording. This procedure is not required in eminent domain actions. CCP §409(c). Instead, a copy of the notice must be recorded at the time of filing suit and must be served with the summons and complaint. CCP §1250.150. Furthermore, a notice of pendency of action may be recorded in a condemnation action without meeting the general requirement that it be issued by the court or by the attorney of record in the action or be accompanied by a certified copy of the certification from the court that an action concerning real property has been filed. CCP §409(b).

California Civil Procedure Before Trial, chap 9 (Cal CEB 1957), discussing lis pendens, has been superseded by California Lis Pendens Practice (Cal CEB 1983). California Real Estate Sales Transactions §§18.30–18.36 (Cal CEB 1967) have been replaced by California Real Property Sales Transactions §§12.86–12.92 (Cal CEB 1981).

CONDEMNOR'S RIGHT TO IMMEDIATE POSSESSION

[§8.7] Statutory Authority

California Constitution art I, §14, which authorized possession before judgment when the condemnation was for a "right of way" or "for reservoir purposes," has been replaced by art I, §19, approved by the voters in the 1974 general election. The new section provides in part:

The Legislature may provide for possession by the condemnor following commencement of eminent domain proceedings upon deposit in court and prompt release to the owner of money determined by the court to be the probable amount of just compensation.

In response, the legislature replaced former CCP §1243.4 with CCP §1255.410, which permits any entity authorized to condemn to obtain an order for immediate possession.

[§8.7A] Form: Notice of Deposit

The following form is used by the California Department of Transportation.

[Title of court]

[Title of case]

No. _ _ _ _
Parcel No. _ _ _ _

NOTICE OF DEPOSIT AND
STATEMENT OF APPRAISAL
CCP §1255.010(a)

TO ALL PARTIES AND THEIR ATTORNEYS OF RECORD:
YOU WILL PLEASE TAKE NOTICE that on _ _ _ _, 19_ _, plaintiff deposited with the State Treasury the sum of $_ _ _ _ under Code of Civil Procedure Section 1255.010(a).

Dated: _ _ _ _ _ _   ___[*Signature of attorney*]___
                                                    _ _[*Typed name*] _ _

STATEMENT OF APPRAISAL

Under Code of Civil Procedure Section 1255.010(b):
1. **Value of parcel(s) $_ _ _ _.]**
[2. **Severance damages $_ _ _ _.]**
[3. **Special benefits $_ _ _ _.]**
[4. **Goodwill $_ _ _ _.]**

Dated: _ _ _ _ _ _   ___[*Signature of appraiser*]___
                                                    _ _[*Typed name of appraiser*] _ _

Comment: Some condemnors will provide a somewhat fuller statement of appraisal in the form of an appraiser's declaration filed together with the notice of deposit. Code of Civil Procedure §1255.010(b) does not specify the detail of statement or summary. Compare CCP §1258.260, concerning statement of valuation for exchange. See Supp §9.10.

[§8.8] Procedure; Deposit of Probable Compensation

The deposit of probable compensation now serves two purposes: (1) It is required before an order of immediate possession (CCP §1255.410), and (2) it fixes the date of deposit as the date of valuation unless it would otherwise be earlier (CCP §1263.110(a); see Supp §§4.19–4.22).

The deposit may be made at any time before entry of judgment. CCP §1255.010(a). The deposit is no longer made on ex parte application (see former CCP §1243.5 (repealed)) and must be based on an appraisal by an expert appraiser. CCP §1255.010(b).

On motion of any party having an interest in the property, the court must determine whether the amount deposited is the probable amount of compensation. CCP §1255.030(a). If the court determines that the deposit is inadequate, plaintiff has 30 days (unless the court grants a longer period) to increase it. If plaintiff does not increase it, the deposit is considered void. CCP §§1255.030(b), 1263.110(b). If plaintiff already has possession, failure to increase the deposit may lead to dismissal of the action and damages for defendant. See CCP §1255.030(c). Evidence of the amount of the deposit or an appraisal connected with it is not admissible on the issue of compensation during the trial. CCP §1255.060.

To provide defendants with a factual basis for seeking an increase in deposit, CCP §1255.020 requires plaintiff to serve notice on defendants stating the amount and date of deposit together with a written statement on the basis of the appraisal made for the deposit.

Homeowners (CCP §1255.040) and owners of rental property (CCP §1255.050) may compel a prejudgment deposit by serving on plaintiff a notice requiring the deposit. The date of the deposit is specified by defendant, but cannot be earlier than 30 days after the date of service of the notice. When a proper deposit is made, plaintiff can obtain an ex parte order for immediate possession 30 days or more after the date specified for the deposit. If, after notice, plaintiff fails to make the deposit, compensation awarded to the defendant homeowner draws interest from the date specified for the deposit without offset for rents or other income received by defendant arising from his continued possession. The home-owner rule applies only to a dwelling containing not more than two residential units and the dwelling for one of the units must be defendant's residence. If plaintiff fails to make a deposit after proper notice by the owner of rental property, interest begins to accrue on the date specified but is offset by the lessor's net rental profits on the property.

The order of immediate possession need no longer state the amount of deposit, the purpose of the condemnation, or the estate or interest sought. The condemnor may request possession of all or part of the property sought. Compare former requirements in Book §8.8.

[§8.8A] Form: Order for Possession Before Judgment

At the time a complaint is filed, or any time thereafter before judgment, on deposit of probable compensation, the condemnor may apply ex parte to the court for an order of immediate possession. The application for that order must reflect that the amount of probable compensation has been ascertained under CCP §§1255.010–1255.080 and has been deposited with the court. Furthermore, the condemnor must explain its need for possession and indicate how any person in possession will be displaced or affected by an order for possession. CCP §1255.410.

The following order for possession form, based on a form of the California Department of Transportation, Legal Division, is an example of the manner in which a condemnor seeks possession of all or a portion of a parcel.

[*Title of court*]

[*Title of case*]   **No. _ _ _ _**
                           Parcel Nos. _ _ _ _

                           ORDER FOR POSSESSION

On consideration of plaintiff's application for an order for possession, and the court determining that plaintiff is entitled to acquire

Parcel Nos. _ _ _ _ by eminent domain and to take possession thereof; and the Court determining that plaintiff has deposited in the State Treasury the probable amount of compensation and filed a statement of appraisal on which the deposit is based, both of which satisfy the requirements of Code of Civil Procedure Section 1255.010;

IT IS ORDERED that plaintiff is authorized and empowered to take possession and use of _ _[a portion of Parcel No._ _ _ _, more particularly described in Exhibit "A" attached and incorporated herein/said property]_ _, and to remove therefrom any and all persons, obstacles, improvements, or structures of every kind or nature thereon situated as of the indicated dates set forth below or on the ninetieth day following the date of service of this order, whichever is later.

PARCEL NUMBER	DATE POSSESSION TO BE TAKEN

Dated: _ _ _ _ _ _

_____
Judge of the Superior Court

Comment: Ninety days' notice is required in cases in which the property is occupied by a person living in a house or by a farm or business; in all other cases 30 days' notice is sufficient. CCP §1255.450(b). Plaintiff, on an appropriate showing, may obtain language in the order that it does not have to serve certain named record owners who are not occupying the property. CCP §1255.450(e).

An order granting prejudgment possession (sometimes referred to as a "quick take") under CCP §1253.410 is not an appealable order. Rather, the proper procedure for review is to seek a stay under CCP §1255.430 or a mandamus action. *City of Morgan Hill v Alberti* (1989) 211 CA3d 1435, 260 CR 42.

[§8.8B] Form: Order for Possession After Defendant's Consent or Withdrawal (CCP §1255.460)

When all defendants entitled to possession have consented in writing to surrender possession or have withdrawn any portion of the deposit, the following order, based on a form of the California Department of Transportation, Legal Division, should be used:

[*Title of court*]

[*Title of case*]   **No. _ _ _ _**
                                        Parcel Nos. _ _ _ _

                                        ORDER FOR POSSESSION
                                        PURSUANT TO CODE OF
                                        CIVIL PROCEDURE §1255.460

IT APPEARING and the Court determining that plaintiff is entitled to acquire Parcel Nos. _ _ _ _ by eminent domain and to take possession thereof;

AND IT FURTHER APPEARING and the Court determining that plaintiff has deposited in the State Treasury the probable amount of compensation and filed a statement of appraisal on which the deposit is based, both of which satisfy the requirements of Code of Civil Procedure Section 1255.010;

AND IT FURTHER APPEARING and the Court determining that each defendant entitled to possession has either expressed in writing his willingness to surrender possession of the property on or after the date set forth hereinafter, or has withdrawn any portion of the deposit;

IT IS ORDERED that plaintiff is authorized and empowered to take possession and use of _ _[*a portion of Parcel No. _ _ _ _, more particularly described in Exhibit "A" attached and incorporated herein/said property***]_ _, and to remove therefrom any and all persons, obstacles, improvements, or structures of every kind or nature thereon situated as of _ _[***insert either the date to which defendants have consented or, pursuant to CCP §1255.450(c), "the 30th day following service of the order"***]_ _.**

Dated: _ _ _ _ _ _   _____
                                  Judge of the Superior Court

Comment: Plaintiff may request a later date than that to which defendants have consented. CCP §1255.460(b)(3). In spite of the 30-day rule of CCP §1255.450(c), for consistency some plaintiffs may choose the 90-day rule of CCP §1255.450(b) in taking possession of houses, farms, or businesses.

[§8.9] Service

The condemnor must give 90 days' notice before possession for properties occupied by a dwelling, business, or farm, and 30 days' notice in all other cases. CCP §1255.450(b). Any defendant or occupant may be able to obtain a stay or limitation of possession in case of hardship by a motion made not later than 30 days after service of an order of possession. However, plaintiff can defeat a stay by a showing of the substantial hardship it would suffer as a result of the stay. CCP §1255.420. If the condemnor can show an urgent need for possession and the court finds possession will not displace any person, the court may order possession effective as soon as three days after service. CCP §1255.410(c).

Service must be made on the record owner and any occupants of the property. CCP §1255.450(b). Personal service is required, except that (1) anyone who has been served with a summons or has previously appeared may be served by mail and (2) persons outside the state or who cannot be found within the state may be served by registered or certified mail at their last known address. CCP §1255.450(d). For good cause, the court may relieve plaintiff of the requirement of serving a record owner not occupying the property. CCP §1255.450(e). Only one of several persons having a common address need receive service or mailing. CCP §1255.450(f).

[§8.9A] Stay of Order Until Ruling on Objections To Take

If defendant has objected to the right to take (see §6.25) and the court finds that there is a reasonable probability that defendant will prevail, the court must stay any order for immediate possession until it rules on the objections. CCP §1255.430.

[§8.10] Effect of Order for Immediate Possession

Interest begins to accrue on the date of entry of judgment or of possession or when plaintiff is authorized to take possession, whichever is earliest. CCP §1268.310. If defendant continues in possession or receives rent or income after that date, there must be an offset against the interest. CCP §1268.330.

The parties may agree to treat a broad right-of-entry agreement between the property owner and the condemnor as equivalent to an order allowing the condemnor to take possession for purposes of calculating interest. *People ex rel Dep't of Pub. Works v Williams* (1973) 30 CA3d 980, 106 CR 795. However, in *County of San Luis Obispo v Ranchita Cattle Co.* (1971) 16 CA3d 383, 94 CR 73, the court held that the condemnor's exceeding a right-of-entry agreement before filing an eminent domain action amounted only to a trespass independent of the eminent domain action.

An order of immediate possession passes the incidents of ownership, including a leasehold interest, to the condemnor. But title does not vest until the recording of the final order of condemnation. Thus a lease that has terminated after the order of immediate possession, but before recordation of the final order, was an interest taken by the condemnor and the lessee was entitled to compensation. *People ex rel Dep't of Water Resources v Gianni* (1972) 29 CA3d 151, 155, 105 CR 248, 251.

Provisions of former Rev & T C §4986(2) concerning the date for proration of taxes are now found in Rev & T C §5082.

[§8.11] Deposit of Probable Compensation; Withdrawal

Generally, the procedure under former CCP §1243.7 is continued in CCP §§1255.210–1255.280. However, repayment of any excess withdrawal over the amount awarded by the judgment does not include interest except for (1) any amount due another defendant and (2) any increase over the original amount deposited resulting from a CCP §1255.030 motion (see Supp §8.8) that was made by a party obligated to repay. CCP §1255.280(b). The Condemnation Deposits Fund is governed by Govt C §16429.

The amount of security deposited is not admissible at trial on the issue of compensation in any fashion. Code of Civil Procedure §1255.060 expands the restriction of former CCP §1243.5(e); see Supp §9.49. The two cases cited in Book §8.11, *People v Cowan* and *People v Douglas,* are overruled by the new law.

Money deposited is placed in the State Treasury or, on written request of plaintiff, in the county treasury. CCP §1255.070.

[§8.12] Form: Application for Withdrawal of Deposit of Probable Compensation

[*Title of court*]

[*Title of case*]   No. _ _ _ _

**APPLICATION FOR WITHDRAWAL
OF DEPOSIT OF PROBABLE
COMPENSATION (CCP §1255.210)**

The undersigned applicant hereby declares:
**That his interest in the property described as Parcel No. _ _ _ _
in the complaint on file in this action is _ _[*e.g., ownership/tenancy*]_ _.
That no other persons have any interest in or right to that property.**

[*or*]

**That the names of other persons having interests in that property,
and their respective interests, are as follows:**

_____

_____

[Continue]

That plaintiff, under Section 1255.010 of the Code of Civil Procedure, has deposited the sum of $_ _ _ _ with this Court as deposit of the probable compensation to be awarded for taking that property.

That applicant is entitled to seek withdrawal of the sum of $_ _ _ _ from the deposit pending trial of the action, under Section 1255.210 of the Code of Civil Procedure.

WHEREFORE, applicant prays for an order of this Court directing that $_ _ _ _ of the deposit be delivered to applicant.

Executed at _ _ _ _ _ _, California, on _ _ _ _, 19_ _.

Dated: _ _ _ _ _ _   ___[*Signature of applicant*]___
                                            _ _[*Typed name*]_ _

Comment: See Book §13.11 for form of verification.

The applicant must serve a copy of his application on plaintiff. No withdrawal may be ordered until 20 days after service. CCP §1255.230(a). If plaintiff wishes to object to the withdrawal, objection must be filed within the 20-day period. CCP §1255.230(b). See CCP §1255.230(c) for more stringent requirements when objections are filed on the basis of other parties' interests in the property.

This form has been modified to meet the requirements of the Eminent Domain Law (CCP §§1230.010–1273.050); see Supp §8.11. Verification is now required by CCP §1255.210. See Book §13.11 for form of verification.

[§8.13] Form: Objection to Withdrawal of Deposit of Probable Compensation

[Title of court]

[Title of case]   No. _ _ _ _

**OBJECTION TO WITHDRAWAL
OF SECURITY DEPOSIT**

Plaintiff in the above-titled action hereby objects to the application of _ _ _ _ _ _ for withdrawal of $_ _ _ _, that amount being _ _[*a portion/all*]_ _ of the money deposited by plaintiff as probable compensation for property described as Parcel No. _ _ _ _ in the complaint on file in this action. This objection is made on the ground that other persons are known or believed to have interests in the property. The names and last known addresses of these persons are:

_ _[e.g., name of title insurance company]_ _

Except as provided below, these persons were served with notice on _ _ _ _, 19_ _, that they may appear within ten days after service and object to this withdrawal and that failure to do so constitutes a waiver of any rights to the amount withdrawn or further rights against the plaintiff to the extent of the sum withdrawn.

Plaintiff has attempted to serve personally _ _[name and last known address]_ _ and has been unable to and will be unable to serve personally within the 20-day period specified in Code of Civil Procedure Section 1255.230.

WHEREFORE, plaintiff prays that the Court hold a hearing after notice to all parties and determine the amount to be withdrawn, if any, and by whom, to a total amount not to exceed the amount deposited by plaintiff as security for taking immediate possession of the property. Plaintiff also prays that this hearing be set only after applicant, _ _[name]_ _, causes personal service to be made on _ _[parties named in preceding paragraph]_ _ of a notice of his application to withdraw funds under Code of Civil Procedure Section 1255.230.

Dated: _ _ _ _ _ _   ___[Signature of plaintiff]___
                                            _ _[Typed name]_ _
                                            Plaintiff

Comment: If the condemnor decides to object to the withdrawal, the objection must allege either that other persons have an interest in the property, that the applicant should file an undertaking, or that the undertaking is insufficient. CCP §1255.230(b). The condemnor must also attempt to notify those other persons having an interest in the property. Unlike former CCP §1243.7(e), new CCP §1255.230(c) permits the court to allow withdrawal even if not all such persons have been served. The applicant may attempt service if the condemnor fails.

[§8.13A] Form: Report of Service of Objections to Withdrawal

In cases in which the objection to withdrawal of the deposit is based on the ground that other parties may have an interest, the plaintiff is required to serve on the applicant for withdrawal a report stating (1) the names of all parties served with the notice of objection and (2) the dates of service. Furthermore, in cases of parties who are believed to have an interest but who were not served, plaintiff must provide the names and last known addresses of such parties. CCP §1255.230(c).

The following form, provided by the California Department of Transportation, Legal Division, accomplishes these purposes.

[*Title of court*]

[*Title of case*]
No. _ _ _ _
Parcel Nos. _ _ _ _

REPORT

COMES NOW the plaintiff and under Code of Civil Procedure Section 1255.230(c) makes the following report:

Name of Party   Date Served With Notice

_ _ _ _ _ _ _ _ _ _ _   _ _ _ _ _ _ _ _ _ _ _ _ _ _ _ _ _ _

[*Add, if applicable*]

The following named parties whose addresses are unknown to plaintiff have not been served: _ _[*list names*]_ _.

Dated: _ _ _ _ _ _
___[*Signature of attorney*]___
_ _[*Typed name*]_ _
Attorney for Plaintiff

[§8.14] Form: Order for Withdrawal

[*Title of court*]

[*Title of case*]
No. _ _ _ _

ORDER FOR WITHDRAWAL
OF DEPOSIT (CCP §1255.220)

Application has been made to this Court for withdrawal of funds in the amount of $_ _ _ _, deposited by plaintiff under Code of Civil Procedure Section 1255.010 as probable compensation for property described as Parcel No. _ _ _ _ in the complaint on file herein. The matter was heard this day, notice having been regularly served, _ _ _ _ _ _ appearing as attorney for the defendant.

[*If objection is made to withdrawal*]

and _ _ _ _ _ _ appearing as attorney for plaintiff.

The Court has found that a copy of the application for withdrawal of funds has been served on the plaintiff, that more than 20 days have elapsed since the filing and service of the application, that the time for filing objections to withdrawal of the funds has expired _ _[*and no objection to the withdrawal having been made/and that plaintiff has entered its objection thereto (state reasons)*]_ _, **and that defendant is the only person having an interest in the parcel and entitled to the funds, and good cause appearing therefor,**

IT IS ORDERED that defendant's application be and the same is hereby granted, and the State Treasurer is hereby authorized and directed to pay to the defendant the sum of $_ _ _ _ from the deposit. This payment shall constitute a waiver by operation of law to all defenses of defendant, except with respect to ascertainment of the value of Parcel No. _ _ _ _ in the manner provided by law. Title to Parcel No. _ _ _ _ shall vest in the plaintiff at the time of payment. The amount so paid shall be credited on any judgment rendered and no interest shall be payable on the amount after the date of its withdrawal.

Dated: _ _ _ _ _ _
                                             Judge

Comment: The court is given discretion to require an undertaking if there are conflicting claims as to the amount to be withdrawn (CCP §1255.240), or if the original deposit was increased under CCP §1255.030 and the withdrawal is greater than the original amount (CCP §1255.250(a)). Unless the primary issue is a dispute over title between the applicant and another party, the bond premium may be recovered as costs. See CCP §1255.240(b).

[§8.14A] Investment of Deposit

A defendant who has an interest in the property may move the court, before entry of judgment, for an order that the deposit of probable compensation be invested in United States government obligations or interest-bearing accounts in an institution whose accounts are insured by an agency of the federal government. Any defendant may make the request, but the investment is for the benefit of all defendants and will be apportioned according to their interests as finally determined. The court must consider the interests of the parties and the effect the investment would have on them, and it may set reasonable conditions for the investment. CCP §1255.075. See CCP §1268.150 for a comparable postjudgment provision.

This procedure allows the defendants to earn more than the statutory rate of interest. However, it applies only to the amount deposited, not to any increase that may be obtained at trial. See generally Supp §10.24 for discussion of interest on award.

[§8.14B] Injunction in Lieu of Order of Possession

A preliminary injunction may issue in a condemnation case to preserve the status quo until trial. In *City of Oakland v Superior Court* (1982) 136 CA3d 565, 186 CR 326, an injunction was sought in lieu of an order of possession by the City of Oakland to prevent a professional football team from moving to another city pending the city's condemnation of that team. The court observed that this remedy was less intrusive than an order of possession, and it allowed the condemnee to remain in possession subject to conditions tailored to the needs of the specific case. See Supp §6.6 for discussion of the supreme court decision in *City of Oakland v Oakland Raiders* (1982) 32 C3d 60, 183 CR 673, concerning a municipality's right to take a professional football franchise, and a later related case, *City of Oakland v Superior Court* (1983) 150 CA3d 267, 197 CR 729.

CONDEMNEE'S PLEADINGS

Disclaimer

[§8.15] Use

A disclaimer is specifically authorized by CCP §1250.325.

[§8.16] Form: Disclaimer

[Title of court]

[Title of case]   **No. _ _ _ _**

DISCLAIMER AS TO PARCEL NO._ _ _ _ (CCP §1250.325)

Defendant, _ _[name] _ _, claims no interest in the property described in the complaint in this action or in any compensation that may be awarded.

Dated: _ _ _ _ _ _   ___*[Signature of defendant]*___
                                          _ _*[Typed name] _ _*
                                          Defendant

Comment: Under CCP §1250.325, a disclaimer need not be a formal document, but it must contain a statement that defendant claims no interest in the property or compensation to be awarded. The disclaimer may be filed at any time during the proceedings and terminates the lawsuit as to that party. A disclaimer must be signed by the party; an attorney's signature is not sufficient.

Answer

[§§8.17–8.18] Statutory Requirements; Contents

Under CCP §1250.320(a) (former CCP §1246), the answer usually need include only a statement of defendant's claimed interest in the property condemned. The requirement that the answer specify the amount of compensation claimed has been deleted because it is usually an "ill-informed guess." 12 Cal L Rev'n Comm'n Reports 1655 (1974).

In special situations, two other requirements apply: A claim for loss of goodwill under CCP §1263.510 must be asserted in the answer. CCP §1250.320(b). Also, a claim for precondemnation damages is properly raised by answer (*People ex rel Dep't of Pub. Works v Peninsula Enters.* (1979) 91 CA3d 332, 353, 153 CR 895, 906), but the Law Revision Commission's Comment has created some uncertainty and the attorney must be wary. See Supp §§4.7–4.7A, 8.18A, 8.24.

If a party is represented by an attorney, the answer does not have to be verified, but it must be signed by the party's attorney or it may be stricken. CCP §1250.330.

[§8.18A] Pleading Precondemnation Damages by Answer or Cross-Complaint

To invoke the rule of *Klopping v City of Whittier* (1972) 8 C3d 39, 104 CR 1, allowing for precondemnation damage (see §4.7, Supp §4.7A), one court suggested that it was necessary to plead special damages caused by the delay (or other unreasonable conduct) preceding the condemnation. See *Redevelopment Agency v Del-Camp Invs., Inc.* (1974) 38 CA3d 836, 847, 113 CR 762, 770. The owner's attorney would be prudent to do so, but it is probably not necessary in view of CCP §1250.320, enacted after *Del-Camp*.

Whether such pleading should be by answer or cross-complaint has been the subject of considerable confusion. Although *Klopping* was an inverse condemnation case, it laid down the rule that such damages must be raised in the direct condemnation action when it finally comes. Because *Klopping* is silent on the procedural aspects of claiming precondemnation damages in a direct condemnation action, some parties, usually condemnors, have argued that these damages must be asserted by cross-complaint. However, the courts have held that the proper way to raise these precondemnation damages is by answer. *Richmond Redev. Agency v Western Title Guar. Co.* (1975) 48 CA3d 343, 349, 122 CR 434, 438.

See *People ex rel Dep't of Pub. Works v Peninsula Enters.* (1979) 91 CA3d 332, 353, 153 CR 895, 906, in which the court stated that the proper method for a condemnee to seek damages for unreasonable precondemnation actions when an eminent domain suit has been begun is by way of answer, but this opinion does not discuss CCP §426.70

or the Law Revision Commission's Comment to that section. See also *Redevelopment Agency v Contra Costa Theatre, Inc.* (1982) 135 CA3d 73, 79 n2, 185 CR 159, 163 n2, approving the seeking of precondemnation damages by answer rather than cross-complaint.

Counsel should also be aware that CCP §426.70 eliminates the claim presentation requirement for cross-complaints in eminent domain actions. Government Code §905.1 eliminates the claim presentation requirement for inverse condemnation actions, thereby invalidating the limitation on recovery laid down in *Stone v City of Los Angeles* (1975) 51 CA3d 987, 996, 124 CR 822, 828 (limiting recovery of precondemnation damages to those accruing within the one year preceding the claim's presentation).

Because the Law Revision Commission suggested in its comments to CCP §426.70 that *Klopping*-type precondemnation damages should be asserted by cross-complaint, some practitioners believe that the safest course for the property owner to follow in a direct condemnation case is to plead *Klopping*-type damages by both answer and cross-complaint and let the condemnor decide if it wishes to challenge the propriety of one of those pleadings and, if so, which one. See 12 Cal L Rev'n Comm'n Reports 1889 (1974).

The Eminent Domain Law (CCP §§1230.010–1273.050) revises and streamlines the contents of an answer; the owner is no longer required to plead value (CCP §1250.320), and the answer need not be verified if signed by an attorney (CCP §1250.330). However, in spite of the evident legislative intent to simplify the answer, it is appropriate to continue pleading *Klopping*-type damages. It would seem an abuse of discretion for a trial court, after sustaining a demurrer to either an answer or a cross-complaint, to refuse to grant permission to amend the answer or to file a cross-complaint. However, these denials have occurred and therefore owners' counsel would be well advised to pursue the safe course, even at the price of increased complexity and paperwork.

[§8.19] Affirmative Defenses

Objections to the right to take (see Supp §§6.25–6.28) may be raised by demurrer or answer, depending on whether an issue of law or fact is presented. The specific ground for the objection must be stated, and if the objection is raised in an answer, the supporting facts must be specifically alleged. CCP §§1250.350–1250.360. Failure to object by answer or demurrer constitutes a waiver. CCP §1250.345. A writ of mandate is available to review the resolution of necessity before the condemnation action is filed. CCP §1245.255(a)(1).

It appears that the correct method of raising the defense that the state has not complied with the California Environmental Quality Act of 1970 (Pub Res C §§21000–21176) is by answer and cross-complaint for injunctive relief rather than demurrer. *People ex rel Dep't of Pub. Works v*

Bosio (1975) 47 CA3d 495, 501, 121 CR 375, 376 (state's failure to file environmental impact report in connection with highway project). In *Bosio*, it eventually became necessary to seek a writ of mandamus. But compare *City of San Jose v Great Oaks Water Co.* (1987) 192 CA3d 1005, 237 CR 845, which allowed the condemnee to challenge the right to take by asserting the environmental defense only in the answer, without an additional assertion in a cross-complaint.

Following *Bosio,* the court in *People ex rel Dep't of Transp. v Sullivan* (1978) 78 CA3d 120, 144 CR 100, held that the need for an Environmental Impact Report (EIR) cannot be raised for the first time on appeal. The state's failure to file an EIR was also rejected as a defense because the land was taken to provide a maintenance easement along an existing highway. When "the proposed use involves no major change in the character of the area," an EIR is not required. 78 CA3d at 123, 144 CR at 101.

If the challenge to the right to take is based on the Political Reform Act of 1974 (Govt C §§81000–91015), it must be asserted by a cross-complaint. *San Bernardino County Flood Control Dist. v Grabowski* (1988) 205 CA3d 885, 252 CR 676, discussed in Supp §6.25.

[§8.20] Form: Answer

[*Title of court*]

[*Title of case*]   **No. _ _ _ _**

ANSWER (CCP §1250.320)

Defendant, _ _[name]_ _, in answer to the complaint on file herein, states:

[*First alternative: When condemnee is sole interest holder*]

1. It is the owner in fee simple absolute and in possession of that certain piece or parcel of land described in plaintiff's complaint and designated there as _ _[e.g., Parcel No._ _ _ _/*the larger parcel of which the parcel taken is a part*]_ _; **answering defendant denies that any other person, firm, or corporation has or claims any valid right, title, or interest in and to** _ _[*Parcel No._ _ _ _/the larger parcel of which the parcel taken is a part*]_ _ **except as** _ _[*e.g., a lessee of this answering defendant/an easement holder for public utility purposes/a holder of a security interest*]_ _.

Comment: Under former law, a verified allegation of exclusive ownership and uncontroverted oral testimony at the time of trial put the property owner in a position to demand that the entire compensation award be paid to him without regard to additional claims that might have been alleged in the complaint. If the answer did not contain such an allegation, the owner might have found the compensation paid into court for the benefit of himself and other persons "as their interests appear." See *People ex rel Dep't of Pub. Works v Shasta Pipe & Supply Co.* (1968) 262 CA2d 520, 537, 70 CR 618, 629. Presumably, the rule remains the same under the new law, although the answer need no longer be verified. CCP §§1260.220, 1268.710.

[Second alternative: When condemnee is lessee, security holder, easement holder, or other party claiming an interest]

1. It owns a _ _ _ _ interest in that certain piece or parcel of land described in plaintiff's complaint and designated there as Parcel No. _ _ _ _, by virtue of that certain _ _[trust deed/deed of easement/ lease]_ _ dated _ _ _ _, 19_ _, by and between _ _[e.g., the owner of Parcel No._ _ _ _]_ _ and this answering defendant.

[If interest claimed is security interest]

This security interest is given to secure payment of an obligation to this answering defendant on which the current balance owing is the sum of $_ _ _ _ and on which interest is accruing from and after _ _ _ _ _ _, 19_ _, at the rate of $_ _ _ _ per day; periodic payments are required to be made on this obligation during the pendency of these proceedings; and this answering defendant will move to amend this answer to set forth the balance and principal due at the time of judgment.

[If objection to right to take]

2. Defendant objects to plaintiff's right to take the property sought herein on the following ground(s); _ _[state specific facts on which the objection is based]_ _.

Comment: Code of Civil Procedure §1250.350 requires that facts supporting each objection to the right to take be specifically stated. See Supp §6.25. Failure to object to the complaint, by answer or demurrer, waives all objections. CCP §1250.345.

[If loss of goodwill claimed]

3. Defendant claims compensation for loss of goodwill under Code of Civil Procedure Section 1263.510.

Comment: Code of Civil Procedure §1250.320 requires only a claim of loss of goodwill; no amount need be specified.

[*If precondemnation damages claimed*]

4. Defendant claims precondemnation damages of loss of rental income resulting from unreasonable delay (or other unreasonable conduct) in commencing the present complaint in eminent domain after prior announcements and actions by plaintiff made clear its intention to acquire the parcel described in the complaint.

Comment: For discussion of precondemnation damages, see Supp §§4.7–4.7A; for rules of pleading such damages, see Supp §8.18A. The opinion in *Redevelopment Agency v Del-Camp Invs.* (1974) 38 CA3d 836, 847, 113 CR 762, 770, appears to indicate that the claim must be specifically pleaded, but detailed facts need not be alleged.

[*Continue*]

WHEREFORE, defendant prays:
(1) Plaintiff take nothing by its complaint; or
(2) This Court determine and award the just compensation to which he is entitled by virtue of the taking of Parcel No. _ _ _ _ _ _[*and for severance damage to the remaining property/or for compensation for loss of goodwill/for precondemnation damages***]_ _.**
(3) For allowable litigation expenses and costs of suit incurred;
(4) For such other and further relief as the Court shall find just and proper.

Dated: _ _ _ _ _ _   ___[*Signature of attorney*]___
                                               _ _[*Typed name*]_ _
                                               Attorney for Defendant

Comment: (a) If affirmative defenses are contemplated to defeat the taking of all or a portion of the property plaintiff seeks to acquire, alternative prayers should request that the court find that plaintiff has no right or power to acquire either certain portions of the property or all of it.

(b) The requests for compensation for loss of goodwill and precondemnation damages are set forth in the prayer based on the requirement that each be specifically claimed in the answer.

[§8.22] Amendment of Answer

Code of Civil Procedure §§464 and 473, permitting amendment of pleadings, are supplemented by CCP §1250.340. In addition, CCP §1250.345 recognizes that the court has discretion to permit an amendment to the answer when the defendant fails to object to the complaint initially by either demurrer or answer. *San Diego Gas & Elec. Co. v 3250 Corp.* (1988) 205 CA3d 1075, 1082, 252 CR 853, 856.

California Civil Procedure Before Trial (Cal CEB 1957) has been replaced by California Civil Procedure Before Trial (3d ed Cal CEB 1990).

[§8.23] Demurrer

When the ground for objection to the right to take (see Supp §§6.25–6.28) appears on the face of the complaint, the objection may be raised by demurrer. CCP §1250.350. Code of Civil Procedure §§1244 and 1266, mentioned in Book §8.23, have been repealed.

Code of Civil Procedure §§1240.320, 1240.350, 1240.420, 1240.510, and 1240.610, regarding the authority under which property is sought to be condemned, each require the complaint and resolution of necessity to refer specifically to the required code section under which the acquisition is authorized. Failure to specify the authority of CCP §1240.610 (acquisition of property already appropriated to public use for a more necessary use) was a fatal defect requiring a judgment of dismissal on demurrer in *PG&E v Superior Court* (1986) 180 CA3d 770, 225 CR 268.

Los Angeles County Flood Control Act §§16–1/2, 16–5/8, cited for illustrative purposes in Book §8.23, have been repealed by Stats 1975, ch 1276, §§7–8.

California Civil Procedure Before Trial §§399–421 (Cal CEB 1957), on demurrers, has been replaced by 2 California Civil Procedure Before Trial, chap 30 (3d ed Cal CEB 1990).

[§8.24] Cross-Complaint

Generally, unless a related cause of action is asserted against the plaintiff, it is barred. CCP §426.30. Code of Civil Procedure §426.70(a) extends this rule to eminent domain proceedings.

The enactment of CCP §426.70(b), which permits the filing of a cross-complaint in a condemnation action without the necessity of presenting a claim, eliminated a possible trap for the condemnee.

The court in *County of San Luis Obispo v Ranchita Cattle Co.* (1971) 16 CA3d 383, 94 CR 73, ruled that the property owner's failure to file a claim for damages resulting from the condemnor's activities that exceeded the scope of a right of access agreement barred the recovery of those damages in a subsequent direct condemnation action. See also *People ex rel Dep't of Pub. Works v Williams* (1973) 30 CA3d 980, 106 CR 795 (prejudgment interest under broad right of entry agreement is incident of award in condemnation action and does not require filing of claim); *City of Oakland v Nutter* (1970) 13 CA3d 752, 92 CR 347 (taking of an air easement to protect approaches of airport was broad enough that claim of damages for excessive noise, vibration, and other interference with remaining land was for severance damages for which no claim was necessary); *City of Fresno v Hedstrom* (1951) 103 CA2d 453, 460, 229 P2d 809, 813 (not necessary to file claim against city in condemnation action brought by that city); *People ex rel Dep't of Parks & Recreation v West-A-Rama, Inc.* (1973) 35 CA3d 786, 111 CR 197 (claim was not necessary for a cross-complaint in a contract action initiated by the state).

A cross-complaint for administrative mandamus was the appropriate remedy to seek "in-lieu moving expenses" under the relocation assistance laws (see §4.53) in a direct condemnation action. *City of Mountain View v Superior Court* (1975) 54 CA3d 72, 126 CR 358. See the discussion of *Mountain View* in Supp §4.53.

The public entity may cross-complain with a direct condemnation action to an inverse suit for delay in commencing the condemnation action. *Stone v City of Los Angeles* (1975) 51 CA3d 987, 990, 124 CR 822, 824.

A cross-complaint is required to challenge the right to take based on a statutory ground other than the California Eminent Domain Law, such as the Political Reform Act of 1974. *San Bernardino County Flood Control Dist. v Grabowski* (1988) 205 CA3d 885, 252 CR 676. See Supp §§6.25, 8.19.

CONSOLIDATION AND SEPARATION

[§8.25] Discretion of Court

All property located in the same county that is sought for the same project may be joined in one complaint. CCP §1250.240. The court, however, may order separate trials if appropriate. CCP §1048.

California Civil Procedure During Trial §§4.25–4.26 (Cal CEB 1960) on consolidation and severance have been replaced by 3 California Civil Procedure Before Trial, chaps 61–62 (3d ed Cal CEB 1990).

[§8.27] Form: Notice of Motion for Order of Consolidation

Comment: The citation in the title of the form should be changed from former CCP §1244 to CCP §1048.

CONDEMNOR'S RIGHT TO ABANDON TAKING

[§8.31] Basis

Code of Civil Procedure §1268.510, concerning a condemnor's right to abandon, is substantially the same as former CCP §1255a.

The court in *City of Torrance v Superior Court* (1976) 16 C3d 195, 127 CR 609, held that, under former CCP §1255a, the condemnor was estopped from abandoning an action for public roads when the defendant, a developer, relying on assurances from the city that it would condemn, bought the affected property, integrated it with adjacent land for subdivision, and omitted that portion required for the public project. But see *Community Dev. Comm'n v Shuffler* (1988) 198 CA3d 450, 243 CR 719, in which the condemnor was permitted to abandon an action because there had been neither assurances that the condemning agency would not abandon the action nor detrimental reliance on the condemnation action for the purchase or construction of replacement property by the landowner. *Shuffler* also concluded that while an appeal is pending a judgment is not final for the purpose of preventing a condemnor from filing a notice of abandonment within 30 days after the final judgment and the trial court retains jurisdiction to rule on a motion to set aside the abandonment. The trial court was not required to make findings in denying a motion to set aside abandonment.

[§8.32] Implied Abandonment

A condemnor whose case was dismissed for failure to bring the case to trial within five years, as required by former CCP §583(b) (now CCP §583.310), has been held not to have abandoned voluntarily. The condemnor had not filed written notice of abandonment, had opposed the motion to dismiss, and had no intention of voluntarily abandoning the action. *City of Industry v Gordon* (1972) 29 CA3d 90, 105 CR 206.

However, in *Alta Bates Hosp. v Mertle* (1973) 31 CA3d 349, 107 CR 277, the court held that failure to appeal a judgment of dismissal with prejudice against plaintiff-hospital was implied abandonment and thus entitled the defendant to costs. *Gordon* was distinguished factually in that failure to appeal established voluntary abandonment of the action. In 1971, after trial of the *Mertle* case, the legislature enacted former CCP §1246.4 (repealed) (see Book §6.2), which allows litigation costs when the condemnor is defeated on its right to take.

The rule of *Gordon* is abrogated by CCP §1268.610(a)(1), which allows owners' litigation expenses on dismissal for any reason. In *Conejo Recreation & Park Dist. v Armstrong* (1981) 114 CA3d 1016, 170 CR 891, the court specifically rejected the contention that CCP §1268.610(a)(1) is limited to voluntary dismissal. In *Armstrong,* a motion for dismissal by the landowner was granted on the grounds that the plaintiff, a park and recreation district, had not given notice to the defendants of its intention to appear before the Board of Supervisors and seek permission to condemn the property under the requirements of Pub Res C §5782.5(c).

In *Cash v Southern Pac. R.R.* (1981) 123 CA3d 974, 177 CR 474, the court discussed the possibility of abandonment of property that had been condemned in a prior proceeding. Property owners whose land had been acquired by defendants as a right-of-way to construct and operate a railroad and to use the land for other purposes necessary and incident to railroad construction and operation sought to recover the property and receive rental payments for the land on the basis that the entire right-of-way had not been used and portions were used for commercial purposes. The court discussed the general property law concerning abandonment of easements and concluded that nonuse of certain portions of the property does not, absent intent to abandon, establish abandonment of right-of-way.

[§8.33] Compensation of Condemnee

Code of Civil Procedure §1255a has been repealed. Under CCP §§1235.140 and 1268.610, litigation expenses (see Supp §1.9) are awarded to defendant on dismissal or defeat of the right to take.

In the case of a partial dismissal or defeat of part of the taking, defendant cannot include in its expenses costs that would have been incurred in any event for defending the remaining action. CCP §1268.610(b).

Reimbursement of defendant's litigation expenses when the complaint is amended to add to the property to be taken is covered by CCP §1250.340(a).

The purpose of these statutes is to reimburse the property owner for litigation expenses that have been paid or to indemnify the owner for fees for which he has become liable. A contingency fee, depending on the particular attorney-client agreement, may not be collected if the contingency on which it is based fails. But if the parties modify a contingency fee contract to compensate the attorney for the reasonable value of his services before any prospect of abandonment, those legal fees can be recovered on abandonment. *People ex rel Dep't of Pub. Works v Metcalf* (1978) 79 CA3d 1, 144 CR 657. A party can also recover reimbursement for fees incurred in unsuccessful, but good faith, motions seeking to resist the abandonment.

It is not appropriate to consider a contingency fee agreement as the basis for determining attorneys' fees on abandonment of an action when the agreement does not provide for fees on abandonment, and the contingencies set forth never occurred. However, the court can award reasonable fees notwithstanding the agreement for a contingency fee. *County of Madera v Forrester* (1981) 115 CA3d 57, 65, 170 CR 896, 900.

In *Glendora Community Redev. Agency v Demeter* (1984) 155 CA3d 465, 202 CR 389, a contingency fee contract specifically relating attorneys' fees to abandonment was properly considered by the trial court when it also considered other factors in awarding attorneys' fees. The court of appeal, however, noted that the trial court was not bound by the terms of the contract. But see *Salton Bay Marina, Inc. v Imperial Irrig. Dist.* (1985) 172 CA3d 914, 218 CR 839, an inverse condemnation case, which criticized the court in *Glendora* for viewing the reasonableness of the attorneys' fees from the client's perspective of agreeing to share a percentage of recovery with the attorney. The court stated that, when a public entity has to pay the property owners' attorneys' fees, the time spent on the case should be considered. See Supp §13.30. See also *Aetna Life & Cas. Co. v City of Los Angeles* (1985) 170 CA3d 865, 216 CR 831, which reversed an award of attorneys' fees based on a contingency fee contract in an inverse condemnation case because the trial court had not considered plaintiff's attorneys' usual hourly rates, the actual amount of the fees, the actual number of hours worked by plaintiff's attorneys, or what relationship the fee award bore to the number of hours worked.

Citing *Glendora Community Redev. Agency v Demeter, supra,* the court in *State v Meyer* (1985) 174 CA3d 1061, 1073, 220 CR 884, 891, held that the factors to consider are hours actually spent, reasonable hourly rate, the difficulty of the issues, and quality of work. The court refused to use a "lodestar multiplier" of four times the hours spent multiplied by the hourly rate.

City of Oakland v Oakland Raiders (1988) 203 CA3d 78, 249 CR 606, approved computing the attorneys' fees by multiplying the number of hours of legal services by the hourly rates charged by top law firms and then raising the fees to account for factors such as novelty, complexity of the issues, and the need for counsel to act quickly in the litigation and defer their fees.

When the condemnation award is not paid to the condemnee because of abandonment, it is not proper to allow the condemnee to recover interest on that award. *Santa Clarita Water Co. v Lyons* (1984) 161 CA3d 450, 207 CR 698. See also *People ex rel Dep't of Transp. v Union Pac. Land Resources Corp.* (1986) 179 CA3d 307, 224 CR 487.

Delay damages (see Supp §4.7A) may not be sought for the first time in a cost bill for abandonment. *State v Meyer, supra.*

Once a condemning agency has abandoned its condemnation proceeding, the owner must file a separate inverse condemnation action to recover precondemnation damages. *Redevelopment Agency v Heller* (1988) 200 CA3d 517, 246 CR 160.

The property owner is not only entitled to be compensated for litigation expenses but can also recover damages proximately caused to the property itself by the proceeding and its dismissal. In such a case, the property owner can pursue damages for loss of use and loss of opportunity. *Community Dev. Comm'n v Shuffler* (1988) 198 CA3d 450, 243 CR 719.

A condemnee that has succeeded in unconditionally dismissing an action can recover the fees not only in the condemnation action but also in a related Public Utilities Commission valuation proceeding, because the fees attributable to the other proceeding were necessitated by the filing of a condemnation action. *City of San Jose v Great Oaks Water Co.* (1987) 192 CA3d 1005, 237 CR 845.

9

Trial Preparation and Trial

INITIAL TRIAL PREPARATION

[§9.1] Factual and Legal Preparation

The Eminent Domain Law (CCP §§1230.010–1273.050) replaced CCP §§1237–1273.06.

The general rules of evidence concerning market value of property (Evid C §§810–823) have been extended to all property valuation cases, including those for eminent domain, except cases concerning ad valorem property tax assessment and equalization. Evid C §810. The practitioner in eminent domain must now take note of developments in the rules of evidence through divorce, property division, contract, and other cases.

[§9.3] Public Use and Necessity Issue

The resolution of condemnation must establish the necessity for the taking before the property may be condemned. CCP §1240.030.

The new condemnation law provides for objections to the right to take

(CCP §1250.350), which should invite more challenges on the public use and necessity issues. See Supp §§6.25–6.28.

A lis pendens must be filed by the plaintiff at the time of filing suit. CCP §1250.150. See Supp §8.5.

[§9.4] Property Interest as an Issue

A defendant must state in the answer the nature and extent of the interest he claims in the property. CCP §1250.320(a). Plaintiff, however, is no longer required to identify, in the complaint, the nature of the various defendants' interests in the property sought to be condemned. CCP §1250.310(b); see former CCP §1244(5).

The apportionment of awards is now governed by CCP §1260.220 (former CCP §1246.1).

DISCOVERY

[§9.5] Conventional Techniques

A survey of California condemnation lawyers conducted by the California Law Revision Commission in 1972 revealed that the discovery devices of interrogatories and statutory exchange are those most often used; depositions are used less often. The survey also revealed that the greatest concern of those responding was the courts' unwillingness to exclude testimony elicited at trial when it was sought but not made known through discovery. See §9.14; Kanner, *Sic Transit Gloria: The Rise and Fall of Mutuality of Discovery in California Eminent Domain Litigation,* 6 Loy LA L Rev 447 (1973).

The law generally provides that an expert witness may require compensation for testifying in a deposition. CCP §2034(i)(2)–(4). One of the primary purposes of the 1978 enactment of the Code of Civil Procedure provisions for discovery of expert witnesses was the exchange of expert witness lists. Since eminent domain law already had a procedure under CCP §1258.210 for exchanging expert witness lists, eminent domain proceedings were excepted from the scope of those Code of Civil Procedure provisions. Code of Civil Procedure §2034(a)(3) excepts eminent domain provisions from the requirement of simultaneous exchange of information concerning expert witnesses.

Under Govt C §68092.5, as amended in 1988, a party requiring testimony of an expert, except one who is a party or an employee of the party, either must accompany the service of subpena or notice with a tender of the expert's fees based on the anticipated length of time the expert is required to remain at the proceeding or must tender the fee at the required time of appearance. The party designating the expert is responsible for any fee charged by the expert for preparing for testimony and for traveling to the place of the civil action or proceeding, unless the court determines otherwise. If a party requiring the appearance of another party's expert deems the fee unreasonable that party may move for an order setting the compensation of the expert.

Although Govt C §68092.5 was amended in 1988 to delete language that the expert's compensation in a deposition is not an allowable cost, note CCP §1033.5(b)(1), which states that the fees of experts not ordered by the court are not allowable as costs unless expressly authorized by law.

[§9.6] Statutory Exchange of Appraisal Data

The exchange of valuation data is now governed by CCP §§1258.210–1258.300, and certain changes have been made in the procedure.

The time of demand must be no later than ten days following the date the trial date is selected. Thereafter, a noticed motion and a showing of good cause is required. CCP §1258.210(a). There is no need to file a cross-demand to reach the initiating party's valuation data, as suggested by former CCP §1272.01(b). When one party makes a demand for exchange, that party must also supply its data to the other party. CCP §1258.230(a). The date of exchange is the time agreed on by the parties; if there is no agreement, the date is either 40 days before trial or the time selected by the court on noticed motion. CCP §1258.220. The superior court of any county may provide a substitute procedure to this scheme by court rule approved by the Judicial Council. CCP §1258.300. Los Angeles County has a system for disclosing valuation information conducted under the court's direction.

After exchange, other discovery remains open until 20 days before trial, notwithstanding the work product rule of CCP §2016. CCP §1258.020(a).

California Pretrial and Settlement Procedures has been replaced by 2 California Civil Procedure Before Trial, chaps 48–54, and 3 California Civil Procedure Before Trial, chaps 68–70 (3d ed Cal CEB 1990).

[§9.7] Limitations on Testimony at Trial

In *Richmond Redev. Agency v Western Title Guar. Co.* (1975) 48 CA3d 343, 122 CR 434, the court allowed incidental use of the reproduction cost method of valuation to check the validity of other approaches, even though the parties had agreed under CCP §1272.02 (replaced by CCP §§1258.250 and 1258.260) that such an approach would not be used.

Code of Civil Procedure §1258.270 (former CCP §1272.04) requires exchanged lists and statements to be supplemented with subsequent data. If a party fails to exchange information, its witness may be prevented from testifying, or valuation data may be excluded from evidence on objection of the other side. CCP §1258.280 (formerly CCP §1272.05).

See *Mehl v People ex rel Dep't of Pub. Works* (1975) 13 C3d 710, 119 CR 625. But see *Nestle v City of Santa Monica* (1972) 6 C3d 920, 101 CR 568. Code of Civil Procedure §1258.280 does not prevent the party from calling the witness or using the data in rebuttal. See *People v Loop* (1954) 127 CA2d 786, 801, 274 P2d 885, 896. In *County of Monterey v W.W. Leasing Unltd.* (1980) 109 CA3d 636, 644, 167 CR 12, 16, however-er, the court cited Book §9.7 and held that appellant could not avoid the requirement that valuation data be exchanged before trial. Appellant had attempted to introduce in rebuttal evidence of comparable sales that would and should have been introduced in the case-in-chief had appellant not failed to exchange that data before trial.

The court can grant relief from the limitation on calling a witness or excluding testimony if it finds that the otherwise delinquent party has made a good faith effort to comply with the exchange requirements and has supplemented the list and statement as provided by CCP §1258.270. CCP §1258.290(a) (former CCP §1272.06). In *City of Fresno v Harrison* (1984) 154 CA3d 296, 201 CR 219, the condemning agency retained an expert witness only one month before the trial, and on being deposed the expert had not yet formed an opinion. The condemning agency also had not exchanged any business goodwill valuation information under CCP §1258.210, and the court held that it was not proper to allow the unexpected testimony of the agency's expert.

[§9.8] Form: Demand for Exchange of Information

[*Title of court*]

[*Title of case*]   No._ _ _ _

DEMAND FOR EXCHANGE OF
INFORMATION (CCP §1258.210)

To _ _[*plaintiff(s)/defendant(s)*]_ _ and to _ _[*its/his/her/their*]_ _ attor-ney(s) of record.

In connection with the above pending action for condemnation of the parcel of property described in the complaint, you are required to deposit with the court clerk and to serve on the undersigned attorney for defendant(s), _ _[*name(s)*]_ _, a list of expert witnesses and statements of valuation data in compliance with Chapter 7, Article 2, of Title 7 of Part 3 of the Code of Civil Procedure, not later than _ _ _ _ _ _, 19_ _, which is ten days before the day this action is set for trial of value. Except as otherwise provided in that article, your failure to do so will constitute a waiver of your right to call unlisted expert witnesses during your case in chief and a waiver of your right to introduce on direct examination during your case in chief any matter that is required to be, but is not, set forth in your statements of valuation data.

The list of expert witnesses to be deposited and served shall include the name, business or residence address, and the business, occupation, or profession of each person intended to be called as an expert witness and a statement of the subject matter to which his testimony relates.

A statement of valuation data shall be deposited and served for each person intended to be called as a witness by you to testify to his opinion on (1) the value of the property or property interest being valued;

[Add, if partial take]

(2) the amount of damage, if any, to the remainder of the larger parcel from which the property is taken; and (3) the amount of the special benefit, if any, to the remainder of the larger parcel from which the property is taken.

[Continue]

_ _[(2)/(4)]_ _ the amount of any other compensation required to be paid by Chapter 9 (commencing with CCP §1263.010) or Chapter 10 (commencing with CCP §1265.010).

Each statement of valuation data shall also set forth in detail all those matters specified in CCP §1258.260 and shall include a statement, signed by the witness, that he has read the statement and that it fairly and correctly states his opinions and knowledge of the matters stated.

An appraisal report prepared by the witness, including information required to be included in the statement of valuation data as defined in CCP §1258.260(e), may be used as a statement of valuation data.

Dated: _ _ _ _ _ _   ___*[Signature of attorney]*___
                                       _ _*[Typed name]*_ _
                                       Attorney for _ _ _ _ _ _

Comment: This form is adapted from the requirements set out in CCP §§1258.210–1258.260.

[§9.9] Form: Responsive List of Expert Witnesses

Comment: The citation in the title of the form to former CCP §1272.03 should be changed to CCP §1258.240.

Code of Civil Procedure §1267 has been repealed. The Eminent Domain Law (CCP §§1230.010–1273.050) does not place any limitation on the number of expert witnesses who may be called to testify on behalf of a party, but the court retains its general control over the number of such witnesses through Evid C §723.

[§9.10] Form: Statement of Valuation Data

Comment: The citation in the title of the form to former CCP §1272.02 should be changed to CCP §1258.260. The statement's description of comparable sales must include the total area and shape of the properties sold. CCP §1258.260(b)(6).

Code of Civil Procedure §1258.250 (former CCP §1272.02(a)(1)–(3)) requires a statement for each person (including the owner) who is to testify concerning an opinion on any of the following:

(a) Value of the property taken;

(b) Severance damage in a partial taking;

(c) Benefits to the remainder; and

(d) Any other compensable item that would include, *e.g.,* goodwill (CCP §1263.510) and leasehold interests (CCP §§1265.110–1265.160).

Pretrial

[§9.11] Purpose

In *Mehl v People ex rel Dep't of Pub. Works* (1975) 13 C3d 710, 718, 119 CR 625, 630, an inverse condemnation case, the condemnees failed to advise the state of an expert's opinion on apportionment of damages between county and state, in violation of a pretrial order to disclose the expert's opinion. The court held that the failure to disclose the opinion, together with other grounds, made the testimony inadmissible.

[§9.13] Pretrial in Los Angeles County

Code of Civil Procedure §1258.300 states that a superior court in any county may provide by court rule a procedure for the exchange of evaluation data to be used instead of the procedure provided by CCP §1258.260, if the Judicial Council finds that the former procedure serves the same purpose as the latter.

In addition to the matters set out in Book §9.13, the first pretrial conference order in Los Angeles County now includes:

(g) Date of valuation;

(h) Dates by which parties will file or exchange opening statement of facts, legal contentions, and points and authorities, and responses to them;

(i) Date of mandatory settlement conference; and

(j) Size of jury, or whether there is to be one.

See Los Angeles Superior Court Eminent Domain Policy Memorandum (Dec. 1988), published by the Los Angeles County Superior Court and available from The Los Angeles Daily Journal, 210 South Spring Street, Los Angeles, CA 90012, or Metropolitan News-Enterprise, P.O. Box 60859, Los Angeles, CA 90060.

[§9.14] Shortcomings of Pretrial Exchange of Valuation Data Procedure

The condemnor's testimony of a direct comparable property was properly excluded when the condemnor did not exchange the information until five days before the pretrial conference and failed to inform the defense of its intended use until one week before trial. In addition, because the improvement on the comparable property was no longer standing, any investigation pertaining to its relevant history would have taken considerable time and effort, making cross-examination extremely difficult if not impossible. The condemnor also failed to explain its lengthy delay in revealing the information. *Redevelopment Agency v First Christian Church* (1983) 140 CA3d 690, 189 CR 749.

On a witness's qualifications to testify concerning a change in zoning as it relates to the property's highest and best use, see §4.14.

For a critique of use of a stripped appraisal report for discovery and a complete report for trial purposes, see Kanner, *Sic Transit Gloria: The Rise and Fall of Mutuality of Discovery in California Eminent Domain Litigation,* 6 Loy LA L Rev 447 (1973).

[§9.14A] Pretrial Offer and Demand

At least 30 days before trial each side must file and serve its final offer and demand for the property taken and any damages to the remainder. CCP §1250.410 (formerly CCP §1249.3). See Supp §§1.9, 10.23A. The new law makes clear that the offer and demand must cover all compensation; the former section spoke of "property sought to be condemned."

The 30-day period is mandatory for the initial final offer and demand. If a property owner does not file a written final demand at least 30 days before trial, the possibility of recovering litigation expenses is forfeited. *People ex rel Dep't of Transp. v Callahan Bros.* (1977) 69 CA3d 541, 138 CR 239. A party can make more than one final offer or demand that the court will consider on the issue of awarding litigation expenses, as long as the revised offer of settlement is made at least 30 days before trial. *Los Angeles Unified School Dist. v C.F. Bolster Co.* (1978) 81 CA3d 906, 146 CR 789. See Supp §9.14B on the 30-day limit.

Noncompliance with the statute by the property owner bars recovery of litigation expenses, despite the agency's corresponding failure to file an offer. In *Santa Clara Valley Water Dist. v Gross* (1988) 200 CA3d 1363, 246 CR 580, a member of the condemnor's board of directors, whose property was condemned, could not avoid this rule on the grounds of conflict of interest under Govt C §1090, which prohibits public officers from entering into transactions with the agency they represent. As soon as the lawsuit was filed, the board member and agency became adversaries and were thus subject to the rules governing eminent domain litigation.

The court in *Coachella Valley County Water Dist. v Dreyfuss* (1979) 91 CA3d 949, 154 CR 467, held that, when an award is based on acceptance of a settlement demand, defendant may also recover ordinary costs and prejudgment interest. Such recovery is not precluded by CCP §1250.410; the court held that "compensation" as used in CCP §1250.410 means compensation for the property taken, severance damage, and other consequential damage, but it does not cover ordinary costs or interest on the award for prejudgment possession.

It is appropriate, in a case in which both a direct and inverse condemnation action are to be tried together, for the property owner to make a lump-sum demand to settle both actions. *People ex rel Dep't of Transp. v Sunshine Canyon, Inc.* (1979) 94 CA3d 599, 156 CR 552.

The court in *City of San Leandro v Highsmith* (1981) 123 CA3d 146, 155, 176 CR 412, 417, held that, unless the parties stipulate otherwise, a recital of the demand and offer in a settlement conference statement or discussion in a deposition is not an adequate substitute for the formal demand and offer contemplated by CCP §1250.410.

Although the parties may stipulate in advance to waive the 30-day requirement, they cannot expressly or impliedly waive the need to make any offer and demand. In the latter situation, the benefits of the statute cannot subsequently be claimed. *Santa Clara Valley Water Dist. v Gross, supra.*

There is no order of filing an offer or demand required by statute. *Santa Clara Valley Water Dist. v Gross, supra.* Thus, the condemnee should not wait for the condemnor's offer. Some condemnee attorneys file early with an explanation of the basis for the offer to lay the groundwork for later demonstrating the reasonableness of the demand and unreasonableness of the responding offer.

A final demand for compensation by the condemnee may be considered reasonable, even though the question of compensation attributable to possible future damage is deferred for future resolution. In *Placer County Water Agency v Hofman* (1985) 165 CA3d 890, 211 CR 894, the condemnee conditioned its offer of settlement on the agency's representations that the project as built would safely support specified vehicle weights. The court held that the conditional offer was reasonable even though there was a substantial dispute in the evidence on the question of reasonableness and it was difficult to predict the damage that would result if there were not adequate support.

However, a final offer subject to the condemnor's reserved right to appeal the trial court's determination of the size of the taking (the state claimed ownership of a 200-foot highway easement, but the trial court ruled that the easement was 100 feet) does not constitute a reasonable offer. If the state were successful on appeal, the total valuation would be nullified. *People v Zivelonghi* (1986) 183 CA3d 187, 228 CR 72.

A condemnee's final demand made without time limitation can be accepted at any time before the commencement of trial. *San Diego Gas & Elec. Co. v Moreland Inv. Co.* (1986) 186 CA3d 1151, 231 CR 274. In this case, 18 months had passed between the making of the demand and its acceptance because of several continuances; but in the meantime, the demand was unrevised, unrevoked, and unsuperseded by any other final demand. The court determined that contract principles are not applicable to offers and demands under CCP §1250.410, and that the condemning agency had acted properly under those statutes in accepting the demand of settlement.

The court in *Coachella Valley County Water Dist. v Dreyfuss, supra,* held that once the parties begin to select jurors, the trial has begun. If defendant's demand is not accepted until after that time, defendant is entitled to litigation expenses because one purpose of CCP §1250.410 is to avoid litigation. Thus, litigation expenses may be awarded even though compensation was not determined by trial. See also *People ex rel Dep't of Transp. v Gardella Square* (1988) 200 CA3d 559, 246 CR 139, which involved settlement of a case, when the original offer and demand were made 30 days before the date first set for trial, but the original demand was not accepted until after the original trial date had been continued.

The court in *Coachella* also held that, when an award is based on acceptance of a settlement demand, defendant also may recover ordinary costs and prejudgment interest. Such recovery is not precluded by CCP §1250.410; the court held that "compensation" as used in CCP §1250.410 means compensation for the property taken, severance damage, and other consequential damage, but it does not cover ordinary costs or interest on the award for prejudgment possession.

Because CCP §998 (which has the effect of automatically terminating an unaccepted offer of compromise when the trial begins) does not apply to eminent domain proceedings, it is recommended that a time limit be set for acceptance when the offer or demand is filed. As an alternative, at the start of trial the attorneys should clarify on the record the status of their respective offer and demand. In *People ex rel Dep't of Transp. v Sunshine Canyon, Inc., supra,* the court held that it is appropriate for a defendant to set a time limit for acceptance of its demand by the condemnor.

In settlement of a direct condemnation proceeding and an inverse condemnation action being tried together, the defendant may properly set a time limit for acceptance of its demand and require payment in a lump sum. *People ex rel Dep't of Transp. v Sunshine Canyon, Inc., surpa.*

For discussion of recovery of attorneys' fees and litigation expenses when the demand is reasonable but the offer is not, see Supp §10.23A.

[§9.14B] The 30-Day Period

In *City of San Leandro v Highsmith* (1981) 123 CA3d 146, 154, 176 CR 412, 416, the court held that the 30-day deadline is mandatory, ruling that the 30 days is measured back from the date the trial was originally scheduled to start, not from the date it is actually held.

Many trial courts take literally the requirement that the offer and demand be *filed* with the court, as well as served, 30 days before trial. On a motion for costs, the statute allows the court to consider revised or superseded offers and demands made any time before and even during trial, but the 30-day period is mandatory for the initial final offer and demand. If a property owner does not file a written final demand at least 30 days before trial, the possibility of recovering litigation expenses is forfeited. *People ex rel Dep't of Transp. v Callahan Bros.* (1977) 69 CA3d 541, 138 CR 239. But see *Lake County Sanitation Dist. v Schultz* (1978) 85 CA3d 658, 149 CR 717, in which the court excused a two-day delay in filing the final demand as "substantial compliance," when the agency made no objection and was late in filing its final offer. A revised final demand served by the defendant on the plaintiff 33 days in advance of the scheduled trial date but not filed with the court until 28 days before the trial substantially complied with the 30-day filing requirement of CCP §1250.410 and was properly considered as a basis for an award of litigation expenses. *Community Redev. Agency v Krause* (1984) 162 CA3d 860, 209 CR 1. See also *People ex rel Dep't of Transp. v Societa Di Unione E Beneficenza Italiana* (1978) 87 CA3d 14, 150 CR 706, in which both parties failed to meet the 30-day deadline.

A subsequent offer by plaintiff within the 30-day period before trial does not constitute a concession that the initial pretrial offer was unreasonable, because under the statute the later offer does not affect the condemnee's right to litigation fees. *Lake County Sanitation Dist. v Schultz, supra.*

A stipulation that the final offer and demand be made at the pretrial conference did not preclude the court from considering the condemnor's revised offer made 30 days before trial to determine whether a party should recover litigation expenses. Revised or superseded offers and demands inside the 30-day period, however, may be considered only to determine the amount of litigation expenses to be awarded. *Los Angeles Unified School Dist. v C.F. Bolster Co.* (1978) 81 CA3d 906, 146 CR 789; *City of Gardena v Camp* (1977) 70 CA3d 252, 138 CR 656.

In *People ex rel Dep't of Transp. v Patton Mission Props.* (1979) 89 CA3d 204, 152 CR 485, the condemnee's final demand made 31 days before trial was held unreasonable because it gave the condemnor only one day in which to evaluate the demand, consider appraisals, and respond with a revised final offer. The condemnor had made its final offer more than six months before the trial. The condemnor's offer was made concurrent with its deposit for prejudgment order of possession. The court rejected the argument that it was common practice for the parties to wait for the 31st day before trial.

This is a harsh result in view of the clear wording of the statute, and many trial courts continue to permit condemnors to make their demands 31 days before trial. The legislature sought to clarify this matter in 1982 by adding subparagraph (c) to CCP §1250.410 to the effect that, if timely made, offers and demands made at least 30 days before the date of trial *shall* be considered by the court on the issue of determining entitlement to litigation expenses.

For discussion of recovery of attorneys' fees and litigation expenses when the demand is reasonable but the offer is not, see Supp §10.23A.

PRELIMINARY TRIAL CONSIDERATIONS

[§9.18] Introduction to Trial Tactics

For an overview of a trial from the viewpoint of the condemnee's attorney, see Fadem, *Trial Tactics To Make the Compensation Just to the Owner,* Planning, Zoning and Eminent Domain Inst 261 (1973); Bishop, *Jury Selection and Trial in Eminent Domain Cases,* Planning, Zoning and Eminent Domain Inst 365 (1974).

For a complete outline of all phases of a trial, see Los Angeles Superior Court Eminent Domain Policy Memorandum (Dec. 1988), published by the Los Angeles County Superior Court and available from The Los Angeles Daily Journal, 210 South Spring Street, Los Angeles, CA 90012, or Metropolitan News-Enterprise, P.O. Box 60859, Los Angeles, CA 90060.

[§9.19] Burden of Proof

Under the current law, the property owner must still present its evidence first, with the right to open and conclude argument. Neither party bears the burden of proof on the issue of compensation (CCP §1260.210) except that the owner must prove matters necessary to recover for loss of goodwill (CCP §1263.510; see Supp §4.61). Accordingly, in *City of Los Angeles v Decker* (1977) 18 C3d 860, 135 CR 640, the court stated that it is no longer appropriate to instruct that the defendant bears the burden of proof on the issue of compensation. Now, BAJI No. 11.98 (rev 1986) provides that, except for the issue of loss of goodwill, neither the plaintiff nor the defendant has the burden of proof. The use note to this instruction states that it may be adapted as well for explaining the burden for precondemnation damage (see Supp §4.7A) and reasonable probability of zone change (see §4.14). However, the law is not so clear. If the court determines that unreasonable delay exists in a case, the property owner should not carry a greater burden for proving the amount of damages; reasonable probability of a zone change is a part of the issue of compensation, for which CCP §1260.210 states that, unless otherwise provided by statute, neither party has the burden of proof.

Decker creates some confusion by setting forth the traditional rule that, the defendant has the burden of proof on the issue of reasonable probability of change of zoning, while at the same time advising the trial court of the neutralizing of the burden of proof by CCP §1260.210. The trial was before the operative date of CCP §1260.210 and the appeal that reversed the case was after that date. However, *Redevelopment Agency v Contra Costa Theatre, Inc.* (1982) 135 CA3d 73, 185 CR 159, a case initiated after the operative date of CCP §1260.210, does not refer to the statute and cites the traditional rule on burden of proof for the issue of reasonable probability of zoning or use changes. Under the Legislative Comment to CCP §1230.065(d), this issue of burden of proof in a retrial after the operative date would be governed by CCP §1260.210.

The 1975 Law Revision Commission Comment to CCP §1260.210 states that a burden of proof in an eminent domain proceeding is not appropriate, because the trier of fact is presented with conflicting opinions of value and supporting data and is then required to fix a value based on the weight it gives to the opinions and supporting data. See, *e.g., City of Pleasant Hill v First Baptist Church* (1969) 1 CA3d 384, 408, 82 CR 1, 16.

[§9.20] Functions of Court and Jury

In order to expedite testimony before a jury, courts routinely conduct hearings in limine to determine the admissibility of evidence. See, *e.g., People ex rel Dep't of Water Resources v Andresen* (1987) 193 CA3d 1144, 1154, 238 CR 826, 832; *Coachella Valley Water Dist. v Western Allied Props.* (1987) 190 CA3d 969, 976 n3, 235 CR 725, 729 n3; *People ex rel Dep't of Public Works v Peninsula Enters.* (1979) 91 CA3d 332, 340, 153 CR 895, 898.

In *Coachella Valley Water Dist. v Western Allied Props.* (1987) 190 CA3d 969, 235 CR 725, the court held that, as part of the determination of the before condition, the jury should determine whether the development of the property depended on the flood control project for which it was being condemned or whether there were less expensive means of providing flood control protection.

[§9.20A] Bifurcation

Because the court decides all questions in a condemnation trial except determination of compensation (see Book §9.20), the parties should consider severing nonjury questions related to compensation, such as loss of access or other severance issues.

The court has authority to sever issues under CCP §1048(b). In *City of Los Angeles v City of Huntington Park* (1939) 32 CA2d 253, 89 P2d 702, the court held that CCP §1048(b), before its 1971 amendment, was applicable to eminent domain proceedings for consolidation.

Separate trials most frequently have been employed to determine the public use issue. *County of San Mateo v Bartole* (1960) 184 CA2d 422, 7 CR 569. Now CCP §1260.110 specifically provides for a hearing on objections to the right to take before the valuation trial. See Supp §§6.27, 9.27–9.29.

The determination of whether there was unreasonable delay in beginning the condemnation action, entitling the landowner to precondemnation damages (see §4.7 and Supp §4.7A), may be properly bifurcated. *Redevelopment Agency v Contra Costa Theatre, Inc.* (1982) 135 CA3d 73, 185 CR 159; *City of Los Angeles v Lowensohn* (1976) 54 CA3d 625, 127 CR 417. See *Stone v City of Los Angeles* (1975) 51 CA3d 987, 124 CR 822 (an inverse condemnation case), which gave the question of unreasonable delay to the jury after the court found there was an issue of fact on the question.

An option holder is not entitled to a jury trial on the bifurcated legal issue of the compensability of its claimed interest in the property. *County of San Diego v Miller* (1980) 102 CA3d 424, 162 CR 480.

Evidence Code §320 gives the court the authority to control the order of proof, and CCP §§597 and 598 allow the court or any party to the litigation to move for separate trials on the issues of special defenses and liability, respectively.

Bifurcation is usually helpful to the condemnor but can add burdensome costs for the property owner. Also, in a bifurcated trial, evidence that casts the condemnor in a bad light may be heard only by the judge. In a nonbifurcated trial this evidence might result in an increased award.

[§9.21] Time for Trial

Code of Civil Procedure §1260.010 maintains the preference for hearing and trial of eminent domain actions formerly set forth in former CCP §1264.

JURY SELECTION

[§9.22] General Considerations

California Constitution art I, §14, cited in Book §9.22, has been renumbered art I, §19. See Supp §8.7.

Trial by jury may be waived by the failure to deposit, 25 days before the date set for trial, a sum equal to one day's jury fees and mileage. CCP §631. In a condemnation case, the jury fees are to be deposited in advance by the plaintiff, no matter who demands the jury. CCP §631.5. See Supp §1.8 on costs.

For a more thorough discussion of trial procedures, see 1.2 California Civil Procedure During Trial (Cal CEB 1982, 1984).

[§9.26] Voir Dire

California Rules of Court 228, which applies to civil cases, now permits the parties to examine prospective jurors outside the judge's presence if all parties so stipulate.

An approved list of questions for examination by the court of prospective jurors in eminent domain cases has been established by the California Judicial Council. California Rules of Court, Appendix—Judicial Administration, §8(d).

Book §9.26 discusses grounds on which a challenge for cause may be based. The law governing qualifications of trial jurors, exemptions from service, voir dire, challenges to jurors, and compensation of jurors was extensively revised in 1988, in the Trial Jury Selection and Management Act (CCP §§190–236).

California Trial Objections, chap 6 (Cal CEB 1967) has been replaced by California Trial Objections, chap 6 (2d ed Cal CEB 1984).

See §1.8 on costs. For a more thorough discussion of trial procedures, see 1, 2 California Civil Procedure During Trial (Cal CEB 1982, 1984).

[§§9.27–9.29] PRIMA FACIE PHASE

There no longer seems to be a need for the traditional prima facie phase to the trial mentioned in Book §§9.27–9.29. This change follows from provisions of three code sections. Objections to the right to take may be raised by answer or demurrer. CCP §1250.350. When such objections are raised, they are heard and determined before determination of the issue of value; on the motion of any party, the court may specially set such objections for trial. CCP §1260.110. Failure to object to the complaint constitutes a waiver. CCP §1250.345. See Supp §§6.25–6.28.

Thus, the prima facie phase is now either a separate trial in which objections to the right to take are asserted or is used only for introducing a resolution of necessity (see Supp §6.18) to which the defendant has already waived any objections by not pleading them.

The prima facie phase should, however, be retained for the purpose of having a condemnor present its engineering witness to describe the physical take and the project for which the property is being acquired. Defendant is cautioned to take steps (*e.g.*, a request at the pretrial conference) to assure that plaintiff presents the engineering witness at the beginning of the trial. Such testimony helps to define the scope of the project and the damage it may cause. It also explains the impact of a partial take on the remainder and is thus important in determining serious damage and special benefits.

WITNESSES

[§§9.31–9.32] Lay Witnesses

"Owner" now includes a tenant or other person entitled to possession of the property and any party to an action or proceeding to determine ownership if the court does not require that the issue of ownership be determined before the admission of the party. Evid C §813(c). In addition to the owner and the owner's spouse, an "officer, regular employee, or partner designated by a corporation, partnership, or unincorporated association that is the owner of the property or property interest being valued" may give opinion testimony on value if the designee is knowledgeable regarding the property's value. Evid C §813(a)(3).

[§9.33] Expert Witnesses

Code of Civil Procedure §1267, permitting only two valuation experts to testify, has been repealed. The court, however, retains general control over the number of expert witnesses under Evid C §723.

California Rules of Professional Conduct 5–310(B) forbids payment of fees to an expert to be contingent on the outcome of the case.

A witness qualified to testify on value is not necessarily qualified to testify on other matters that may be foundational to his opinion of value. In *Redevelopment Agency v First Christian Church* (1983) 140 CA3d 690, 189 CR 749, it was held proper to exclude testimony of an expert who was both a real estate appraiser and building contractor concerning the extent and cost of bringing a church into compliance with current earthquake standards, when the expert testified that he was unfamiliar with the actual structural changes made in the church after a previous earthquake and unaware of any actual tests that had been undertaken to measure the shear strength of the walls. He also admitted that he was not a structural engineer and that that type of person was necessary to assess the actual structural deficiencies and best use of the property.

Conclusions of an expert based on assumptions not supported by the record are not proper evidence. The trial court must review the factors considered and reasoning employed in allowing an expert's conclusion to go to the jury. *PG&E v Zuckerman* (1987) 189 CA3d 1113, 234 CR 630.

PRESENTATION OF DIRECT EXAMINATION

[§9.34] General Tactics

See Fadem, *Trial Tactics To Make the Compensation Just to the Owner,* Inst on Planning, Zoning and Eminent Domain Inst 261 (1973).

[§§9.35–9.39] Direct Examination of Appraisal Witness

See Searles, *Examination and Cross-Examination of Appraiser in Eminent Domain,* Planning, Zoning and Eminent Domain Inst 339 (1973).

Subjects of Examination

[§9.45] Reproduction/Replacement Cost Study

For discussion of the reproduction/replacement cost method as it relates to a church, see *Redevelopment Agency v First Christian Church* (1983) 140 CA3d 690, 189 CR 749. There the court determined that replacement costs, less depreciation or obsolescence, provided a more just and equitable approach than the fair market value method for certain special use properties, such as churches.

Objections

[§9.49] Matters on Which Opinion of Value Cannot Be Based

In *People ex rel Dep't of Pub. Works v Amsden Corp.* (1973) 33 CA3d 83, 109 CR 1, the owner and lessee had an agreement that, should the subject property be condemned, the owner would be entitled to the first $270,000 in compensation. In the action for condemnation, the owner and the state stipulated that the property was worth $274,350; lessee's experts testified to values of $449,000 and $490,000. The court held that the stipulation was not a compromise or settlement, because there was no bona fide dispute between the owner and the state on the value, and it was admissible in evidence.

Evidence Code §1152 provides that offers to settle a claim of damage or statements of damages made in negotiation are inadmissible to prove liability. This section was designed to undo the rule of *People ex rel Dep't of Pub. Works v Forster* (1962) 58 C2d 257, 23 CR 582, which distinguished concessions made for the purpose of an offer of compromise in an eminent domain case from statements of independent facts, holding the latter admissible against the party making them. See also *People ex rel Dep't of Pub. Works v Glen Arms Estate, Inc.* (1964) 230 CA2d 841, 41 CR 303. In *People ex rel Dep't of Pub. Works v Southern Pac. Transp. Co.* (1973) 33 CA3d 960, 109 CR 525, it was pointed out that there was an inherent conflict between Evid C §822(b) (now renumbered Evid C §822(a)(2)), which allows offers as a limited admission, and Evid C §1152. The appellate court, relying on the strong public policy of §1152 to encourage settlement of lawsuits, treated offers in condemnation cases the same as any other settlement offer that is barred from evidence.

This principle is carried even further in *Georgia-Pacific Corp. v California Coastal Comm'n* (1982) 132 CA3d 678, 693, 183 CR 395, 404, a beachfront access easement case concerning Coastal Commission permits.

The parties had tried to settle conditions of the permits during the administrative proceedings. The court held that, although literally applied, Evid C §1152 appears to refer to settlement offers in a trial setting, the public policy in favor of settlement of disputes should govern, and the evidence of settlement attempts before filing the action should be excluded.

Cross-examination of condemnor's expert on an offer made for comparable property is prohibited by Evid C §822. *People ex rel Dep't of Pub. Works v Amsden Corp., supra,* disapproving *People ex rel Dep't of Pub. Works v Union Mach. Co.* (1955) 133 CA2d 167, 284 P2d 72. Evidence Code §822 does not preclude cross-examination on inadmissible matters for the limited purpose of determining whether a witness based his opinion in whole or in part on a matter that is a proper basis for opinion. It also does not preclude the use of an unrelated appraisal report to impeach the credibility of the expert witness. *City of Los Angeles v Waller* (1979) 90 CA3d 766, 776, 154 CR 12, 17.

Effective in 1988, Evid C §822(a)(1) created an exception to the prohibition against using sales to condemning agencies as comparable sales. In the case of a public agency acquiring land already devoted to a public use, the sale of that property to the public agency for the same purpose for which the property could have been taken by condemnation may be admissible. The reason for this exception is the difficulty of finding market transactions when, *e.g.,* a municipality acquires the facilities of a water company. Thus, the exception is most applicable to the condemnation of utility properties or special districts. See CEB Real Prop L Rep 29 (Jan. 1988) for additional discussion.

The sale of all or part of property condemned after a lis pendens has been filed may not be taken into account in the evaluation of the property. Evid C §815. This provision applies, however, when only the property or property interest being taken, or a part of it, is the subject of the sale or the contract to sell. In a case involving a bankruptcy sale of a fee interest in a 4000-acre ranch after the lis pendens, when the condemnation action sought only to acquire a nonexclusive easement across that ranch, Evid C §815 did not prohibit consideration of the sale. *San Diego Gas & Elec. Co. v 3250 Corp.* (1988) 205 CA3d 1075, 1084, 25CR 853, 858. This case also addressed the proper exclusion of a sale of adjoining land from the state to the condemnee because the sale was part of a larger transaction involving an exchange for property that the state could have taken by eminent domain for a new prison site. The court ruled that Evid C §822 prohibited admissibility of the exchange as an integrated transaction involving property that could have been taken by eminent domain. See generally *People ex rel Dep't of Pub. Works v Reardon* (1971) 4 C3d 507, 515, 93 CR 852, 857, allowing evidence of an exchange of properties in which the parties to the transaction had fixed a monetary value as a proper sale under Evid C §816.

An opinion on value may not be based on the amount of property taxes due on the property or on its assessed valuation. Evid C §822(a)(3) (replacing former Rev & T C §4986(2)(b)). The final clause of Evid C §822(a)(2) contains this limitation: "Nothing in this subdivision permits an admission to be used as direct evidence upon any matter that may be shown only by opinion evidence under Section 813."

By implication, Evid C §801(b) prohibits experts from forming opinions based on speculative matters. This section was cited in *City of Los Angeles v Tilem* (1983) 142 CA3d 694, 191 CR 229, to exclude testimony regarding tax benefits flowing to the property owner from a sale in determining the value of a lease option. The evaluation of property must focus on the marketplace and not the personal worth of the seller or buyer or the personal benefits that might result from a particular transaction.

Code of Civil Procedure §1255.060(a) (similar to former CCP §1243.5(e)) provides that the amount deposited or withdrawn cannot be used in evidence in the compensation phase of the trial. Furthermore, a witness cannot be impeached by any written summary made in connection with the deposit or withdrawal; nor can the opposing party call the person who made the written summary as a witness over objection of the other party. CCP §1255.060(b)–(c). This section specifically overrules *People v Cowan,* cited in Book §9.49. Revenue and Taxation Code §4986(b) has been amended to delete the provision that mention of the current taxes due on the property during the course of a jury trial is grounds for a mistrial.

Evidence Code §822(a)(4), which provides that an opinion of value for the property condemned may not be based on an opinion of value of other property, does not preclude use of the cost-of-reproduction approach (see §4.38). Evidence "relative to estimated cost of acquiring comparable property (cost of reproduction) based on the average cost of other property in the area was properly admissible." *People ex rel Dep't of Transp. v Southern Pac. Transp. Co.* (1978) 84 CA3d 315, 327, 148 CR 535, 542.

Nor does Evid C §822(a)(5) preclude evidence on the rental value; and Evid C §822(a)(6) does not preclude evidence of the capitalized rental value of the condemnee's own property. *People ex rel Dep't of Water Resources v Andresen* (1987) 193 CA3d 1144, 238 CR 826.

For special purpose properties, there may be no true comparables and greater latitude regarding admissibility may be warranted. But property cannot be considered comparable when it was sold with fixtures, rights, improvements, and personal property that are not included in the condemned property. *PG&E v Zuckerman* (1987) 189 CA3d 1113, 234 CR 630.

[§9.51] "Backdooring" Sales

The testimony of the federal government's expert on the sales range of other properties was ruled admissible to determine the fair market value of the right to mine and remove clay from certain property, despite the absence of a showing that those other properties were similar to condemnee's interest in the subject property. Counsel for the claimants had in their possession the list of comparable sales and leases considered by the government's experts and had full opportunity to show lack of comparability or similarity on cross-examination, which they did not do. *U.S. v 45,131.44 Acres of Land* (10th Cir 1973) 483 F2d 569.

The trial court properly exercised its discretion in admitting price increases of land that was nearby but not directly comparable to the condemned parcel when the testimony did not include the actual prices and was for the limited purpose of showing the basis of the expert's opinion concerning price trends. *City of Los Angeles v Retlaw Enters.* (1976) 16 C3d 473, 128 CR 436. The court distinguished *City of Rosemead v Anderson,* cited in Book §9.51, because there was no use of average sales prices of noncomparable properties, only percentage increase in sales of other properties.

An appraisal witness may examine ground leases in the general area of the subject property for the sole purpose of determining the prevailing percentage-rate relationship between the value of the underlying vacant land and the rent it will bring from a tenant developing the property. That evidence may be used to show what property owners in the general area expect as a return on their investment, but not to establish absolute rental values for noncomparable properties. *People ex rel Dep't of Pub. Works v Peninsula Enters.* (1979) 91 CA3d 332, 350, 153 CR 895, 904.

See generally Stubbs, *How to Admit Into Evidence Sales That Are Noncomparable—Use of Subdivision and Small Sales Use of Noncomparable Sales to Indicate Trends,* Planning, Zoning and Eminent Domain Inst 259 (1980).

CROSS-EXAMINATION

[§9.53] General Points of Exploration

See Searles, *Examination and Cross-Examination of Appraiser in Eminent Domain,* Planning, Zoning and Eminent Domain Inst 339 (1973).

Cross-Examination on Value

[§9.54] Market Data/Comparable Sales Approach

It was not proper to cross-examine the condemnor's expert appraiser on a sale that was not used by either side as a "comparable," to show it was similar to a comparable sale. *Richmond Redev. Agency v Western Title Guar. Co.* (1975) 48 CA3d 343, 122 CR 434.

Cross-examination of the condemnor's expert on an offer made for comparable property is prohibited by Evid C §822. *People ex rel Dep't of Pub. Works v Amsden Corp.* (1973) 33 CA3d 83, 109 CR 1. However, it is proper to cross-examine a witness on an unrelated appraisal to impeach the credibility of the expert. *City of Los Angeles v Waller* (1979) 90 CA3d 766, 154 CR 12. See Supp §§9.49, 9.51.

The tax benefits flowing to the condemnee are properly excluded in appraising the value of an option. *City of Los Angeles v Tilem* (1983) 142 CA3d 694, 191 CR 229. Compare *Tilem* with *Regents of Univ. of Cal. v Morris,* cited in Book §9.54.

[§9.62] DEMONSTRATIVE EVIDENCE

Photographs of the condemned property and comparable properties used by the condemnor's expert witness were admissible as summaries of the expert witness's testimony, but not as substantive evidence. Notations made on the margins of the photographs of purchase dates, and prices of comparable sales that were accurate but did not reflect the dissimilarities shown by the landowners on cross-examination, did not preclude admission of the photographs. *U.S. v 633.07 Acres of Land* (MD Pa 1973) 362 F Supp 451.

Video recording has become more popular as an evidentiary tool and is admissible in the same manner as photographs of the condemned property and its surrounding area. Photographs, films, and videotapes are "writings" as defined in Evid C §250 and, thus, subject to requirements of proper foundation, relevancy, and hearsay rules. They are, however, admissible. See *People v Moran* (1974) 39 CA3d 398, 407, 114 CR 413, 418. A party may videotape a deposition if the notice of the deposition advises of the videotaping. CCP §§2020(c), 2025(d)(5).

On use of videotapes of depositions, see German, Merin & Rolfe, *Videotape Evidence at Trial,* 6 Am J Tr Adv 209 (Fall 1982); Murray, Jr., *Videotaped Depositions: Putting Absent Witnesses in Court,* 68 ABA J 1402 (1982); Kornblum, *Videotape in Civil Cases,* 24 Hastings LJ 9 (1972); Miller, *Videotaping the Oral Deposition,* 18 Prac Law 45 (Feb. 1972); and Salomon, *The Use of Video Tape Depositions in Complex Litigation,* 51 Cal SBJ 20 (1976).

[§9.63] VIEW OF PREMISES

In 1975 the legislature replaced CCP §610 with CCP §651. That section provides that the court may order a view of the property subject to litigation on its own motion or the motion of any party. If a view is ordered, the judge, all court personnel, and the jury, if any, view the property;

the court is in session throughout the view and may permit testimony
by witnesses on site.

[§9.64] FINAL ARGUMENT

Although the defendant no longer bears the burden of proof (neither
party does), he has the burden of going forward. Thus, he is entitled
to open and close the argument. CCP §1260.210.

The supreme court granted a new trial in a condemnation action on
the ground that a city attorney committed misconduct in his argument
to the jury by denying a need for airport parking when he knew of an
environmental impact report indicating the contrary. See *City of Los Angeles v Decker* (1977) 18 C3d 860, 135 CR 647.

See Bishop, *Jury Selection and Trial in Eminent Domain Cases*, Planning, Zoning and Eminent Domain Inst 365, 391 (1974).

VERDICT

[§9.66] Statutory Requirements

The requirement of separate assessment of value, severance damages,
and any special benefits, formerly set out in CCP §1248, is now found
in CCP §1260.230. The list now includes compensation for loss of goodwill (see Supp §4.61).

[§9.67] Form: Verdict

Comment: Add to the form of verdict:

4. The loss of goodwill is $_ _ _ _ _ _.

[§9.67A] Special Verdict To Ascertain Specific Amounts on Claims of Severance Damage

It is the responsibility of the party who seeks appellate review challenging the admissibility of some element of severance damage to submit
special verdict forms to the trial court, in order to establish the extent
to which the jury relied on the alleged erroneously admitted evidence.
San Diego Gas & Elec. Co. v Daley (1988) 205 CA3d 1334, 1343, 253
CR 144, 154.

[§9.68] Basis of Award

In *Aetna Life & Cas. Co. v City of Los Angeles* (1985) 170 CA3d
865, 216 CR 831, the court approved application of BAJI No. 11.80
and the holdings in *Redevelopment Agency v Modell* (1960) 177 CA2d
321, 2 CR 245, and *People v McCullough* (1950) 100 CA2d 101, 223

P2d 37, to an inverse condemnation case. The court thus held that the jury hearing an inverse condemnation action must determine the fair market value of the subject property only from the opinions of qualified witnesses and the property owners. Furthermore, the court held that the jury "may not disregard the evidence as to value and render a verdict that either exceeds or falls below the limits established by the testimony of the witnesses." 170 CA3d at 877, 216 CR at 838.

LOS ANGELES COUNTY SHORT CAUSE

[§9.70] Official Form: Stipulation and Order

Former CCP §1272.02, referred to in the form in Book §9.70, was repealed. Its subject matter now is found at CCP §§1258.240–1258.250.

10

Apportionment, Judgment, and Posttrial

PART ONE: APPORTIONMENT OF THE AWARD

[§10.1] INTRODUCTION

The rule of *City of Pasadena v Porter,* cited in Book §10.1, requiring continuation of the lessee's full rental obligation for the duration of the lease in cases of a partial taking, was abolished by CCP §1265.120. That section requires a prorata abatement of the rental obligation. See Supp §4.59.

[§10.2] APPORTIONMENT PROCEDURE

Code of Civil Procedure §1260.220 has replaced former CCP §§1246.1 and 1248 dealing with apportionment. The statutory scheme is unchanged.

The right to a jury trial in condemnation activities goes only to the compensation issue (see Book §9.20), but this includes the apportionment phase of a bifurcated trial. *People ex rel Dep't of Water Resources v Gianni* (1972) 29 CA3d 151, 105 CR 248. However, the reasonableness of a condemnor's conduct in delaying condemnation in a *Klopping*-type situation (see Supp §§4.7–4.7A) is a jury question. *Stone v City of Los Angeles* (1975) 51 CA3d 987, 997, 124 CR 822, 828.

LEASEHOLDS

[§10.3] Value of Lessee's Right to Possession and Use

When the entire property is taken, leases on the property terminate. CCP §1265.110. In a partial taking, the lease terminates on the part taken and rent allocated to the part taken is extinguished. CCP §1265.120. In either case, the lessee may also seek compensation for the taking of its leasehold interest. CCP §1265.150. A valid lease provision will supersede these statutory rules. CCP §1265.160. See Supp §§4.58–4.59. American

Institute of Real Estate Appraisers, The Appraisal of Real Estate (5th ed 1967) is updated periodically.

[§10.5] Machinery and Equipment Used in Place

The lessee in a month-to-month tenancy may recover the value of its fixtures as part of the realty, rather than only its removal value. *Concrete Serv. Co. v State ex rel Dep't of Pub. Works* (1972) 29 CA3d 664, 105 CR 721. Under CCP §1263.205, the phrase "improvements pertaining to realty" includes "any machinery or equipment" installed on the property taken or the remainder if the improvements cannot be removed without substantial loss in value, or substantial damage to the property itself, regardless of the method of installation. Thus, the condemnor acquires title to the improvements. Former CCP §1248b had specified that only equipment designed for manufacturing or industrial purposes would be considered fixtures.

However, if the owner of the improvements elects to remove any or all of the improvements and the condemnor does not object, the owner would receive compensation for their reasonable removal and relocation cost, if cost does not exceed the value of the improvements. CCP §1263.260. See Supp §4.52.

[§10.7] Use of Condemnation Provisions in Leases

For an example of a condemnation clause in a lease agreement, see *People ex rel Dep't of Pub. Works v Amsden Corp.* (1973) 33 CA3d 83, 109 CR 1. The lease provided for a "true value" of the property and that the lessee would receive any amount in excess of that value. See Supp §4.56 for further discussion of *Amsden*.

[§10.10] CONTRACTORS, MANAGERS, AND SUPPLIERS

California Constitution art I, §14, cited in Book §10.10, has been renumbered art I, §19. See Supp §8.7.

GRANTOR-GRANTEE

[§10.11] Title Transfer During Pendency of Condemnation

The right to take possession under an order of immediate possession before judgment is now stated in CCP §1255.410 (former CCP §1243.5). Possession after judgment is governed by CCP §§1268.210–1268.230. See former CCP §§1253–1254 and CCP §1268.240 permitting a public entity to exercise its police powers in an emergency.

[§10.12] Option To Purchase

The supreme court disapproved *People v Ocean Shore R.R.* and

East Bay Mun. Util. Dist. v Kieffer, cited in Book §10.12, and held that the owner of an unexercised option to purchase property holds a compensable property right. The measure of damage to the option holder is the excess of the total award over the optioned purchase price. *County of San Diego v Miller* (1975) 13 C3d 684, 693, 119 CR 491, 496. This decision was interpreted in a later appeal of the same case after retrial in *County of San Diego v Miller* (1980) 102 CA3d 424, 162 CR 480. The court held that the supreme court had not decided the factual issue of whether the optionee had a valid compensable interest. The court held further that the optionee was not entitled to a jury trial on the bifurcated issue of its claimed interest in the property.

Although *Miller* allows the option price to be received to show the value of the option, Evid C §822(a)(2) states that the option price is not admissible, except as an admission against interest, to show the value of the property itself. In addition, *People ex rel Dep't of Water Resources v Gianni* (1972) 29 CA3d 151, 105 CR 248, held that an unexercised option of a lessee may be considered in determining the value of a lease. See also Book §4.56.

In general, if the option expires before the condemnation action is filed, the option holder is not entitled to share in the condemnation award even when the option had been held throughout a major portion of the precondemnation planning activities. *City of Walnut Creek v Leadership Hous. Sys.* (1977) 73 CA3d 611, 140 CR 690. However, if unreasonable precondemnation activities occurred during the option period, the option holder may recover if he can show that the option was lost by reason of the improper conduct. *Toso v City of Santa Barbara* (1980) 101 CA3d, 934, 949, 162 CR 210, 218.

Note that, when property that is the subject of a real estate sale agreement providing for a broker's commission is taken by eminent domain before close of escrow, the broker is not entitled to a commission. The broker's right to compensation depends on performance of the sales contract. *City of Turlock v Zagaris* (1989) 209 CA3d 189, 256 CR 902.

[§10.13] Reversionary Interests

Code of Civil Procedure §1265.410 nullifies the rule of *Romero v Department of Pub. Works* (1941) 17 C2d 189, 109 P2d 662, by allowing compensation for contingent future interests, such as rights of reentry and possibilities of reverter.

If the property is subject to a life tenancy, the court is given broad authority to make an equitable solution. Code of Civil Procedure §1265.420 allows the court to order any of the following:

(a) Apportionment based on the value of the life estate and the remainder;

(b) Compensation to be used to purchase comparable property to be held subject to the life estate;

(c) Compensation to be held in trust and invested to provide income to the life tenant for the remainder of the tenancy; and

(d) Any other equitable arrangement.

See *Estate of Giacomelos* (1961) 192 CA2d 244, 13 CR 245, in which a trust was imposed on the proceeds.

[§10.14] ENCUMBRANCES; LIENS

A lien is defined as a "mortgage, deed of trust, or other security interest in property whether arising from contract, statute, common law, or equity." CCP §1265.210. When property is encumbered by a lien and the indebtedness is not due at the time of entry of judgment, plaintiff may deduct the amount of this indebtedness from the judgment and allow the lien to continue until the indebtedness is paid, or pay the full amount. CCP §1265.220 (former CCP §1248(8)).

In a partial taking, the lienholder can share in the award only to the extent of the impairment of the security; the lien continues on the part not taken. CCP §1265.225. This codifies the holding of *Milstein v Security Pac. Nat'l Bank,* cited in Book §10.14. If there are senior and junior lienholders and the compensation in a partial taking is not sufficient to satisfy both liens, the court may adjust the portion of the award available to the lienholders so that each will retain security interests proportionate to those existing before the condemnation. CCP §1265.230 (former CCP §1248(9)).

For discussion of impaired security and apportionment among lienholders, see *People ex rel Dep't of Transp. v Redwood Baseline, Ltd.* (1978) 84 CA3d 662, 149 CR 11, which arose before the 1975 revision to the Eminent Domain Law (CCP §§1230.010–1273.050).

The lienholder is not entitled to any prepayment penalty in a condemnation action. CCP §1265.240 (former CCP §1246.2).

A building restriction constitutes "property" within the meaning of Cal Const art I, §14 (now art I, §19). Consequently, whenever damage results to the landowner from violation of the restriction, compensation must be paid. *Southern Cal. Edison Co. v Bourgerie* (1973) 9 C3d 169, 107 CR 76. The court stated that its ruling applies whether the condemnor is a private or a public entity.

There is dictum in *Mosesian v County of Fresno* (1972) 28 CA3d 493, 500, 104 CR 655, 660, suggesting that a trust deed beneficiary alone might not be able to maintain an inverse condemnation action; he must be joined by the owner of the land. It would seem, however, that if security is impaired (*i.e.,* the property's value is inadequate to satisfy the lien) and the owner is unable or unwilling to sue, the owner of a security interest can sue because his property has been taken or damaged.

The beneficiary under a deed of trust has a compensable interest in property under condemnation even in cases in which the underlying obligation has become barred by the statute of limitations. *Carson Redev. Agency v Adam* (1982) 136 CA3d 608, 186 CR 615. The statute of limitations bars an action to enforce the note and an action for judicial foreclosure, but the power of sale under a deed of trust is not barred.

The seller under a land sales contract retains legal title to the property until the buyer completes the purchase and therefore may execute a deed of trust secured by the seller's interest in the property. In distributing condemnation proceeds, if the beneficiary of a trust deed executed by the seller following a land sales contract has notice of the land sale contract, the beneficiary is entitled to only an amount representing the seller's interest in the contract, rather than to the beneficiary's entire lien. *Alhambra Redev. Agency v Transamerica Fin. Serv.* (1989) 212 CA3d 1370, 261 CR 248.

See generally California Mortgage and Deed of Trust Practice (2d ed Cal CEB 1990), which has replaced California Real Estate Secured Transactions (Cal CEB 1970); Miller, *Valuation of the Mortgagee's Interest Upon Partial Condemnation*, 15 Loy LA L Rev 227 (1982).

[§10.15] PROPERTY TAXES

The provisions governing the apportionment, payment, and cancellation of ad valorem property taxes on property subject to eminent domain proceedings are found in the Code of Civil Procedure and the Revenue and Taxation Code. In an attempt to make these provisions more understandable and well organized, the legislature, following the California Law Revision Commission's recommendations, revised and relocated various provisions of the law, effective January 1, 1980.

Proration of property taxes is governed by CCP §1268.410 and Rev & T C §5082 (former Rev & T C §4986(b)). A property owner remains liable for ad valorem taxes, penalties, and costs prorated to the date of apportionment on property in a condemnation proceeding. CCP §1268.410. Revenue and Taxation Code §5082 defines the date of apportionment as the earlier of:

(1) The date conveyance or the final order of condemnation is recorded;

(2) The date of actual possession by condemnor; or

(3) The date condemnor may, as authorized by the order, take possession.

Revenue and Taxation Code §5082.1 requires that a public agency that acquires property do the following:

(1) Provide the local assessor and auditor a copy of the instrument by which the property was acquired;

(2) State the date of apportionment on that instrument;

(3) Request the auditor to cancel taxes as of the date of apportionment; and

(4) Provide a map of the acquired property.

Revenue and Taxation Code §5086 requires the auditor, if the amount of taxes or special assessment liens is unknown, to compute the portion of current taxes attributable to a fiscal year that ends on the day before the date of apportionment on a prorata basis of the previous year's taxes, and that amount shall be paid to the tax collector.

Revenue and Taxation Code §5086.1 requires the auditor to cancel taxes on the date of apportionment as stated in the notice required by Rev & T C §5082.1.

A property owner remains liable for ad valorem taxes assessed against the property pending an unsuccessful appeal by the condemnor from a judgment entered on the jury's award. When there is no order of immediate possession, taxes continue to be the owner's responsibility until the time title is transferred, *i.e.*, recordation of the final order of condemnation. *City of Ontario v Kelber* (1973) 35 CA3d 751, 111 CR 222.

Any party to a condemnation action may apply for a separate valuation on the assessment roll if the property being acquired is not separately valued. CCP §1268.450 (former CCP §1252.2). That section has been interpreted to require the condemnor to reimburse a property owner for the taxes he paid that were subject to cancellation under Rev & T C §4986(a)(6) (taxes are cancelled on property acquired by government entity) and puts the burden on the condemnor to obtain that cancellation and the reimbursement of taxes from the taxing authority. *City of Los Angeles v Southern Pac. Transp. Co.* (1979) 90 CA3d 379, 153 CR 379. See Supp §10.15A for a CalTrans form for a property owner to apply for a refund of property tax.

Attorneys should be aware that this area is replete with organizational revisions in the name of clarity. To avoid confusion, one should heed the pertinent code section legislative histories to determine the exact changes that have occurred. See *Recommendation Relating to Ad Valorem Property Taxes in Eminent Domain Proceedings,* 14 Cal L Rev'n Comm'n Reports 291 (1978).

In June, 1982, California voters adopted a proposition effective January 1, 1983, which provides that the purchase of a "comparable property" as a replacement for property acquired by eminent domain proceedings or acquisition by a public entity, or by governmental action resulting in an inverse condemnation action, does not qualify as a "change in ownership" under Cal Const art XIIIA, §2(a) to establish a new base for the assessed valuation of the replacement property. "Comparable property" must be similar in size, utility, and function to the property replaced, or it must conform to regulations governing the relocation of persons displaced by governmental actions. Implementing Cal Const art XIIIA, §2(a), Rev & T C §68 provides that the adjusted base-year value is the lower of the replacement property's fair market value or the sum of (1) the adjusted base year value of the property from which the person was displaced and (2) the amount, if any, by which the full cash value of the property acquired exceeds 120 percent of the amount received by the person for the property from which the person was displaced.

The following form is used by Santa Clara County to determine the appropriate value on real property that replaces property taken by the condemning agency.

Office of the County Assessor
Assessment Standards Division
County Government Center, East Wing
70 West Hedding Street
San Jose, California 95110
299-3941   Area Code 408

County of Santa Clara

California

APPLICATION FOR VALUATION RELIEF
Real Property Replacing that taken by Government Agency

I.   GENERAL INFORMATION

A.   Among the provisions of Article XIIIA which was added to the California Constitution by Proposition 13 in June 1978 is the reappraisal of real property
when it changes owership. The passage of Proposition 3 in June 1982 added
Section 2(d) to Article XIIIA. This section provides that the term "change
in ownership" shall not include the acquisition of real property which replaces comparable property from which the owner was displaced by eminent domain proceedings, acquisition by a public entity, or by governmental action
which has resulted in a judgment of inverse condemnation.

B.   The adjusted base year value of the replacement property shall be the lesser
or (1) the fair market value of the comparable replacement property or (2)
the sum of the adjusted base year value of the property from which the person
was displaced plus the amount, if any, by which the full cash value of the
comparable replacement property exceeds 120 percent of the amount received
for the property taken or acquired by the acquiring entity. This amount received from the acquiring entity shall not include amounts paid for relocation assistance and other non-real estate items.

C.   Factors to be considered for comparability would be size, utility and function. If the two properties are not totally comparable, adjustments will be
made in the valuation process to account for characteristics in the replacement property which are not comparable to those of the property from which
the person was displaced.

D.   Valuation relief for the replacement property shall affect the 1983-84 tax
bill and thereafter. There shall be no reassessments or refunds for years
prior to 1983-84. Once valuation relief for a particular replacement property has been requested by the applicant and approved by the Assessor, that
relief cannot be transferred to another property, nor to another person.

II. REQUIREMENTS

A.   Displacement must have occurred on or after March 1, 1975.

B.   When to apply with the Assessor.
     1.   For replacement property acquired after March 1, 1975 and before
          January 1, 1983, application must be made by January 1, 1987.
     2.   For replacement property acquired on or after January 1, 1983,
          application must be made within four years of displacement from
          the formerly owned property.

C.   The applicant must provide documented evidence of displacement. Such
     documentation may include one of the following:
     1.   A certified recorded copy of the final order of condemnation.
     2.   A certified copy of a final judgment of inverse condemnation.
     3.   A copy of a recorded deed showing acquisition by a public entity.

D.   The applicant must complete the questionnaire on the back of this letter, sign
     the request to apply their Proposition 3 benefits to the new property, and
     return this form to the address shown above within the time limit.

Form 5268 Front (9-83)

A. PROPERTY FROM WHICH APPLICANT WAS DISPLACED

   1. Assessor's Parcel Number _____, County of _____

   2. Property Address _____

   3. Property Type (Single family, apartment, commercial, agriculture, etc., or combination of uses). _____

   4. Date property was acquired by government entity _____

   5. Entity acquiring property _____

   6. Purchase price or award paid by acquiring entity (Excluding amounts paid for relocation assistance and other non-real estate items). $_____

   7. Taxable value as of the fiscal year property taken. If available, please attach a copy of the tax bill for that year. $_____

B. REPLACEMENT PROPERTY

   1. Assessor's Parcel Number _____

   2. Property Address _____

   3. Property Type _____

   4. Date Acquired _____

   5. Recorder's Deed Number _____

   6. Full Purchase Price $_____. Amount of Cash Down $_____

   7. Details concerning loans

	Amount	Rate	Term	New Loan	Assumed	Type of Loan (FHA, VA, Seller, S&L, etc.)
1st	$_____	___%	___yrs	__	__	_____
2nd	$_____	___%	___yrs	__	__	_____

   8. If trade was involved, what was the value of the equity traded? $_____

   9. Amount of outstanding improvement bonds assumed, if any $_____

   10. If price included personal property, please estimate value $_____

I have read the general information and requirements on the front side of this application. I declare under penalty of perjury that, to the best of my knowledge and belief, the information provided above is true and correct. I request that the property identified in item B(1) be valued in accordance with Section 2(d) of Article XIII A of California Constitution.

_____ Telephone_____ Date_____
Signature of owner or authorized agent
(Agent's authorization must be attached)

REMINDER - PLEASE ATTACH DOCUMENTED EVIDENCE OF DISPLACEMENT
(Certified recorded copy of the final order of condemnation, certified copy of a final judgment of inverse condemnation or a copy of a recorded deed showing acquisition by a public entity, whichever is applicable.)

ASSESSOR'S USE ONLY

A. Full Cash Value of the Replacment Property $_____
B. Net Purchase Price of Property Taken $_____ x 1.20 $_____
C. Subtract B from A (if B is more than A, enter zero) $_____
D. Base Value of Property Taken, factored to FY:____ $_____
E. Adjusted Base Year Value of Replacement Property (C plus D) $_____
F. Full Cash Value of Non-comparable Portion, if any $_____
G. Total Value for Enrollment (E plus F) $_____

Appraiser_____ Date_____ Approved_____ Disapproved_____

Form 5268 Back (9-83)

[§10.15A] Form: Application for Refund of Tax

Comment: CalTrans' procedure in acquiring property by agreement allows the property owner to apply for a tax refund. After close of escrow, CalTrans instructs the property owner to complete the following form and send it to the appropriate tax office, the address of which will be supplied by a representative of the state:

APPLICATION FOR TAX REFUND BY PROPERTY OWNER

State Reference:
APN No. _ _ _ _

I. Enclosed is receipted bill showing taxes paid on property described therein. Part of said taxes covers a period during which the State of California was the owner of (a portion) (all) of said property, (including the improvements thereon).

II. Under the provisions of Section 5096.7 of the Revenue and Taxation Code, I/we are entitled to a refund of those prepaid taxes which apply to: 1. The portion acquired by the State, and 2. The period following the State's purchase.

III. ( ) Please send the refund to the undersigned at the address indicated, or
( ) Please send the refund to:

Name:

_____

Address:

_____

Who actually paid the taxes.
I hereby declare under penalty of perjury that the foregoing is true and correct.
Dated this _ _ day of _ _ _ _, 19 _ _.

_____
Name

_____
Name

_____
Address

The attorney representing the property owner should contact the local county tax collector or recorder to see if there is a specific form applicable to that county.

Revenue and Taxation Code §4986(2)(b) has been repealed. Now see Rev & T C §5084. See generally Rev & T C §§5081–5091.

PART TWO: JUDGMENT AND POSTTRIAL

[§10.16] FINDINGS AND CONCLUSIONS

Waiver of findings of fact and conclusions of law submitted on stipulation by all parties in the first phase of a trial, bifurcated under former CCP §1246.1 (now CCP §1260.220; see §10.2), does not constitute an intentional or voluntary waiver in the second phase. *People ex rel Dep't of Water Resources v Gianni* (1972) 29 CA3d 151, 105 CR 248.

Code of Civil Procedure §632 no longer requires findings of fact and conclusions of law when the court is the trier of fact. The parties may request the court for a statement of decision as defined in CCP §632.

[§10.17] JUDGMENT

Judgment is defined in CCP §1235.130 (former CCP §1264.7) as the judgment determining the right to condemn the property and fixing the amount of compensation. It is final when "all possibility of direct attack by way of appeal, motion for a new trial, or motion under section 663 to vacate the judgment has been exhausted." CCP §1235.120.

The judgment must conform to the extent of the taking described in the resolution of necessity. *County of San Diego v Bressi* (1986) 184 CA3d 112, 229 CR 44. See Supp §6.18.

[§10.18] Form: Judgment

The citation in the caption of the form should be changed from CCP §1264.7 to CCP §1235.130. The citation in the form in Book §10.18 to Rev & T C §4986(2)(b) should be changed to Rev & T C §5082.

IT IS FURTHER ORDERED AND ADJUDGED that $_ _ _ _ be paid to the Tax Collector of the County of _ _ _ _ _ _ for unpaid taxes (and penalties) due as of_ _[*insert earlier of date of actual possession or order of immediate possession under Rev & T C §5082*]**_ _.**

Comment: The above paragraph should be used in place of the paragraph just before the Comment in Book §10.18 at page 272 when there has been actual possession or an order for immediate possession before the date of the final order of condemnation. See Rev & T C §5082.

[§10.19] Possession After Judgment

After entry of judgment, the condemnor is entitled to an order for possession of the property, pending conclusion of the litigation if (1) the judgment finds that plaintiff is entitled to take and (2) the plaintiff paid to or deposited for defendants an amount equal to the award, together with any interest due. CCP §1268.210 (former CCP §1254). A writ of mandate properly lies against a superior court that denies a condemnor such an order. *PG&E v Superior Court* (1973) 33 CA3d 321, 109 CR 10. The condemnor is also entitled to possession after judgment notwithstanding its failure to comply with relocation acts requirements. *City of Los Angeles v Decker* (1976) 61 CA3d 444, 132 CR 188.

Thirty days' notice of an order of possession is required when the property is occupied by a person dwelling on it or by a farm or business; ten days' notice is required in all other cases. CCP §1268.220. Taking of possession does not waive plaintiff's rights to appeal, move for a new trial, or abandon. CCP §1268.230.

[§10.19A] Postjudgment Procedure for Increase of Deposit for Ongoing Prejudgment Possession

Code of Civil Procedure §1268.110(a) allows the condemnor at any time after entry of judgment to deposit with the court the full amount of the judgment, together with interest due, less any amounts already paid or deposited. This is a permissive statute, and CCP §1268.130 provides that, at any time after the plaintiff has made the deposit, the court may require an increase in the deposit to secure the payment of any further compensation, costs, or interest that may be recovered. Code of Civil Procedure §1255.030 sets forth the procedure for a redetermination of probable compensation for a prejudgment order of possession. See Supp §8.8. The latter procedure does not apply to cases involving a prejudgment possession that continues past judgment when the condemnor has not paid the judgment while pursuing an appeal. See *People ex rel Dep't of Transp. v Zivelonghi* (1986) 181 CA3d 1035, 226 CR 748. However, the court concluded in *Zivelonghi* that the trial court has inherent power, as well as authority under CCP §187 (providing the court the means necessary to carry into effect the exercise of its jurisdiction), to adopt a suitable procedure in the face of a legislative gap. It was thus proper to require the plaintiff to deposit as probable compensation the amount of the judgment for the land and improvements, plus interest. The court could not require payment of litigation expenses in the order, because there is no constitutional requirement to pay such costs. Finally, the appellate court advised that the trial court could also devise a procedure, including a judgment of dismissal and abandonment, under CCP §187 to enforce its order requiring deposit after redetermination if the plaintiff refused to increase the deposit after the redetermination.

[§10.20] Finality of Judgment

A judgment becomes final when "all possibility of direct attack by way of appeal, motion for a new trial, or motion under [CCP §] 663 to vacate the judgment has been exhausted." CCP §1235.120 (former CCP §1264.7).

[§10.21] Time of Payment

The Eminent Domain Law (CCP §§1230.010–1273.050) eliminates the one-year delay for payment of a judgment, permitting the state and public corporations to market bonds to pay the judgment under former CCP §1251, and establishes a uniform 30-day period for payment. CCP §1268.010. That period begins 30 days after final judgment or 30 days after the conclusion of any federal or state court proceeding challenging the judgment or condemnation proceedings, whichever is later.

If the judgment is not paid within the period prescribed by CCP §1268.010 by a plaintiff that is a public entity, defendant may enforce the judgment as provided in CCP §1268.020(a)(1). Govt C §§810–996.6. The Regents of the University of California do not constitute a public entity under CCP §1268.020. CCP §1268.020(d). If a plaintiff is not a public entity, the judgment is enforced by defendant as in normal civil cases. CCP §1268.020(a)(2).

If plaintiff's action is dismissed, or if the judgment denies plaintiff the right to acquire the subject property, defendant is entitled to litigation expenses. CCP §1268.610. To obtain a dismissal, defendant must show by noticed motion that the judgment has not been paid within the 30 days specified in CCP §1268.010 and that, within 20 days after service of written notice by registered or certified mail, plaintiff continued to fail to pay. CCP §1268.020(b).

When plaintiff deposits the full amount of the award, it must serve notice of the date and amount of the deposit on the other parties. CCP §1268.120.

Payment of the award terminates the accrual of interest (CCP §1268.320(b)) and allows the court to issue a final order of condemnation (CCP §1268.030(a)).

Code of Civil Procedure §690.8, exempting the condemnee's award from attachment and execution by creditors, has been repealed. Now only relocation benefits for displacement from a dwelling paid as "relocation assistance" are exempt. CCP §704.180.

[§10.21A] Installment Payments

Payment of a settled claim or a judgment against a local public entity (see Govt C §970(c)) may now be made in up to ten equal annual installments if plaintiff and claimant agree in writing (Govt C §912.6(c)) or if the court so orders as part of the judgment. Govt C §970.6. The court must order payment in no more than ten equal annual installments if the local public entity's governing board adopts a resolution or ordinance finding that unreasonable hardship will result unless the judgment is payable in installments and if the court so finds after hearing. Govt C §970.6(a).

Code of Civil Procedure §1263.015, relating generally to public entities acquiring property by eminent domain, and Govt C §15854.1, relating to the State Public Works Board acting under the Property Acquisition Law (see Govt C §§15850–15866), establish rules for reporting income in a condemnation action in which the public entity and owner agree to payment of the judgment over a period not to exceed ten years from the date the owner's right to compensation accrues. The agreement may also provide for the payment of interest at a rate agreed on not to exceed the maximum rate authorized by Govt C §16731 or §53531, as applicable, in connection with the issuance of bonds. At the same time, Rev & T C §17551 allows property owners who have entered into a contract for installment payments to elect to have the income derived from the disposition of the property taken into account as an installment sale.

FINAL ORDER OF CONDEMNATION

[§10.22] Contents and Effect

The final order of condemnation, when recorded, transfers title of the condemned property. CCP §1268.030(c). It is issued when the judgment authorizing the taking becomes final and the award has been paid. CCP §1268.030(a). The order must describe the condemned property and identify the judgment authorizing the taking. CCP §1268.030(b).

[§10.23] Form: Final Order of Condemnation

The citation in the caption of the form in Book §10.23 should be changed from CCP §1253 to *CCP §1268.030.*

The first paragraph of the form on Book p 276 should be replaced with the following:

IT IS FURTHER ORDERED AND ADJUDGED that $_ _ _ _ be paid to the County of _ _ _ _ _ _ for unpaid taxes (and penalties) due under California Revenue and Taxation Code Section 5084, and that the plaintiff's portion of the current taxes are cancelled as of _ _[*insert earliest applicable date under Rev & T C §5082***]_ _.**

Comment: See also Rev & T C §4986(a)(6). The statutory law on interest is now set forth in CCP §§1268.310–1268.360.

[§10.23A] Assessment of Costs and Litigation Expenses

Defendants are entitled to recover costs, including the cost of determining any apportionment of the award. CCP §1268.710. Ordinary costs include filing fees, reporter's fees for depositions, witness's fees, and mileage for parties under subpena, jury fees (required to be advanced by condemnor under CCP §631.5), court reporter's fees, and transportation costs for jury visits to the site. See CCP §1033.5.

If defendant has paid real property taxes for which plaintiff is liable, reimbursement is claimed by cost bill. CCP §1268.430. If plaintiff has taken possession before judgment, the claim must be made at the time provided for claiming costs; otherwise the time is 30 days after plaintiff takes title.

Code of Civil Procedure §1250.410 (former CCP §1249.3) permits the court (on defendant's motion within 30 days after entry of judgment) to award litigation expenses, including attorneys' fees, appraisal, and other experts' fees necessary to the preparation and conduct of the case, when the court finds that the condemnor's offer was unreasonable and the condemnee's demand was reasonable. See Supp §9.14A.

In *Coachella Valley County Water Dist. v Dreyfuss* (1979) 91 CA3d 949, 154 CR 467, the court held that a defendant may also recover ordinary costs and prejudgment interest when an award is based on acceptance of a settlement demand. "Compensation" as used in CCP §1250.410 means compensation for the property taken, severance damage, and other consequential damage, but it does not cover ordinary costs or interest on the award for prejudgment possession.

See *People ex rel Dep't of Transp. v Gardella Square* (1988) 200 CA3d 559, 246 CR 139, which involved settlement of a case when the original offer and demand were made 30 days before the date first set for trial, but the original demand was not accepted until after the original trial date had been continued. It is not necessary to proceed to trial to recover litigation expenses.

The courts have attempted to provide guidelines to define the reasonableness of an offer and demand. But the statute itself establishes the initial point of reference. The offer and demand are to be "viewed in the light of the evidence admitted and the compensation awarded in the proceeding." CCP §1250.410(b). Thus, it is not enough simply to rely on one's own appraisal expert; one must recognize the possible consequences of trial and the position of the other side. In *County of Los Angeles v Kranz* (1977) 65 CA3d 656, 660, 135 CR 473, 475, the court observed that the condemnor "should have realized that a jury would give some weight to the opinion of each expert, and fix the fair market value of the property somewhere between the two." Another court, in *City of Gardena v Camp* (1977) 70 CA3d 252, 257, 138 CR 656, 659, also concluded that "unyielding adherence" to its own appraisal "was incompatible with that spirit of compromise one would expect of a reasonable condemnor." Failure to give any weight to large differences between experts' opinions on the amount of severance damage shows lack of good faith by the condemning agency. *San Diego Gas & Elec. Co. v Daley* (1988) 205 CA3d 1334, 253 CR 144.

The first case interpreting the former statute, CCP §1249.3, appeared to stress the good faith nature of the offer in judging reasonableness. But it is doubtful that the opinion intended to require bad faith on the condemnor's part for the condemnee to recover its litigation expenses. Actually, the court spoke of a broader standard: "Reasonableness depends also on the *good faith, care and accuracy"* of how the amounts of the offer and demand were determined. (Emphasis added.) *City of Los Angeles v Cannon* (1976) 57 CA3d 559, 562, 127 CR 709, 712.

In the later case of *County of Los Angeles v Kranz* (1977) 65 CA3d 656, 659, 135 CR 473, 475, the court set forth three standards for defining reasonableness, all of which must be viewed in light of the adjudicated value of the property:

(1) The proportional difference between the offer and the demand;

(2) The absolute monetary amounts; and

(3) The good faith, care, and accuracy used in determining the offer and demand.

In *Kranz* the court ruled for the property owner when the condemnor's offer was $63,000, the demand $72,500, and the award $79,077.55. Under the above three-pronged test, the offer was 13 percent less than the demand, it was significantly lower than the award, and it ignored the condemnee's expert's appraisal of $96,750. The substantial difference between appraisals was an important factor in the court's consideration of the accuracy of the condemnor's offer. See also *Redevelopment Agency v First Christian Church* (1983) 140 CA3d 690, 189 CR 749; *Lake County Sanitation Dist. v Schultz* (1978) 85 CA3d 658, 149 CR 717; *Community Redev. Agency v Friedman* (1977) 76 CA3d 188, 143 CR 160.

If the condemnee claims precondemnation *Klopping* damages (see Supp §4.7A), it is not unreasonable for the condemnor to exclude from its offer of settlement any amount for such damages when there is no evidence that property owners lost rental income because of the delay. *City of Fresno v Shewmake* (1982) 129 CA3d 907, 181 CR 451. In *Shewmake,* the court noted that, if there had been evidence of actual rental loss with a dispute on its precise amount, failure by the condemnor to offer any *Klopping* damages could have been considered unreasonable.

The offer of the condemnor was found to be unreasonable in *City of Commerce v National Starch & Chem. Corp.* (1981) 118 CA3d 1, 19, 173 CR 176, 187, because it failed to take into account substantial reduction in the market value of the remainder property due to impairment of the useful life of the fixtures, and the offer was only 33 percent of the final award, which did take into account that reduction of market value.

In *City of San Leandro v Highsmith* (1981) 123 CA3d 146, 176 CR 412, the court, although stating that the condemnor's final offer amounting to 61 percent of the verdict appeared mathematically to be unreasonably low, found that the offer was made in good faith and with care and accuracy and was, therefore, reasonable. The court relied on a declaration of the condemnor's attorney, showing that plaintiff did not ignore the information it received through depositions of defendant's experts, and apparently relied on the fact that the condemnee did not introduce any contradictory evidence. Moreover, the condemnee's demand exceeded the award.

In *City of El Monte v Ramirez* (1982) 128 CA3d 1005, 180 CR 690, the court denied litigation expenses to a condemnee who failed to submit the appraisal information to plaintiff that would have justified an increase in the offer. Citing *City of San Leandro v Highsmith, supra,* the court found plaintiff's refusal to increase its offer reasonable because the valuation data submitted by the defendant lacked essential supporting data and because the condemnee failed to give its reasons for its opinion on the amount of severance damages. 128 CA3d at 1012, 180 CR at 694. In *County of San Diego v Woodward* (1986) 186 CA3d 82, 230 CR 406, defendant was denied litigation expenses because the court found that the county's offer was reasonable and defendant's was not. The county based its offer on information from a well-qualified appraiser and defendant's demand was based on his ownership of the property, his personal experience, and the opinions of others, but not on comparable sales.

The condemnor's amended offer to accept the property owner's original demand more than 30 days before the rescheduled trial does not qualify as a reasonable offer. The offer must be judged by the circumstances that prevailed 30 days before the time originally set for trial. *People ex rel Dep't of Transp. v Gardella Square* (1988) 200 CA3d 559, 246 CR 139. But see, *Community Redev. Agency v Matkin* (1990) 220 CA3d 1087, 272 CR 1, which distinguished *Gardella Square* and ruled that the property owner did not forfeit its right to recover litigation expenses under CCP §1250.410 when it failed to serve a demand 30 days before the original scheduled trial date, but filed a timely demand before a rescheduled trial date. The *Matkin* court observed that the *Gardella Square* court decided that the original trial date was appropriate for determining the reasonableness of the final offer and demand.

The trial court's determination of the reasonableness of plaintiff's offer will not be overturned if supported by substantial evidence, and the supreme court has stated that it must presume there was substantial evidence to support the trial court's determination if a reporter's transcript of the trial is not supplied on appeal. *Redevelopment Agency v Gilmore* (1985) 38 C3d 790, 214 CR 904, citing *City of El Monte v Ramirez, supra.*

From these cases it would appear that the phrase "good faith, care and accuracy," does not simply mean general reliance on one's own experts. More recent cases have held that the mathematical approach of *Camp, Kranz,* and *Friedman* to examination of the offer and demand is useful only when the condemnor has shown little or no willingness to compromise in the face of a reasonable position by the condemnee. See *People ex rel Dep't of Transp. v Patton Mission Props.* (1979) 89 CA3d 204, 152 CR 485. In *State ex rel Pub. Works Bd. v Turner* (1979) 90 CA3d 33, 153 CR 156, the court held that the state acted in good faith when (1) it used a well-qualified appraiser who considered proper comparables, (2) there was no evidence he tried to keep the values low, and (3) defendants did not offer any expert assistance to counter the state's offer. Under the holding of *People ex rel Dep't of Transp. v Societa Di Unione E Beneficenza Italiana* (1978) 87 CA3d 14, 150 CR 706, the fact that a plaintiff's offer is closer in dollar amount to the verdict than is the defendant's demand does not in itself ensure a finding that the offer was reasonable or that the demand was unreasonable. An offer by the condemnor that was 82 percent of the verdict did not compel a finding of reasonableness when the appraiser used noncomparable properties as the basis for the opinion of value and the condemnor both refused to negotiate and ignored the property owner's qualified expert. *Community Redev. Agency v Krause* (1984) 162 CA3d 860, 209 CR 1. A final demand for compensation by the property owner qualified for consideration in determining litigation expenses, even though the question of compensation attributable to possible future damage, on which there was substantial dispute, was deferred for future resolution. *Placer County Water Agency v Hofman* (1985) 165 CA3d 890, 211 CR 894, discussed further in Supp §9.14A.

In *Los Angeles Unified School Dist. v C.F. Bolster Co.* (1978) 81 CA3d 906, 146 CR 789, the court, relying primarily on a formula approach, determined that a plaintiff's offer, which was 87 percent of the verdict, constituted a high enough percentage of the award to make the offer reasonable.

The court in *Lake County Sanitation Dist. v Schultz, supra,* established several points concerning the amount of litigation fees: (1) The 30-day period mentioned in former CCP §1249.3 (now CCP §1250.410) affects only entitlement and does not serve as a threshold date for determining which expenses can be collected; (2) the property owner is entitled to fees in presenting its motion and appeal to recover litigation expenses; and (3) the attorney's fees for a successful motion cannot be reduced on the basis that future clients of an attorney specializing in condemnation may benefit from his research in the present case, or that the attorney has already received substantial fees for services in the trial itself.

An original offer and demand made at least 30 days before trial affects the entitlement to litigation expenses; revised or superseded offers affect only the amount of expenses—not the entitlement. *City of Gardena v Camp* (1977) 70 CA3d 252, 138 CR 656. The court must consider the prelitigation offer required to be made under Govt C §7267.2 (see Supp §§7.4, 8.2), together with any other written offers and demands filed in the case. CCP §1250.410(b).

Litigation expenses may be allowed when a condemnation action is conditionally settled after the first phase of a bifurcated trial. *Los Angeles County Flood Control Dist. v Mindlin* (1980) 106 CA3d 698, 165 CR 233.

A property owner who testifies to the value of his property cannot recover litigation expenses for the time he spends preparing and presenting his own testimony. Appraisal fees can be awarded as costs only if paid to an expert testifying on the owner's behalf. *County of Madera v Forrester* (1981) 115 CA3d 57, 62, 170 CR 896, 898. However, in *Leaf v City of San Mateo* (1984) 150 CA3d 1184, 198 CR 447, an inverse condemnation case, the court allowed the recovery of the reasonable value of necessary professional services to an attorney who acted for himself in prosecuting the case.

See Supp §9.14A for discussion of the procedure used in making final offers of settlement.

It is within the court's discretion to provide an evidentiary hearing on a motion for recovery of litigation expenses. In *Community Redev. Agency v Krause, supra,* the judge who heard the case in chief was not required to consider additional evidence when the transcripts of the hearing revealed that the court was familiar with the nature of the litigation and the property owner's expert. The court also had before it a declaration of the property owner's attorney stating the amount of fees, his background and qualifications, and his opinion that the fees were reasonable. Moreover, the condemnor submitted no evidence showing that the fees were unreasonable, only its opinion to that effect. *Los Angeles Unified School Dist. v C.F. Bolster Co., supra,* held that findings of fact and conclusions of law under CCP §632 (now providing for a statement of decision specifying its factual and legal basis rather than findings of fact and conclusions of law) were unnecessary under former CCP §1249.3 (now CCP §1250.410). See also *People ex rel Dep't of Transp. v Sunshine Canyon, Inc.* (1979) 94 CA3d 599, 156 CR 552 (motion for litigation costs under former CCP §1249.3 was not the type of proceeding requiring findings under CCP §632).

A final offer of settlement made subject to the condemnor's reserved right to appeal from a court-tried issue before jury trial on compensation was unreasonable. *People v Zivelonghi* (1986) 183 CA3d 187, 228 CR 72. In *Zivelonghi,* the state reserved the right to appeal from a bifurcated issue concerning the size of the taking. The state claimed ownership of a 200-foot highway easement, which the trial court determined was only 100 feet. Based on that determination, the state made a final offer of settlement for the valuation trial, subject to its right of appeal on the issue of size of the taking. The court held that, if the state were successful on appeal, the offer would be nullified, leaving no settlement.

[§10.24] INTEREST ON AWARD

The procedure for calculating interest on condemnation awards was revised by the legislature effective January 1, 1987. Interest must now be computed as described by new CCP §1268.350. CCP §1268.310. Under CCP §1268.350 the rate of interest for each six-month period (January 1 to June 30 and July 1 to December 31) or fraction of a six-month period for which interest is due is the "apportionment rate" for the immediately preceding six-month period. The apportionment rate is that calculated by the Controller as the rate of earnings of the Surplus Money Investment Fund for each six-month period. Interest awards in inverse condemnation cases must also be computed under CCP §1268.350. CCP §1268.311.

Under Cal Const art XV, §1, the legal rate of interest on a judgment in California may be set by the legislature at no more than 10 percent per annum (or 7 percent if the legislature fails to act). In 1982, CCP §685.010 was enacted, effective January 1, 1983, increasing to 10 percent per annum the rate applying to interest that accrues after the operative date of the statute. But for condemnation cases after 1987, as noted above, the legislature has provided a means of calculating interest (CCP §1268.350).

In *Redevelopment Agency v Gilmore* (1985) 38 C3d 790, 807, 214 CR 904, 916, the supreme court ruled that the California statutory interest ceiling provided in Cal Const art XV, §1 cannot prevail when it falls short of constitutional just compensation, which requires an award of interest "at a proper rate." To determine the proper rate of interest, the trial court must examine the rates prevailing during the period a condemnation payment was delayed for all forms of money market obligations, government and private, that prudent depositors and investors normally purchase for income purposes and whose terms and maturities fall within the period of delay. 38 C3d at 806, 214 CR at 916. See also *Aetna Life & Ins. Co. v City of Los Angeles* (1985) 170 CA3d 865, 879, 216 CR 831, 840 (applying *Gilmore* to inverse condemnation case). *San Bernardino County Flood Control Dist. v Grabowski* (1988) 205 CA3d 885, 901, 252 CR 676, 685, did declare that interest was not to be calculated based on market rates when they fell below statutory rates.

Gilmore did not address the question of whether the condemnee was limited to the statutory rate on amounts that were placed on deposit to secure an order of possession and left with the court pending trial and judgment, because the property owners had withdrawn the full amount of their respective deposits. Nor did *Gilmore* decide the issue of whether the legal rate prevails when it is *higher* than the market rate. 38 C3d at 802 n13, 214 CR at 913 n13. It should be noted that the former 7 percent ceiling on interest (with a provision allowing parties to contract for up to 10 percent interest) arose in the mid–1930s when prevailing market interest rates were below that figure. See former Cal Const art XX, §22, adopted November 6, 1934. By prescribing the use of the rate of earnings of the Surplus Money Investment Fund, the legislature has apparently attempted to satisfy the requirements of *Gilmore* as well as prescribe the use of an interest rate lower than the "legal" rate of CCP §685.010 when the rate of earnings is lower.

Redevelopment Agency v Erganian (1989) 211 CA3d 166, 259 CR 213, held that the property owner was entitled to interest at the legal rate for the period of time during which moneys remained in a security deposit under an order of possession, but had the right to interest at the prevailing market rate on all amounts in excess of the deposit for probable compensation until the judgment was paid. The *Erganian* court observed that, in some instances, the market rate might be applicable to deposited funds, *i.e.,* if respondents had raised a claim or defense that would have been waived by withdrawal of the security deposit. See Supp §6.25 about waiver of objections to right to take on withdrawal of probable compensation. See *Smith v County of Los Angeles* (1989) 214 CA3d 266, 262 CR 754, on consideration of rates of return on various investments, which supported a trial court's conclusion that the state's surplus money fund reflects the consequence of actual investment decision making rather than speculation. In other words, this court found that the statutory rate was the market rate. In this case, the court ruled that CCP §1268.350 applies to interest calculations after January 1987, but not retroactively.

Other procedures regarding the payment of interest in condemnation cases were revised in 1980. Government Code §906 has been added providing that, when a public entity makes an offer in settlement or compromise of a claim, interest on judgments begins to accrue 30 days after the claimant accepts that amount in writing. Govt C §906(b)(2)–(3). If, however, the claim is subject to approval of an appropriation by the legislature, interest on the amount appropriated for the claim begins to accrue 30 days after the effective date of the law by which the appropriation is enacted. Govt C §906(b)(1). The public entity and claimant may agree in writing to vary the terms prescribed by Govt C §906(b). Govt C §906(c)–(d). Government Code §906 does not affect the claimant's rights to interest under a judgment. Govt C §906(e).

There can be no recovery of interest on a judgment if, after entry of judgment but before taking possession, there is a timely abandonment (see Supp §§8.31–8.33). *People ex rel Dep't of Transp. v Union Pac. Land Resources Corp.* (1986) 179 CA3d 307, 224 CR 487.

[§10.25] When Interest Begins To Accrue

If the parties, by the terms of the agreement, treat a broad right-of-entry agreement as equivalent to a taking under an order for immediate possession, the interest begins to accrue on that date of entry under former CCP §1255b(a)(3). *People ex rel Dep't of Pub. Works v Williams* (1973) 30 CA3d 980, 106 CR 795.

If the property owner raises an affirmative defense of inverse condemnation, alleging precondemnation activity that constituted an earlier taking of the property, the owner is entitled to interest from the date of the constructive taking, provided the owner has proof of being deprived of the use or value of the property by the government's precondemnation activity. *People ex rel Dep't of Transp. v Gardella Square* (1988) 200 CA3d 559, 246 CR 139.

Code of Civil Procedure §1268.310 continues the same dates for beginning accrual of interest as former CCP §1255b(a).

Some reported federal cases allow the property owner to seek the prevailing rate of interest rather than the legal rate. See Supp §11.19.

See Supp §10.24 for discussion of new provisions on interest.

[§10.26] When Interest Ceases To Accrue

Code of Civil Procedure §1268.320 continues the same dates for terminating interest as under former CCP §1255b(c).

Under current law, notice of any postjudgment deposit must be served on defendants. CCP §1268.120. Under former CCP §1254, notice of deposit was required only when served with an order for possession.

See Supp §10.24 for discussion of new provisions on interest.

[§10.26A] Withdrawal of Deposit

On application to the court, defendant may withdraw from the deposit of the award the amount to which he is entitled on filing either a satisfaction of judgment or receipt for the money. The filing of a receipt waives all claims and defenses except a claim for greater compensation. CCP §1268.140(a).

If the award has not been apportioned, the applicant must give notice to all other defendants who have appeared. When apportionment has occurred, the court may require notice to be given to certain defendants. CCP §1268.140(b).

When the judgment is reversed, vacated, or set aside, the deposit (CCP §1268.110) and withdrawal (CCP §1268.140(d)) are governed by the procedures governing deposit and withdrawal before judgment. See Supp §§8.7–8.14.

Any excess withdrawal must be repaid. Interest is included only on the amount repaid to other defendants, but not to plaintiff. CCP §1268.160.

Defendant must reimburse the amount withdrawn in excess of the final award on a retrial after appeal, whether that appeal was taken by defendant or plaintiff. *City of Downey v Johnson* (1978) 79 CA3d 970, 145 CR 298, interpreting former CCP §1254.

See Supp §10.24 for discussion of new provisions on interest.

[§10.27] Offset of Interest

As was true under former CCP §1255b(b), there can be an offset against interest when defendant remains in possession or receives income from the property after interest begins to accrue. CCP §1268.330.

The new provision clarifies that only net income may be offset; it establishes a presumption affecting the burden of proof that the value of continued occupancy after interest begins will equal the rate of interest as calculated under CCP §1268.350. See Supp §10.24 for discussion of calculation of interest rates under that section. This rule also applies to inverse condemnation cases. CCP §1268.311, effective January 1, 1987. *Holtz v San Francisco BART Dist.* (1976) 17 C3d 648, 131 CR 646. There cannot be an offset against interest for the value of possession when the condemnor is seeking an easement. The taker of an easement obtains the right to use the land in a specified manner and to bar its owner from uses that are inconsistent. Therefore, once taken, the property right is no longer possessed by the owner, regardless of its continued possession of other property rights in the same land. *Placer County Water Agency v Hofman* (1985) 165 CA3d 890, 211 CR 894.

The amount of interest and any offset is assessed by the court, not the jury. CCP §1268.340.

See Supp §10.24 for discussion of new provisions on interest.

APPEAL AND NEW TRIAL

[§10.28] Application of General Civil Rules

The right to move for a new trial or to appeal is not affected by deposit of judgment (CCP §1268.170), withdrawal of deposit (CCP §1268.140(a)(2)), or taking of possession (CCP §1268.230). After withdrawal, however, the new trial or appeal may concern only the amount of compensation. CCP §1268.140(a)(2).

The court in *Redevelopment Agency v Goodman* (1975) 53 CA3d 424, 125 CR 818, upheld the constitutionality of former CCP §1255b (now CCP §1268.310) and former CCP §1254(f) (now CCP §1268.140), which terminate interest on an award if there is an appeal on the right to take.

It was proper to grant a new trial in a case in which there was unexpected testimony of the city's expert on the question of goodwill loss (the only issue tried) and the condemnor had not complied with the statutory exchange of valuation information provisions of CCP §1258.210 (see

Supp §9.6). *City of Fresno v Harrison* (1984) 154 CA3d 296, 201 CR 219. New trials were directed in *City of Los Angeles v Decker* (1977) 18 C3d 860, 135 CR 640, and *County of San Diego v Bressi* (1986) 184 CA3d 112, 229 CR 44. In *Decker* the condemnor took a position in trial contradictory to evidence it knew about in a draft environmental impact report concerning the airport project for which it condemned the land. In *Bressi* the trial court allowed the condemnor to introduce evidence of future plans for the airport project contradictory to the scope of the taking described in the resolution of necessity. See Supp §6.18.

Code of Civil Procedure §§1256–1257, providing general rules relating to new trials and appeals in condemnation actions, were replaced by CCP §1230.040.

California Civil Procedure During Trial §§20.14–20.41 (Cal CEB 1960) have been replaced by California Civil Procedure During Trial §§19.11–19.36 (Cal CEB 1984). California Civil Appellate Practice (Cal CEB 1966) has been replaced by a second edition published in 1985. 5 Witkin, California Procedure, *Attack on Judgment in Trial Court* §§16–21 (2d ed 1971) have been replaced by 8 Witkin, California Procedure, *Attack Judgment* §§18–24 (3d ed 1985); 6 Procedure, *Appeal* has been replaced by 9 Procedure, *Appeal,* in the new edition.

[§10.29A] Appeal of Judgment and Orders

The most common appeal is from the judgment of condemnation. A judgment in a direct condemnation, conditioned on the finality of a judgment in a corresponding inverse condemnation action, is itself a final, appealable judgment because it is self-executing. *Taper v City of Long Beach* (1982) 129 CA3d 590, 181 CR 169. Although in condemnation proceedings the judgment is sometimes referred to as an interlocutory judgment or decree, it is final as to all issues between the parties; it determines their rights and fixes the amount of compensation to be paid the condemnee. See *Baldwin Park Redev. Agency v Irving* (1984) 156 CA3d 428, 202 CR 792. The final order of condemnation (CCP §1268.030, formerly CCP §1253) is a special order made after final judgment and is appealable apart from the judgment. *City of Los Angeles v Pomeroy* (1901) 132 C 340, 64 P 477.

The following orders have also been held appealable:

(1) An order striking a cross-complaint directed against codefendant. *People ex rel Dep't of Pub. Works v Buellton Dev. Co.* (1943) 58 CA2d 178, 136 P2d 793.

(2) An order after judgment authorizing possession. *San Francisco Unified School Dist. v Hong Mow* (1954) 123 CA2d 668, 267 P2d 349. An order denying immediate possession before judgment, however, was nonappealable. *Central Contra Costa Sanitary Dist. v Superior Court* (1950) 34 C2d 845, 848, 215 P2d 462, 464. Likewise, an order granting

prejudgment possession under CCP §1255.410 (so-called "quick take" procedure) is not an appealable order. The correct procedure would be to seek a stay under CCP §1255.430, or a mandamus action. *City of Morgan Hill v Alberti* (1989) 211 CA3d 1435, 260 CR 42.

(3) A judgment of abandonment (CCP §1268.510(c) formerly CCP §1255a). *Oak Grove School Dist. v City Title Ins. Co.* (1963) 217 CA2d 678, 32 CR 288.

(4) After the judgment has become final, a court order setting aside the condemnor's abandonment. *Taper v City of Long Beach* (1982) 129 CA3d 590, 181 CR 169.

(5) An order determining litigation expenses under CCP §1250.410. *City of Los Angeles v Aalbers* (1977) 67 CA3d 80, 136 CR 396.

(6) An order denying a motion to recover litigation expenses. *City of San Leandro v Highsmith* (1981) 123 CA3d 146, 152, 176 CR 412, 416.

(7) An order determining probable compensation when prejudgment possession continues after judgment. *People ex rel Dep't of Transp. v Zivelonghi* (1986) 181 CA3d 1035, 226 CR 748.

(8) Denial of the challenge on the right to take. *San Bernardino County Flood Control Dist. v Grabowski* (1988) 205 CA3d 885, 252 CR 676.

[§10.30] Costs on Appeal

Effective January 1, 1987, CCP §1034 was repealed and replaced with a new CCP §1034, which provides that prejudgment costs and costs on appeal shall be determined under rules adopted by the Judicial Council.

See *People ex rel Dep't of Pub. Works v Amsden Corp.* (1973) 33 CA3d 83, 109 CR 1, in which appellant-condemnees were not allowed to recover their costs on an appeal concerning admission of evidence of a lease agreement for valuation purposes.

In cases under CCP §1268.720, however, defendant is entitled to costs on appeal against plaintiff, whether defendant is the prevailing party, unless the court directs otherwise. Former CCP §1254(k) did not allow costs of a new trial to defendant if he did not receive greater compensation than awarded in the first trial. Code of Civil Procedure §1268.710 eliminates this restriction.

11

Federal Condemnation Practice

INTRODUCTION

[§11.2] SPECIAL FEATURES OF FEDERAL SUBSTANTIVE LAW

California Constitution art I, §14, cited in Book §11.2, has been renumbered art I, §19. See Supp §8.7.

[§11.3] FEDERAL POLICY ON REAL PROPERTY ACQUISITION

When a redevelopment authority filed a declaration of taking and acquired the condemned property before the date provided in the Uniform Relocation Assistance and Real Property Acquisition Policies Act of 1970 (42 USC §§4601–4655), an owner had no cause of action based on violation of the Act. The Act does not create rights in landowners to sue in federal district courts, it merely establishes policy guidelines. *Rubin v HUD* (ED Pa 1972) 347 F Supp 555. See also *Barnhart v Brinegar* (WD Mo 1973) 362 F Supp 464, discussed in Supp §11.18.

[§11.4] BASIC PROCEDURAL PROVISIONS; JURISDICTION AND VENUE

Allegations that no condemnation suit has been filed, at the time plaintiff initiated an inverse suit because of defendant's delay in filing its action, raise constitutional questions that create federal jurisdiction. If this jurisdiction is proper when the complaint is filed, a change or clarification of state law (*Klopping v City of Whittier* (1972) 8 C3d 39, 104 CR 1; see Book §4.7, Supp §4.7A) does not affect the federal action. *Eleopoulos v Richmond Redev. Agency* (ND Cal 1972) 351 F Supp 63.

[§11.5] PUBLIC USE AND NECESSITY

Before a landowner is required to vacate his homestead, he is entitled to a hearing on his objections to the condemnation. It is improper to delay this hearing until determination of just compensation. *U.S. v 58.16 Acres of Land* (7th Cir 1973) 478 F2d 1055.

Federal courts have jurisdiction to determine whether the purpose for which the property is sought is a congressionally authorized public use, but not whether particular property is necessary for that use. "Only in cases of egregious bad faith will the right to condemn be denied." *U.S. v 416.81 Acres of Land* (7th Cir 1975) 514 F2d 627, 632. "To allege bad faith a party must charge facts rather than conclusions, and such facts must suggest actual malevolence by the officer towards the complaining party." *U.S. v Southerly Portion of Bodie Island* (ED NC 1953) 114 F Supp 427, 430.

In an action by local merchants seeking injunctive relief and damages on the ground that the location and design of a garage is contrary to an urban renewal plan, the title of the purchaser of the garage cannot be collaterally attacked. If a governmental agency considers it necessary, it may take full title to property in an urban renewal area and convey it to a private corporation in order to carry out a redevelopment project. *Gibson & Perin Co. v City of Cincinnati* (6th Cir 1973) 480 F2d 936. See also *Gardner v Housing Auth.* (6th Cir 1975) 514 F2d 38.

The holder of federal geothermal leases was entitled to an injunction prohibiting condemnation of leaseholds when the lessee demonstrated probable success on the issue of whether the condemnation by the Northern California Power Agency was barred by the supremacy clause (US Const art VI, cl 2). *Grace Geothermal Corp. v Northern Cal. Power Agency* (ND Cal 1985) 619 F Supp 964, aff'd (9th Cir 1985) 770 F2d 170.

Under the provisions of the former Federal Insecticide, Fungicide and Rodenticide Act (FIFRA), the Environmental Protection Agency was authorized to use data submitted by an applicant for the registration of a pesticide in evaluating the application of another manufacturer and to disclose publicly some of the submitted data. In an action seeking to enjoin the data disclosure as a taking of property for private rather than public purpose, the Supreme Court held that, according to the provisions of the Act between 1972 and 1978, the taking was for a public use, even though subsequent applicants might be the direct beneficiaries. An injunction was not an appropriate remedy for the taking. *Ruckelshaus v Monsanto Co.* (1984) 467 US 986. Congress properly provided a procedure in FIFRA for binding arbitration concerning the right to compensation for data submitted by previous registrants of similar products with the right of judicial review only for fraud, misrepresentation, or other misconduct, without violating US Const art III (establishment of the federal court system). *Thomas v Union Carbide Agricultural Prods. Co.* (1985) 473 US 568.

PLEADING

[§11.8] Answer

The defendant's appearance or answer is governed by Fed R Civ P 71A. If a defendant has no objection or defense to the taking, the defendant may simply serve a notice of appearance designating the property in which the defendant claims to be interested. Thereafter, the defendant will receive notice of all proceedings affecting that property. If a defendant has any objection or defense, however, the defendant must serve an answer within 20 days after service of notice on the defendant. That answer must identify the property in which the defendant claims to have an interest, state the interest claimed, and state all objections and defenses to the taking. Defenses and objections not presented are waived. The defendant may always present evidence at the trial on the issue of just compensation for the amount to be paid for the property.

California procedure on raising objections to the right to take (CCP §1250.350; see Supp §6.25) now generally parallels federal procedure.

[§11.12] POSSESSION AND TITLE

When the federal government condemned land to save costs with no immediate need for possession of the property, a district court properly continued its stay of the order of possession pending final judgment. *U.S. v 58.16 Acres of Land* (7th Cir 1973) 478 F2d 1055.

When the government's occupancy of premises is under claim of contractual right and not a seizure of the premises under *U.S. v Dow* (1958) 357 US 17, cited in Book §11.12, the owner is only entitled to just compensation from the date that the government files its condemnation action and not earlier. *U.S. v Bedford Assoc.* (2d Cir 1981) 657 F2d 1300.

Under 25 USC §357, a condemning authority must institute formal condemnation proceedings to gain title to Indian trust lands and may not gain title through inverse condemnation by way of prior physical invasion. *U.S. v Clarke* (1980) 445 US 253. But when the Alyeska Pipeline Service Company did initiate formal condemnation proceedings, a prior physical invasion by way of trespass did not convert the formal proceedings into an action for inverse condemnation. *Etalook v Exxon Pipeline Co.* (9th Cir 1987) 831 F2d 1440.

California Constitution art I, §14, cited in Book §11.12, has been renumbered art I, §19. See Supp §8.7.

[§11.13] Declaration of Taking

Under 40 USC §257, the government can obtain a judicial valuation of the property without committing itself to condemn it. In the case of unimproved, vacant land, such a condemnation judgment can force the owner to hold the property. This generates liabilities and offers no benefits, because condemnees are not entitled to interest before the date of taking. *Danforth v U.S.* (1939) 308 US 271, 286.

The enactment of legislation authorizing a condemnation is not a taking, nor is the announcement of the intent to acquire. There must be an actual taking of the property. *U.S. v 3.95 Acres of Land* (ND Cal 1979) 470 F Supp 572, 574.

[§11.14] Deposit

Failure to deposit in advance as much money as plaintiffs demanded as compensation for their properties did not violate their constitutional rights under the Civil Rights Act (42 USC §1983). *Gigliotti v Redevelopment Auth.* (WD Pa 1973) 362 F Supp 764, aff'd (3d Cir 1974) 492 F2d 1238.

VALUATION

[§11.16] Fair Market Value

The date of valuation is the time of trial for a case in which no declaration of taking is filed. *U.S. v Land in Worcester* (D Md 1972) 354 F Supp 1233.

In a 5–4 decision, the Supreme Court held that value resulting from an actual or potential use of condemned property in conjunction with grazing lands under revocable permits cannot be considered an element of compensation. *U.S. v Fuller* (1973) 409 US 488. Compare *U.S. v Citrus Valley Farms, Inc.* (9th Cir 1965) 350 F2d 683 (diminution in value of cotton allotment compensable); and *U.S. v Certain Land Situated in City of Detroit* (ED Mich 1982) 547 F Supp 680 (when adjoining land might increase the value of a condemnee's land and a government permit is not relevant, *Fuller* does not apply).

It was held permissible to use two different methods of evaluation on one condemned parcel when the commission fixing compensation used a comparable sales method to value the farm and recreational portion, and an income approach to value the gravel portion of the condemned property. *U.S. v 1,629.6 Acres of Land* (D Del 1973) 360 F Supp 147 (reversed in part on other grounds (3d Cir 1974) 503 F2d 764).

In determining the royalty rate for condemned land having the highest and best use for mining, a commission appointed under Fed R Civ P 71A properly relied on testimony of an expert qualified in the field of mineral appraisal and economic geology in the absence of any comparable royalty leases. *U.S. v 100.80 Acres of Land* (MD NC 1987) 657 F Supp 269. See also *U.S. v 22.80 Acres of Land* (9th Cir 1988) 839 F2d 1362 on the use of methods of valuation other than comparable sales and capitalization of income in the case of valuation of mineral deposits.

In valuing a permanent and exclusive easement, the award must consider all possible uses to which the government could put the land, including possible encroachment on the remaining rights of the condemnee in its land. *U.S. v 201.19 Acres of Land* (9th Cir 1973) 478 F2d 1042.

On condemnation of an easement over a road for which the government had previously paid the owner a use fee, the expectation of continued government payments for the use privilege could not be considered in valuing the easement. Just compensation does not include elements of value created by the needs of the condemnor. *U.S. v Weyerhaeuser Co.* (9th Cir 1976) 538 F2d 1363.

Dictum in *Brown v U.S.* (1923) 263 US 78, suggested that, in the condemnation of municipal property by the federal government, the best measure for making the defendant whole is the cost of acquiring substitute property. In *U.S. v 50 Acres of Land* (1984) 469 US 24, however, the Supreme Court rejected this suggestion, finding that the same principles of just compensation apply to both private and public condemnees. The Court held that there was no requirement that the United States pay a public condemnee compensation measured by the cost of substitute property when the market value of the condemned property is ascertainable and there is no showing of manifest injustice. The Court noted that in *Brown v U.S., supra,* the Court was interpreting the scope of the government's condemnation power, not the compensation required by the fifth amendment. See also *U.S. v 564.54 Acres of Land* (1979) 441 US 506, in which the Supreme Court held that the fair-market-value approach should apply to the condemnation by the United States of property of a private nonprofit organization operating a community facility for a public purpose (Lutheran Church summer camp). See Comment, *"Substitute Facilities" Compensation for Private Condemnees: U.S. v 564.54 Acres of Land,* 92 Harv L Rev 514 (1978), discussing the lower court's decision.

[§11.17] Enhancement and Blight

Changes in property value due to the effect of the condemnation project itself are to be disregarded. Citing *U.S. v Miller* (1943) 317 US 369, the court in *U.S. v 5.27 Acres of Land* (WD Pa 1972) 354 F Supp 1346, avoided finding loss of value caused by the project by evaluating the affected property in terms of its condition before the scope of the project was announced.

In *Richmond Elks Hall Ass'n v Richmond Redev. Agency* (9th Cir 1977) 561 F2d 1327, the court held that a de facto taking (see Supp §§4.7, 13.21) occurred from the effect of certain precondemnation activities: classifying subject property within the redevelopment area; acquiring and demolishing surrounding properties; informing a tenant of scheduled acquisition; and forming an option agreement with a developer that called for use of the property as a parking lot. All these activities rendered the property unsalable and caused commercial lenders to refuse to make loans on the property. Although the agency decided it no longer wanted to acquire the property because of funding difficulties, it was bound to the acquisition by inverse condemnation.

In an action to acquire an explosive safety hazard zone around wharves used to load and unload explosives, the court held that diminution in value caused by the fear of a hazard in the mind of a knowledgeable and prudent buyer may be recovered as part of just compensation. *U.S. v 760.807 Acres of Land* (9th Cir 1984) 731 F2d 1443.

[§11.18] Relocation Assistance; Moving Costs

The legislative history of the Uniform Relocation Assistance and Real

Property Acquisition Policies Act of 1970 (42 USC §§4601–4655) shows an intent to preclude judicial review of federal and state agency actions under §301 of the Act (42 USC §4651). Thus, federal courts cannot entertain suits based on noncompliance by a state or federal agency with the real property acquisition practices under §301. *Barnhart v Brinegar* (WD Mo 1973) 362 F Supp 464. See also *U.S. v 416.81 Acres of Land* (7th Cir 1975) 525 F2d 450, 454. But see *Tullock v State Highway Comm'n* (8th Cir 1974) 507 F2d 712, in which the court enjoined the State Highway Commissioner's efforts to evict the tenants without providing relocation assistance. *Tullock* apparently distinguishes between court action affecting the condemnation itself and that forcing the government to provide relocation assistance. Although the court cites *Barnhart* with approval, *Barnhart* did not allow judicial review of federal and state agency actions under the real property acquisition practices of §301 of the Act. The court in *Barnhart v Brinegar* (WD Mo 1973) 362 F Supp 464, 477, did say that an action on a contract claim could be brought under the Tucker Act (28 USC §§1346(2) and 1491(4)), but *Tullock* was not a Tucker Act case. See also *Bethune v HUD* (WD Mo 1972) 376 F Supp 1074.

United States Code Title 23 §§501–512 (Federal-Aid Highway Act of 1968), discussed in Book §11.18, was repealed and incorporated into the Uniform Relocation Assistance Act (42 USC §§4601–4638).

The United States Department of Housing and Urban Development publishes a handbook titled "Relocation and Real Property Acquisition," setting forth the basic HUD rules governing real property acquisition and relocation under HUD assisted programs. A copy may be obtained by writing to: Department of Housing and Urban Development, Regional Office, Region IX, 450 Golden Gate Avenue, San Francisco, CA 94201.

[§11.19] Other Direct Losses

If the condemnor has taken buildings for one year with short term options for renewal, the condemnees must show direct economic loss caused by the existence of these options. This may be difficult if the options are exercised and the risk of a vacancy does not materialize. Although the costs of litigating the yearly condemnation award impose a significant burden, they are not compensable, because they are an indirect, consequential result of the takings. *U.S. v Improved Premises* (SD NY 1973) 359 F Supp 528.

[§11.20] Severance Damages and Special Benefits

Severance damages do not include any diminution in value of the subject property arising solely from the acquisition and use of adjoining lands. *Campbell v U.S.* (1924) 266 US 368, 372. However, damages can arise in a case in which there is reduced accessibility of the land not taken by reason of a project on the lands of others. *U.S. v Pope & Talbot,*

Inc. (9th Cir 1961) 293 F2d 822. Three factors can negate the application of *Campbell:* (1) The land taken from the condemnee landowner was indispensable to the project; (2) the land taken constituted a substantial part of the tract devoted to the project; and (3) the damages resulting to the remaining land were inseparable from those to the same land flowing from the government's use of its adjoining land as a part of the project. See discussion in *U.S. v 15.65 Acres of Land* (9th Cir 1982) 689 F2d 1329.

When the government condemned land on which there were easements serving other land, the easement owners were entitled to compensation for their easements and severance damages representing the reduction in value of their properties served by the easements. Contiguity of the benefited land and the condemned tract is not essential; there need only be unity of ownership and use between the easement and the property that the easement serves. *U.S. v 57.09 Acres of Land* (9th Cir 1983) 706 F2d 280.

[§11.22] TRIAL

When a commission is appointed to determine just compensation, it must report how it arrived at the award, *i.e.,* with evidence of the reasoning used, standard of valuation followed, line of testimony adopted, and measure of severance damage used, if any. *U.S. v 20.53 Acres of Land* (10th Cir 1973) 478 F2d 484 (following *U.S. v Merz* (1964) 376 US 192).

An inadequate award of just compensation after a judicial determination is not a violation of plaintiff's constitutional rights under the Civil Rights Act (42 USC §1983). *Gigliotti v Redevelopment Auth.* (WD Pa 1973) 362 F Supp 764, aff'd (3d Cir 1974) 492 F2d 1238.

Although *U.S. v Reynolds,* cited in Book §11.22, held that most issues in a condemnation proceeding must be decided by the court rather than the jury, the court in *Washington Metropolitan Area v One Parcel of Land* (4th Cir 1982) 691 F2d 702, 705 n2, commented that it is unsettled whether the issue of potential unity of use between the land taken and the land retained is for judge or jury. Furthermore, the court in *U.S. v Certain Land Situated in City of Detroit* (ED Mich 1982) 547 F Supp 680, determined that *Reynolds* merely held that Fed R Civ P 71A(h) requires the judge to decide "preliminary matters," ruling that the issue of a parcel's highest and best use in an evaluation proceeding is not a preliminary matter solely for the decision of the judge.

[§11.23] COSTS

Under 28 USC §2412, condemnees are "prevailing parties" and are entitled to an award of fees and costs when the government's right to take was not actively litigated and the award of compensation substantially exceeded the amount deposited by the condemnor. *U.S. v 101.80 Acres of Land* (9th Cir 1983) 716 F2d 714, rejected the contention that a land-owner can never be a prevailing party in a condemnation case. The Ninth Circuit extensively reviewed the legislative history of the Equal Access to Justice Act of 1979 (Pub L 96–481, 94 Stat 2325, revised by Pub L 99–80, 99 Stat 183 (1985)) and commented that few actions of the government are as drastic as taking one's property. The court also distinguished the contrary holding of *U.S. v Bodcaw Co.* (1979) 440 US 202, on the grounds that it was based on an earlier version of 28 USC §2414 and that the Supreme Court did not provide any reasons for holding that the condemnee cannot be a prevailing party.

The Ninth Circuit's rule in *101.80 Acres of Land* was rejected in *Kreimes v Department of Treasury* (6th Cir 1985) 764 F2d 1186 and *U.S. v 341.45 Acres of Land* (8th Cir 1984) 751 F2d 924. Generally, the rule in those courts is simpler than in the Ninth Circuit: a landowner who recovers more at trial than the government offered is the "prevailing party." The size of the excess recovery is not relevant.

The Court of Claims mentioned in Book §11.23 has been renamed United States Claims Court. 28 USC §171.

[§11.23A] Interest

Interest is not available on a judgment against the United States in the absence of a statute (*DeLucca v U.S.* (9th Cir 1982) 670 F2d 843), but the fifth amendment makes interest available when the taking precedes payment. In two cases in which the government filed a condemnation action without a declaration of taking or entering into possession, the Ninth Circuit computed interest from (1) the date of the judgment in *U.S. v 156.81 Acres of Land* (9th Cir 1982) 671 F2d 336 and (2) the stipulated date of valuation in *U.S. v 15.65 Acres of Land* (9th Cir 1982) 689 F2d 1329. In both cases, the property was taken for the Golden Gate National Recreation Area. It was unimproved land that, because of the government's action, could not be developed or otherwise put to economic use.

In *Kirby Forest Indus. v U.S.* (1984) 467 US 1, the Supreme Court rejected two Ninth Circuit decisions, *U.S. v 15.65 Acres of Land, supra,* and *U.S. v 156.81 Acres of Land, supra,* which held that interest must be paid for the period before the award is made and title passes in cases under 40 USC §257. Rather, the Supreme Court concluded that, absent statutory provisions to the contrary, interest runs only from the time of taking. The Court determined, however, that when the date of valuation precedes payment and the value changes between those dates, the owner is constitutionally entitled to some supplemental procedure to determine any increase in the property's value until the time of payment.

The statutory 6 percent interest rate contained in the Declaration of Taking Act (40 USC §258a) does not preclude the court from requiring payment at a higher rate reasonably related to the prevailing money market. *U.S. v Blankinship* (9th Cir 1976) 543 F2d 1272. On remand, the trial court considered rates of federal treasury bonds and rates suggested by Treasury Bulletin statistics. *U.S. v Blankinship* (D Ore 1977) 431 F Supp 403. See also *U.S. v 429.59 Acres of Land* (9th Cir 1980) 612 F2d 459, 465, in which the court held that the interest on a deficiency award in condemnation cases should be fixed at a rate that "a reasonably prudent person investing funds so as to produce a reasonable return while maintaining safety of principal would receive." For a discussion of *Blankinship* in a California case, see *Redevelopment Agency v Erganian* (1989) 211 CA3d 166, 259 CR 213.

The condemnee is entitled to a proper and reasonable rate of interest as an element of loss for a delay in compensation payment. Determination of the proper rate of interest is a factual question and should be decided by the trier of fact. *U.S. v 100 Acres of Land* (9th Cir 1972) 468 F2d 1261. In that case, the issue of interest rate was not raised during the valuation trial but was introduced only after the amount of just compensation had been determined by the jury. The court ruled that the condemnees could not then present new evidence to show additional elements of compensation, because it had been possible to introduce such evidence at the original trial. In *U.S. v Blankinship* (9th Cir 1976) 543 F2d 1272, the proper interest rate was held to be the rate commanded by federal Treasury instruments issued for periods similar to the period of delay in payment, during the time of the delay.

See also *U.S. v 97.19 Acres of Land* (D Md 1981) 511 F Supp 565.

LOCAL PRETRIAL RULES

[§11.24] Northern District

This district court repealed its Local R 127, mentioned in Book §11.24, concerning special pretrial procedures for condemnation actions. Now the general rule (ND Cal Local R 235–7) governs.

[§11.25] Eastern District

The general pretrial rules for the Eastern District are now found at ED Cal Local R 281. Special information is required in the pretrial statement for eminent domain actions. ED Cal Local R 281(b)(6)(i).

[§11.26] Central and Southern Districts

In the Central District, the pretrial rules for eminent domain require service and filing of a Memorandum of Contentions of Fact and Law at least 21 days before the pretrial conference. CD Cal Local R 9.5. For special rules relating to eminent domain actions, see CD Cal Local R App B, subsection (g).

The names of impeaching witnesses are omitted from the "Memorandum of Contentions of Fact and Law" in both the Central District (CD Cal Local R 9.6) and the Southern District (SD Cal Local R 235–4(d)(4)).

In the Southern District, a Statement of Comparable Transactions must be filed with the trial judge by each party no later than five days before the pretrial conference. SD Cal Local R 235–4(e)(4). A Statement as to Just Compensation must be served and filed by each party at least five days before trial. SD Cal Local R 235–4(e)(4).

The Southern and Central District Rules have been renumbered and revised as follows:

SOUTHERN DISTRICT RULES

Former	*Present*	*Comments*
9(d)	None	But see Fed R Civ P 16(b)(3)
9(e)	235–4(c)	
9(f)	235–4(d)	
9(f)(6)	235–4(d)(1)	
9(f)(7)	235–4(d)(2)	
9(f)(8)	235–4(d)(3)	
9(f)(9)	235–4(d)(4)	
9(f)(4)(a)	235–4(e)(4)	
9(f)(4)(b)	235–4(e)(4)	
9(j)	235–4(g)(2)	Order must be lodged no later than 5 p.m. five days before pretrial hearing

CENTRAL DISTRICT RULES

Former	Present	Comments
9(c)	9.4.8	Discovery to be completed at least 20 days before conference
9(d)	9.4, 9.4.4–9.4.6, 9.4.10, 9.5, 9.6, 9.7	
9(e)	9.5	Serve and file memorandum no later than 21 days before trial
9(e)(4)(A)–(B)	App B(g)	Now requires (1) valuation testimony, market data, and reproduction analysis detail or (2) an appraisal report
9(e)(6)	9.5.2	
9(e)(7)	9.5.6	
9(e)(8)	9.7	Requires all parties to jointly file a single document listing exhibits expected to be offered at trial for direct tesimony; filed at the same time as memorandums of contentions of fact and law
9(e)(9)	9.5.6, 9.6, App B(g)	
9(g)	9.8.1	Order must be lodged 7 days before pretrial conference

[§11.27] SOVEREIGN IMMUNITY

An action by a municipality to condemn property held in the name of the Secretary of Housing and Urban Development was barred by sovereign immunity. Although the National Housing Act (12 USC §§1701–1750g) permits the Secretary to sue and be sued, the defense of a condemnation action is not contemplated by the Act. *City of Sacramento v Secretary of HUD* (ED Cal 1972) 363 F Supp 736.

If certain constitutional violations occur, government officials may be sued in their individual capacities for damages under *Bivens v Six Unknown Federal Narcotics Agents* (1971) 403 US 388, 91 S Ct 1999, 29 L Ed 2d 61. In *Trotter, Inc. v Watkins* (9th Cir 1989) 869 F2d 1312, private defendants engaged in a federal action with the United States Navy in the joint preparation of an air installation compatible use zone plan for a naval station are not entitled to qualified immunity. The scope of immunity for private defendants in a *Bivens* claim is the same as in a 42 USC §1983 (civil rights) case.

[§11.28] Tucker Act

The Tucker Act (28 USC §§1346, 1491) waives the immunity of the United States to allow a property owner to petition for damages for violation of the fifth amendment's prohibition against a governmental taking of private property without prior compensation. The Act confers jurisdiction on the United States Claims Court (formerly the United States Court of Claims) and the district courts; the jurisdiction of the claims court is unlimited on amount, but that of the district court is limited to claims of no more than $10,000.

In either case, the condemnor is not entitled to a jury trial on the issue of just compensation. 28 USC §2402; US Ct Cl R 13, 14. See also *U.S. v 21.54 Acres of Land* (4th Cir 1973) 491 F2d 301.

The Tucker Act is only a jurisdictional statute; it does not create any substantive right against the federal government for money damages. Plaintiff must overcome sovereign immunity by showing that the government has specifically consented to be sued in the particular situation. *Vorhauer v U.S.* (ED Pa 1976) 426 F Supp 839, 843.

When a plaintiff who was denied reversion rights in a railroad right of way adjacent to its property under the National Trails System Act Amendments of 1983 (16 USC §§1241–1251) made a taking claim, the United States Supreme Court concluded that a taking claim is premature until the property owners use the process provided by the Tucker Act. Although the 1983 amendments did not mention the Tucker Act, there was no evidence of legislative intent to withdraw the Tucker Act grant of jurisdiction on such a claim. Thus, the holder of the reversionary interest has a recognized procedure for recovery of compensation. *Preseault v Interstate Commerce Comm'n* (Feb. 21, 1990) 110 S Ct 914, 108 L Ed 2d 1.

Federal regulatory enactments amounting to a taking may be valid as regulations and yet entitle an owner to recovery in inverse condemnation in the United States Claims Court. *Blanchette v Connecticut Gen. Ins. Corp.* (1974) 419 US 102. See Kanner, *Developments in Eminent Domain: A Candle in The Dark Corner of the Law,* 52 J Urb L 861 (1975).

[§11.29] State and Municipal Corporations

Under the 11th amendment, a state cannot be sued for damages or injunctive relief in federal court. See *Pennhurst State School & Hosp. v Halderman* (1984) 465 US 89. The main holding in *Pennhurst* was that the 11th amendment bars federal court jurisdiction of injunctive suits seeking to order state officials to conform their conduct to state law. However, *Pennhurst* also recognized the exception established by *Ex parte Young* (1908) 209 US 123, that federal courts may enjoin a state official from enforcing an unconstitutional state statute. See also *Hoohuli v Ariyoshi* (9th Cir 1984) 741 F2d 1169. The *Young* exception is only applicable, however, when prospective injunctive relief is sought. *Edelman v Jordan* (1974) 415 US 651.

In *Beck v State* (CD Cal 1979) 479 F Supp 392, the court held that the 11th amendment extended to state agencies sued under 42 USC §1983. Because the state had not consented to be sued, the court dismissed the action. See also *Clallum County v Department of Transp.* (9th Cir 1988) 849 F2d 424.

In *Doe by Gonzales v Maher* (9th Cir 1986) 793 F2d 1470, aff'd in *Honig v Doe* (1988) 404 US 305, 108 S Ct 592, 98 L Ed 2d 686, the court applied *Atascadero State Hosp. v Scanlon* (1985) 473 US 234 in concluding that California had not waived its 11th amendment immunity by participating in a federally funded and regulated special education program for handicapped children.

The 11th amendment barred a suit against the Governor of Hawaii, based on allegations that the state purchased property subject to the plaintiff's option under threat of condemnation. The court ruled that the action against the Governor was really intended to recover damages from the state treasury rather than from the Governor. *Windward Partners v Ariyoshi* (9th Cir 1982) 693 F2d 928.

In *Lake Country Estates, Inc. v Tahoe Regional Planning Agency* (1979) 440 US 391, the Supreme Court noted that a state's political subdivisions, such as counties and municipalities, are not afforded immunity under the 11th amendment from federal suit and concluded that the bi-state Tahoe Regional Planning Agency (TRPA) was not entitled to immunity either. The court held that the federal courts had jurisdiction over petitioner's inverse condemnation action under the Civil Rights Act (42 USC §1983, 28 USC §1343), which provides a remedy for individuals deprived of rights under color of state law. However, the court in *Tahoe-Sierra*

Preservation Council, Inc. v Tahoe Regional Planning Agency (D Nev 1985) 611 F Supp 110, held that the states of California and Nevada did not waive their 11th amendment immunity by forming the TRPA and by enacting TRPA's provisions for litigation.

Federal Rules of Civil Procedure 71A(k) provides that its practice governs actions concerning the exercise of the power to condemn under the law of a state, "provided that if the state law makes provision for trial of any issue by jury . . . that provision shall be followed." In California, all issues but compensation must be tried by the court. *People v Ricciardi* (1943) 23 C2d 390, 144 P2d 799. However, Rule 71A(k) relates only to direct condemnation actions. Therefore, the question arises whether a landowner's election to sue under the federal Constitution instead of Cal Const art I, §19 waives the benefit of the latter's guaranty of the right to a jury. In *U.S. v Reynolds* (1970) 397 US 14, 18, the court declared that the seventh amendment does not grant the right to a jury trial in federal courts for condemnation proceedings. See also *Georgia Power Co. v 138.30 Acres of Land* (5th Cir 1979) 596 F2d 644, 647. To attempt to gain a jury trial, plaintiff should allege that the taking violates the constitutional guaranties of both the United States and California.

[§11.30] Abstention

The federal courts may abstain in cases in which state action is challenged in federal court as contrary to the federal Constitution if there are unsettled questions of state law that may dispose of the controversy without reaching federal constitutional issues. See Wright, Miller & Cooper, Federal Practice and Procedure, *Relation of State and Federal Courts* §4242 (1978).

Inverse condemnation, *i.e.,* the taking of private property for a public use without the prior payment of just compensation, can present substantially the same constitutional question at both federal and state levels. When the federal and state constitutional provisions are similar, abstention is inappropriate. *Donohoe Constr. Co. v Maryland-National Capital Park & Planning Comm'n* (D Md 1975) 398 F Supp 21; *M.J. Brock & Sons v City of Davis* (ND Cal 1975) 401 F Supp 354.

In land use cases challenging state law on both state and federal grounds, a federal court should abstain from deciding the merits of state law claims. In *Kollsman v City of Los Angeles* (9th Cir 1984) 737 F2d 830, the Ninth Circuit held that the federal district court should have abstained from deciding a developer's action challenging the refusal of the City of Los Angeles to accept and process a subdivision application.

In *Richardson v Koshiba* (9th Cir 1982) 693 F2d 911, 915, the court delineated three criteria for applying the abstention doctrine enunciated in *Railroad Comm'n v Pullman Co.* (1941) 312 US 496: (1) The complaint must touch a sensitive area of social policy into which the federal courts should not enter unless there is no alternative to adjudication; (2) a definitive ruling on the state issues by a state court could obviate the need for constitutional adjudication by federal court; and (3) the proper resolution of the potentially determinative state law issue is uncertain.

See generally Harris, *Application of the Abstention Doctrine to Inverse Condemnation Actions in Federal Court,* Pepperdine L Rev 1 (1977).

12

Income Taxation Consequences of Condemnation Awards

Note: Legislative Changes

The Tax Reform Act of 1976 (Pub L 94–455, 90 Stat 1525) included changes that affect the entire discussion of the federal income tax consequences of condemnation awards in this chapter. The most significant changes were the amendments to IRC §§1033 and 1231. These amendments are outlined briefly below; no attempt has been made to relate the amendments to each section of this chapter.

Section 1231 was amended by changing the holding period of property used in a trade or business and capital assets to which the section applies from six months to nine months for taxable years beginning in 1977, and to one year for taxable years beginning after December 31, 1977. This period was reduced by the Tax Reform Act of 1984 (see below) to six months for assets acquired after June 22, 1984, and before January 1, 1988. It appears that condemned property had to be acquired after June 22, 1984, to qualify for the shorter holding period. See also IRC §1223(1)(A). Effective January 1, 1988, the holding period to obtain long term capital gain or loss treatment on the disposition of a capital or §1231 asset is one year. See IRC §1222(3).

Section 1033(a)(2) was deleted, and §1033(a)(3) was redesignated as §1033(a)(2).

Section 1033(b) was deleted and subsections (c) through (h) were redesignated as subsections (b) through (g).

A new subparagraph (E) was added to §1033(a)(2), which defines the terms "control" and "disposition of the converted property" for purposes of §1033(a)(2).

A new paragraph (3) was added to §1033(f), providing for an election to treat outdoor advertising displays as real property for purposes of subsection (f). Since then, IRC §§1033(f), (g) were redesignated §§1033(g), (h) by the Revenue Act of 1978 (Pub L 95–600, 92 Stat 2763), and a new §1033(f) was enacted.

The Foreign Investment in Real Property Tax Act (Pub L 96–499, 94 Stat 2682 (FIRPTA)) imposes United States income tax on sales of United States real property by nonresident aliens. FIRPTA denies application of the nonrecognition provisions of the Internal Revenue Code when the tax could be avoided. See IRC §897(e). Apparently, this statutory rule prevents a nonresident alien from benefiting from the IRC §1033 nonrecognition provisions unless he reinvests the condemnation proceeds in United States real property. See IRS Letter Ruling 8128010. (In a situation before enactment of IRC §897, the IRS allowed a nonresident alien to reinvest proceeds from the condemnation of United States real property in real property located outside the United States.)

There seems to be no direct authority for the position of the California Franchise Tax Board on whether a taxpayer whose land is condemned in California could avoid California tax on the condemnation proceeds if the replacement property is in some other state. In a legal ruling in a somewhat similar area, the Franchise Tax Board stated that it would not impose a California income tax when a resident sold a home in California and purchased a new residence outside California. Legal Ruling 329 (July 25, 1968), CCH California Tax Reports ¶16–557.40.

Two major pieces of tax legislation were enacted in 1981 and 1982: The Economic Recovery Tax Act of 1981 (Pub L 97–34, 95 Stat 172 (ERTA)) and the Tax Equity and Fiscal Responsibility Act of 1982 (Pub L 97–248, 96 Stat 320 (TEFRA)). This legislation does not affect IRC §1033. TEFRA amended IRC §165, adding another restriction on the deductibility of a casualty loss: aggregate nonbusiness casualty losses are deductible only to the extent they exceed 10 percent of adjusted gross income. IRC §165(h). For disaster losses, the facts at the time of the loss, and not in the year the deduction is claimed, control. IRC §165(i).

Another piece of major federal tax legislation was the Tax Reform Act of 1984 (Pub L 98–369, 98 Stat 494, 1210). Relevant provisions are discussed throughout the chapter.

Under the Tax Reform Act of 1984, IRC §1031 was amended to limit when a nonsimultaneous exchange will be treated as a tax-exempt exchange. The replacement property must be identified as property to be received in the exchange within 45 days after the date the taxpayer transfers his property, and the taxpayer must receive the exchange property the earlier of (1) 180 days after the date of the taxpayer's transfer of his property or (2) the due date, determined with regard to extension, for the taxpayer's return for that taxable year in which the taxpayer transferred his property. This provision is in direct response to *Starker v U.S.* (9th Cir 1979) 602 F2d 1341.

Any transfer of property to a public entity on the installment basis (a very rare occurrence) must also consider the provisions relating to the imputation of interest, adjustment of basis, and the recognition of income. The Tax Reform Act of 1984 imposed the original issue discount rules when debt instruments were issued for property. See IRC §§1271–1275. In essence, the statute requires that any deferred payment obligation provide for a statutorily determined rate of interest that is deductible or includable in income as mandated by the statute. Public Law 98–612, §2, 98 Stat 3180 (1984), amended those provisions of the Tax Reform Act of 1984 relating to imputed interest and original issue discount. The Internal Revenue Service determines the imputed interest rate monthly and publishes it in the Internal Revenue Bulletin. See, *e.g.,* Rev Rul 89–65, 1989–20 Int Rev Bull 4.

The Tax Reform Act of 1984 also added IRC §1445, which requires that the buyer of any United States real property interest, as defined in IRC §897(c), from a foreign person must withhold a tax equal to 10 percent of the amount realized on any transfer on or after January 1, 1985. Several exceptions are provided by the statute.

Major federal tax legislation now includes the Tax Reform Act of 1986 (Pub L 99–514, 100 Stat 2085) (TRA 86), which was enacted on October 22, 1986. TRA 86 made numerous changes to existing condemnation law, important aspects of which are summarized below:

1. Renames the Internal Revenue Code of 1954 the Internal Revenue Code of 1986, even though most of the provisions are not effective until tax years beginning in 1987. TRA 86 §2. Therefore, all references to the Internal Revenue Code of 1954 are now references to the Internal Revenue Code of 1986.

2. Reduces maximum tax rates for both corporations and individuals effective in 1988 with transitional rules applicable for the year 1987. In 1988 the maximum corporate tax rate (34 percent) will be higher than the maximum individual rate (28 percent). See amended IRC §§1, 11.

3. Repeals the 60 percent long term capital gain deduction (IRC §1202), causing the tax rate that applies to gain from the sale or exchange of capital assets and IRC §1231 assets to be the same rate that applies to all income. There were transitional rules for 1987.

4. Extends the application of the "at risk" rules to real property losses to the extent the real property is subject to nonrecourse debt in favor of qualified lenders, *i.e.,* sellers. Thus, certain real estate losses will be limited to the amount at risk. See amended IRC §465.

5. Amends IRC §§336 and 337 to disallow avoidance of the recognition of gain or loss on certain sales and exchanges made in connection with or on the liquidation of a corporation. Under the 1986 Act, gain or loss will be recognized at the corporate level if there is a corporate liquidation, except for property distributed in a complete liquidation of a subsidiary. See amended IRC §§332, 337.

6. Extends the useful life of real property for depreciation purposes

to 27.5 years for residential real property and 31.5 years for nonresidential real property. See amended IRC §168(c).

7. Denies deductions for "tax shelter" losses against other income in determining income subject to tax. The new law announces the concept of "passive activity" as a separate activity for determining gains and losses. Real estate rental, *e.g.*, is considered to be a passive activity, but there is a limited offset of nonpassive income with losses and credits for "active participation" in the rental. Disallowed losses may be used as a deduction against income when there is a disposition of the taxpayer's entire interest in the property. See IRC §469.

8. Phases out deduction for personal interest, except for "qualified residence interest." IRC §163(h).

Although many changes were made by the 1986 Act, the primary provisions dealing with condemnation and involuntary conversion were not changed. More particularly, no changes of substance were made to IRC §§1031, 1033, 1231, and 165.

The Revenue Act of 1987 (Pub L 100–203, 101 Stat 1330) was enacted on December 22, 1987. This Act again changed the provisions of IRC §163(h) relating to the deduction of personal interest.

The Revenue Act of 1987 repealed IRC §453C. Further, concomitant with the repeal was the enactment of the rule that dealers in real property cannot elect to report gain from the disposition of the property under the installment method. See IRC §453(b)(2).

The Technical and Miscellaneous Revenue Act of 1988 (Pub L 100–647, 102 Stat 3342) made technical corrections to the Tax Reform Act of 1986 as well as to prior acts. It did not include a provision relating to IRC §1031 exchanges, but it did enact a taxpayer's bill of rights. CAVEAT: Many Revenue and Taxation Code sections cited in Book chap 12 have been renumbered as shown in Supp Appendix C.

The California Personal Income Tax was heavily amended and renumbered by Stats 1983, ch 488. Those provisions that conform to federal law now specifically incorporate the applicable Internal Revenue Code sections. The State of California advanced further toward conformity with the Internal Revenue Code by the enactment of the California Personal Income Tax Fairness, Simplification and Conformity Act of 1987 (Stats 1987, ch 1138) and the California Bank and Corporation Tax Fairness, Simplification and Conformity Act of 1987 (Stats 1987, ch 1139). Through these acts, California adopted the federal Tax Reform Act of 1986 and presumably the Revenue Act of 1987, except as otherwise provided. Technical amendments intended to clarify and correct issues relating to the 1987 enactments relating to tax conformity are set forth in Stats 1988, ch 11, which was signed on February 18, 1988.

Section 122 of the California Personal Income Tax Fairness, Simplification and Conformity Act of 1987 specifically provides that Rev & T C §18037 is not in conformity with IRC §1033(g)(3)(A) in that for California purposes a taxpayer can take advantage of IRC §1033 even though he claimed an investment credit or elected to expense the asset on the taxpayer's federal return. Otherwise, it appears that the State of California provisions in the Revenue and Taxation Code follow the provisions of the Internal Revenue Code.

A proper tax election filed in accordance with the provisions of the Internal Revenue Code must be considered a proper election under the Revenue and Taxation Code unless regulations of the Franchise Tax Board provide otherwise. Rev & T C §17024.5(d)(1).

INTRODUCTION

[§12.1] Importance of Early Study of Tax Consequences

Internal Revenue Code §56(c), added by the Tax Reform Act of 1986 (Pub L 99–514, 100 Stat 2085) (TRA 86) provides that a book income adjustment should be taken into account in determining the alternative minimum taxable income for a corporation. More specifically, IRC §56(f) states that alternative minimum taxable income of any corporation must be increased by 50 percent of the amount the adjusted net book income of the corporation exceeds alternative minimum taxable income for the taxable year. The important phrase is "adjusted net income," which means the net income or loss of a taxpayer as set forth in the taxpayer's applicable financial statement. Presumably, a corporation would financially account for a condemnation as a sale and the reinvestment as a purchase while treating it as a nontaxable event for federal income tax purposes. Thus, it appears possible that the amount of unrecognized gain for federal income tax purposes would constitute an adjustment in determining alternative minimum taxable income for a corporation.

In addition to the sources mentioned in Book §12.1, additional information on the tax aspects of condemnations and IRC §1033 is available from the following sources:

(1) Robinson, Gerald J. Federal Income Taxation of Real Estate, chap 13. 5th ed. Boston: Warren, Gorham & Lamont, 1988.

(2) Douglas, James A., Benton, Donald S., & Haley, Robert E. Real Estate Tax Digest. Boston: Warren, Gorham & Lamont, 1984. Supplemented semi-annually. Contains digests of recent cases, revenue rulings, and private letter rulings.

(3) Bureau of National Affairs, Inc. Tax Management Portfolio. Involuntary Conversions, vol 33–7th. Washington, D.C.: Tax Management, Inc., 1987.

(4) Research Institute of America. Federal Tax Coordinator 2d. 26 vols, looseleaf. New York: Research Institute of America, 1955–1988. Discusses condemnation in vol 13 beginning at ¶I–3000.

(5) Both Commerce Clearing House and Prentice-Hall looseleaf tax services discuss IRC §1033 in accordance with each publication's organiza-

tion based on code section. These tax publications are supplemented week-ly and revised annually.

(6) The Internal Revenue Service publishes pamphlets on the subjects of depreciation (Depreciation, Pub. No. 534, 11–88), condemnation (Con-demnation in Business Casualties and Thefts, Pub. No. 549, 11–88), and casualty and disaster losses (Non-Business Disasters, Casualties and Thefts, Pub. No. 547, 11–88). Washington, D.C.: U.S. Printing Office. Its publica-tions are available at no cost and are updated as the Internal Revenue Service determines.

(7) Mertens, Jacob, Jr., Mertens Law of Federal Income Taxation. 18 vols, looseleaf. Chicago, Ill.: Callaghan & Co., 1942–1990. See vol 3, chap 20A, for analysis of IRC §1033.

On California tax aspects of condemnation, see:

(8) Peterson, Plant & Eager, California Taxation. San Francisco: Mat-thew Bender & Co., 1983.

(9) Commerce Clearing House. State Tax Reporter, California. 4 vols, looseleaf. Chicago: Commerce Clearing House, Inc. See ¶16.554 on in-come tax aspects and ¶21.123 on property tax aspects.

(10) Prentice-Hall. California State and Local Tax Service. 4 vols, loose-leaf. Paramus, N.J.: Prentice-Hall, Inc. See ¶55,400 on recognition of gain or loss on an involuntary conversion and ¶55,449 on basis.

It appears that the Internal Revenue Service will provide written rulings on issues relating to the application of IRC §1033 to any particular transaction. Among other rulings, the IRS will rule on whether (1) there is a threat or imminence of condemnation, (2) the party reinvesting the proceeds can take advantage of IRC §1033, and (3) the property is of like-kind or similar in service or use. Rulings will be issued on a completed transaction basis as well as a proposed transaction basis if the completed transaction is subject to question by the IRS. The Service is now authorized to charge a fee in connection with applications for ruling requests. Procedural rules for obtaining a ruling from the IRS are set forth in Reg §601.201 as well as Rev Proc 89–1, 1989–1 Int Rev Bull 8, and Rev Proc 89–2, 1989–1 Int Rev Bull 21. The provision for fees is set forth in Rev Proc 89–4, 1989–3 Int Rev Bull 18. Further, previously issued private letter rulings are available from commercial publishers, e.g., Commerce Clearing House, as well as direct-ly from the Internal Revenue Service. See IRC §6110. It should be noted that the taxpayer can rely unequivocally on a published revenue ruling but not on a private letter ruling unless the taxpayer is the recipient of that ruling.

[§12.2] Taking Is a Sale

Legal, accounting, and other fees incurred by the owner in a condem-nation action are normally not deductible. These fees are treated as capital expenditures and thus as a reduction of the sales price. See *Madden v Commissioner* (9th Cir 1975) 514 F2d 1149 (legal fees incurred in unsuccessful defense of condemnation action treated as reduction in sales price). There are indications that the Franchise Tax Board is following this case rather than *Charlie Sturgill Motor Co.,* TC Memo 1973–281, in which the Tax Court allowed fees incurred in an unsuccessful defense of a condemnation action to be deducted as a business expense. *Sturgill* relied on the Tax Court's earlier decision in *Madden,* which was later reversed by the Ninth Circuit. However, in *James Mosby* (1986) 86 TC 190, the Tax Court followed *Madden* in holding that legal fees incurred with prosecuting an inverse condemnation suit against the United States are not deductible but are properly added to basis of the property under IRC §263. The Tax Court rejected the "primary purpose test" and held that the "origin of claim test" is the appropriate test to determine deductibility of legal fees in both direct and inverse condemnations; in *James Mosby* the origin of the claim was the disposition of a capital asset (taking of mineral rights). Although the Tax Court did not discuss whether only successful litigants would be allowed to capitalize legal fees in a condemnation case, Mosby had been a successful litigant in his claim for inverse condemnation. Thus, legal fees incurred in connection with successful defense of a condemnation would also appear to be a proper addition to the basis of the property sought to be condemned.

Government Code §7363 now provides for the reimbursement of increased loan interest incurred in acquiring replacement property on being compelled to sell the family residence. The portion of the award constituting the additional interest is probably taxable interest. The taxpayer would deduct his increased interest cost under IRC §163, unless he chooses not to itemize his deductions.

Because of the repeal of IRC §1202 by the Tax Reform Act of 1986 (Pub L 99–514, 100 Stat 2085), the effective tax rate applied on gain from the disposition of IRC §1231 property for taxable years after 1986 (except for 1987, to which transitional rules apply) is the same as the gain from the sale of any other kind of property. See IRC §§1, 11, 1201. However, it is still important to maintain the IRC §1231 property distinction when determining losses because a §1231 loss still retains its character as an ordinary loss and is therefore not subject to the limitations on capital losses under IRC §1211.

In *Wood v U.S.* (DC La 1988) 1988–2 USTC ¶9399, 62 AFTR2d ¶5174, property forfeited because of use in violation of the Internal Revenue Code was deemed to be not involuntarily converted. However, the court did not address the issue of whether the forfeiture constituted a sale, because the property forfeited was cash. If the Internal Revenue Service seized real property used in violation of the Internal Revenue laws it might argue that gain resulted, *i.e.,* the fair market value of the property was more than the property's basis. The IRS might be able to collect a tax on the gain caused by the seizure. The court in *Wood* did state that there is no offsetting expense or loss because of the forfeiture. Although it is a loss, the loss will not be allowed, because there is a defined national policy against the very acts that result in the forfeiture.

CONDEMNATION GAIN RECOGNIZED; NO REPLACEMENT PROPERTY ACQUIRED

[§12.3] Normal Rules

It is now undisputed that a notice or a threat of condemnation is a neutral factor in determining the character of property for income tax purposes. See *William B. Daugherty* (1982) 78 TC 623.

A property owner may take depreciation on his improvements and reduce their useful life to reflect total obsolescence by the expected date of condemnation or of sale under threat of condemnation. Whether the depreciation taken or the property's estimated useful life was proper is a question of fact based on the property's value at the time of sale or condemnation. To avoid recapture of depreciation, the sale price or condemnation award must be limited exclusively to the value of the land, and the improvements must lack any salvage value whatsoever. *Edward F. Brylawski,* TC Memo 1983–622. The property owner in *Brylawski* learned that his land and improvements were going to be condemned and that he could either submit his own plan for redevelopment, sell his property to an approved private developer, or await condemnation by the public agency. As a result, the owner reduced the improvements' useful life and increased his depreciation deductions. After five years, he sold the property to an approved developer for the land's value alone. Because the improvements, slated for demolition, had virtually no value, the court allowed the deductions.

Repeal of IRC §1202 by the Tax Reform Act of 1986 (Pub L 99–514, 100 Stat 2085) has eliminated the distinction between capital gain income (IRC §1231 gain) and ordinary income because under the Act the effective tax rate for taxable years after 1986 (except for 1987, to which transitional rules apply) will be the same for all types of income. See IRC §§1, 11, 1201. The rules relating to the deduction of losses, however, still require identification of the nature of the loss.

[§12.4] IRC §1231 Rules

Because IRC §1202 was repealed by the Tax Reform Act of 1986 (Pub L 99–514, 100 Stat 2085), the effective tax rate applied on gain from the disposition of IRC §1231 property for taxable years after 1986 (except for 1987, to which transitional rules apply) is the same as the gain from the sale of any other kind of property. See IRC §§1, 11, 1201.

However, it is still important to maintain the IRC §1231 property distinction when determining losses.

Internal Revenue Code §1231 was amended to provide that an asset for the purpose of this section must be either of the following: "property used in the trade or business, or any capital asset which is held for more than six months and is held in connection with a trade or business or a transaction entered into for profit." Accordingly, capital assets not used in a trade or business or in a transaction entered into for profit will fail to qualify for IRC §1231 treatment. Thus, personal assets can never benefit from IRC §1231, but are now covered by IRC §165.

Previously, any capital asset that was held longer than the required time was an IRC §1231 asset. Now, the section provides for the recapture of previously deducted losses under IRC §1231 if the losses occurred after December 31, 1981. Under IRC §1231(c), a taxpayer is required to recapture as ordinary income that portion of an IRC §1231 gain that is less than his nonrecaptured §1231 losses for the previous five years. The five-year period begins January 1, 1982. For example, if a taxpayer has a net §1231 gain of $50,000 in 1985 and has accumulated net §1231 losses of $40,000 for the years starting January 1, 1982, the taxpayer is required to report as ordinary income the sum of $40,000 as recaptured §1231 losses. The balance, $10,000, is treated as §1231 gain, *i.e.,* long term capital gain. The effect of this provision is that gain under IRC §1231 is converted from capital gain to ordinary income to the extent of these previously deducted losses. A condemnation seller must take this new provision into consideration in determining whether he will proceed under IRC §1033 or recognize gain and reinvest the proceeds in a taxable transaction.

Internal Revenue Code §165(k) has been amended to allow a taxpayer a disaster loss when he is ordered to demolish or relocate his personal residence in a disaster area because of the disaster. This provision applies to taxable years ending after December 31, 1981. Thus, a taxpayer might be entitled to a refund for a loss under IRC §165(k) occurring in a previous year.

A change in ownership occurs for property tax purposes on condemnation and reinvestment of the proceeds if the transaction qualifies as a transfer under Rev & T C §60.

CONDEMNATION GAIN DEFERRED; QUALIFIED REPLACEMENT PROPERTY ACQUIRED

Tax-Free Replacement Under IRC §1033

[§12.5] Basic Operation

In *Estate of Benjamin F. Seltzer,* TC Memo 1987–568, the Tax Court held that that portion of a condemnation award attributable to the delay by the condemning authorities in making prompt payment constituted interest that was taxable as ordinary income. The interest could not be reinvested under IRC §1033. The court stated that the additional compensation was for delay in payment rather than the increase in value of the property occurring between the time of condemnation and the time of payment.

The basis of the replacement property is its cost (cash paid plus liabilities assumed or taken subject to) less the amount of the gain not taxed on the condemnation sale of the prior property. IRC §1033(b); Rev & T C §18031 (replacing former Rev & T C §18088). On the computation of basis when amounts have been received for severance damages, see Rev Rul 83–49, 1983–1 Cum Bull 191.

In Rev Rul 88–103, 1988–2 Cum Bull 304, the issue is whether property purchased by a taxpayer's grantor revocable trust would qualify as replacement property acquired by the taxpayer whose property had been involuntarily converted. The Internal Revenue Service held that the purchase by a taxpayer's grantor trust is equivalent to a purchase by the taxpayer, with the result that IRC §1033 can shield the gain. This ruling is consistent with Rev Rul 70–376, 1970–2 Cum Bull 164, which stated that it was the taxpayer and not the trustee who is eligible to elect deferred gain under §1033. The individual is the taxpayer through the entire analysis.

In IRS Letter Ruling 8810054, the Internal Revenue Service stated that the acquisition of replacement property under IRC §1033 must occur after the condemnation or other act of involuntary conversion. Here, the taxpayer purchased like-kind property in anticipation of the eminent domain proceedings. He then sold the original property under eminent domain. It was held that the acquisition of the replacement property before the condemnation was premature and that §1033 did not apply.

The citation to IRC §1033(c), in Book §12.5, should be to IRC §1033(b). See Note at the beginning of this supplement chapter.

See the discussion of IRC §1033 and involuntary conversions in Taxation of Real Property Transfers §§3.129–3.154 (Cal CEB 1981).

[§12.6] Depreciation Recapture

Internal Revenue Code §1245(b)(4) provides for the recapture of depreciation for involuntarily converted IRC §1245 property defined in IRC §1245(a)(3), to the extent that replacement property does not consist of IRC §1245 property.

A condemnation may also result in recapture of investment credits. IRC §§46(a)(2)(A), 48(a)(1)(E). Counsel should note that the Tax Reform Act of 1986 (Pub L 99–514, 100 Stat 2085) repealed the regular investment tax credit for property placed into service after December 31, 1985. See new IRC §49(a).

[§12.10] Holding Period of Replacement Property

As stated in Book §12.10, the holding period of the condemned property is tacked onto the holding period of the replacement property (except in the case of failure to replace recapture property). IRC §1223(1).

[§12.12] Involuntary Exchange of Property for Property

The holding period of the replacement property would include that of the condemned property. IRC §1223(1); Rev & T C §18151.

Involuntary Conversions Qualifying for Tax-Free Replacement Treatment

[§12.13] Introduction

In *Eugene H. Koziara* (1986) 86 TC 999, the Tax Court held that a unitization order issued under state law did not qualify as an involuntary conversion of the taxpayer's property. As a result, the royalty payments received in this respect are not entitled to capital gain treatment under IRC §1231. In so holding, the Tax Court relied on the case of *Dorothy C. Thorpe Glass Mfg. Corp.* (1968) 51 TC 300, an IRC §1033 case cited in Book §12.13.

Chemical contamination was held to constitute an involuntary conversion in Rev Rul 89–2, 1989–1 Cum Bull 259.

Moreover, the sale of the contaminated property to a governmental authority to protect public health may constitute a sale under threat of condemnation. The taxpayer must establish that the proceeds represent compensation for the taking of the property by the government, not compensation for the destruction caused by the contamination. In this ruling, the purchasing city passed an ordinance authorizing eminent domain proceedings of the contaminated property. The amount paid by the city was based on an appraised value of the property that did not take into account the diminution of value caused by the chemical contamination. Accordingly, it would appear that only the fair market value, after giving consideration to the contamination, would qualify as proceeds taken under the threat of condemnation.

An involuntary conversion occurred when the city contaminated the taxpayer's property with toxic street-cleaning chemicals. See IRS Letter Ruling 8524023.

"Condemnation" does not include every act of a governmental body having eminent domain authority. If a municipality requires a developer of a subdivision to "contribute" a park or a school site to get subdivision map approval, the dedication of the site to public purposes is not a condemnation for purposes of IRC §1033. Rev Rul 69–654, 1969–2 Cum Bull 162.

Similarly, if a municipal authority closes down a restaurant for unsanitary conditions, or an apartment house because of fire hazards, the action taken by the municipality is not a condemnation within the meaning of IRC §1033.

A more significant question is whether the dedication qualifies as a charitable deduction contribution under IRC §170. It appears that qualification depends on the determination that the motive for the dedication was altruistic or to gain goodwill, rather than a matter of direct economic benefit. Whether there is donative intent depends on several factors. Economic benefit to the donor will not defeat donative intent if the donation benefits the community and the property owner merely benefits as a member of the community. In *Citizens & S. Nat'l Bank v U.S.* (WD SC 1965) 243 F Supp 900, a bank donated property for a road. The road was desired by many members of the community and the fact that the bank would be particularly benefited was held not to defeat donative intent.

If a local ordinance requires dedication of a portion of the taxpayer's property as a condition to developing the remainder of the property, donation of the required portion in anticipation of his developing the part he retains results in direct economic benefit; thus, the taxpayer lacks donative intent. *Larry G. Sutton* (1971) 57 TC 239. In *Sutton,* the property owner wished to build on his property. He was aware that a local ordinance would require dedication of land for road widening before he could build. He donated the land for widening the road and ten months later began the project. The court held that he did not have a donative intent because his reason for donating was to permit the building. But in *Collman v Commissioner* (9th Cir 1975) 511 F2d 1263, the deduction was allowed under somewhat similar circumstances because the court found no evidence that, at the time of the deduction, he was aware of the ordinance requiring the deduction or that he intended to develop at that time. The court was strongly influenced by the fact of a 17-month delay between the dedication and first steps toward development, and that other steps were still necessary before the land could be developed (annexation and dedication of more land for streets and sidewalks). On the other hand, the donation was conditioned on the county's performing certain additional street work. The value of this work was held to be consideration to the property owner and its value was deducted.

In Rev Rul 73–339, 1973–2 Cum Bull 68, the IRS ruled that a farmer who gave the government a prescriptive easement preventing development but permitting farming could take a charitable deduction for the difference between the value of the property before and after granting the prescriptive easement. The ruling states ambiguously that the government "secured" the easement to preserve open space. It further indicates that the taxpayer had no reasonable expectation of economic gain as a result of the transfer, as distinguished from *Larry G. Sutton, supra.* However, the ruling does not clearly cover a charitable deduction claimed for dedicating a prescriptive easement in response to a threat of downzoning.

See also *John L. Connell,* TC Memo 1986–333 (dedication of right-of-way qualified for charitable contribution deduction when increase in value of remainder tract resulted from alignment of right-of-way and change in zoning by county).

In *Billy J. Gaines,* TC Memo 1982–731, the court disallowed the taxpayer's claimed loss deduction when the taxpayer constructed a road and dedicated it to the county in return for a rezoning of certain land for apartment use. The court found that no involuntary conversion occurred and implied that no charitable deduction could be allowed because the construction and dedication were capital expenses relating to the apartment building's construction. See also *Richard H. Foster* (1983) 80 TC 34, aff'd and vacated on other grounds (9th Cir 1985) 756 F2d 1430 (bargain sale to church did not entitle seller to a charitable deduction when seller obtained economic benefit for private land development).

Whether a taxpayer holding land subject to condemnation should attempt to dedicate it and claim a charitable deduction depends on individual circumstances, including the value of the tax deduction to the owner versus the expected net proceeds from condemnation, the importance of avoiding condemnation proceedings, the need for an immediate decision on the fate of the property, the desirability and likelihood of a successful defense to the condemnation, and the possibility of a dispute with the IRS over the deduction.

From a public policy view it should be noted that, although avoiding the expense of condemnation proceedings is beneficial to the government, dedication has the effect in nonfederal cases of switching the cost of the acquisition from local to federal government.

In Rev Rul 76–376, 1976–2 Cum Bull 53, the IRS ruled that the value of a *voluntary* charitable easement was measured by the "before-and-after" test, *i.e.,* by comparing the fair market value before granting of the easement (in this case an open-air easement in perpetuity) with the value of the land after granting of the easement.

Claiming a charitable deduction in response to downzoning is similar to filing an inverse condemnation action. If either is successful, the property owner receives compensation based on diminution of market value. But inverse condemnation actions are seldom successful in this context. It should also be noted that, if a property owner unsuccessfully contests downzoning of his property, the charitable deduction will probably not be available. Once downzoning occurs, it would appear that the property owner cannot donate an easement of equivalent effect.

If downzoning seems inevitable, the property owner may be well advised to claim the charitable deduction, as this may be the only means of obtaining a tax benefit. (The only alternative would be to sell and claim the capital loss, but sale may be impractical or incur too much tax if the owner has a low basis in the property.) The charitable deduction is based on reduction in current market value rather than basis. Therefore the major factors to consider in deciding whether to take the deduction or fight the downzoning are the likelihood of defeating the downzoning attempt, the difference between basis and the current market value of the property, the loss in potential future profits if the property is downzoned or an easement is granted, and the willingness of the property owner to sell.

Occasionally, an inverse condemnation action may be an available alternative. See Supp §13.2.

Internal Revenue Code §170(e) provides special rules for charitable contributions of certain ordinary income and capital gain property. A gift of a portion of real property may require a basis allocation. See IRC §170(e)(2).

In *Drey v U.S.* (ED Mo 1982) 535 F Supp 287, aff'd (8th Cir 1983) 705 F2d 965, the taxpayer owned real property located on a river. He granted the United States a scenic easement to the riverside property and he granted his remaining interest in the property to a private foundation. As a result of these gifts, contiguous real property was denied access to the river. The issue was the fair market value of the gift to the private foundation. The IRS argued that the charitable deduction is limited to the fair market value of the property given. The taxpayer argued that the decrease in value to the contiguous property resulting from denial of access to the river must be valued and considered part of the charitable contribution. The taxpayer contended that fair market value must take into consideration severance damages that would arise if the property were condemned, *i.e.*, that fair market value is what the condemning authority would pay. In finding for the IRS, the district court noted that Rev Rul 76–376, 1976–2 Cum Bull 53, states the position of the IRS but did not control the decision. The court noted that the Tax Court in *Benjamin Klopp,* TC Memo 1960–185, held that the fair market value of real property included severance damages when the gift was made under threat of condemnation. The district court implied that a different valuation rule applies if the property is voluntarily transferred to a condemning authority rather than transferred under threat of condemnation.

A homeowner's inability to use his or her house because of a physical disability does not constitute a condemnation within the meaning of IRC §1033. IRS Letter Ruling 8851021.

In certain instances, a sale may occur at the taxpayer's own election without the taxpayer's receiving any consideration, either from a buyer or from an insurance company. In IRS Letter Ruling 8544001, the IRS ruled that damage to standing timber by southern pine beetles, their larvae, and other wood-destroying insects constitutes sufficient destruction to qualify as an involuntary conversion under §1033. Therefore, in that situation gain from the election and constructive sale under IRC §631(a) could be deferred by investing an amount equal to that gain in additional timber.

See §12.5. However, the IRS specifically held that the destruction by the insects did not cause a casualty loss under IRC §165.

In Rev Rul 86–12, 1986–1 Cum Bull 290, the Internal Revenue Service ruled that it will consider the underwriting and actuarial data and any other information used in writing insurance to determine whether the insurance is designed to reimburse for a loss of profits and fixed charges. Thus, written terms of a contract described as a "use and occupancy" are not the sole basis for determining whether the proceeds from an insurance contract may constitute proceeds from an involuntary conversion of property that may be reinvested in like-kind property under IRC §1033 without the recognition of gain. If the amounts received under the insurance policy are for lost profits, the proceeds are taxable as ordinary income.

[§12.13A] Period To Replace

The period within which condemned real estate must be replaced to qualify for nonrecognition of gain under IRC §1033 is three years for property held for investment or for productive use in a trade or business (IRC §1033(g)(4)) and two years for other property (IRC §1033(a)(2)(B)(i)).

[§12.14] Sale Under Threat or Imminence of Condemnation

In *815 Riverside Co.*, TC Memo 1987–524, the Tax Court addressed the question of fact whether the sale was under the threat or imminence of condemnation when the taxpayer was willing to sell and the condemning authority never threatened condemnation in its negotiations to acquire the property. In holding for the Internal Revenue Service, the court applied a subjective test because the seller was a willing seller and did not act under any threat or imminence of condemnation.

In IRS Letter Ruling 8406048 the Internal Revenue Service restated its rule in determining whether a sale was under threat or imminence of condemnation. The issue is whether the vendor has reasonable grounds to think the city would condemn the property.

A sale to the condemning authority qualifies prima facie for condemnation gain deferral. Nevertheless, in this situation the landowner's attorney should ask the condemning authority to state by letter that it will refer the matter to its attorneys for institution of condemnation proceedings unless the owner sells the property to the condemning authority. Such a letter is sufficient evidence of the "threat or imminence" test required. IRS Letter Ruling 8840022. Newspaper articles or oral testimony of telephone calls or conferences are much less convincing.

The Internal Revenue Service has ruled that a sale made by the owner to an agent for a public utility was a sale made under the threat or imminence rule cited in Book §12.14. The agent had disclosed the identity of the utility and had stated that the utility could readily acquire a certificate of public convenience and necessity to authorize it to condemn the property. But if the identity of the condemning authority had not been disclosed, the sale would have been treated as a voluntary sale not under the threat or imminence rule. Rev Rul 74–8, 1974–1 Cum Bull 200.

The Internal Revenue Service has also ruled that the sale of a scenic easement to the government after written notice from the Department of Agriculture of its intention to condemn is an involuntary conversion of real property for purposes of IRC §1033(g). Rev Rul 76–69, 1976–1 Cum Bull 219.

Revenue Ruling 63–221, 1963–2 Cum Bull 332, was followed in Rev Rul 81–180, 1981–2 Cum Bull 161. The IRS apparently follows an objective test in determining whether a "threat or imminence" of condemnation exists when property has been sold to other than the condemning authority. Does the taxpayer have reasonable grounds to believe that the necessary steps to condemn the property eventually will be taken? In Rev Rul 81–180, a sale to a third party constituted a sale under a "threat or imminence" of condemnation when the taxpayer read a newspaper report that the property was to be acquired by condemnation and the taxpayer then confirmed that report.

In IRS Letter Ruling 8234048, the IRS held that a threat of condemnation cannot arise until the condemning authority has the funds to proceed with the condemnation. In that ruling, the plan of condemnation was premised on obtaining consent of the voters to a bond approval. The proceeds from the sale of the bonds would have been used to acquire the condemned property. Thus, the ability to carry out the condemnation is apparently necessary to create a "threat" under IRC §1033.

Under IRS Letter Ruling 8226066, a threat of condemnation exists when a taxpayer has reasonable grounds to believe that the property will be condemned. This is a question of fact based on all the evidence in support of the taxpayer's position. See *Joseph P. Balistrieri,* TC Memo 1979–115.

In *J. Robert King, Jr.* (1981) 77 TC 1113, the Tax Court held that interest on warrants issued by a condemning authority was part of the condemnation award and therefore subject to federal income tax. However, the Tax Court also held that interest on warrants arising from the voluntary sale to a governmental authority is exempt from federal income tax. IRC §103(a)(1).

It is now established in the Ninth Circuit that interest, which by operation of law must be paid by the condemning authority as a result of an acquisition resulting from either condemnation or the threat of condemnation, is subject to federal income tax. *Stewart v Commissioner* (9th Cir 1983) 714 F2d 977 (condemnation); *Stewart v U.S.* (9th Cir 1984) 739 F2d 411 (threat of condemnation).

[§12.15] Irrigation and Reclamation Districts

Former Reg §1.1033(d)–1 is now numbered Reg §1.1033(c)–1. TD 7625, 1979–2 Cum Bull 298.

Qualified Replacement Property

[§12.17] "Like-Kind" Test

The Internal Revenue Service takes the position that land is not of the same nature or character as a building. Rev Rul 76–390, 1976–2 Cum Bull 243; Rev Rul 76–391, 1976–2 Cum Bull 243. Furthermore, the Service will allow a taxpayer to attempt to shield gain by applying either the "like-kind" test or the "similar or related in service or use" test on the replacement property.

The Service has ruled that the following replacement property does not satisfy the like-kind test of IRC §1033(g): replacement of rental residence with personal residence (Rev Rul 76–84, 1976–1 Cum Bull 219); replacement of unimproved farm land held for leasing with building also held for leasing (Rev Rul 76–391, 1976–2 Cum Bull 243); replacement of mobilehome park with motel (Rev Rul 76–390, 1976–2 Cum Bull 243).

The Tax Court has held that the investment of condemnation proceeds in a joint venture that purchased real property did not satisfy the like-kind test. The joint venture created a partnership that was personal property and not "of a like-kind" with the condemned real estate. *M.H.S. Co.,* TC Memo 1976–165, aff'd (6th Cir 1978) 575 F2d 1177.

Internal Revenue Code §1031(a)(2) was amended, effective July 18, 1984, to preclude partnership interests from qualifying as like-kind property, except that the amendment does not apply to any exchange under a binding contract in effect on March 31, 1984, and at all times before the exchange. In a case arising before that amendment, the Ninth Circuit held that an exchange of real property for a tenancy-in-common interest in other real property followed by a contribution of that tenancy-in-common interest for a general-partnership interest constituted a tax-free transaction under IRC §§1031 and 721. *Magneson v Commissioner* (9th Cir 1985) 753 F2d 1490. The position taken by the Service in the *Magneson* case was the same as that taken in IRS Letter Ruling 8424099 in which it ruled that the purchase of another partner's interest in a partnership with the proceeds from an involuntary conversion (*e.g.,* fire damage or condemnation) did not constitute the acquisition of like-kind property. In so holding, the Service relied on Rev Rul 57–154, 1957–1 Cum Bull 262, in which it ruled that replacement of condemned property with tenancy-in-common interest in similar real property was a like-kind replacement, but that replacement with an interest in a partnership owning similar property was not. The Ninth Circuit in the *Magneson* case found little difference between a tenancy-in-common interest and a general-partnership interest for purposes of the application of §1031.

Internal Revenue Service Letter Rulings 8901031 and 8911034 explore IRC §§1071 and 1033 and resolve issues relating to the taxpayer corporation's interaction with affiliated corporations in acquiring replacement property under IRC §1033. The general rule is that any transaction between a taxpayer and an affiliate must be at arm's length as to terms and price. It is appropriate to use an appraiser. See also IRS Letter Ruling 8803088. Apparently if the corporations file a consolidated return, the reinvestment is treated as a deferred intercompany transaction under Reg §1.1502–13(a)(2)(1).

Like-kind property also includes outdoor advertising displays, if an election is made to treat the sign, display, or device as permanently affixed to the ground or permanently attached to a building or other inherently permanent structure. IRC §1033(g)(3)(C). Rev & T C §§18031, 18037.

In IRS Letter Ruling 8808025, the Service held that the taxpayer could revoke an election to treat billboards as real property.

The period of replacement of an outdoor advertising display or sign is three years rather than two. IRC §1033(g)(4); Rev & T C §§18031, 18037; see Willis & Steinmann, *Davis Decision May Increase Flexibility in Replacing Involuntarily Converted Real Property*, 56 Taxes 272 (May 1978).

In IRS Letter Ruling 8119029, the IRS stated that investing the proceeds from the condemnation of land and building in a building alone is not a reinvestment in like-kind property. IRC §1033(g)(1). However, the building may be "property similar or related in service or use," thus qualifying the investment under IRC §1033(a)(1). Similarly, proceeds received from the condemnation of raw land cannot be invested in buildings or land previously owned by the taxpayer to qualify as a like-kind reinvestment. IRS Letter Ruling 8307007. Further, the "service or use" test is not satisfied unless there is a substantial continuity of investment.

When a taxpayer took the proceeds from the condemnation of raw land and acquired other raw land and a put option, the IRS held that the put option did not qualify as like-kind property, with the result that there had to be an allocation of the purchase price to determine whether gain is recognized on the initial condemnation. IRS Letter Ruling 8807029.

[§12.18] "Similar or Related in Service or Use" Test; Functional Use

The issue of like-kind property is always present when there is a reinvestment of condemnation proceeds. In IRS Letter Ruling 8411044, the Internal Revenue Service held that, if the rental of the newly acquired property is similar to the rental of the condemned property, the like-kind rule will be satisfied. In that ruling, the proceeds from the sale of a commercial building that was rented out were used to (1) rehabilitate another rental building, (2) demolish still another building, and (3) construct a new building on the site of the demolished building. The new buildings were going to be put to the same use as the old building. In Letter Ruling 8852009, the IRS found rented farm land to be equivalent to a rented office building and land; apparently, they were related in service or use.

Like-kind property includes improvements on leased land that were acquired as replacement for a condemned land and building. The taxpayer used the property for the same purposes. See IRS Letter Ruling 8509075.

The transactions described in Rev Rul 76–390, 1976–2 Cum Bull 243, and Rev Rul 76–391, 1976–2 Cum Bull 243, in Supp §12.17, also failed to satisfy the "similar or related in service or use" test of IRC §1033(a)(1). The Internal Revenue Service ruled that whether property is similar or related in use to other property depends on the physical characteristics of the properties. Accordingly, a bowling center was held not to be similar or related in use to a billiard center, because the physical characteristics of a bowling center are not similar to those of a billiard center. Rev Rul 76–319, 1976–2 Cum Bull 242. However, the functional use test was used by the IRS to approve a reinvestment of the proceeds from the condemnation of a leasehold into a fee simple. Rev Rul 83–70, 1983–1 Cum Bull 189. See Falk & Singer, *Planning for Real Estate Condemnation Awards in Light of Recent Favorable Rulings,* 59 J Tax 400 (Dec. 1983).

In determining what constitutes "related in service or use," the IRS looked at certain personal property used in the taxpayer's leasing business. Measuring standards applied by the IRS included the business risks involved, management of the property, users of the property, and other similarities. It held that replacement property subject to lease was similar to involuntarily converted property within the meaning of IRC §1033(a). See IRS Letter Ruling 8820055.

In one case, a taxpayer's manufacturing plant burned down. The taxpayer used the insurance proceeds to build a new plant that manufactured a different product. The Internal Revenue Service held in IRS Letter Ruling 8844049 that §1033 applied to shield gain.

In Letter Ruling 8851034, the IRS held that standing timber on seldom logged land was real property under IRC §3033(g)(1). This holding should be compared with Letter Ruling 8707022, in which condemned growing timber was impliedly held not to be property under §1033(g)(1).

Other transactions failing to satisfy the "similar or related in use" test include the replacement of rental property with unimproved land (*Bratton v Rountree* (MD Tenn 1976) 76–1 USTC ¶9198, 37 AFTR2d ¶76–438) and the replacement of a building held for investment with shares of a publicly held real estate investment trust (*Lakritz v U.S.* (ED Wis 1976) 418 F Supp 210).

[§12.19] Investments in Improvements to Other Property

The Ninth Circuit has applied the "similar use" test in allowing the receipt of proceeds from the condemnation of agricultural property to be reinvested tax free in improvements to industrial property already owned by the taxpayer. *Davis v U.S.* (9th Cir 1979) 589 F2d 446. See Willis & Steinmann, *Davis Decision May Increase Flexibility in Replacing Involuntarily Converted Property*, 56 Taxes 272 (May 1978). This result is consistent with Rev Rul 71–41, 1971–1 Cum Bull 223, cited in Book §12.19. See also Rev Rul 80–184, 1980–2 Cum Bull 232. *Davis* was also applied by the Internal Revenue Service to support the conclusion that a 15-year lease was related in service or use to a fee simple in real property used for the same purpose by the taxpayer. Rev Rul 83–70, 1983–1 Cum Bull 189.

Internal Revenue Service Letter Ruling 7903064 points out that "like-kind" as used in IRC §1033 only applies to real estate owned in a business or by a landlord, not a dealer or homeowner. The phrase "similar or related in use or service" can apply to a dealer or homeowner.

Special Problems of Tax-Free Replacement

[§12.21] Tenant's Interest in Lease

Former 18 Cal Adm C §18081 (now called the California Code of Regulations) has been repealed. California law now conforms to IRC §1031. See Rev & T C §18031.

Anderson, Tax Planning of Real Estate (6th ed 1970) has been replaced by a seventh edition published in 1977.

The IRS declared IT 3793 (cited in Book §12.21) obsolete in Rev Rul 69–45, 1969–1 Cum Bull 313.

[§12.23] Effect of Mortgage and Other Liens Against Condemned Property

In *Harsh Inv. Corp. v U.S.* (D Ore 1970) 323 F Supp 409, an attempt was made to reconcile the conflict between *Fortee Props.* and *Babcock,* discussed in Book §12.23, by distinguishing those cases on their facts. In *Fortee Props.,* the taxpayer-condemnee was personally liable on the mortgage note; in *Babcock,* the taxpayer-condemnee was not liable on the mortgage note.

If partnership property is involuntarily converted, the partnership must make the reinvestment. For tax purposes, the partnership is treated as a separate entity. However, although the partnership may avoid tax on involuntary conversion, a partner may recognize gain if the proceeds from the involuntary conversion are used to reduce the partnership's liabilities in an amount in excess of the partner's basis for his interest in the partnership. A reduction in partnership liabilities is treated as a cash distribution to a partner. If the cash constructively distributed to a partner exceeds his basis in the partnership, the partner recognizes gain. IRC §§731(a)(1), 752. The partner's recognition of gain occurs even if the partnership later reinvests in replacement property. Rev Rul 81–242, 1981–2 Cum Bull 147. A partner faced with this problem might wish to negotiate a three-way exchange with the condemning authority to avoid taxable income to the partners.

In determining the amount realized on a sale of property, it is necessary for the seller to take into consideration the amount of nonrecourse debt that exceeds the fair market value of the property. *Commissioner v Tufts* (1983) 461 US 300. Gain on a condemnation sale is shielded only to the extent that the amount reinvested in the appropriate type of property equals or exceeds the amount realized on the sale of the condemned property. See IRC §§1033(a)(2)(A), 1033(g).

The Tax Reform Act of 1986 (Pub L 99–514, 100 Stat 2085) phases out income tax deductions for personal interest except "qualified residence interest." IRC §163(h). See Supp §12.31 for discussion.

[§12.24] Single Economic Unit Rule

In *Graphic Press, Inc.* (1973) 60 TC 674, the California Division of Highways condemned the owner's lithography printing press operation, including land and building. The owner was agreeable to the land and building condemnation, but could not accept the state's offer of 10 percent of cost on its presses. The agreement finally reached required (1) removal of presses by tenant, (2) no payment for loss of profits or moving expenses in excess of $3000, and (3) waiver of compensation for the presses. The entire amount paid to the owner was invested in a new lithography plant site. The Tax Court held that the amount allocable to the owner's *waiver* of his right to receive compensation for his presses was ordinary income and could not be sheltered under IRC §1033. The problem could have been avoided had the taxpayer given a bill of sale to the state for the presses and then bought replacement presses. The court of appeals reversed and found that the excess portion of the award was for moving expenses and business interruption costs that flowed from the condemnation, and that the whole award qualified under IRC §1033. *Graphic Press, Inc. v Commissioner* (9th Cir 1975) 523 F2d 585. See also *Buffalo Wire Works Co.* (1980) 74 TC 925 (reimbursement of moving expenses for fixtures held to constitute part of nontaxable condemnation award).

For the single economic unit rule to apply, the taxpayer must show that the involuntarily converted property could not be easily replaced and that a substantial economic relationship existed between the condemned property and the property sold that made them constitute one economic unit. Rev Rul 78–377, 1978–2 Cum Bull 208. This expands Rev Rul 59–361, 1959–2 Cum Bull 183, cited in Book §12.24.

The value of contiguous parcels is substantially greater than the individual value of any one parcel if the condemning authority contemplates acquiring all the contiguous parcels. *Charles Ivey,* TC Memo 1983–273.

[§12.25] Depreciation on Replacement Property

The Tax Reform Act of 1986 (Pub L 99–514, 100 Stat 2085) repealed the regular investment tax credit for property placed into service after December 31, 1985. See new IRC §49(a). However, in Rev Rul 86–89, 1986–2 Cum Bull 4, the Internal Revenue Service ruled that the basis of any new tangible personal property acquired to replace property destroyed in a casualty must be reduced for purposes of computing the investment credit by the amount of gain deferred under IRC §1033(a)(2). This rule is similar to the rule applicable to determining the basis for depreciation.

[§12.26] Successor to Owner of Condemned Property

The question of who can reinvest the proceeds from a condemnation sale is bothersome. In Letter Ruling 8834075, the IRS stated that the surviving corporation after a statutory merger could take advantage of IRC §1033 on behalf of the disappearing corporation. The disappearing corporation sold its assets under threat of condemnation and merged into the surviving corporation.

In *Appeal of the Estate of Howard W. Chase & Estate of Gladys C. Chase* (SBE 1976) CCH Cal Tax Rep ¶16–554.60, P-H State & Local Tax Serv ¶¶55,400.504, 55,400.506, the State Board of Equalization held that no gain would be recognized when an individual's receipt of condemnation proceeds from the disposition of land was reinvested by his executors in land and a commercial building. The State Board stated that not only did the executors acquire like-kind property but they were also the proper people to make the reinvestment because they were acting on behalf of the deceased.

Internal Revenue Code §2032A allows for reducing the fair market value of certain real property for federal estate tax purposes. If reduced value property is involuntarily converted, special rules come into play relating to preservation of the reduction in value. The executor and his attorney are directed to IRC §§2032A(h) and 2032A(e)(14).

Although an estate may elect to replace property taken from a decedent (see Book §12.26), his widow cannot. *Estate of George W. Jayne* (1974) 61 TC 744.

The Technical and Miscellaneous Revenue Act of 1988 (TAMRA) (Pub L 100–647, 102 Stat 3342) amended IRC §1034(g) (deferral of gain from personal residence) to provide that a deceased spouse will be deemed to have consented if the surviving spouse consents to the application of the rollover provisions of IRC §1034. It is unclear whether including this provision in §1034 regarding a deceased spouse's consent would apply under §1033 if the surviving spouse proceeds under that section.

Estate of John E. Morris, cited in Book §12.26 as *Estate of Morris,* was affirmed (4th Cir 1972) 454 F2d 208. See also *Estate of Harry A. Gregg* (1977) 69 TC 468; Elder & Beckett, *When may deceased's spouse make a valid §1033 involuntary conversion replacement,* 40 J Tax 370 (1974).

What happens if property under probate administration is condemned? An estate is a taxpayer, but the heirs are the real parties in interest. As beneficiaries, the heirs are technically different taxpayers. Theoretically, therefore, the estate must reinvest. But practical problems can be very difficult, as illustrated by the following hypothetical case:

Suppose unimproved real estate is appraised at $250,000 in light of restrictions on its use as beach property in Monterey. The California State Parks and Beach Department buys it from an estate for $1,250,000. The two heirs both want to purchase qualified property under IRC §1033. One wants to purchase an office building and the other wants to purchase ranch acreage for raising cattle. The executor of the estate is faced with an impossible problem: Can the executor refuse to purchase the "similar or related in use or service" property, pay the tax, and distribute the net after taxes? That would be the conservative approach, but the heirs might threaten suit.

The executor then agrees to purchase the designated properties. To protect himself, however, the executor insists on withholding the full federal capital gains tax for three years and the full California capital gains tax for four years. (The statute of limitations on an honest mistake is three years for federal income tax purposes and four years for California income tax purposes. IRC §6501; Rev & T C §18586. See Rev & T C §18586.7, tolling statute of limitations during period of proceedings to quash a subpena.) During that period, who should hold, own, and manage the properties? The executor does not want the responsibility, and the heirs are anxious to obtain the properties. The executor is liable for any deficiencies and must retain substantial assets during the period of limitations in case the replacement property does not qualify. This problem has always been present for an individual, but for an estate, it is complicated by the questions of (1) management of the replacement property during the three- or four-year limitation period after the year of reacquisition and (2) payment of trustee and other professional fees in the interim.

The author's experience has been that a guaranty by the heirs is insufficient. Distribution of the replacement property should be made only after the statute has run or the heirs secure their maximum tax liability by a certificate of deposit pledged to the representative.

The Tax Reform Act of 1986 (Pub L 99–514, 100 Stat 2085) repealed the 12-month liquidation provision of IRC §337. Under IRC §336 gain or loss is generally recognized on complete liquidation. However, no gain or loss is recognized by a liquidating corporation on the distribution of property in complete liquidation to a corporation that owns shares constituting at least 80 percent of the voting rights of the liquidating corporation. IRC §337 as amended, generally effective for distributions after July 31, 1986. See also IRC §332. Distributions to minority shareholders in the course of a liquidation are treated as nonliquidating redemptions and thus gain (but not loss) is recognized by the distributing corporation. See IRC §336(d)(3).

The IRS has filed nonacquiescence to *Estate of John E. Morris* (1971) 55 TC 636, 1978–2 Cum Bull 4.

Internal Revenue Code §334(b)(2) is no longer an exception to IRC §332. See now IRC §338.

Internal Revenue Code §331(a)(1) has been redesignated IRC §331(a).

[§12.27] Replacement by Investment in Corporate, Partnership, or Commonly Owned Property

The actual owner of the property at the time of condemnation may be the one entitled to reinvest the proceeds under IRC §1033. In IRS Letter Ruling 8527090, the Internal Revenue Service held that the partners independently could elect to take advantage of the provisions of §1033. The partnership had conveyed its property, apparently raw land, to its partners. The partners then held the property as tenants in common and the property was condemned.

If partnership property is condemned, the partnership must elect to defer recognition of gain under IRC §1033(a) in order for the individual partners to benefit from the statute. Even if a partnership is dissolved at the time its property is condemned, individuals cannot make the election unless the partnership was also terminated under IRC §708(b)(1)(A). Termination generally requires cessation of all partnership business and the complete distribution of assets. *Morton Fuchs* (1983) 80 TC 506.

The Service apparently ignored the existence of a partnership in IRS Letter Ruling 8818029, holding that the two partners could independently purchase replacement property after assets of the partnership were condemned. It would appear that the partners stood in the shoes of the partnership in proceeding under §1033.

One partner did not want to roll over the proceeds of condemned partnership property under §1033 but the other partners did. In Letter Ruling 8735026, the Service stated that both the remaining partners and the other partner could be satisfied if there was a double escrow and a double deed (first to the partnership and then to the partner) in liquidating the one partner's interest in return for a designated parcel of land. Neither step transaction nor agency arguments destroyed the §1033 rollover.

An interest in a partnership is no longer treated as like-kind property, effective March 1, 1984. IRC §1031(a)(2). On like-kind property, see §12.17.

The distinction discussed in Book §12.27 between tenants in common and a partnership was reinforced in *Roy P. Varner,* TC Memo 1973–027. If the property is held in the name of a partnership, the partnership is the owner and it is the entity that must acquire the replacement property. Replacement of a partner's prorata interest in the partnership property will not qualify, according to the Service. Rev Rul 66–191, 1966–2 Cum Bull 300. See also *Demirjian v Commissioner* (3d Cir 1972) 457 F2d 1. However, IRC §701 states that partners are liable "for income tax only in their separate or individual capacities," so there may be room to maneuver. See IRS Letter Ruling 8735026, discussed above.

In IRS Letter Ruling 8750001, the Service held that a tenant in common's gain was sheltered under IRC §1033 when he reinvested in like-kind property but held title as a joint tenant.

Similarly, a revocable grantor trust can purchase replacement property on behalf of the grantor and shelter gain on the condemnation. See IRS Letter Ruling 8729023.

The Service has privately ruled on certain factual situations in which the owner of the property has acquired stock in another corporation in order to satisfy the requirements under IRC §1033(a)(2)(A). The Service takes the position that the acquisition of stock must be in a corporation not previously owned by the purchaser and further that the corporation must already own like-kind property. The Service held in IRS Letter Ruling 8420087 that §1033 was not satisfied when the purchase was of new stock issued by the parent's subsidiary and the subsidiary was to use the funds to acquire like-kind property. On the other hand, in IRS Letter Ruling 8707022, the Service allowed the taxpayer to acquire stock in another corporation's subsidiary when the subsidiary already owned property similar or related in use to the converted property (§1031 property). Finally, IRS Letter Ruling 8648052 specifically stated that the taxpayer could avoid the recognition of gain on the purchase of like-kind property directly from a related corporation as long as the purchase was made at fair market value.

The taxpayer's transfer of condemnation proceeds to his corporation in exchange for stock did not qualify for nonrecognition when the corporation later purchased other real estate from the taxpayer. The court held that the taxpayer failed to establish that his purpose was to replace the condemned property. *Frank G. Templeton* (1976) 66 TC 509, aff'd (4th Cir 1978) 573 F2d 866. Moreover condemnation proceeds advanced to a corporation by the person that owns the corporation must be invested in assets consisting principally of similar property. Failure to comply with that rule will result in recognition of gain to the taxpayer. See *Lester Howard Kahl,* TC Memo 1986–240. In IRS Letter Ruling 8707022, the Service held that §1033 applied when the taxpayer's growing timber was condemned and the proceeds therefrom used to buy stock in a corporation doing the same business. The stock qualified as replacement property because the underlying assets of the corporation constituted property similar or related in service or use to the property converted. It appears that the growing of timber was not considered to be real property held for productive use in a trade or business, because the acquisition of stock would not have constituted the acquisition of like-kind property. See IRC §1033(g)(2).

If a corporation's property is condemned, the corporation can proceed to acquire replacement property and then transfer that property to a wholly owned subsidiary under IRC §351 without exposing the transfer to income tax. See Rev Rul 84–29, 1984–1 Cum Bull 181 (involuntary transfer replacement property under IRC §1033 transferred to subsidiary).

[§12.28] Replacement Period

The replacement period begins at the end of the tax year the gain is realized by the taxpayer. See IRS Letter Ruling 8424099. It is the position of the Internal Revenue Service that replacement occurs when the taxpayer designates the replacement property. See IRS Letter Ruling 8422005.

A taxpayer can make his designation of replacement property on an amended return if there is no designation made on his originally filed return. See IRS Letter Ruling 8424026.

See Reg §1.1033(g)–1(c), which extends the replacement period from two years to three years after the taxable year in which taxable gain is recognized. In *Casalina Corp.* (1973) 60 TC 694, aff'd (4th Cir 1975) 511 F2d 1162, the court held that gain is first recognized in the year in which the owner withdraws amounts from escrow in excess of his basis. The fact that the final condemnation price has not been determined is not controlling. See also *Lino Scolari*, TC Memo 1973–116, aff'd *Scolari v Commissioner* (9th Cir 1974) 497 F2d 962.

In *Casalina Corp., supra,* the owner had obtained extensions of time to replace, but he had not disclosed the withdrawals at the time he requested the extensions. The extensions were held invalid because of the owner's failure to disclose a material fact.

The Service has ruled that a sewer moratorium is reasonable cause for extending the replacement period, provided the taxpayer has obtained adequate information that obstacles to the acquisition of the replacement property will be removed within a reasonable extension period. Rev Rul 76–540, 1976–2 Cum Bull 245, distinguishing Rev Rul 76–488, 1976–2 Cum Bull 244.

Internal Revenue Code §1033(g)(4), added by the Tax Reform Act of 1976 (Pub L 94–455, 90 Stat 1525) extends the replacement period to three years for involuntary conversions described in IRC §1033(g)(1), *i.e.*, property held for a productive use in trade or business or for investments. See Reg §1.1033(g)–1(c).

Request for extension of time to replace involuntarily converted property held by a partnership must be made by the partnership and not by an individual partner. *Estate of Jerome K. Goldstein,* TC Memo 1976–19.

The mere notation on the owner's federal income tax return for the year of taking that the owner elects to defer recognition of the gain is not an "automatic" application for an extension of time within which to replace. *Lino Scolari, supra.*

In *Scolari,* the owner testified that he had instructed his accountant to file a request for an extension. However, because the accountant was not called to corroborate, the Tax Court rejected the owner's testimony. But in Rev Rul 72–27, 1972–1 Cum Bull 226, the Service ruled that an owner can rely on the "good faith" representations of both a "reputable" attorney and a "reputable" accountant that no gain was realized on a condemnation as "reasonable cause" for failure to apply for an extension of the period for replacement. In *Theron M. Lemly,* TC Memo 1973–147, a division of the Tax Court held that a rejection by the Service of a late-filed application for extension of time to reinvest was an abuse of discretion because the accountant of the firm responsible for making the application on or before the end of the year died unexpectedly on December 19.

Reliance on erroneous advice of an accountant is not reasonable cause for extending the replacement period when an application for extension is filed three months after the end of the taxable year in which gain was realized. *Marco S. Marinello Assocs. v Commissioner* (1st Cir 1976) 535 F2d 147.

An extension of time under IRC §1033 can be granted only by the District Director of the Internal Revenue Service for the particular district in which the taxpayer files his or her return. The national office of the Service cannot grant an extension of time to reinvest the proceeds. See IRS Letter Ruling 8840022.

The Service advises that the following information should be submitted with an application for an extension of time under IRC §1033(a)(2)(B)(ii) to reinvest involuntary conversion proceeds:

(1) The year and form number of the tax return on which the election not to recognize gain was made;

(2) The taxpayer's identification number as shown on that return;

(3) The date of the condemnation;

(4) The name of the condemning authority;

(5) A legal description of the property condemned, including a street address;

(6) The total amount of proceeds received from the condemning authority and whether this amount constituted full or part payment;

(7) The date the payment was received from the condemning authority;

(8) The adjusted basis of the property condemned; and

(9) A statement reciting the specific action taken by the taxpayer to purchase replacement property. This would include statements about offers made to acquire replacement property, the names of agents worked with in acquiring property, specific listings and requests made of agents, and all other evidence of a serious intent and interest in acquiring replacement property.

The Service will usually act favorably on an application for additional time to reinvest involuntary conversion proceeds but may grant an extension of one year or less.

Replacement property may be subject to property tax reassessment. See Rev & T C §60.

[§12.29] Elections on Tax Return

In *Laverne Cerny,* TC Memo 1987–599, the Tax Court addressed the issue of whether a divorced wife was liable for tax on a condemnation gain when the previously filed joint return failed to report the condemnation gain. First, the court treated the failure to report the condemnation gain as an election to reinvest the proceeds from the gain. Although the wife did receive her share of the condemnation proceeds, she turned them over to her husband on threats of violence. The wife was held liable for the tax on her half of the condemnation proceeds but excused from any liability for tax on the ex-husband's portion; because she was considered an innocent spouse under IRC §6013.

Internal Revenue Code §6045(e) requires specified people to report sales transactions to the Internal Revenue Service. To date, the reporting requirements have been limited to transactions for single family residences and apartments consisting or four or fewer units. The statute does not limit reporting requirements to any particular units or types of property. Accordingly, it is expected that the Service will broaden its regulations to include all types of property. Thus, the Service will be on notice for all real property sales transactions. Previously, this was not the case.

Internal Revenue Code §280B added by the Tax Reform Act of 1984 (Pub L 98–369, 98 Stat 494, 1210) specifically provides that neither the cost expended for demolition nor any loss sustained on account of demolition shall be deductible. Such amounts must be charged to the land's capital account; accordingly, they are not added to the basis of the building and are not subject to depreciation. The question arises whether such charges are properly includable as replacement property under §1033. In IRS Letter Ruling 8307007 the IRS held that the use of condemnation proceeds, to demolish other property does not constitute the acquisition of like-kind property. The use of condemnation proceeds, however, to remodel other units may constitute like-kind property. See IRS Letter Ruling 8329014.

A revocation of the taxpayer's election not to recognize gain under IRC §1033 may not be made after the condemned property has been replaced. *John McShain* (1976) 65 TC 686.

Once a taxpayer designates replacement property, he cannot substitute another piece of property unless the originally selected property is not qualified replacement property. Rev Rul 83–39, 1983–1 Cum Bull 190.

[§12.31] CONDEMNATION OF A HOME

An interesting issue arises when a building owned by a nonprofit residential cooperative association is condemned. The condemnation proceeds are then received by the corporation. The cooperative shareholders choose not to rebuild but wish to receive cash. The corporation liquidates, and the cash is distributed to the cooperative shareholders. Some of the cooperative shareholders used their cooperative units for their personal residence while others used theirs for rental purposes. Some of its shareholders use liquidation proceeds to purchase a new personal residence while others use the proceeds to acquire new commercial property. What is the tax effect of receipt of the proceeds by the cooperative corporation, the distribution of the proceeds to the shareholders, and the eventual use of the proceeds by the shareholders? Further, are these problems alleviated if the cooperative association elects to be taxed in accordance with the provisions of subchapter S of the Internal Revenue Code? Similarly, what advice should be given to the cooperative when it receives insurance proceeds after the building is destroyed by fire? It appears that IRC §1034(f) may answer some of the questions.

The Revenue Act of 1987 (Pub L 100–203, 101 Stat 1330) amended IRC §163(h)(3) by redefining "qualified residence interest" for years after 1987. This interest includes interest on (1) acquisition indebtedness that is subject to a $1 million limitation and (2) home equity indebtedness that is subject to a $100,000 limitation. Acquisition indebtedness is debt generated to acquire, construct, or substantially improve a qualified residence and includes refinancing indebtedness to the extent of the refinanced debt. Home equity indebtedness means any other indebtedness secured by a qualified residence. There are special rules for debts incurred before October 13, 1987.

The Internal Revenue Service has ruled, in effect, that a prior casualty loss cannot be sheltered under IRC §1034 (Rev & T C §18031). In 1972 a taxpayer's house was destroyed by flooding. The taxpayer took a $15,000 casualty loss. In 1973, the taxpayer's property was taken by condemnation for a redevelopment project. The taxpayer received $40,000, the preflood value of the property. The taxpayer then purchased a new residence for $45,000. The Service ruled that there was a recovery of a "tax benefit," *i.e.,* the prior casualty loss, and despite the taxpayer's investment in a qualified principal residence under IRC §1034, the "tax benefit" rules prevailed. For that reason, the prior casualty loss was taxable as ordinary income when received. Rev Rul 74–206, 1974–1 Cum Bull 198. These principles have been extended to property held in a trade or business within the meaning of IRC §1231(b). Rev Rul 80–65, 1980–1 Cum Bull 183, amplifying and clarifying Rev Rul 74–206. The rationale of Rev Rul 74–206, 1974–1 Cum Bull 198, was followed in *Mager v U.S.* (MD Pa 1980) 80–1 USTC ¶9236, 45 AFTR2d ¶80–503.

In the author's opinion, Rev Rul 74–206 is erroneous because IRC §1034 shelters all gain realized on the sale of a personal residence, not merely that portion of the gain that is capital gain. Gain is defined as the excess of the sales price over the cost or other basis of the property, whether that gain be taxed as ordinary, capital, recapture, or IRC §1231 gain. IRC §1001(a). At the time of sale the basis of the property had been reduced by the amount of the prior casualty loss. IRC §1016(a)(1).

The replacement period of a personal residence under IRC §1034(a) is now two years, effective July 20, 1981, not one year as stated in Book §12.31 for both existing and newly constructed replacement property. Internal Revenue Code §1034(c)(5) has been repealed. The replacement period for condemnation replacement is two years, not one. IRC §1033(a)(2)(B)(i).

The Revenue Act of 1978 (Pub L 95–600, 92 Stat 2763) changed the scheme for excluding gain on the sale of a personal residence. To qualify, a taxpayer must be 55 years old rather than 65 and have lived in the residence for three of the past five years at the time of the sale. The taxpayer may elect to exclude up to $125,000 of gain regardless of the sale price, and the amount excluded is no longer a tax preference item. The election may be made only once, but a person who has excluded $20,000 ($35,000 under the Tax Reform Act of 1976, Pub L 94–455, 90 Stat 1525) on a sale before July 27, 1978, as previously allowed is still eligible for this election. IRC §121.

Revenue and Taxation Code §17154 was repealed in 1979 and replaced with Rev & T C §17155, which was itself replaced, effective July 28, 1983, with Rev & T C §17131, which incorporates the comparable federal law (IRC §121) by reference into California law. Section 121 excludes gain up to $125,000 ($62,500 if a married person files a separate return) if the condemned property was the principal residence of the taxpayer for at least three of the five years preceding the condemnation. IRC §§121(a)(2), (b), (d)(4).

The two-year period in which to replace a principal residence under IRC §1034 may be extended for up to four years after the sale of the residence if, after the sale of the residence, the taxpayer has a tax home (as defined by IRC §911(d)(3)) outside the United States. IRC §1034(k).

The California provision similar to IRC §1034 is Rev & T C §18031.

[§12.32] EASEMENTS

Under *Inaja Land Co.* (1947) 9 TC 727, proceeds from a condemnation of an easement are treated as recovery of basis on the underlying land. If the taxpayer can reasonably determine the exact land affected by the easement, then only the basis of the portion that is affected by the easement is reduced. *James Iske,* TC Memo 1980–61.

The Internal Revenue Service has clarified one of the uncertainties noted in Book §12.32. A taking of a nonexclusive easement can be sheltered from tax on the gain. In Rev Rul 72–433, 1972–2 Cum Bull 470, the IRS ruled that a farmer qualified for nonrecognition of gain when he granted a flowage easement to a flood control authority and retained the right to grow rice on the land subject to the flowage easement. The fact that the easement was nonexclusive was immaterial.

The Internal Revenue Service has ruled that proceeds received on threat of condemnation of a utility power line and exclusive right-of-way easement may be shielded from tax by the purchase of property that was also to be used in the condemnee's trade or business. The owner had also reserved rights to the property that would not interfere with the easement including the right to cultivate the property beneath the utility towers. Rev Rul 72–549, 1972–2 Cum Bull 472.

[§12.33] SEVERANCE DAMAGES

Revising past policy, the Internal Revenue Service now allows the taxpayer the choice of either reinvesting the proceeds of severance damages in other real property or using the proceeds to restore the retained property. Rev Rul 83–49, 1983–1 Cum Bull 191.

For a case relating to the allocation of a portion of the award to severance damages, see *Emory D. Stine,* TC Memo 1976–339.

[§12.35] Tax Treatment

For detailed rules on the determination of basis for land affected by severance damages and also by newly acquired land, see Rev Rul 83–49, 1983–1 Cum Bull 191. See also Falk & Singer, *Planning for Real Estate Condemnation Awards in Light of Recent Favorable Rulings,* 59 J Tax 400 (1983).

See Clurman, *Condemnation Severance Damages may be Tax-deferred under 1033 if they are Identified,* 43 J Tax 100 (1975).

INVERSE CONDEMNATION

[§12.39] Casualty Loss Deduction Taken

If the owner obtained an emergency loan that was later cancelled, the Internal Revenue Service exacts the same price; the cancellation of indebtedness is treated as the recovery of a prior tax benefit. Rev Rul 73–408, 1973–2 Cum Bull 15. This ruling was based on the cancellation of a loan to a farmer who was in a drought area and lost crops valued at $8000. Revenue Ruling 71–160, 1971–1 Cum Bull 75, cited in Book §12.39, was distinguished because it concerned destruction of property and no loan had been made to the taxpayer. Under Rev Rul 76–500, 1976–2 Cum Bull 254, the cancelled portion of an emergency loan represents the replacement of lost profits; the cancelled portion of the loan is part of the owner's net earnings from self-employment.

[§12.41] Lost Profits

In Rev Rul 75–381, 1975–2 Cum Bull 25, the Internal Revenue Service illustrates the allocation of indemnity payments between compensation for loss of profits and compensation for loss of property.

13

Inverse Condemnation

[§13.1]   INTRODUCTION: DIRECT CONDEMNATION CONTRASTED WITH INVERSE CONDEMNATION

California Constitution art I, §14, cited in Book §13.1, has been renumbered art I, §19. See Supp §8.7.

There is no substantive difference between direct and inverse condemnation. *Klopping v City of Whittier* (1972) 8 C3d 39, 43, 104 CR 1, 5; *Breidert v Southern Pac. Co.* (1964) 61 C2d 659, 663 n1, 39 CR 903, 905 n1.

[§13.2] FAILURE TO USE DIRECT CONDEMNATION MAY RESULT IN INVERSE CONDEMNATION ACTION

Code of Civil Procedure §1245.260 continues the general rule of former CCP §1243.1, allowing an inverse condemnation action if the condemnor fails to file a condemnation proceeding within six months after adopting the resolution or to make a diligent effort to serve the summons and complaint within six months after filing the action. Note the following changes:

(1) The property owner can elect to bring an inverse condemnation action or to seek a writ of mandate to compel the public entity to rescind the resolution or to file a condemnation action.

(2) Submission of a claim is not a prerequisite. See §13.7. This rule supersedes the holding to the contrary in *Stone v City of Los Angeles* (1975) 51 CA3d 987, 124 CR 822, which held that CCP §1243.1 did not do away with the requirement of filing a claim before instituting an inverse condemnation action. But a limitation period is established requiring the inverse condemnation action to be instituted within one year after the six months given to the public entity to implement its resolution of necessity. The limitation period does not apply to a writ of mandate.

(3) The public entity can begin its proceeding or rescind the resolution of necessity as a matter of right before the property owner institutes any action. But see *Klopping v City of Whittier* (1972) 8 C3d 39, 104 CR 1, concerning the property owner's constitutional right to sue for precondemnation damages; see §§4.7, 4.7A, 13.21. Such a rescission is subject to the same rules and has the same consequences as abandonment of a direct condemnation action. See Supp §§8.31–8.33.

The holding in *Richmond Elks Hall Ass'n v Richmond Redev. Agency* (9th Cir 1977) 561 F2d 1327, follows *Foster v City of Detroit* (6th Cir 1968) 405 F2d 138, cited in Book §13.2.

[§13.3] ELEMENTS OF INVERSE CONDEMNATION ACTION

(a) *Interest in property.* A trustee of the property under a testamentary trust (*Leppo v City of Petaluma* (1971) 20 CA3d 711, 97 CR 840), an executor of the property owner's estate (*Blau v City of Los Angeles* (1973) 32 CA3d 77, 107 CR 727), or a mortgagor whose interest has been foreclosed (*Klopping v City of Whittier* (1972) 8 C3d 39, 104 CR 1) may institute an action in inverse condemnation. Dictum in *Mosesian v County of Fresno* (1972) 28 CA3d 493, 104 CR 655, suggests that if the mortgage is outstanding, a joint suit by mortgagor and mortgagee is necessary. However, this appears incorrect if the taking or damaging impairs the mortgagee's security interest. See also *Brown v Critchfield* (1980) 100 CA3d 858, 868, 161 CR 342, 348 (mortgagee may share in condemnation award obtained by mortgagor).

The holder of an unexercised option to purchase the affected property has a compensable property right. *County of San Diego v Miller* (1975) 13 C3d 684, 119 CR 491. If the unexercised option has not been renewed before the condemnation action is filed, however, the option holder has no compensable property right (*City of Walnut Creek v Leadership Hous. Sys.* (1977) 73 CA3d 611, 140 CR 690), unless he or she can show that the unreasonable precondemnation activity constituted a de facto taking during the option period. *Toso v City of Santa Barbara* (1980) 101 CA3d 934, 162 CR 210.

An insurer of a merchant whose premises and merchandise were damaged when a water main broke can bring an inverse condemnation action as the merchant's subrogee. *McMahan's of Santa Monica v City of Santa Monica* (1983) 146 CA3d 683, 194 CR 582.

A revocable permit may be sufficient to establish a property right if the permittee makes substantial expenditures for permanent improvements in reliance on the permit. But in *Belmont County Water Dist. v State* (1976) 65 CA3d 13, 135 CR 163, the court did not find evidence under the facts presented to qualify the property under this principle.

Class actions have been permitted (*Bohannan v City of San Diego* (1973) 30 CA3d 416, 106 CR 333), but plaintiffs must show they are all members of the affected class (*Associated Home Builders, Inc. v City of Walnut Creek* (1971) 4 C3d 633, 635 n1, 94 CR 630, 632 n1, in which only some members of the nonprofit corporation bringing the action owned lands in Walnut Creek). In *Associated Home Builders,* composition of the class was not discussed. For a case holding plaintiffs' community of interest and adequacy of representation inadequate to constitute a class, see *City of San Jose v Superior Court* (1974) 12 C3d 447, 115 CR 797 (discussed and distinguished in *Dhuyvetter v City of Fresno* (1980) 110 CA3d 659, 168 CR 61).

Several individual plaintiffs may seek relief in a joint action for damages arising from the same public project. *Aaron v City of Los Angeles* (1974) 40 CA3d 471, 115 CR 162. In *Nestle v City of Santa Monica* (1972) 6 C3d 920, 101 CR 568, the court adopted a procedure by which plaintiffs selected ten representative parcels from many affected to determine damages. However, in another overflight case, it was held that the development, use, and topography of the area in the flight path were so diverse that the interest of all the landowners in the area could not be properly represented in one class action. *City of San Jose v Superior Court, supra.*

A public entity holding an interest in property may state a cause of action in inverse condemnation against another public entity. *Marin Mun. Water Dist. v City of Mill Valley* (1988) 202 CA3d 1161, 249 CR 469. In this case, a water district's franchise interest that provided the right to lay and maintain pipes under city streets was sufficient to support a cause of action in inverse condemnation when there was a destruction of the street by a landslide resulting from the city's failure to maintain the street properly.

(b) *Defendant engaged in public project.* Approval and acceptance of an improvement, such as a street or drainage system offered for dedication, may subject the public entity to liability to a third party whose property is damaged. Approval and acceptance by the public agency may be implied by official acts of dominion or control of the property and by continued use of the improvement by that agency for many years. *Marin v City of San Rafael* (1980) 111 CA3d 591, 168 CR 750; *Sheffet v County of Los Angeles* (1970) 3 CA3d 720, 735, 84 CR 11, 21.

However, the court in *Ellison v City of San Buenaventura* (1976) 60 CA3d 453, 131 CR 433, held that a municipality with no part in the private development of upstream property other than approval of plans and issuance of permits was not liable for subsequent sediment buildup in downstream waterways. In *Yox v City of Whittier* (1986) 182 CA3d 347, 227 CR 311, the court concluded that there was no inverse condemnation when water from uphill lots ran down a *private* street and collected in front of plaintiff's property. In *Chatman v Alameda County Flood Control Dist.* (1986) 183 CA3d 424, 228 CR 257, a flood control district was held not liable for subsidence damage caused by a culvert that it periodically inspected but neither owned nor controlled.

A county's approval of a subdivision map that included a drainage course was not sufficient to create inverse liability for landslides caused by drainage from the water course when the public agency expressly rejected an offer of dedication and did not maintain or control the creek. *Ullery v Contra Costa County* (1988) 202 CA3d 562, 248 CR 727.

Pacific Gas & Electric, having contracted with the developer of a subdivision to supply the lots with gas and electricity, did not need prior governmental approval or a declaration of necessity to construct a trench beneath a private road in which to place its gas and electric lines. Thus, it was not liable in inverse condemnation for a landslide caused by the PG&E trench conducting water to slope supporting residences. The trench was installed to provide utility service line extensions to interruptible customers in a private development under rules authorized by the Public Utility Commission; this was not the same as a permanent power line designed to serve a general area. *Cantu v PG&E* (1987) 189 CA3d 160, 234 CR 365. See *Belair v Riverside County Flood Control Dist.* (1988) 47 C3d 550, 566, 253 CR 693, 703, discussed in Supp §13.17, categorizing these cases as involving a diversion or obstruction of waters from their natural channels or drainages.

When a storm drain ruptured and allowed water to seep into the soil adjacent to plaintiff's property, causing massive subsidence, inverse condemnation was a proper remedy because the public purpose served by the storm drain was to collect and divert surface water and the injury occurred while the improvement was operating as intended. *Yee v City of Sausalito* (1983) 141 CA3d 917, 190 CR 595. See also *McMahan's of Santa Monica v City of Santa Monica, supra,* holding that the damage caused by certain maintenance of an improvement, rather than the improvement itself, can engender liability for inverse condemnation. Negligence in ordinary, daily operations is insufficient to render a party liable. However, the principles of "construction" and "maintenance" are synonymous when maintenance entails a deliberate act that serves to fulfill the purpose of the improvement as a whole. Thus, a city was held liable for inverse condemnation when it adopted a plan of pipe replacement and maintenance that it knew was inadequate and damage proximately resulted.

A public agency may be liable in inverse condemnation, even though it does not have the authority to exercise the power of eminent domain. See *Baker v Burbank-Glendale-Pasadena Airport Auth.* (1985) 39 C3d 862, 218 CR 293, in which the supreme court held that an airport authority that did not have the power to condemn air easements nonetheless could be held liable in inverse condemnation for damages caused by noise, smoke, and vibrations from airplane flights over property owners' homes.

(c) *Property taken or damaged.* In an inverse condemnation action, the burden of alleging and proving the owner's property right and its infringement is on the owner. *People ex rel Dep't of Pub. Works v Romano* (1971) 18 CA3d 63, 72 n4, 94 CR 839, 845 n4.

A cable television installation within existing easements for electrical energy and telephone lines does not constitute a taking; cable television equipment use comes within the scope of the easements as a part of the natural evolution of communication technology. *Salvaty v Falcon Cable Television* (1985) 165 CA3d 798, 212 CR 31. But see *Group W Cable, Inc. v City of Santa Cruz* (ND Cal 1988) 679 F Supp 977, holding that a city could charge a cable television company for the use of a street easement, although that company was already making payments to utility companies to use their telephone poles, because the utilities had franchises and not easements or other property interests.

In a case involving a New York State statute that required landlords to permit cable television companies to install lines on their buildings and that directed that compensation be fixed by a state commission at a reasonable rate, at which time the commission awarded a one-time payment of $1, the United States Supreme Court declared that, because there was a physical intrusion, there could not be a formula approach to compensation. The statute was not declared invalid; rather, the case was remanded for a full trial on valuation. *Loretto v Teleprompter Manhattan CATV Corp.* (1982) 458 US 419. See Rabin, *A Comment on Loretto v Teleprompter Manhattan CATV Corp.,* 6 CEB Real Prop L Rep 136 (1983).

Loretto was distinguished in *FCC v Florida Power Corp.* (1987) 480 US 245, in which the Supreme Court held that the FCC's significant reduction of pole rental rates paid by cable television companies to public utilities to use their poles did not constitute a taking. The distinction was made on the basis of the power companies not being *required* to permit the use of the poles while the landlords in *Loretto* were required to allow the passage of television cable. The rate charged by the public utilities was legally subject to government scrutiny.

INVERSE CONDEMNATION AND TORT LAW

[§13.4] Confusion Between Theories of Recovery

The absolute liability rule for interference with land stability proximately caused by a public project as deliberately designed or constructed, as stated in *Albers v County of Los Angeles* (1965) 62 C2d 250, 42 CR 89, discussed in Book §13.4, is modified in flooding cases if the damaged property was subject to historic flooding before the public flood protection project. The California Supreme Court in *Belair v Riverside County Flood Control Dist.* (1988) 47 C3d 550, 567, 253 CR 693, 703, declared that, in cases involving damages from the construction, operation, or maintenance of a flood control project, failure to function is not sufficient to impose liability. There must also be unreasonable conduct by the public agency. See discussion in Supp §13.17.

Liability against a public agency for damage to property from a landslide, allegedly caused by the faulty design and construction of adjacent municipal streets, may be based on concurrent substantial causes. In *Blau v City of Los Angeles* (1973) 32 CA3d 77, 107 CR 727, error was found in the following jury instruction regarding proximate cause: "In case you find that a substantial cause of said landslide was attributable to conduct on the part of plaintiffs or their predecessors in interest in the subject property, then you may not award damages against the defendant City of Los Angeles." The instruction misstated the law. Although plaintiffs and their predecessors in interest may have contributed to the landslide by development of the building site, the concurrent development of adjacent streets also may have been a substantial factor in causing the earth movement. "[e]ach such important causal element is legally responsible notwithstanding the contribution of another." 32 CA3d at 85, 107 CR at 733. See also *Ingram v City of Redondo Beach* (1975) 45 CA3d 628, 119 CR 688; *Aaron v City of Los Angeles* (1974) 40 CA3d 471, 487, 115 CR 162, 173.

Blau v City of Los Angeles, supra, recognized the rule of *Sheffet v County of Los Angeles* (1970) 3 CA3d 720, 84 CR 11, that a public entity that approves and accepts for a public purpose work performed by a subdivider or private property owner may be liable in inverse condemnation for damage to property caused by the improvement. Streets, utilities, and drainage systems, when accepted and approved by a municipality, become a public improvement and part of its system of public works. See also *Marin v City of San Rafael* (1980) 111 CA3d 591, 168 CR 750 (further discussed in Supp §13.3); *Frustuck v City of Fairfax* (1963) 212 CA2d 345, 28 CR 357; *Steiger v City of San Diego* (1958) 163

CA2d 110, 329 P2d 94. This liability of the public agency does not necessarily exonerate the subdivider.

In *Fisher v Morrison Homes, Inc.* (1980) 109 CA3d 131, 139, 167 CR 133, 137, a developer negligently constructed a bikepath and then dedicated it to a city as a condition of subdivision approval. The court held that whether such a developer should be held liable in tort for injuries resulting from that negligence depends on the nature of the relationship between the developer and the city through the process of design, construction, dedication, and acceptance. The developer is not liable for damages when the work is done in accordance with officially sanctioned plans and specifications and under the supervision and direction of the public body. In *County of San Mateo v Berney* (1988) 199 CA3d 1489, 245 CR 738, however, a public agency that had been sued in inverse condemnation based on a claim that the county planned and constructed a public street affecting the lateral support of adjacent property was allowed to cross-complain against the developer to seek indemnification from the party whose negligent or fraudulent conduct caused the damage. In *Berney,* the public agency alleged in the cross-complaint that the developer had fraudulently concealed the use of improper fill material and that the plans and permits submitted to the county for approval did not disclose such information, all of which caused or contributed to the homeowner's injury.

See also *County of Mariposa v Yosemite W. Assocs.* (1988) 202 CA3d 791, 248 CR 778, in which the county's minimal participation in development under a subdivision agreement did not preclude an action against the developer for defective construction. This court distinguished *Sheffet v County of Los Angeles, supra,* on the basis that there was active negligence on the part of the developer, and the developer had a contract with the public agency to install certain improvements.

Negligent maintenance, as opposed to construction, of an improvement can often serve as the basis for inverse condemnation liability. *McMahan's of Santa Monica v City of Santa Monica* (1983) 146 CA3d 683, 194 CR 582. For further discussion, see Supp §13.3.

Although a utility may be immune from inverse condemnation liability for a defectively designed trench that does not involve public use, owners of damaged property could have pursued a negligence cause of action. *Cantu v PG&E* (1987) 189 CA3d 160, 234 CR 365.

A nuisance arising from a public project may be so intense as to allow a property owner to seek damages under both nuisance and inverse condemnation theories. In *Varjabedian v City of Madera* (1977) 20 C3d 285, 142 CR 429, a sewage facility produced recurring odors that were carried by prevailing winds directly across plaintiff's farm. The burden on the property was sufficiently direct, substantial, and peculiar to constitute a taking of the property. See also *Smith v County of Los Angeles* (1989) 214 CA3d 266, 262 CR 754, combining a claim of nuisance in order to assert damages for emotional distress with inverse allegations for physical damage to property.

California Constitution art I, §14, cited in Book §13.4, has been renumbered art I, §19. See Supp §8.7.

[§13.5] Choice of Action

Miller v City of Burbank, cited in Book §13.5, was vacated in *Miller v Los Angeles County Flood Control Dist.* (1973) 8 C3d 689, 106 CR 1. The supreme court did not discuss the issues mentioned in Book §13.5.

Although the pleadings of a particular action do not expressly characterize the proceeding as one for inverse condemnation, the case may be converted into one by the evidence presented and submitted to the jury solely on an inverse theory. *Blau v City of Los Angeles* (1973) 32 CA3d 77, 89, 107 CR 727, 735. See also *Ingram v City of Redondo Beach* (1975) 45 CA3d 628, 119 CR 688.

In an inverse condemnation action arising from noise from aircraft using an airport, plaintiffs were not allowed to proceed under a tort theory, because they made no allegation that the flights did not comply with federal laws and regulations, which preempt local control of aircraft in flight. (Preemption does not apply to damages arising from tortious management and maintenance of the airport facilities rather than aircraft in flight.) Inverse condemnation was available if an owner could have shown that the flights resulted in a taking. *San Diego Unified Port Dist. v Superior Court* (1977) 67 CA3d 361, 136 CR 557.

It was appropriate to join a nuisance and inverse condemnation theory for damages arising by reason of recurring odors from a nearby sewage treatment plant when the burden was peculiar to the property in question. *Varjabedian v City of Madera* (1977) 20 C3d 285, 142 CR 429, further discussed in Supp §13.4. See also *Greater Westchester Homeowners Ass'n v City of Los Angeles* (1979) 26 C3d 86, 160 CR 733, which involved causes of action in inverse condemnation for property damage and for nuisance for personal injuries allegedly caused by the noise, smoke, and vibration from aircraft using Los Angeles International Airport; and *Institoris v City of Los Angeles* (1989) 210 CA3d 10, 258 CR 418, combining causes of action for inverse condemnation and a nuisance action regarding a claim of damages against an airport caused by overflights.

Loss of business goodwill may now be recoverable in an inverse condemnation action. CCP §1263.510; *Hladek v City of Merced* (1977) 69 CA3d 585, 589 n1, 138 CR 194, 196 n1. A private carrier's loss of business to competition from a bus system operated by a public metropolitan transit district, however, is not compensable. *Peerless Stages, Inc. v Santa Cruz Metropolitan Transit Dist.* (1977) 67 CA3d 343, 136 CR 567.

In *Kachadoorian v Calwa County Water Dist.* (1979) 96 CA3d 741,

158 CR 223, the court held that abandonment by the county of a public alley, under which a public utility had maintained a water pipeline, terminated the county's right-of-way easement for use of the alley. However, 50 years of use of that water pipeline as a part of a community system was sufficient to establish the necessity of maintaining the pipeline use and thus to prevent the property owner from quieting title or seeking injunctive relief. The only remedy was damages under inverse condemnation.

On the other hand, a public entity was permitted to quiet title to a public beach recreation easement across private property that had been used by the public for years. The property owner did not establish inverse condemnation for unreasonable precondemnation delay by arguing that the public entity had a duty to advise the owner of the public access easement (see Supp §§4.7A, 13.21). *County of Los Angeles v Berk* (1980) 26 C3d 201, 161 CR 742.

Government Code §830.6, part of the California Tort Claims Act of 1963 (Govt C §§810–996.6), has been expanded to grant immunity to a public agency that is reasonably attempting to remedy a deficient construction plan or design.

California Constitution art I, §14 has been renumbered art I, §19. See Supp §8.7.

California Government Tort Liability §6.65 (Cal CEB 1964) has been replaced with California Government Tort Liability Practice §§2.08–2.14 (Cal CEB 1980).

INITIATING THE ACTION

Claims

[§13.7] Prerequisite to Litigation

A formal notice of a permanent taking by a governmental agency is not necessary before filing a claim in inverse condemnation. The cause of action accrues once the damage or taking is "apparent and discoverable." Under former law, an inverse condemnation suit was barred by failure to file a timely claim. *Mosesian v County of Fresno* (1972) 28 CA3d 493, 104 CR 655, further discussed in Supp §13.10. See also *People ex rel Dep't of Pub. Works v Peninsula Enters.* (1979) 91 CA3d 332, 356, 153 CR 895, 908, in which the court held that adoption of a formal resolution of condemnation is not a prerequisite to the injured party's proceeding with an inverse condemnation action based on direct and special interference with the owner's property by unreasonable precondemnation activities.

In 1975, the legislature adopted CCP §426.70(b), which provides that a cross-complaint in a direct condemnation action need not be preceded by a claim. See Supp §§8.18A, 8.24. In 1976, the legislature abolished the claims requirement for inverse condemnation actions. Govt C §905.1. When a tort claim such as nuisance is combined with an inverse cause of action, the claims statute will apply to the nuisance claim. *Smith v County of Los Angeles* (1989) 214 CA3d 266, 262 CR 754. If a claim is presented, however, it must be processed in the usual manner. Govt C §905.1.

Government Code §905.1, effective January 1, 1977, applies to litigation pending on that date. *City of Los Angeles v Superior Court* (1977) 73 CA3d 509, 142 CR 292. In that case the court of appeal determined that this statute protected the plaintiff in an inverse condemnation action, even though the complaint had been filed before the effective date of the statute; however, the timeliness of plaintiff's allegedly late claim had not yet been adjudicated. This decision was followed in *Wedding v People ex rel Dep't of Transp.* (1979) 88 CA3d 719, 152 CR 181.

California Government Tort Liability, chap 8 (Cal CEB 1964) has been replaced with California Government Tort Liability Practice, chap 5 (Cal CEB 1980).

[§13.8] Form: Claim

Comment: Claims are no longer a prerequisite for actions filed after December 31, 1976. See *City of Los Angeles v Superior Court* (1977) 73 CA3d 509, 142 CR 292, discussed in Supp §13.7.

[§13.9] Period During Which Suit Must Be Instituted

Because the claims requirement has been abolished in inverse condemnation cases (Govt C §905.1; see Supp §13.7), these cases are no longer governed by the time limits in Govt C §945.6. They are now governed by the ordinary statutes of limitation in the Code of Civil Procedure. Govt C §945.8.

Effective January 1, 1990, CCP §338(j) requires that an action for "physical damage to private property" under Cal Const art I, §19 be filed within three years. Previously, it was not clear under case law whether a three-year period or a five-year period was applicable. See, *e.g., Wilson v Beville* (1957) 47 C2d 852, 306 P2d 789, cited in Book §13.9. But note that the statute only speaks of *damaging,* not *taking.* Since five years are necessary to establish a prescriptive right, a similar period would be logical for bringing a taking action.

[§13.10] Accrual of Cause of Action

The demise of the claims requirement for inverse condemnation cases (see Supp §13.7) means that these cases are now governed by the three-year period of CCP §338(j). See Supp §13.9. Generally, it would appear that the same considerations governing accrual of the cause of action discussed in *Pierpont Inn, Inc. v State* (1969) 70 C2d 282, 74 CR 521, and its progeny still apply, and that principles set forth in these cases will probably continue to be followed. See *Leaf v City of San Mateo* (1980) 104 CA3d 398, 163 CR 711, which discusses accrual of an inverse condemnation cause of action joined with a tort action concerning subsidence that resulted from a latent defect in the city's sewage and drainage systems. The court held that the cause of action accrued at the time of discovery of the negligent cause of the damage rather than at the time of the discovery of the damage itself. The settlement of a prior action against the developer was not a bar to the inverse condemnation action against the city.

Reviewing several cases, including *Pierpont Inn, Inc. v State, supra,* the court in *Mosesian v County of Fresno* (1972) 28 CA3d 493, 501, 104 CR 655, 660, rejected plaintiffs' position that "though a taking is objectively total and the improvement complete, the time for filing a claim is postponed until the claimant is subjectively convinced the taking is permanent rather than temporary." Presumably, now that no claim need be filed, this holding would be applied in a determination of when the statute of limitations begins to run. *Mosesian* also held that a letter by one of the plaintiffs more than a year before the claim was filed indicated that plaintiffs believed the taking to be permanent. Compare *Mehl v People ex rel Dep't of Pub. Works* (1975) 13 C3d 710, 717 n2, 119 CR 625, 629 n2.

In a case concerning overflights (see §13.20), although plaintiffs were annoyed by jet noise and hired attorneys and appraisers more than a year before claims were filed, the cause of action did not accrue until the flights substantially interfered with the use and enjoyment of their properties and resulted in a diminution of their market value. Plaintiffs were not required to sue at the time the damaging flights began but under the rule of *Pierpont Inn* could wait until the situation stabilized. *Aaron v City of Los Angeles* (1974) 40 CA3d 471, 115 CR 162.

The courts in *Mehl v People ex rel Dep't of Pub. Works* (1975) 13 C3d 710, 717, 119 CR 625, 629, and *Oakes v McCarthy Co.* (1968) 267 CA2d 231, 73 CR 127, have held that the date of accrual occurs when the consequential damage is clear to a "reasonable man." *Pierpont Inn,* however, goes further and holds that time does not start running until the public project is completed *and* the damage stabilizes.

In *Smart v City of Los Angeles* (1980) 112 CA3d 232, 169 CR 174, an inverse condemnation action resulting from airport noise, the court extended the date of accrual beyond the date of stabilization. The noise level impact from the airport was found to have stabilized in 1966, but the property, which had been vacant, did not suffer any detriment until 1972, when the owner tried to sell it and discovered that it was redlined by lending institutions because of the high noise level. The court held that the cause of action accrued at the time the owner learned of the redlining. Compare *Smart* with *Institoris v City of Los Angeles* (1989) 210 CA3d 10, 258 CR 418, which held that the date of accrual of a cause of action against an airport was when the aircraft created noise sufficient to cause the taking and damaging of the property, not when the noise fell below that level. The court distinguished the *Pierpont Inn* case discussed above; here the noise was sufficient to effect a taking in 1967 and by 1972 a prescriptive aviation easement was acquired before the lawsuit was filed in 1973.

[§13.10A] Date of Valuation

When a taking of property by a public agency occurs by physical invasion rather than by formal condemnation, the established rule is that the time of taking is the time of the invasion, and it is that event that fixes the date of valuation for a claim of compensation. *Leaf v City of San Mateo* (1984) 150 CA3d 1184, 1191, 198 CR 447, 451, citing *McDougald v Southern Pac. R.R.* (1912) 162 C 1, 120 P 766. However, because hardship to the property owner may result when that valuation date is used if the property value has since increased, the property may be valued at the time of trial if the property owner has promptly pursued the remedy of inverse condemnation. *Mehl v People ex rel Dep't of Pub. Works* (1975) 13 C3d 710, 719, 119 CR 625, 630, citing *Pierport Inn, Inc. v State* (1969) 70 C2d 282, 296, 74 CR 521, 530; *Leaf v City of San Mateo, supra.*

[§13.11] Form: Complaint

Comment: Judicial Council form complaints for property damage are optional. See CCP §425.12. An inverse condemnation action for damages qualifies as a property damage case, but the Judicial Council form complaint is not complete, and allegations for individual causes of action must be attached.

Paragraph VII is no longer necessary. See Supp §13.7.

[§13.12] Prepayment of Costs Undertaking

On due process grounds, the supreme court struck down Govt C §947, which required an undertaking for costs by a private party instituting an action against a public agency. *Beaudreau v Superior Court* (1975) 14 C3d 448, 121 CR 585. Government Code §947 was then repealed in 1980.

[§13.12A] Two-Phase Trial

Before plaintiff can raise the issue of compensation for inverse condemnation, he must plead and prove that there has been a taking or damaging under Cal Const art I, §19. Such a case, therefore, has two phases: The first phase may be determined by the pleadings through demurrer, or by court trial as a mixed question of fact and law; the second phase, if there is one, fixes compensation.

Consequently, as a practical method of disposing of the issues, inverse condemnation cases are usually bifurcated, particularly when compensation is to be decided by a jury. There can be no decision by a jury jury on the first phase, because in eminent domain the purpose of a jury is to assess value. *People v Ricciardi* (1943) 23 C2d 390, 144 P2d 799. Unless the plaintiff establishes liability, *i.e.*, that a taking or damaging occurred, there can be no second phase. See *Niles Sand & Gravel Co. v Alameda County Water Dist.* (1974) 37 CA3d 924, 112 CR 846, in which there was a cross-complaint in inverse condemnation; and *United Cal. Bank v People ex rel Dep't of Pub. Works* (1969) 1 CA3d 1, 81 CR 405. See also Supp §9.20A for discussion of bifurcation of issues in a condemnation trial. Often the parties stipulate to a bifurcated trial. See, *e.g., Turner v County of Del Norte* (1972) 24 CA3d 311, 101 CR 93. If the parties do not stipulate, however, the court properly bifurcates the inverse condemnation action under CCP §598, leaving the liability issue to be determined by the trial court and the damages, if any, by the jury. *Orpheum Bldg. Co. v San Francisco BART Dist.* (1978) 80 CA3d 863, 146 CR 5. See also *Marshall v Department of Water & Power* (1990) 219 CA3d 1124, 268 CR 559; *Redevelopment Agency v Tobriner* (1984) 153 CA3d 367, 376, 200 CR 364, 370; *Wagner v State* (1975) 51 CA3d 472, 124 CR 224.

Whether plaintiff is entitled to precondemnation damages (see §§4.7–4.7A, 13.21) is an obvious issue for bifurcation. *City of Los Angeles v Lowensohn* (1976) 54 CA3d 625, 127 CR 417. However, in *Stone v City of Los Angeles* (1975) 51 CA3d 987, 124 CR 822, the trial court gave the question of unreasonable delay to the jury after determining that the question presented an issue of fact.

CAUSES OF ACTION

[§13.13] Types of Compensable Damages

(1) Interference with land stability. *Yee v City of Sausalito* (1983) 141 CA3d 917, 190 CR 595; *Blau v City of Los Angeles* (1973) 32 CA3d 77, 107 CR 727.

(4) Injury by escaping sewage. *Amador Valley Investors v City of Livermore* (1974) 43 CA3d 483, 117 CR 749. Recurring odors from sewage facility. *Varjabedian v City of Madera* (1977) 20 C3d 285, 142 CR 429.

(5) Loss of or interference with access. *City of Los Angeles v Ricards* (1973) 10 C3d 385, 110 CR 489.

(6) Interference with access caused by raising or lowering street grade. *England v San Francisco,* cited in Book §13.13, should not be cited in any proceeding. Cal Rules of Ct 977.

(12) Interference with exercise of substantial property right secured in contract or deed. See *Southern Cal. Edison Co. v Bourgerie* (1973) 9 C3d 169, 107 CR 76, in which the court held that a building restriction constituted property.

(13) Cost of minimizing damages in a reasonable manner. *Albers v County of Los Angeles* (1965) 62 C2d 250, 42 CR 89; *Sheffet v County of Los Angeles* (1970) 3 CA3d 720, 730, 84 CR 11, 17.

(14) Land regulation enacted in bad faith, *e.g.,* to depress the value of property for subsequent acquisition by the public agency. *Peacock v County of Sacramento* (1969) 271 CA2d 845, 77 CR 391; see Supp §13.22F. Governmental regulation of land having the effect of removing all reasonable use of the property may also be compensable. See Supp §§13.22B–13.22C.

(15) Injury by fire caused by sparks from electric power transmission lines. *Aetna Life & Cas. Co. v City of Los Angeles* (1985) 170 CA3d 865, 216 CR 831.

In *Beaty v Imperial Irrig. Dist.* (1986) 186 CA3d 897, 231 CR 128, the court held that property owners who have successfully prosecuted an inverse condemnation action that is a substitute for a direct condemnation action and who have been displaced from their property by a public entity's appropriation or acquisition of their property are entitled to relocation benefits under Govt C §§7260–7277. See §4.53 for discussion of compensation for moving and relocation costs.

The correct title of the first case in the last paragraph of Book §13.13 is *Brandenburg v Los Angeles County Flood Control Dist.*

[§13.14] Water Damage

Damages to the premises and merchandise of a store caused by a water main's breaking is compensable in inverse condemnation. *McMahan's of Santa Monica v City of Santa Monica* (1983) 146 CA3d 683, 194 CR 582, discussed in Supp §13.3.

For further discussion of *Keys v Romley* (1966) 64 C2d 396, 50 CR 273, mentioned in Book §13.14, see *Weaver v Bishop* (1988) 206 CA3d 1351, 254 CR 425, and *Ellison v City of San Buenaventura* (1976) 60 CA3d 453, 131 CR 433.

See generally Shoaf & Aklufi, *A Summary of the Rules of Liability in Water Damage Cases,* 55 Cal SBJ 459 (1980).

[§13.16] Stream Water; Alteration by Public Project

A regulatory scheme by the State Water Resources Control Board that prohibited direct diversion of water from the Napa River for frost protection during the crucial winter period was a valid exercise of the police power, not a taking. *People ex rel State Water Resources Control Bd. v Forni* (1976) 54 CA3d 743, 126 CR 851.

A city was not liable for sediment buildup in downstream waterways at a faster rate than would have occurred without upstream development when the municipality played no part in the private development of upstream property other than approval of plans and issuance of permits. *Ellison v City of San Buenaventura* (1976) 60 CA3d 453, 131 CR 433.

[§13.17] Flood Damage

Miller v City of Burbank, cited in Book §13.17, has been vacated. *Miller v Los Angeles County Flood Control Dist.* (1973) 8 C3d 689, 106 CR 1. The supreme court did not discuss the issues mentioned in Book §13.17.

In an action to recover damages from the flooding of a river, when the state had constructed a levee along the river bank opposite plaintiffs' lands and partially completed a dam upstream, the evidence showed that the flooding was greater than would have occurred had only the dam been present. Nevertheless, because the net result of the total project was less flooding than would have occurred without the entire improvement—dam and levee system—recovery was denied. *Shaeffer v State* (1972) 22 CA3d 1017, 99 CR 861 (disapproved on other grounds in *County of San Diego v Miller* (1975) 13 C3d 684, 693, 119 CR 491, 496).

An irrigation district was liable in inverse condemnation because a constructed drain, conceived and designed to accommodate only the minimal average yearly rainfall in the county, was inadequate to accommodate the rainwater runoff from tropical storms. *Imperial Cattle Co. v Imperial Irrig. Dist.* (1985) 167 CA3d 263, 213 CR 622. A city's use of a natural channel or creek as part of a storm drainage system did not preclude a finding that the system was a public improvement subjecting the city to inverse condemnation liability. However, because the city's storm drainage system added only a minimal amount of water to the creek and the erosion that occurred was a natural phenomenon, a causal connection between the conduct of the city and the damage was not established. *Souza v Silver Dev. Co.* (1985) 164 CA3d 165, 210 CR 146.

In *Belair v Riverside County Flood Control Dist.* (1988) 47 C3d 550, 253 CR 693, the supreme court sought to clarify the standards for proximate causation and liability in flood cases. A levee controlled by the defendant agency failed while it was operating well below its designed capacity, which resulted in flooding the plaintiff's property.

Plaintiff never pleaded negligence in the design, construction, or operation, and produced no evidence to that effect. Although plaintiff's property was subject to flooding before construction of the levee, the court concluded that that fact was irrelevant to the question of causation because the plaintiff had reasonably relied on the levee's containing the river waters within the channel and had made substantial expenditures based on that reliance. For there to be recovery, however, there must first be proof that the failure was attributable to unreasonable conduct on the part of the defendant agency. The rule of *Albers v County of Los Angeles* (1965) 62 C2d 250, 42 CR 89, discussed in Book and Supp §13.4, regarding absolute liability for damages proximately caused by a public project as deliberately designed or constructed, is not applicable to flooding cases. The supreme court summarizes its *Belair* rule as follows (47 C3d at 567, 253 CR at 703):

> It is sufficient for our purposes here to hold that when a public flood control improvement fails to function as intended and properties historically subject to flooding are damaged as a proximate result thereof, plaintiff's recovery in inverse condemnation requires proof that the failure was attributable to some unreasonable conduct on the part of the defendant public entities.

The court did not, however, define unreasonable conduct. If unreasonable conduct is found, liability does not require proof that the public agency's improvement diverted waters onto property not previously affected.

This case interprets both *Shaeffer* and *Imperial Cattle Co.*, discussed above. *Shaeffer* is interpreted to hold that proximate cause was not found, because there was no evidence in that case that the project failed to function as intended. The holding in *Imperial Cattle Co.* is probably still valid because it can be argued that the design of the drain in that case was unreasonable in that it could accommodate only minimal average yearly rainfall.

Subsequently, the appellate court in *Bunch v Coachella Valley Water Dist.* (1989) 214 CA3d 203, 262 CR 513, concluded that *Belair* holds liability can be established "only when there is a conjunction of substantial causation and unreasonableness." 214 CA3d at 209, 262 CR at 515. Furthermore, the *Belair* rule should not be limited to the "common enemy doctrine" but should apply to "all flood control inverse condemnation cases involving unintended physical damage to property." 214 CA3d at 213, 262 CR at 519. The court further observed that *Belair* applies to public agencies, intentional diversion of waters from a natural course or channel; the focus must be on "whether water is unintentionally diverted to a particular place—without regard to whether water is intentionally diverted from a particular place." 214 CA3d at 215, 262 CR at 520.

In a case concerning flooding after the failure of a levee operated by a local levee maintenance district, the state was held not liable in inverse condemnation because it had no duty to review the plan for the project. *Galli v State* (1979) 98 CA3d 662, 159 CR 721.

When a city street was washed out by flood, destroying access to private property, the city was obligated, within a reasonable time, either to restore the street or pay the owner for the loss of access. *Clay v City of Los Angeles* (1971) 21 CA3d 577, 98 CR 582. But see *City of Los Angeles v Ricards* (1973) 10 C3d 385, 110 CR 489, which denied compensation for an acknowledged temporary taking of the sole means of access by a diversion of waters that destroyed a private bridge, when the city reconstructed the bridge two years after the flooding and the property would not have been used during the interim in any event. When a flood control project benefits the property, causing less flooding than would have occurred without the project, no action for inverse condemnation arises by reason of waters flowing onto the property and causing damage. *Tri-Chem, Inc. v Los Angeles County Flood Control Dist.* (1976) 60 CA3d 306, 132 CR 142. The supreme court's decision in *Belair* qualifies this rule to the effect that there is no damage as long as the project functioned as designed.

In *Ingram v City of Redondo Beach* (1975) 45 CA3d 628, 119 CR 688, the court held that the city was liable for water damage caused by the collapse of its sump wall. But see *Tri-Chem, Inc. v Los Angeles County Flood Control Dist., supra,* in which the court denied compensation on similar facts absent evidence indicating that flooding would have resulted even if the county's dike had not broken.

Under 33 USC §702c, the federal government is immune from damage caused by floods. This immunity protects it from backwater damage. *Pierce v U.S.* (9th Cir 1981) 650 F2d 202.

Agreements and easements that purported to absolve an irrigation district and county from all liability for flooding damage from an irrigation reservoir were contrary to public policy and void. *Salton Bay Marina, Inc. v Imperial Irrig. Dist.* (1985) 172 CA3d 914, 218 CR 839.

[§13.18] Rights in Water

The condemnor of the water rights of a mutual water company may not repudiate the company's contract obligation to supply water to its shareholders. In *San Bernardino Valley Mun. Water Dist. v Meeks & Daley Water Co.* (1964) 226 CA2d 216, 38 CR 51, the condemnor attempted to condemn only the water rights and diversion facilities. However, the court held that the condemnor must also condemn the transportation facilities and diversion structures, although located in different counties, to continue water services to the shareholders of the condemned water company.

The owners of land above percolating waters do not have an absolute right to pump and discharge those waters under CC §829, granting to the fee owner of land "the right to the surface and to everything permanently situated beneath or above it." The property is subject to a public servitude, and its owner is governed by the doctrine of "correlative rights," under which the rights to the water by each owner of land having water percolating below the surface are limited, in correlation with those of others, to his reasonable use when the water is insufficient to meet the needs of all.

In *Niles Sand & Gravel Co. v Alameda County Water Dist.* (1974) 37 CA3d 924, 112 CR 846, a water district's water replenishment program raised the water table, flooding a company's sand and gravel pits. The water district obtained an injunction to stop the company from pumping out and discharging the water, and the company filed a cross-complaint in inverse condemnation. The court held that, under the correlative rights doctrine, discharge of the water was an unreasonable use, and also noted that the company was operating under a use permit, one of the conditions of which was that it cooperate with the water district in not discharging or wasting water. As an alternative ground for denying inverse condemnation, the court held that the water district's taking was an exercise of police power and thus not compensable. See §13.22 for discussion of police power.

When a county water district establishes a public use relative to sub-basin groundwater surplus against private landowners, inverse condemnation for damages, not an injunction, is the proper remedy. See *Wright v Goleta Water Dist.* (1985) 174 CA3d 74, 219 CR 740.

A regulatory scheme by the State Water Resources Control Board that prohibited direct diversion of water from the Napa River for frost protection during a crucial winter period was a valid exercise of police power, not a taking. *People ex rel State Water Resources Control Bd. v Forni* (1976) 54 CA3d 743, 126 CR 851. A landowner who was denied access to a water district's facilities on the basis of an initiative ordinance establishing a moratorium on new service connections during drought conditions cannot recover in inverse condemnation for diminution in value of property caused by lack of water. *Gilbert v State* (1990) 218 CA3d 234, 266 CR 891; *Hollister Park Inv. Co. v Goleta County Water Dist.* (1978) 82 CA3d 290, 147 CR 91. See Supp §§13.22K (temporary regulations) and 13.22L (emergency regulations).

Tidelands in San Francisco Bay that were conveyed to private parties by the State Board of Tide Land Commissioners under an 1870 act are not free of the public trust for commerce, navigation, and fishing. But those lands so conveyed that have been filled under applicable land use regulations are free of the trust to the extent that they are not subject to tidal action. *City of Berkeley v Superior Court* (1980) 26 C3d 515, 162 CR 327. See *Summa Corp. v California* (1984) 466 US 198, in which the United States Supreme Court held that the public trust in tidelands does not extend to lands directly conveyed by the Mexican government to private ownership unless the public trust was raised during federal court proceedings to confirm Mexican land grants shortly after California became a state. On remand to the California court by the Supreme Court, the *Summa* decision was implemented in *City of Los Angeles v Venice Peninsula Props.* (1988) 205 CA3d 1522,

253 CR 331. See also *State v Superior Court* (Lyon) (1981) 29 C3d 210, 172 CR 696, concerning Clear Lake; and *State v Superior Court* (Fogerty) (1981) 29 C3d 240, 172 CR 713, concerning Lake Tahoe. These cases applied the public trust doctrine to lands between low and high water marks of navigable lakes.

[§13.19] Land Stability

A public entity is liable for damage to real property caused by a landslide when the faulty design and construction of street improvements accepted and approved by defendant-city was a concurrent substantial cause of the earth movement. *Blau v City of Los Angeles* (1973) 32 CA3d 77, 107 CR 727; see Supp §13.4.

A public entity may be liable in inverse condemnation for any physical injury to real property proximately caused by a deliberately designed and constructed improvement even if there is no negligence on the entity's part and the injury was not foreseeable. See *City of Mill Valley v Transamerica Ins. Co.* (1979) 98 CA3d 595, 600, 159 CR 635, 637, in which an insurance policy indemnifying the City of Mill Valley for property damages neither intended nor expected by the city was held to cover damages from a landslide triggered by surface water discharged from the city's drainage system. In *Yee v City of Sausalito* (1983) 141 CA3d 917, 190 CR 595, liability was found when a storm drain ruptured, allowing surface water to seep into the soil and cause subsidence of neighboring land because the improvement was operating as it was intended, *i.e.,* to collect and divert surface water.

A county's approval of a subdivision map that included a drainage course was not sufficient to create inverse liability for landslides caused by drainage from the water course when the public agency expressly rejected an offer of dedication and did not maintain or control the creek. *Ullery v Contra Costa County* (1988) 202 CA3d 562, 248 CR 727.

See also *Barnhouse v City of Pinole* (1982) 133 CA3d 171, 183 CR 881, in which a determination was made that the damages stemmed not from public improvement but from the subdivision developer's placement of fill and inadequate repair of preexisting slides on the property. When a city's storm drainage system added only a minimal amount of water to a creek and the erosion that occurred was a natural phenomenon, the evidence did not establish a causal connection between the conduct of the city and the damage. *Souza v Silver Dev. Co.* (1985) 164 CA3d 165, 210 CR 146.

When a county removes slide debris across a roadway without providing replacement stabilization, thus reactivating a landslide that contributed to damages to nearby residents, the defense of responding to an emergency under the police power in order to keep the road open to traffic was not available because alternative routes were available. *Smith v County of Los Angeles* (1989) 214 CA3d 266, 262 CR 754.

On situations in which landslide or subsidence is caused by flooding, see *Belair v Riverside County Flood Control Dist.* (1988) 47 C3d 550, 253 CR 693, discussed in Supp §13.17. Because it relies on the "common enemy" doctrine of handling overflowing waters from other lands, *Belair* applies only to landslides proximately caused by a failed flood control project that does not divert more waters than existed before the project. *Albers v County of Los Angeles* (1965) 62 C2d 250, 42 CR 89, discussed in Book §13.19, regarding strict liability for interference with land stability proximately caused by a public project as deliberately designed or constructed, otherwise remains viable and is recognized in *Belair.*

See generally Landslide and Subsidence Liability (Cal CEB 1974).

[§13.20] Overflying Aircraft

A municipal operator of an airport is liable for a taking or damaging of property when the owner of property in the vicinity of the airport can show a measurable reduction in market value resulting from the operation of the airport in such a manner that the aircraft noise causes a substantial interference with the use and enjoyment of the property, and the interference is sufficiently direct and peculiar that the property owner would contribute more than his fair share to the public undertaking. *Aaron v City of Los Angeles* (1974) 40 CA3d 471, 493, 115 CR 162, 177. The appellate court reached this conclusion from a thorough review of both federal and other state case law, as well as California decisional and statutory law, and found that its conclusion was implied in prior decisions of the California Supreme Court.

In particular, the court considered *Loma Portal Civic Club v American Airlines, Inc.* (1964) 61 C2d 582, 39 CR 708, in which the court denied plaintiff, residents of a neighborhood in the flight path of a jet aircraft using Lindbergh Field in San Diego, an injunction to prevent airlines from flying at low altitudes near their residences. The *Aaron* court found support in the holding of *City of Oakland v Nutter* (1970) 13 CA3d 752, 92 CR 347, that noise and other interference with remaining property from the use of an air easement, taken by direct condemnation to protect the approaches of an airport, could be considered in determining severance damages. See also *County of San Diego v Bressi* (1986) 184 CA3d 112, 229 CR 44 (effect of avigation easements on highest and best use in direct condemnation case).

The court rejected the two primary contentions of defendant-city by concluding that (1) the rule of *Batten v U.S.,* cited in Book §13.20, that damages must result from a physical invasion by the aircraft of the air space directly over plaintiff's property should not be followed by California and (2) the extensive pattern of federal regulation of air transportation does not absolve the owner and operator of the airport from liability when its operation is one of the substantial causes of the damages.

Finally, *Aaron* declared that whether the interference meets the standard of being sufficiently direct and peculiar so that an owner suffers more than incidental damages, such as are suffered by the general public, is a mixed question of fact and law for the trial judge to determine. See Supp §13.12A.

In an action by a neighboring town and individual homeowners against a city airport operator and airlines for injunctive relief and damages from the operation of the city airport, plaintiffs were awarded compensation on the theory that the defendant had taken permanent flight easements. *Town of East Haven v Eastern Airlines, Inc.* (2d Cir 1972) 470 F2d 148.

Flights by government helicopters over a landowner's property at altitudes of less than 500 feet were judged a compensable taking of an avigation easement when the flights constituted direct and substantial interference with the use and enjoyment of the property. The landowners were allowed recovery for the temporary taking of the avigation easement, which terminated when the military airfield was closed. *Speir v U.S.* (Ct Cl 1973) 485 F2d 643.

An airline itself is not liable to property owners in inverse condemnation for the taking of an avigation easement. The easement is a part of the airport, and only the airport is liable. Whether the airline has a duty of indemnification to the airport depends on the contract between them. *City of Los Angeles v Japan Air Lines Co.* (1974) 41 CA3d 416, 116 CR 69.

In *Parker v City of Los Angeles* (1974) 44 CA3d 556, 118 CR 687, it was not necessary to allocate damages between two units or phases of a taking (airport runway), because the difference in the effects of the two takings was minimal. See Book §4.6 regarding separate public projects.

In *San Diego Unified Port Dist. v Superior Court* (1977) 67 CA3d 361, 136 CR 557, the court held that property owners could not recover damages in tort from the operator of a municipal airport for harm caused by aircraft in flight, because federal laws and regulations preempt local control of aircraft in flight. See *City of Burbank v Lockheed Air Terminal, Inc.* (1973) 411 US 624, holding that the Federal Aviation Administration and the Environmental Protection Agency have preemptive and sole control over aircraft noise and striking down a local noise abatement ordinance forbidding nighttime takeoffs by jets. However, in *Santa Monica Airport Ass'n v City of Santa Monica* (9th Cir 1981) 659 F2d 100, the court held that federal exemption was inapplicable when the city was a proprietor of the airport and enacted its own noise control ordinance.

In *San Diego Unified Port Dist. v Superior Court, supra,* the court held that nearby homeowners could recover in tort if damages were caused by the proprietary operation of the airport facility itself and that recovery for damage from aircraft flights could be pursued in inverse condemnation if the flights resulted in a taking. See also *Greater Westchester Homeowners Ass'n v City of Los Angeles* (1979) 26 C3d 86, 160 CR 733, in which an action for inverse condemnation was joined with a nuisance action. The court pointed out that it was the city, not the federal government, that chose the location of the airport and elected to expand the facility with knowledge of the residential character of the area, and it held that the plaintiffs could recover in inverse condemnation for damages to their real property and under a nuisance theory for personal injuries. Relying on *Westchester,* the appellate court in *Andrews v County of Orange* (1982) 130 CA3d 944, 182 CR 176, held that the proprietor of an airport is not immune from liability for personal injuries and emotional distress caused by noises from aircraft in flight. Although airport proprietors cannot regulate aircraft in flight, they are responsible for operation of the airport and for land use planning designed to minimize the effects of noise.

In *Baker v Burbank-Glendale-Pasadena Airport Auth.* (1985) 39 C3d 862, 218 CR 293, the supreme court held that property owners may bring an inverse condemnation action against a public airport for damage from noise, smoke, and vibrations from flights over their homes, even if the airport lacks the power of eminent domain. The court also held that the property owners could elect to treat the damaging activities as a continuing, rather than a permanent nuisance, and thus bring successive suits for damages until the nuisance is abated. This case is distinguished in *Institoris v City of Los Angeles* (1989) 210 CA3d 10, 258 CR 418, in which the court commented that *Baker* did not specify that its holding permitted actions for inverse condemnation and for nuisance to compensate for damage to real property. Rather, the court in *Baker* assumes that the nuisance cause of action addressed personal injuries and that the inverse action addressed personal damage. Moreover, *Institoris* held that emotional distress cannot be recovered in an inverse cause of action but it may in a case in which public nuisance can be shown. 210 CA3d at 21, 258 CR at 425.

See Berger, Michael M., *Airport Noise in the 1980's: It's Time for Airport Operators to Acknowledge the Injury They Inflict on Neighbors,* Institute on Planning, Zoning & Eminent Domain, Southwestern Legal Foundation (1987), which discusses the above-mentioned California cases concerning inverse liability from the operation of airports.

[§13.21] Impact of Impending Project

Under CCP §1245.260 (former CCP §1243.1; see Supp §13.2), a property owner may bring an inverse condemnation action against a public entity that has adopted a resolution of condemnation against a particular parcel but fails to begin its action within six months.

Under Health & S C §33399, when a public agency has adopted a redevelopment plan but has not instituted a condemnation action to acquire any property under the plan within three years of its adoption, the owner of any affected parcel may offer in writing to sell the property to the agency at its fair market value. Then, if the agency does not acquire or commence proceedings within 18 months, the owner may file an inverse action for damages for any interference with possession and use of the property caused by the plan.

A decrease in market value, resulting from unreasonable delay of an eminent domain action following an announcement of intent to condemn or other unreasonable conduct by a public agency before condemnation, gives rise to an inverse condemnation cause of action. In *Klopping v City of Whittier* (1972) 8 C3d 39, 104 CR 1, the city adopted resolutions to condemn, filed suits, and then dismissed the actions because of other litigation seeking to enjoin the assessment necessary to fund the project. In dismissing the suits in condemnation, the condemnor declared it would reinstate the proceedings once the assessment matter was resolved. Klopping and Sarff, two property owners affected, filed inverse condemnation actions for loss of rental value because of the on-again, off-again conduct of the city. Klopping was precluded from recovering his damages because, after he instituted his inverse action, the city filed a second condemnation suit, which proceeded to judgment before the inverse case. Thus the claim for damages was barred by res judicata. Sarff, though he lost his property through foreclosure a few months after filing his inverse condemnation case, was allowed to seek recovery of loss of rents. The supreme court also concluded that plaintiffs' receipt of their costs and disbursements on abandonment of the first condemnation actions under CCP §1268.610 (former CCP §1255a; see §8.33) did not prevent recovery for the damages claimed in the inverse condemnation action. The decrease in market value is not compensable as a cost or disbursement under former CCP §1255a, but rather compensation for it is required by the constitution. For further discussion of *Klopping* on the issue of blight, see §4.7 and Supp §4.7A.

The planning for a project does not have to culminate in a resolution of condemnation in order to show unreasonable precondemnation activity. *People ex rel Dep't of Pub. Works v Peninsula Enters.* (1979) 91 CA3d 332, 356, 153 CR 895, 908.

In *Eleopoulos v Richmond Redev. Agency* (ND Cal 1972) 351 F Supp 63, plaintiff's allegations that (1) the city designated plaintiff's property as part of redevelopment area which it declared blighted, (2) the city redevelopment agency denied plaintiff's application for a permit to improve the property, and (3) the city then delayed condemnation proceedings, were sufficient to state a claim for de facto taking (see §4.7, Supp §4.7A).

A redevelopment agency's plans may so affect a particular property that the agency is liable for taking that property even though it decided not to acquire the property because of a cutback in federal funds. In

Richmond Elks Hall Ass'n v Richmond Redev. Agency (9th Cir 1977) 561 F2d 1327, the agency adopted a plan that included the property in a redevelopment area; it began acquiring and demolishing surrounding properties, with the result that the owner was unable to obtain insurance or loans on the property, and tenants who were told of the scheduled acquisition vacated the premises. These factors resulted in a reduction of rental income. Further, the agency undertook street improvements that caused flooding in the subject property's basement. Thereafter, the agency announced that it preferred not to acquire the property. The court concluded that the agency, acting in furtherance of a public project, directly and substantially interfered with the property rights of the landowner and significantly impaired the value of the property and, therefore, had effected a compensable taking.

A city's mere inclusion of certain property in a general neighborhood renewal plan area, however, is not, absent other conduct by the city, a taking. *Sayre v City of Cleveland* (6th Cir 1974) 493 F2d 64. The California Supreme Court has ruled that enactment of a general plan for future development of an area, including potential public uses for private land, does not amount to inverse condemnation of affected property. *Selby Realty Co. v City of San Buenaventura* (1973) 10 C3d 110, 109 CR 799. For further discussion of *Selby,* see Supp §13.22G. See also *Cambria Spring Co. v City of Pico Rivera* (1985) 171 CA3d 1080, 217 CR 69, which held that a city's adoption of a redevelopment plan was not an announcement of intention to condemn property and thus did not give rise to inverse condemnation or precondemnation damages.

In *Stone v City of Los Angeles* (1975) 51 CA3d 987, 124 CR 822, unreasonable delay was found when the city adopted a resolution to create an airport in August 1968, enacted an ordinance to take plaintiff's property in early 1969, but did not file an action until August 1972, after plaintiff had filed an inverse condemnation action in April 1972. Code of Civil Procedure §1245.260 (continuing the general rule of former CCP §1243.1), however, establishes a statute of limitations for filing an inverse condemnation action of one year after the six months given the condemnor to file suit after its resolution. See Supp §13.2.

In sustaining a demurrer, the court in *Smith v State* (1975) 50 CA3d 529, 123 CR 745, concluded that a delay of approximately seven years from the announcement of a tentative intent to acquire a proposed freeway route to the time of the action in inverse condemnation, with the prospect of acquisition not occurring for eight additional years, was not unreasonable in view of the requirements for public hearing and environmental studies. Similarly, *Elgin Capital Corp. v County of Santa Clara* (1975) 57 CA3d 687, 129 CR 376, held that a delay of 22 months while the condemnor was obtaining federal or state assistance was not an unreasonable delay. The appellate court in *Elgin* ruled that there was substantial evidence to support the trial court's finding that the delay was reasonable.

See also *Stone v City of Los Angeles, supra,* in which the question of unreasonable delay was given to the jury. See Supp §13.12A. No unreasonable delay in the acquisition of property for open space resulted from waiting for a bond election to establish whether funds would be available to purchase the property and from taking the time necessary to appraise the property, negotiate with the owner, and realize the necessary funds from the sale of bonds before beginning condemnation proceedings. *City of Walnut Creek v Leadership Hous. Sys.* (1977) 73 CA3d 611, 140 CR 690. The court also noticed that part of the delay was attributed to the plaintiff, who was seeking permission to develop some of the property in return for donating 100 acres to the city.

If the evidence shows only that the city had, six months before initiating the condemnation action, denied the tenant's request for a use permit to expand its operation of a drive-in theater without a corresponding showing of intent to diminish the value of the property, there is no precondemnation liability. *Redevelopment Agency v Contra Costa Theatre, Inc.* (1982) 135 CA3d 73, 185 CR 159. Even in a case in which there was a finding by the trial court that, the property was unmarketable and unusable from April 1973 to the time of filing the condemnation proceeding in 1977 due to publicly disseminated precondemnation announcements and activities by the city to acquire the property for a park in disregard of a prior agreement between the owner and the city for development of the property, the appellate court did not find a taking in fee, only precondemnation damages. It directed the lower court to reconsider the evidence and determine how long the property owners were unreasonably denied the right to develop their property, deleting any period of delay attributable to proper land use and fiscal planning. *Taper v City of Long Beach* (1982) 129 CA3d 590, 181 CR 169. This case cited *Peacock v County of Sacramento* (1969) 271 CA2d 845, 77 CR 391, as illustrating how unreasonable conduct can give rise to a de facto taking. See discussion at Supp §13.22F.

In *Redevelopment Agency v Heller* (1988) 200 CA3d 517, 246 CR 160, the court permitted the condemnor to abandon its action (see Supp §8.31) and denied the condemnee leave to file an amended answer seeking precondemnation damages, observing that the owner should seek such damages in a separate inverse condemnation action.

A city's delay in acting on a developer's building permit application in order to study the possible acquisition of the property as a city park was held not to constitute a governmental taking of the property. *Guinnane v City & County of San Francisco* (1987) 197 CA3d 862, 241 CR 787. The first building permit application was cancelled because the property owner delayed in providing necessary information, and the second application had not yet been ruled on. This was not the unreasonable delay of *Klopping.* The temporary suspension of land use that occurs during the normal governmental decision-making process does not constitute a taking. In contrast, *First English Evangelical Lutheran Church v County of Los Angeles* (1987) 482 US 304, recognized liability under an interim ordinance for flood protection that prohibited all building. See discussion in Supp §13.22B.

First English involved an interim ordinance that did not terminate, but the case did acknowledge that there is no liability for normal delays in the planning process. Subsequent cases will focus on what is a normal delay; meanwhile, the practitioner can look to precondemnation damage cases for guidance on what is a reasonable planning process.

The taking for a public project of residential property adjacent to a shopping center, which caused former residents who patronized the shopping center to move elsewhere, was not a taking or damaging supporting an inverse condemnation action. *Hecton v People ex rel Dep't of Transp.* (1976) 58 CA3d 653, 130 CR 230. Even under CCP §1263.510, allowing compensation for loss of goodwill, plaintiff could not have recovered because the affected property was neither the property taken nor a remainder.

It is very difficult to prove liability for precondemnation activities. The public agency's conduct must be proved to have gone beyond mere general planning to show that it placed obstacles in plaintiff's path regarding the land's use. Compare *Jones v People ex rel Dep't of Transp.* (1978) 22 C3d 144, 148 CR 640, in which the state went beyond the announcement of a freeway plan and denied the property owners a right of access to local streets for the subdivision of property (damages awarded), with *Jones v City of Los Angeles* (1979) 88 CA3d 965, 152 CR 256, in which an ordinance of condemnation was repealed to avoid the liability of CCP §1245.260 requiring the filing of a condemnation action within six months after the legislative determination of necessity (no damages awarded because there was no showing of an invasion of valuable property right). Even if unreasonable conduct is shown, damages cannot be awarded unless there is a substantial impairment of plaintiff's property rights. *City of Los Angeles v Waller* (1979) 90 CA3d 766, 778, 154 CR 12, 19. In *City of Los Angeles v Property Owners* (1982) 138 CA3d 114, 187 CR 667, the appellate court reversed an award of precondemnation damages when the trial court did not find a de facto taking, only unreasonable conduct. Because there was no demonstration of conduct on the part of the city that defeated the highest and best use of the property, there could be no actual damages, and the court reversed an award of interest for the period of so-called unreasonable delay to the date of payment.

The statement in Book §13.21 that under the 11th amendment a state cannot be sued in a federal court is correct. *Hans v Louisiana* (1890) 134 US 1; *Southern Ry. v South Carolina Highway Dep't* (ED SC 1965) 246 F Supp 435. Although theoretically this rule does not apply to subordinate government entities and state officials, a state official cannot be sued if he acted as an alter ego of the state. *Ex parte Young* (1908) 209 US 123. In *Young*, however, the court avoided the effect of this rule. The court held that the attacked action was state action for 14th amendment purposes, but for 11th amendment purposes the official's action was not official state action that would make him an alter ego of the state. Although the right to compensation under the fifth amendment has been held to be secured by the 14th amendment, the author has been unable to find any eminent domain case to which the *Young* reasoning has been applied. See *Windward Partners v Ariyoshi* (9th Cir 1982) 693 F2d 928, in which the court held that the 11th amendment barred the plaintiff's action against state employees, when the real purpose of the action to recover damages arising out of a state purchase of property under threat of condemnation was to recover funds from the state treasury.

In *Lake Country Estates, Inc. v Tahoe Regional Planning Agency* (1979) 440 US 391, the United States Supreme Court interpreted the immunity of the 11th amendment narrowly, indicating that a subordinate state subdivision could be sued in federal court for inverse condemnation under the Civil Rights Act (42 USC §1983). The Court, however, ruled that members of the Tahoe Regional Planning Agency, to the extent they were acting in a legislative capacity, were immune from federal damage liability.

DEFENSES

[§13.22] Police Power

Today, the defense that the public entity's activity is a proper exercise of the police power occurs most frequently in disputes concerning regulation of land use. See Supp §§13.22A–13.22M.

Despite increased litigation, it is still true that "judicial efforts to chart a usable test for determining when police power measures impose constitutionally compensable losses have, on the whole, been notably unsuccessful." Van Alstyne, *Taking or Damaging by Police Power: The Search for Inverse Condemnation Criteria,* 44 S Cal L Rev 1 (1970). See also Sax, *Takings, Private Property and Public Rights,* 81 Yale LJ 149 (1971); Epstein, Takings: Private Property and the Power of Eminent Domain (1985).

California Constitution art I, §14, cited in Book §13.22, has been renumbered art I, §19. See Supp §8.7.

[§13.22A] Types of Land Use Regulation

Land use regulation takes on many forms, *e.g.,* subdivision controls, dedication on development, building moratoriums, environmental controls, and several types of zoning. See generally California Zoning Practice (Cal CEB 1969). In Supp §§13.22B–13.22L some of these controls are examined in light of recent case law, with the cautionary note that this area of the law is rapidly changing.

In considering these cases, the court's frame of reference is the reasonableness of the land use regulation, which has been explained as follows in Broadhead & Rosenfeld, Open Space Zoning Handbook 15 (California Assembly Select Committee on Open Space Lands 1973):

There are four aspects of the term "reasonable" which courts consider. (1) The regulation must promote an objective which is a proper topic of governmental concern and there must be a demonstrable relationship between the regulation and the objective. (2) The objective, though a proper subject of government concern, must not be one ordinarily attained through eminent domain. (3) Landowners who are similarly situated must receive equal treatment. (4) The extent to which the regulation reduces the economic value of the land must not be "too severe," but the extent of permitted devaluation may be . . . related to the objective of the regulation.

[§13.22B] Zoning

Zoning is the division of a community into zones of land use. It separates a municipality into categories of types of land use, such as residential, commercial, industrial, and open space, to provide for orderly development. Govt C §65850(a). See California Zoning Practice §§6.4–6.5 (Cal CEB 1969). Zoning ordinances also regulate buildings and structures within the zones created. See, *e.g.,* Zoning §§6.33–6.73.

Zoning originated from common law nuisances that recognized certain restrictions on the right to use land to the detriment of adjacent and neighboring lands. Zoning §§1.3, 3.24; 1 Anderson, American Law of Zoning §1.02 (3d ed 1986). Nuisance gave way to the broader standard of general health and safety in *Village of Euclid v Ambler Realty Co.* (1926) 272 US 365, in which the Supreme Court declared comprehensive zoning constitutional. See also California's seminal decision of *Miller v Board of Pub. Works* (1925) 195 C 477, 234 P 381. Since then zoning has spread, with the court's sanction, into areas such as aesthetics, historic preservation, planned unit communities, flood plains, and open space controls.

Monetary loss alone does not invalidate a zoning restriction. In *Hadacheck v Sebastian* (1915) 239 US 394, a Los Angeles ordinance prohibiting brick kilns in residential areas was alleged to decrease property values, and in *Village of Euclid v Ambler Realty Co., supra,* there was a similar decrease in value. However, a zoning law must be reasonable in its purpose and application.

Restrictive zoning for the public's general welfare may be applied to one parcel of property and not to another parcel of property carrying on identical operations, if there is a difference in the character of the two properties and the nature of their surrounding terrain and neighboring uses. *Consolidated Rock Prods. Co. v City of Los Angeles* (1962) 57 C2d 515, 20 CR 638. The questioned ordinance in that case forbade rock and gravel operations on property that had no other economic use;

the court, in deference to the legislative judgment that quarrying operations were a health hazard to nearby residents and sanitariums, refused to find the ordinance invalid. However, in *San Leandro Rock Co. v City of San Leandro* (1982) 136 CA3d 25, 185 CR 829, an ordinance that barred trucks over 4.5 tons from using certain city streets was found invalid as applied to a rock company for which the route was essential, because the ordinance deprived the company of substantially all use of its land and thus constituted an excessive regulation of land in violation of both the fifth amendment and Cal Const art I, §19.

In recent years, the California Supreme Court has addressed the question of inverse condemnation liability claimed to result from the effect of a zoning regulation on property. First, in *HFH, Ltd. v Superior Court* (1975) 15 C3d 508, 125 CR 365, the court refused to find inverse condemnation liability for the downzoning of property from a commercial district to a residential designation, although it was alleged that the property suffered a decline in value from $400,000 to $75,000. Diminution in market value was held neither a taking nor a damaging. The court in a footnote indicated, however, that there might be an important exception: "This case does not present, and we therefore do not decide, the question of entitlement to compensation in the event a zoning regulation forbade substantially *all* use of the land in question. We leave the question for another day." 15 C3d at 518 n16, 125 CR at 372 n16. In *Eldridge v City of Palo Alto* (1976) 57 CA3d 613, 129 CR 575, the court decided in claimant's favor under that exception.

Then, in 1979, the California Supreme Court forthrightly declared that inverse condemnation is not available to an owner whose property loses value because of downzoning. *Agins v City of Tiburon* (1979) 24 C3d 266, 157 CR 372. The court held that a landowner objecting to the downzoning must seek to invalidate the ordinance. The inverse condemnation remedy was held to present an inhibiting financial force on the degree of freedom that should be available to municipalities in land use planning. In *Agins v City of Tiburon* (1979) 24 C3d 266, 273, 157 CR 372, 375, the court disapproved *Eldridge v City of Palo Alto, supra,* but offered the footnote of *HFH, Ltd. v Superior Court, supra,* as the test for invalidation of a zoning ordinance; it is invalid when its effect is to deprive the landowner of substantially all reasonable use of his property. 24 C3d at 277, 157 CR at 378.

In light of the United States Supreme Court decision in *First English Evangelical Lutheran Church v County of Los Angeles* (1987) 482 US 304, discussed below, this test is again applicable to an overly restrictive land use regulation in an inverse condemnation action.

Subsequently, the United States Supreme Court reviewed *Agins v City of Tiburon* (1980) 447 US 255, and affirmed the California decision, but from a more narrow view. The Supreme Court concluded that the city's zoning ordinance that permitted the landowners to build between one to five single family dwellings on their five-acre parcel, with density to be established after review of a particular development plan, did not on its face take the property without just compensation. In effect, the plaintiffs were attacking the enactment of the ordinance, not its application to their land, and were still free to submit a development plan to local officials. Thus, the Court did not consider whether an inverse action would be permissible if an overly restrictive application of a land regulation unconstitutionally deprives a landowner of property without just compensation.

The Ninth Circuit court did consider that question in *American Sav. & Loan Ass'n v County of Marin* (9th Cir 1981) 653 F2d 364, holding that, when there are allegations that a zoning ordinance singled out one parcel for more restrictive zoning than adjacent land also owned by plaintiff and substantially lowered the density of the former parcel to preserve its open space characteristics, there may be a taking of that parcel. When no development plan is submitted to the county, however, it is impossible to ascertain whether there are one or two parcels because the county could provide for a density transfer between the two parcels.

There is an indication in *Agins* that a regulation extinguishing a fundamental attribute of ownership, such as that involved in *Kaiser Aetna v U.S.* (1979) 444 US 164, may constitute a taking. See 444 US at 262. *Kaiser Aetna* held that the extinguished fundamental attribute was the right to exclude others from the property (the government had declared a privately developed marina to be a navigable waterway open to public access).

Following this case, *Hodel v Irving* (1987) 481 US 704, held that a provision of the Indian Land Consolidation Act of 1983 (25 USC §§2201–2211) that precluded descent of an undivided fractional interest of Indian land in favor of escheat to the tribe effected a taking.

Since the *Agins* decision in 1980, the United States Supreme Court has dealt with the question of whether the application of land use regulations could constitute a taking in three key cases, discussed below, before it made that determination in *First English Evangelical Lutheran Church v County of Los Angeles, supra.*

First, in *San Diego Gas & Elec. Co. v City of San Diego* (1981) 450 US 621, a California appellate court, in an unpublished opinion, had dismissed an action in inverse condemnation based on the downzoning of property from industrial to agricultural after the California Supreme Court had directed it to reconsider its earlier decision in light of *Agins.* On appeal to the United States Supreme Court, a bare majority of the Court refused to hear the case on the grounds that there was no final judgment in the California courts. Four justices dissented in an opinion written by Justice Brennan arguing that there was a final judgment and that the California Supreme Court's decision in *Agins v City of Tiburon, supra,* was incorrectly decided. Those justices would hold that exercise of police power regulation through zoning laws may constitute a taking for public use that requires compensation under the fifth amendment. A fifth justice, while agreeing with the majority on the procedural issue, generally agreed with the reasoning of the dissent. See *Hernandez v City of Lafayette* (5th Cir 1981) 643 F2d 1188, 1198, which follows Justice Brennan's analysis in the dissent in *San Diego Gas & Elec. Co. v City of San Diego, supra.*

Courts in other states have followed the substantive majority in *San Diego Gas & Elec. Co. v City of San Diego, supra.* See, *e.g., Burrows v City of Keene* (NH 1981) 432 A2d 15 (holding based on New Hampshire Constitution); *Sheerr v Township of Evesham* (NJ Super 1982) 445 A2d 46 (rezoning of land for public park and recreation uses that was subsequently amended to specify no permitted uses, but making available by permit limited conditional uses, all of which was later strengthened by master plan and other ordinances); and *Rippley v City of Lincoln* (ND 1983) 330 NW2d 505 (rezoning of land from residential to public use, which permitted only public recreation, education, and other governmental use). See also *In re Air Crash in Bali, Indonesia* (9th Cir 1982) 684 F2d 1301, in which the Ninth Circuit rejected *Agins* on the basis of *San Diego Gas & Elec. Co.* and held that a governmental legislative act, in this case the Warsaw Convention, which purports to limit the dollar amount of recovery against international air carriers, constituted a taking compensable under the fifth amendment. The case involved a series of wrongful death actions brought against an airline by survivors of passengers killed in an airplane crash. See Pflueger, *Takings Law—Is Inverse Condemnation an Appropriate Remedy for Due Process Violations?—San Diego Gas & Elec. Co. v City of San Diego (1981) 450 US 621,* 57 Wash L Rev 551 (1982); Berger & Kanner, *Thoughts on the White River Junction Manifesto: A Reply to the "Gang of Five's" Views on Just Compensation for Regulatory Taking of Property,* 19 Loy LA L Rev 685 (1986).

Nonetheless, California courts continued to rely on *Agins* to deny the remedy of inverse condemnation. In *Aptos Seascape Corp. v County of Santa Cruz* (1982) 138 CA3d 484, 493, 188 CR 191, 195, the court observed that the United States Supreme Court in *San Diego Gas & Elec.* did not address the question directly in the majority opinion and thus *Agins* is controlling. See also *Baker v Burbank-Glendale-Pasadena Airport Auth.* (1985) 39 C3d 862, 868 n4, 218 CR 293, 296 n4.

Second, in 1985 the United States Supreme Court was presented with an opportunity to focus on the question of when land regulation constitutes a taking in *Williamson County Regional Planning Comm'n v Hamilton Bank* (1985) 473 US 172. However, the Supreme Court determined that the claim was premature. The property owner's predecessor had obtained approval of a preliminary subdivision plat of a large residential development in 1973, for which substantial money was spent to develop roads and utility lines and to build a golf course on a permanent open-space easement conveyed to the county. In 1977 the county changed its zoning to provide a new means of calculating density, but gave final approval under the pre–1977 ordinance to phases of the development from 1973 to 1979. In 1979, however, the county decided that all renewal plats were to be evaluated under the zoning ordinance in effect when the renewal was sought. Thus, in 1981 the county disapproved the owner's revised preliminary plat for the remaining section of the subdivision for various reasons, including density noncompliance under the new ordinance. The regulations governing the process provided a variance procedure that could have tested the objections to the plat. The Court held that, because the property owner did not pursue this remedy, the taking issue was not ripe for decision. Justice Brennan together with Justice Marshall concurred in this decision, but noted that they were not departing from Justice Brennan's views set forth in *San Diego Gas & Elec. Co. v City of San Diego, supra.*

The Supreme Court had a third opportunity to review California's *Agins* rule in *MacDonald, Sommer & Frates v County of Yolo* (1986) 477 US 340, but concluded that the claim of excessive land use regulation was not ripe for decision. In that case, the county planning commission and board of supervisors denied subdivision of agricultural property into 159 residential units, while at the same time refusing to provide any of the public services of streets, sewers, and water to make the property usable, even for agricultural uses. However, because the property owner did not seek approval for a less intense development, no final decision was reached on how the county's regulations would be applied.

Finally, in *First English Evangelical Lutheran Church v County of Los Angeles* (1987) 482 US 304, the United States Supreme Court declared that property owners are entitled to just compensation, including *interim damages* (as noted in Justice Brennan's dissent in *San Diego Gas & Elec. Co. v City of San Diego, supra*). The Supreme Court sent the matter back to trial to resolve the factual issue of whether the regulation in question denied the property owner all use of its land. In this case, the challenge was to the validity of a Los Angeles County flood protection regulation that prevented a church from rebuilding a camp on the hillside that had been destroyed by flooding. The regulation also precluded any other use of the property.

On remand of *First English* to determine whether the Los Angeles County ordinance constitutes an unlawful taking, the court of appeal upheld the trial court's dismissal of the inverse condemnation action because the restriction was properly related to health and safety and did not deprive the plaintiff of all use of the property. *First English Evangelical Lutheran Church v County of Los Angeles* (1989) 210 CA3d 1353, 258 CR 893. The ordinance did not prevent occupancy of any remaining structures nor did it prohibit uses of the campground for recreational activities without reconstruction. *First English Evangelical Lutheran Church v County of Los Angeles* (1989) 210 CA3d 1353, 258 CR 893. The Supreme Court's holding in *First English* did not make a moratorium a temporary taking requiring compensation, unless the interim measure was unreasonable, which the court did not find in this case. The county was reasonably acting to protect life and health.

See Berger, *Happy Birthday, Constitution: The Supreme Court Establishes New Ground Rules For Land-Use Planning,* 20 Urban Lawyer 735 (1988).

Thus, the remedy of inverse condemnation is available in land use regulation. But the United States Supreme Court does not favor a facial challenge that an ordinance or statute has deprived an owner of all reasonable use of the land; an as-applied challenge is easier to sustain at the pleading stage. In *Keystone Bituminous Coal Ass'n v DeBenedictis* (1987) 480 US 470, the Court reaffirmed the facial challenge tests announced in *Agins* to the effect that the adoption of an ordinance can constitute a taking only if (1) it does not substantially advance a legitimate state interest or (2) it denies all "economically viable use" of the property. In *Keystone,* a mining subsidence and land conservation act prohibited coal mining that causes subsidence to certain pre-existing structures and authorized the Pennsylvania Department of Environmental Resources to revoke mining permits when operators damaged protected structures and failed to remedy the damages. There was a strong public interest in preventing harmful environmental effects, and the property owners had failed to show any economic impact on their property. See also *Hodel v Virginia Surface Mining & Reclamation Ass'n* (1981) 452 US 264.

Recent decisions affirm that the challenged regulation must deny the property owner "economically viable use" of the land. See, *e.g., Lake Nacimiento Ranch Co. v County of San Luis Obispo* (9th Cir 1987) 830 F2D 977, modified at 841 F2d 872. In *Ellison v County of Ventura* (1990) 217 CA3d 455, 265 CR 795, rezoning property from industrial and agricultural to open space did not deprive the owner of all beneficial use of the land because the trial court found that the property had doubled in value since it had been acquired. See also *Griffin Dev. Co. v City of Oxnard* (1985) 39 C3d 256, 217 CR 1, and *Terminals Equip. Co. v City & County of San Francisco* (1990) 221 CA3d 234, 270 CR 329 (redevelopment plan did not constitute a taking because existing use of land for offices and warehousing continued).

Compounding the difficulty of seeking damages in land regulation cases, the Supreme Court in *Williamson County Regional Planning Comm'n v Hamilton Bank, supra,* and *MacDonald, Sommer & Frates v County of Yolo, supra,* emphasized satisfying the *ripeness test* before finding that a regulation can constitute inverse condemnation. In *Kinzli v City of Santa Cruz* (9th Cir 1987) 818 F2d 1449, modified at 830 F2d 968, a taking claim based on a voter-adopted greenbelt initiative was not ripe for decision due to the owner's failure to seek administrative relief. The Ninth Circuit states that under recent Supreme Court decisions a final and authoritative decision requires (1) a rejected development plan and (2) denial of a variance. The futility doctrine (see Supp §13.27) is not applicable without "at least one meaningful application." See *Barancik v County of Marin* (9th Cir 1988) 872 F2d 834, regarding application of these concepts concerning ripeness for review and facial challenge to the transfer of development rights.

[§13.22C] Open Space Zoning

This section relates closely to the section above, Supp §13.22B; here, the primary focus is on the test of all "economically reasonable use" of the land.

"Rollback" and "downzoning" describe the rezoning of land that was previously zoned for a more intense use or density to a more restrictive use. The present focal point of this type of zoning is open space zoning. Municipalities and counties are reconsidering existing zoning districts that allow urban growth on lands as yet undeveloped, and rezoning those lands for large-lot agricultural use or low-density residential use.

The position of landowners that zoning, once given, cannot be taken back is not legally viable. The vesting of rights requires more than merely holding land and planning for its development under a particular zoning designation. See discussion in Supp §13.22N.

In 1970, Govt C §§65560–65570, concerning open space lands, were enacted. These sections defined open space (Govt C §65560) and, as amended in 1973, required all cities and counties to prepare and adopt open space plans by December 1, 1973 (Govt C §65563). Each plan must include an action program (Govt C §65564), and zoning ordinances, building permits, and subdivision maps may not be passed or approved unless they are consistent with the open space plan (Govt C §65567). Government Code §65860 requires that all zoning be consistent with the general plan by January 1, 1974.

In 1953, the California Supreme Court held that the rezoning of land from single family residential to a beach recreational zone was not confiscatory. *McCarthy v City of Manhattan Beach* (1953) 41 C2d 879, 264 P2d 932. The ordinance allowed the landowner to charge an admission fee, and there was no evidence that plaintiff could not make a profit from the land as regulated. The ordinance was supported by the additional factors that the city's general plan identified the beach as an important community asset and that the area was not suited for residential use because of the likelihood of high waves and storms.

In *Morse v County of San Luis Obispo* (1967) 247 CA2d 600, 55 CR 710, the court sustained minimum five-acre zoning to encourage open space development by promoting and retaining agricultural uses.

A county zoning district requiring exclusive agricultural use of lands and setting a minimum parcel size of 18 acres was "reasonable in object, not arbitrary in operation, and a proper exercise of the police power." *Gisler v County of Madera* (1974) 38 CA3d 303, 307, 112 CR 919, 921. The property in the area had always been used for agricultural purposes. Although a subdivision map, recorded in 1913, divided plaintiffs' land on paper into 2.5-acre residential lots, no residential buildings had been constructed on the land, none of the streets had been developed, and no money had been spent to convert the property to residential use. The county was not obligated to compensate the property owners for losses as a result of changes in zoning.

The California Supreme Court has reaffirmed the principle that mere reduction of value by zoning is not enough to require compensation for inverse condemnation; the zoning must have the effect of depriving the private owner of his property for a public use. *HFH, Ltd. v Superior Court* (1975) 15 C3d 508, 518, 125 CR 365, 372. However, the court left open the possibility that a zoning restriction so severe that it forbids all reasonable use of the land might constitute a taking. 15 C3d at 518 n16, 125 CR at 372 n16.

The California Supreme Court in *Agins v City of Tiburon* (1979) 24 C3d 266, 157 CR 372, declared that inverse condemnation is not available to attack the enactment of the zoning regulation. However, in *First English Evangelical Lutheran Church v County of Los Angeles* (1987) 482 US 304, inverse condemnation was allowed for governmental deprivation of use of property through regulation.

The difficulty California property owners had in alleging or proving that their property lacked any residual value after downzoning before the decision in *Agins v City of Tiburon, supra,* is expected to continue after the decision in *First English.* On difficulties before *First English,* see, *e.g., Friedman v City of Fairfax* (1978) 81 CA3d 667, 146 CR 687 (land had recreational value); *Pan Pac. Props. v County of Santa Cruz* (1978) 81 CA3d 244, 146 CR 428 (agricultural or residential use possible); *Orsetti v City of Fremont* (1978) 80 CA3d 961, 146 CR 75 (no facts shown to support finding of diminution in value); *Sierra Terreno v Tahoe Regional Planning Agency* (1978) 79 CA3d 439, 144 CR 776 (complaint admitted that property retained 25 percent of its former value); *Pinheiro v County of Marin* (1976) 60 CA3d 323, 131 CR 633 (complaint alleged only diminution in value). See also *Cormier v County of San Luis Obispo* (1984) 161 CA3d 850, 207 CR 880, in which a property owner filed a writ of mandate to compel the county to reclassify and rezone his property, which had been downzoned from commercial to rural-residential by an amendment to the county general plan, resulting in a 75 percent decrease or more in the value of his property. The court found that the validity of the amendment was "fairly debatable" and thus constitutional. 161 CA3d at 859, 207 CR at 886.

Compare *Toso v City of Santa Barbara* (1980) 101 CA3d 934, 162 CR 210, which held that a court generally cannot compel a city to rezone land, and *Kinzli v City of Santa Cruz* (ND Cal 1982) 539 F Supp 887. In the latter case, the court questioned whether estoppel could be asserted to force a government entity to permit a landowner to build in a manner contrary to its zoning ordinance, but nevertheless found sufficient evidence to support a claim of detrimental reliance on the city's representations, in settling a prior condemnation action for a portion of the land, that construction of a new street would enhance the residential development value of the remainder. That development was prevented by a later initiative ordinance for open space preservation, which was upheld against an unlawful taking challenge on grounds of balancing public interest against temporary economic impact (the ordinance limited land use until 1990), in *Kinzli v City of Santa Cruz* (ND Cal 1985) 620 F Supp 609. See subsequent history of case in Supp §§13.22B, 13.27.

An ordinance that deprived an owner of a property's best use by limiting conversion of apartments to condominium units was not a taking in that a reasonable use of rental apartments remained. *Traweek v City & County of San Francisco* (ND Cal 1984) 659 F Supp 1012.

In *Griffin Dev. Co. v City of Oxnard* (1985) 39 C3d 256, 217 CR 1, the supreme court held that a city ordinance regulating the conversion of apartments to condominium units was within the scope of the city's police power and that the denial of a special use permit under the ordinance was not an unconstitutional taking of property.

On its face, the rezoning of land from recreational to rural does not constitute a taking when the property has been held for investment and leased for grazing and equestrian purposes. The owner failed to show that any beneficial permissible uses were not available through a variance or waiver of restriction. *Lake Nacimiento Ranch Co. v County of San Luis Obispo* (9th Cir 1987) 830 F2D 977, modified at 841 F2d 872. The case noted that the Supreme Court had not clarified the meaning of "economically viable use" (see discussion in Supp §13.22B).

In *Twain Harte Assocs. v County of Tuolomne* (1990) 217 CA3d 71, 265 CR 737, an undeveloped 1.7 acre portion of a larger parcel that had been developed as a shopping center was downzoned from light commercial to open space to the effect that (1) open space zoning allows only recreational, public utitility, or agricultural uses, but prohibits building any structures; (2) downzoning prevented plaintiffs from receiving a fair return on their investment-backed expectations when it precluded property development; and (3) the development and zoning history of the overall parcel presented evidence of economic deprivation of use sufficient to defeat the condemnor's motion for summary judgment.

A county ordinance providing for transfer of development rights among property owners for individual parcels but limiting total development throughout the area was upheld in *Barancik v County of Marin* (9th Cir 1988) 872 F2d 834.

An initiative banning development of housing on a former golf course in order to preserve the parcel as open space was ruled invalid on the basis of the Equal Protection Clause because it singled out only this property. *Fry v City of Hayward* (ND Cal 1988) 701 F Supp 179.

In enacting open space zoning, local government often bases its ordinance on several goals. It may serve not only to support open space needs but also to protect an important natural resource, *e.g.*, San Francisco Bay (*Candlestick Props. v San Francisco Bay Conserv. & Dev. Comm'n* (1970) 11 CA3d 557, 89 CR 897), or to avoid the hazards of flooding, earth movement, or fire (*Turner v County of Del Norte* (1972) 24 CA3d 311, 101 CR 93).

In *Furey v City of Sacramento* (9th Cir 1986) 780 F2d 1448, the Ninth Circuit ruled that landowners who initiated the formation of an assessment district acted in a voluntary manner. Thus, the assessment was a private investment not compelled by local government and for which there could be no taking. Plaintiff's neighbors initiated the creation of the sewer district and plaintiff consented to the inclusion of his property in the district. If the construction of the improvements had been compelled by the city, plaintiff would have had to have been given the opportunity to make beneficial use of the improvement or be refunded the amount of the assessment. The Ninth Circuit decision effectively limits the California Supreme Court decision in *Furey v City of Sacramento* (1979) 24 C3d 862, 157 CR 684, which held that, although owners were not entitled to relief in inverse condemnation, they were entitled to some form of relief, suggesting that the trial court permit the defendants to use their reassessment powers to redress the inequity.

[§13.22D] Protective Zoning in Hazardous Areas

Land development may be severely restricted in areas subject to dangers such as flooding, substantial earth movements, and fire. In *Turner v County of Del Norte* (1972) 24 CA3d 311, 101 CR 93, plaintiffs instituted an action in inverse condemnation for the alleged taking of their property as a result of imposition of zoning regulations severely limiting the uses to which their property could be put (*e.g.*, no permanent buildings were allowed). The zoning ordinance was held to be a proper exercise of police power in that the restrictions were necessary because of the existing flood conditions in the area.

In *Helix Land Co. v City of San Diego* (1978) 82 CA3d 932, 147 CR 683, land subject to flooding had been scheduled to be benefited by a flood control project. The flood control project was abandoned and the city changed the land's agricultural zoning classification from temporary to permanent, but the owners were unable to state a cause of action for inverse condemnation.

A Pennsylvania statute requiring coal mining operators to leave a certain amount of coal in the ground for support under certain surface structures, including publicly used buildings, cemeteries, and perennial streams, and to repair subsidence damage to such structures, or lose their mining permits did not, on its face, constitute a taking of property under the fifth amendment. *Keystone Bituminous Coal Ass'n v DeBenedictis* (1987) 480 US 470. In this case the Supreme Court was motivated by the strong public interest of preventing harmful environmental effects to land from subsidence. Four justices dissented, arguing that the support estate is a separate property interest and, because it was recognized by Pennsylvania law, must be honored as a property right. From this perspective, requiring a certain percentage of the coal to remain beneath the surface to protect the structures constituted a taking from the holder of the mineral and support estates. See *Pennsylvania Coal Co. v Mahon* (1922) 260 US 393, holding that a Pennsylvania state limitation on coal mining to prevent subsidence was an unconstitutional taking of property without just compensation.

In *Rose v City of Coalinga* (1987) 190 CA3d 1627, 236 CR 124, inverse condemnation was available because the city intentionally destroyed the property in the absence of an emergency. The city notified the owner of a building damaged in an earthquake that it had to be demolished for health and safety reasons although the official structural report showed that it was repairable. See also *Smith v County of Los Angeles* (1989) 214 CA3d 266, 262 CR 754, holding that removal of slide debris in order to keep a road open to traffic when alternative routes were available is not an emergency that can justify the taking of private property without compensation.

[§13.22E] Aesthetic Zoning

The most common examples of regulations related to aesthetic considerations are those affecting sign structures, *e.g.,* billboards. Aesthetic considerations in themselves are not enough to uphold the ordinance; there must be other justification. However, economic benefit arising from the area's enhanced attractiveness to tourists, settlers, and industry is sufficient justification. *Desert Outdoor Advertising, Inc. v County of San Bernardino* (1967) 255 CA2d 765, 63 CR 543. A regulation based on highway safety and aesthetic value is valid. *City of Escondido v Desert Outdoor Advertising, Inc.* (1973) 8 C3d 785, 106 CR 172. See generally California Zoning Practice §§8.53–8.58 (Cal CEB 1969).

Since 1982 state law has prohibited removal of lawfully erected off-site signs (billboards) without compensation except for nonfreeway-oriented agricultural and residentially zoned signs (Bus & P C §§5412–5412.3) and signs subject to litigation at the time the law was enacted (Bus & P C §5412.4). This law followed the state supreme court's holding that the California Outdoor Advertising Act (Bus & P C §§5200–5486) preempted local law and required compensation for removal of billboards in existence (or removed subject to litigation) on November 6, 1978, and located within 660 feet of federal interstate and primary highways. *Metromedia, Inc. v City of San Diego* (1980) 26 C3d 848, 164 CR 510. The 1982 law encourages relocation agreements as an alternative to compensation.

The ordinance in *Metromedia,* prohibiting the erection of outdoor advertising displays, was held invalid on its face on review by the United States Supreme Court. The ordinance permitted on-site commercial advertising for goods or services available on the property where the sign was located, but forbade other commercial advertising and noncommercial advertising, with certain exceptions (*e.g.,* temporary political signs, signs within shopping malls, religious symbols, signs located at public bus stops, and for sale or for lease signs). Four justices ruled that the ordinance was unconstitutional on its face because it constituted a general ban on signs carrying noncommercial advertising. Two other justices concluded that the city ordinance constituted a total ban on the use of billboards, whether commercial or noncommercial, and that the city had not shown sufficient, substantial governmental interest in drawing such a restriction, even though the stated purpose of the ordinance was to eliminate hazards to pedestrians and motorists and to preserve and improve the city's appearance. Two separate dissents were filed, generally indicating that the ordinance was a permissible, impartial, total ban on billboards. *Metromedia, Inc. v City of San Diego* (1981) 453 US 490. On remand, the California Supreme Court determined that the constitutionality of the ordinance could not be preserved by judicial construction limiting its reach to prohibit only commercial signs. *Metromedia, Inc. v City of San Diego* (1982) 32 C3d 180, 185 CR 260.

Previous law held that zoning legislation may properly provide for the termination of nonconforming signs without compensation if the legislation provides a reasonable amortization period for the investment involved. *National Advertising Co. v County of Monterey* (1970) 1 C3d 875, 877, 83 CR 577, 578; Zoning §§9.25–9.29 (Cal CEB 1969). The burden of establishing the unreasonableness of the amortization period for a nonconforming structure is on the owner of the advertising sign. *City of Salinas v Ryan Outdoor Advertising, Inc.* (1987) 189 CA3d 416, 234 CR 619.

Effective 1984, Bus & P C §§5491 and 5494 were added to prohibit municipalities from ordering removal of on-premise advertising displays without payment of compensation, unless ordinances introduced or adopted before March 12, 1983, provide for amortization.

Even though a sign is visible from the highway, it is exempt from the California Outdoor Advertising Act if the copy of the sign is not visible from the travelled way because of the angle of the sign. *City of Salinas v Ryan Outdoor Advertising, Inc., supra.* The compensation requirements of Bus & P C §5412, however, equally apply to billboards not visible from the freeway.

The zoning ordinance involved in *Bohannan v City of San Diego* (1973) 30 CA3d 416, 106 CR 333, was designed to preserve and enhance the cultural and historic aspects of a state park known as "Old Town" by regulating the architectural design of structures and signs in the immediate area. Although the ordinance was based primarily on aesthetic considerations, the court upheld the ordinance, reasoning that preservation of the area's historic image contributed to the city's general welfare by encouraging economically beneficial tourism.

A parcel designated as a historical landmark was not inversely condemned by its rezoning from general commercial to commercial recreational, a classification designed to preserve existing open space use, when the land had been used as a commercial recreational property and retained some value for that purpose. Although the property owner had terminated the commercial recreational use of the property for economic reasons, evidence showed that certain cottage apartment units on the property continued to be leased and that a tennis club could be established on the property. *Friedman v City of Fairfax* (1978) 81 CA3d 667, 146 CR 687.

See *Penn Cent. Transp. Co. v New York City* (1978) 438 US 104 (court held that restriction on use of air space over Penn Central Terminal under a landmark preservation law was not a taking); Marcus, *The Grand Slam Grand Central Terminal Decision: A Euclid for Landmarks, Favorable Notice for TDR and a Resolution of the Regulatory/Taking Impasse,* 7 Ecology LQ 731 (1979).

A property owner seeking to develop a highrise residential development found that new regulations restricted the building height to 40 feet, but could not recover in inverse condemnation even though the new zoning restrictions prevented recovery of the property owner's investment. Regulatory changes are not a compensable taking merely because they frustrate economic expectations. *Haas & Co. v City & County of San Francisco* (9th Cir 1979) 605 F2d 1117.

[§13.22F] Answer to Police Power Defense: Zoning in Bad Faith

If zoning can be shown to be a subterfuge to reduce the acquisition price in a subsequent condemnation action, it constitutes a taking. In *Peacock v County of Sacramento* (1969) 271 CA2d 845, 77 CR 391, plaintiff's property was near an airport being studied for expansion; he was not given permission to extend sewers or to subdivide his property. The county then imposed flight path zoning for the area in addition to the conventional zoning affecting the property. Later, it changed the conventional zoning to impose more restrictive height limitations and adopted a land use plan for the airport environs. When the airport expansion was later abandoned, the property owner filed an inverse condemnation action. The court noted the trial court's finding that the county's actions were for the purpose of depressing or preventing an increase in property value and concluded that the planning-zoning actions of the County of Sacramento amounted to a taking of plaintiff's land.

When a city's policy is to acquire abandoned railroad rights-of-way or to prevent their development, zoning of these strips for unintensive use with a view to future condemnation is improper; the zoning may be collaterally attacked in a condemnation proceeding by the city, and evidence of the restrictive zoning should be excluded in determining property value to prevent the city from benefiting from the resulting reduced value. However, when the condemnor is a different public agency from the authority imposing the zoning, the effect on value of the improper restrictions cannot be disregarded. *People ex rel Dep't of Pub. Works v Southern Pac. Transp. Co.* (1973) 33 CA3d 960, 109 CR 525. In this case the state, acting separately from the city, acquired the property for its own purpose. To exclude evidence of the zoning for valuation purposes would shift the responsibility for the disguised taking from the city to the state. The property owner must pursue the remedy for inverse condemnation against the responsible agency.

The enhancement of a governmental asset is an improper motive to invoke the police power. Adoption of an emergency ordinance rolling back zoning from multiple to one-family residential on property in an airport flight zone at the same time the city is considering condemnation cannot be sustained. *Kissinger v City of Los Angeles* (1958) 161 CA2d 454, 327 P2d 10. Likewise, airport height limitations for approaches and clear zones constitute an attempt to acquire an easement for flight in the guise of regulation; traditional height limitation in zoning does not contemplate invasion of the air space above the restricted zone. *Sneed v County of Riverside* (1963) 218 CA2d 205, 32 CR 318. Zoning in the vicinity of airports under a comprehensive plan seeking both to protect the surrounding lands and to improve the utility of the airport has been approved. *Morse v County of San Luis Obispo* (1967) 247 CA2d 600, 55 CR 710; *Smith v County of Santa Barbara* (1966) 243 CA2d 126, 52 CR 292.

When, after several years of precondemnation activity that included study, interim moratoriums, and exploration of means to acquire the land, a city adopted an open space zoning district changing the density for residential dwellings from one unit per acre to one per ten acres, the zoning was held to be a taking. "The plain and admitted object of the open space ordinances was to achieve the same result, to the full extent possible, as would have been achieved through purchase of the land itself." *Arastra Ltd. Partnership v City of Palo Alto* (ND Cal 1975) 401 F Supp

962, 975. Although this decision was "vacated, set aside and expunged" under stipulation of the parties as a part of the settlement purchasing the property ((ND Cal 1976) 417 F Supp 1125), its analysis and reasoning have been considered in subsequent cases. See *Frisco Land & Mining Co. v State* (1977) 74 CA3d 736, 759, 141 CR 820, 834.

The court in *Pinheiro v County of Marin* (1976) 60 CA3d 323, 327, 131 CR 633, 636, observed there was a notable exception to the general rule that the motives of city officials are irrelevant to the inquiry of the reasonableness of the zoning ordinance; motive may be explored when there are precondemnation activities intended to freeze or lower property value. See also *Redevelopment Agency v Contra Costa Theatre, Inc.* (1982) 135 CA3d 73, 82, 185 CR 159, 163. In a later case, *Viso v State* (1979) 92 CA3d 15, 23, 154 CR 580, 586, without discussing the "notable exception" of *Pinheiro,* the court raised some question of whether the *Pinheiro* general rule is still valid. See *Cormier v County of San Luis Obispo* (1984) 161 CA3d 850, 207 CR 880 (motives of city officials are irrelevant when considering reasonableness of zoning ordinance). For discussion of *Viso v State, supra, Friedman v City of Fairfax* (1978) 81 CA3d 667, 146 CR 687, and another case concerning motive, see *Toso v City of Santa Barbara* (1980) 101 CA3d 934, 954, 162 CR 210, 221.

When a city did not downzone land (see Supp §13.22C) but preserved the status quo by denying an application for change from single family to multifamily residential on the basis of adverse impacts on public services, there was no abuse of discretion, even though there was also evidence that the city was considering the site for a public park but lacked available funds. *Mira Dev. Corp. v City of San Diego* (1988) 205 CA3d 1201, 252 CR 825.

See §§4.11–4.16 for further discussion of zoning as it affects value.

[§13.22G] Planning

Municipal planning and zoning are closely related but distinct processes. Planning connotes the overall policy for development and control of a community's land use. Zoning relates to actual regulation of the use of property. Ideally, zoning follows planning.

Government Code §65300 mandates that each city and county adopt a general plan which is a long range, comprehensive policy statement of a community's physical development. It must include land use, circulation, housing, conservation, open space, noise, and safety elements (Govt C §65302) and it may address any other subjects relating to the physical development of the local jurisdiction (Govt C §65303). To strengthen planning, Govt C §65860(a) requires zoning to be consistent with the local government's general plan. "Consistency" does not mean there must be absolute conformity but rather general compatibility. The two processes are not meant to become one. See California Zoning Practice §2.29 (Cal CEB 1969); Comment, *"Zoning Shall be Consistent With the General Plan"—A Help or a Hindrance to Planning?* 10 San Diego L Rev 901 (1973).

Chartered cities are generally exempted from the requirement of consistency between zoning and the general plan (Govt C §65803), but Govt C §65860 requires that Los Angeles zoning ordinances adopted before 1979 be consistent with the city's general plan by July 1, 1982.

As planning becomes increasingly comprehensive through mapping and policy statements, and certain areas are designated for future public use, it can have an adverse impact on the value of particular properties. Claims of inverse condemnation are a natural reaction of affected property owners. The court in *Peacock v County of Sacramento* (1969) 271 CA2d 845, 77 CR 391, found planning combined with zoning for airport purposes so restrictive as to constitute a taking. For discussion of *Peacock*, see Supp §13.22F.

The court in *Klopping v City of Whittier* (1972) 8 C3d 39, 104 CR 1 (see §§4.7–4.7A), held that excessive delay in bringing an action in eminent domain and other oppressive precondemnation activity by a public agency can result in a taking. Although *Klopping* did not involve planning, general plan designation of a particular area for a proposed public use could also cloud marketability of affected properties. See discussion of *San Diego Gas & Elec. Co. v City of San Diego* (1981) 450 US 621, in Supp §13.22B.

Any implication of liability by reason of enacting or amending a general plan, however, raises serious concern among local governments. The first test of the issue came when the *Klopping* decision was invoked by a property owner in an inverse condemnation action in which a city-county general plan showed a new major traffic corridor extending through plaintiff's property. In *Selby Realty Co. v City of San Buenaventura* (1973) 10 C3d 110, 109 CR 799, the city, based on the general plan's designation, had refused a building permit for apartment construction on the property, although zoned for such use, unless the resulting street were dedicated and improved. If the owner had done so it would have left the site with insufficient area for the proposed development. The supreme court refused to accept the contention that a mere indication of a potential public use of privately owned land constitutes a taking.

The *Selby* court noted that the city and county were required to adopt a general plan that includes a circulation element, and that long range planning is necessary for California's orderly progress of community growth. It further declared that there was no action taken against plaintiff's land other than adoption of the plan, which is, by its nature, tentative. "The adoption of a general plan is several leagues short of a firm declaration of an intention to condemn property [as was the case in *Klopping*]." 10 C3d at 119, 109 CR at 805. See also *Rancho La Costa v County of San Diego* (1980) 111 CA3d 54, 168 CR 491. The court allowed plaintiff to proceed on an alternative cause of action in mandamus to question the reasonableness of the dedication requirement. See discussion in Supp §13.28. See also *Navajo Terminals, Inc. v San Francisco Bay Conserv. & Dev. Comm'n* (1975) 46 CA3d 1, 120 CR 108.

The key distinctions the court drew between *Klopping* and *Selby* are that (1) announcement of a specific acquisition in the near future is different from potential public use of properties in an area sometime in the future and (2) excessive delay in bringing a condemnation action contrasts with long-range planning activity, which in theory does not place obstacles in the path of the owner's use of his land.

Citing both *Selby* and *Navajo Terminals,* the court in *Dale v City of Mountain View* (1976) 55 CA3d 101, 127 CR 520, held that the general plan designation as open space of a golf course under lease until the year 2011 was not a taking. The mandate of consistency between zoning and general plan (Govt C §65860) was not applicable in *Dale.* 55 CA3d at 108 n5, 127 CR at 524 n5.

A general plan singling out certain properties for purchase if a proposed bond issue is successful is not sufficiently unequivocal to give rise to an inverse condemnation action. *City of Walnut Creek v Leadership Hous. Sys.* (1977) 73 CA3d 611, 622, 140 CR 690, 696.

Following the rule of *Selby,* the court in *Orsetti v City of Fremont* (1978) 80 CA3d 961, 146 CR 75, held that a mere declaration of intent to amend the general plan as open space and to take appropriate action regarding the zoning does not give rise to an inverse condemnation action. Adoption of a general plan with areas designated for acquisition cannot give rise to a claim for inverse condemnation. *Sierra Terreno v Tahoe Regional Planning Agency* (1978) 79 CA3d 439, 144 CR 776. The court noted that the Tahoe Regional Planning Agency was empowered by legislation to regulate but was not given the power to condemn directly, and therefore could not be liable in inverse condemnation. But see *Baker v Burbank-Glendale-Pasadena Airport Auth.* (1985) 39 C3d 862, 218 CR 293, discussed in Supp §13.3, which permitted an inverse condemnation action against an entity that did not have the power to condemn.

The California Coastal Commission's refusal to certify a county general plan, which would have permitted oil and gas development and some residential use of the plaintiff's property, did not give rise to inverse condemnation. The commission recommended changes in the plan that would have prohibited energy development and that would have limited residential development to 21 units. *Pier Gherini v California Coastal Comm'n* (1988) 204 CA3d 699, 251 CR 426.

Denial of an application to rezone land from single family to multifamily residential, when the land was considered for possible purchase as a city park, was not an abuse of discretion. The council's action on the zoning request simply preserved the status quo and there was other evidence of adverse impacts on public services from the project. *Mira Dev. Corp. v City of San Diego* (1988) 205 CA3d 1201, 252 CR 825.

The enactment of legislation authorizing condemnation is not a taking of property, because it may be repealed. *U.S. v 3.66 Acres of Land* (ND Cal 1977) 426 F Supp 533; Golden Gate National Recreation Area Act (16 USC §§460bb–460bb–5). But see *Drakes Bay Land Co. v U.S.* (Ct Cl 1970) 424 F2d 574, which involved other actions as well as legislation.

The California courts have been reluctant to extend *Klopping* to land use planning activities. Generally, *Klopping* has been distinguished whenever an agency has taken no particular condemnation acts against a specific property or has not relied on land use restrictions to suppress property values. See *Helix Land Co. v City of San Diego* (1978) 82 CA3d 932, 947, 147 CR 683, 691; *Frisco Land & Mining Co. v State* (1977) 74 CA3d 736, 757, 141 CR 820, 833.

The point at which steps taken to implement planning become a taking was examined in a freeway planning case, *Jones v People ex rel Dep't of Transp.* (1978) 22 C3d 144, 148 CR 640, in which *Selby* was distinguished. The court found a taking when a freeway route was adopted, designating plaintiff's land for future acquisition, and the state denied access to the property necessary to its development as a residential subdivision. See Str & H C §100.2, forbidding any road from opening into a freeway without approval of the California Highway Commission. The state went beyond mere planning. See Supp §4.7A for discussion of when a public agency's conduct goes beyond mere general planning.

Relying on *Agins v City of Tiburon* (1979) 24 C3d 266, 157 CR 372, the court in *Rancho La Costa v County of San Diego* (1980) 111 CA3d 54, 60, 168 CR 491, 494, ruled that the county's enactment of a general plan indicating the potential public use of privately owned land coupled with refusal to rezone, and opposition to an annexation petition to LAFCO, is not an inverse condemnation.

Note that the *Agins* rule on nonavailability of the remedy of inverse condemnation for land regulation cases was effectively overruled in *First English Evangelical Lutheran Church v County of Los Angeles* (1987) 482 US 304. See Supp §13.22B. But *Agins* and *First English* were both analyzed in *Guinnane v City & County of San Francisco* (1987) 197 CA3d 862, 241 CR 787, which held that a municipality's delay in acting on a developer's building permit application in order to study the possible acquisition of the property for a public park did not constitute a taking. The first application for a building permit was cancelled because the property owner failed to submit required information for environmental review, and the second application was in process. This was not unreasonable delay.

[§13.22H] Controlled Growth

The first significant case dealing with the concept of "controlled growth" or "timed development" was *Golden v Planning Bd.* (NY 1972) 285 NE2d 291. The town's ordinances were amended according to an 18-year development plan. Subdivision development was not permitted unless public services and facilities would be available. The purpose of the ordinances was to provide for a balanced community for the efficient use of land through a system of sequential development. The highest court of New York upheld the ordinances, stating that there was a rational basis for the "phased growth," because it was clear that the community's existing physical and financial resources were inadequate to furnish the essential public services required by a substantial increase in the population.

Recent challenges to the validity of zoning ordinances adopted to implement controlled growth plans have looked to other constitutional provisions for support, in addition to the traditional method of attack based on the taking of property without just compensation and the deprivation of property without due process. In *Town of Los Altos Hills v Adobe Creek Props.* (1973) 32 CA3d 488, 108 CR 271, an ordinance prohibiting the commercial development of recreational areas was challenged as a denial of equal protection by a claim that the zoning was exclusionary because it virtually eliminated all commercial use of property within the city. The zoning ordinance was upheld on the basis that there is a valid distinction between commercial and noncommercial uses as well as the burdens each imposed on the city.

Another important California case on controlled growth is *Construction Indus. Ass'n v City of Petaluma* (9th Cir 1975) 522 F2d 897, in which the court held that a limited growth plan permitting construction of not more than 500 dwelling units per year to protect the small town character and surrounding open space of the city was valid. See also *Village of Belle Terre v Boraas* (1974) 416 US 1, in which the Supreme Court approved of an ordinance prohibiting boarding houses and other multifamily dwellings to preserve the character of a small New York village. But see *City of Santa Barbara v Adamson* (1980) 27 C3d 123, 164 CR 539, which held that a city ordinance prohibiting more than five unrelated persons from living together in a house in a single family residential zone violates the right of privacy guaranteed by Cal Const art I, §1.

In *Associated Home Builders, Inc. v City of Livermore* (1976) 18 C3d 582, 135 CR 41, the supreme court upheld an ordinance prohibiting issuance of further building permits for residential development until local educational, sewage, and water supply facilities complied with specific standards. The court suggested that the standard for testing land use restrictions must measure the impact on the welfare of the surrounding region as well as on the enacting community.

A county ordinance permitting the transfer of development rights under a scheme that defines a limit on overall development of an area, but allows a residential developer of a given parcel to purchase from another owner development rights in order to increase the number of units for the developer's project, was upheld in *Barancik v County of Marin* (9th Cir 1988) 872 F2d 834.

[§13.22I] Rent Control

The enactment of rent control ordinances by several California cities has produced challenges to the constitutionality of those ordinances.

The court may review rent control legislation before it becomes operative and actual rent ceilings are imposed to determine on the face of the ordinance whether it has confiscatory effects. *Oceanside Mobilehome Park Owners Ass'n v City of Oceanside* (1984) 157 CA3d 887, 204 CR 239. A reasonable return on fair market value is not a constitutional requirement for sustaining a rent control ordinance. *Cotati Alliance for Better Hous. v City of Cotati* (1983) 148 CA3d 280, 287, 195 CR 825, 829. But the ordinance cannot deny a "fair return on investment," defined in *Cotati* as a rent that generates sufficient income to cover the cost of operation and servicing of reasonable financing and to ensure a reasonable profit. See also *Birkenfeld v City of Berkeley* (1976) 17 C3d 129, 130 CR 465; *Searle v City of Berkeley Rent Stabilization Bd.* (1988) 197 CA3d 1251, 243 CR 449.

The United States Supreme Court in *Fisher v City of Berkeley* (1986) 475 US 260, upheld the constitutionality of a city's rent control ordinance against a charge that it violated the federal antitrust provision of the Sherman Antitrust Act (15 USC §1), because of the lack of the necessary element of concerted action. The California Supreme Court had also taken this position, but further held that the ordinance provisions for fair return based on a landlord's investments rather than on the value of their property were valid and did not result in a confiscatory taking of the property, even though the value of the property may decrease because of regulation. *Fisher v City of Berkeley* (1984) 37 C3d 644, 209 CR 682.

In *Carson Mobilehome Park Owners' Ass'n v City of Carson* (1983) 35 C3d 184, 197 CR 284, the California Supreme Court ruled that an ordinance imposing mobilehome rent controls and establishing that a nonexclusive list of 12 factors for a rental review board to determine whether any requested rent increase would be "just, fair, and reasonable," was valid. The court held that the method of fixing rents is immaterial as long as the result achieved is constitutionally acceptable. The fact that the ordinance did not articulate a formula for determining just what constitutes a just and reasonable return did not make it unconstitutional.

In *Pennell v City of San Jose* (1986) 42 C3d 365, 228 CR 726, the California Supreme Court upheld a portion of a rent control ordinance requiring consideration of the hardship to low income tenants of a rent increase over an automatic 8 percent yearly increase allowed by the ordinance. The United States Supreme Court affirmed this decision in *Pennell v City of San Jose* (Feb. 24, 1988) 108 S Ct 849, 99 L Ed 2d 1, stating that, based on the face of the ordinance, it would be premature to determine that consideration of the hardship provision of the ordinance would cause a hearing officer to reduce rent below what the rent would have been, based on other factors set forth in the ordinance. The lack of a concrete factual setting did not present a case that was ripe for decision. The Supreme Court also held that the provision did not violate the Equal Protection Clause because a rational basis existed for protecting tenants. See also *Berman v Downing* (1986) 184 CA3d Supp 1, 229 CR 660 (rent rollback provisions and rent control ordinance did not violate contract clause of either the United States or California Constitutions).

An ordinance that prohibited the removal of rental units from the housing market by conversion or demolition without a permit was held not to constitute a taking of the landlord's property, because the ordinance did not interfere with the owner's primary investment-backed expectations and did not render the owner unable to receive a reasonable return on his investment. *Nash v City of Santa Monica* (1984) 37 C3d 97, 207 CR 285. See also *McMullan v Santa Monica Rent Control Bd.* (1985) 168 CA3d 960, 214 CR 617. However, the Ellis Act (Govt C §§7060–7060.7), operative July 1, 1986, prohibits a public entity from enacting or administering any legislation that would require an owner of any residential property to offer, or continue to offer, accommodations in the property for rent or lease. These sections overrule *Nash v City of Santa Monica, supra,* to the extent the decision is contrary. Govt C §7060.7. See also *City of Santa Monica v Yarmark* (1988) 203 CA3d 153, 249 CR 732, and *Javidzad v City of Santa Monica* (1988) 204 CA3d 524, 251 CR 350 concerning preemption of the Ellis Act.

The approval of a tentative map for condominium conversion did not lead to a vested right exemption from a later rent control ordinance that required a permit for conversion of controlled rental units. *Blue Chip Props. v Permanent Rent Control Bd.* (1985) 170 CA3d 648, 216 CR 492. Similarly, in *Briarwood Props. v City of Los Angeles* (1985) 171 CA3d 1020, 217 CR 849, the court held that tentative map approval for a condominium conversion did not lead to a vested right to be free from later tenant relocation assistance ordinances. See also Supp §13.22O.

In *Gregory v City of San Juan Capistrano* (1983) 142 CA3d 72, 191 CR 47, a rent control law that required a mobilehome park owner who desired to sell the park to first offer it to park residents was held unconstitutional.

Likewise, a rent control ordinance applicable to mobilehome parks that required operators to give tenants leases of unlimited term, terminable by the tenant at will but by the landlord only for causes specified in the ordinance, and that gave the tenants the right to convey their leasehold interest to others, constituted a taking of property. The landlords were effectively stripped of their reversionary interests. *Hall v City of Santa Barbara* (9th Cir 1986) 833 F2d 1270 (originally published as 813 F2d 198). See also *Ross v City of Berkeley* (ND Cal 1987) 655 F Supp 820, involving an ordinance that required the lessors to give lessees an indefinite leasehold interest (the ordinance listed specific reasons for eviction, and owner occupation was not given as good cause for eviction or nonrenewal of a lease).

An ordinance that precluded unregistered landlords and their successors from recapturing annual rent increases lost during the time they were unregistered was not confiscatory, because the ordinance also allowed the landlords, on registration, to petition for an individual rent adjustment to obtain a fair return on their investment. *Searle v City of Berkeley Rent Stabilization Board* (1988) 197 CA3d 1251, 243 CR 449.

[§13.22J] Regulation for Protection of a Natural Resource

Several planning agencies have been established to set up environmental controls in the development of land around land resources of environmental concern. Three are discussed below.

The San Francisco Bay Conservation and Development Commission (BCDC) prepared a plan for the conservation of water and development of the shoreline of San Francisco Bay in 1968. The BCDC has authority to grant or deny fill permits and permits for the extraction of materials, and generally to exercise control over the development of shoreland surrounding the bay 100 feet inland from the highest tide line. Govt C §§66600–66661. See Govt C §66610(b).

Restrictions imposed by the BCDC on the development of land around San Francisco Bay have been ruled valid. In *Candlestick Props. v San Francisco Bay Conserv. & Dev. Comm'n* (1970) 11 CA3d 557, 89 CR 897, the preservation of a natural resource was held to be sufficient justification for denial of a permit to fill land in the bay. Refusal of the fill permit was not such a severe restriction as to amount to a taking considering the results of the extensive studies conducted on the bay showing that a change in one part of the bay would produce detrimental effects on all other parts of the bay. See discussion of *City of Berkeley v Superior Court* (1980) 26 C3d 515, 162 CR 327, in Supp §13.18.

The interstate (California and Nevada) Tahoe Regional Planning Agency (TRPA) was created under the Tahoe Regional Planning Compact (Govt C §§66800–66801). This agency is responsible for the formulation of land development plans for the Lake Tahoe region, including establishment of environmental standards. The agency is authorized to adopt ordinances, rules, and regulations for implementing and enforcing the adopted plans. The constitutionality of this law was upheld in *People ex rel Younger v County of El Dorado* (1971) 5 C3d 480, 96 CR 553. See California

Zoning Practice §2.18A (Cal CEB 1969). The opinion in *Sierra Terreno v Tahoe Regional Planning Agency* (1978) 79 CA3d 439, 442, 144 CR 776, 777, appears to indicate that, because the TRPA was not granted the power of direct condemnation, only the power to plan and regulate, it cannot be liable in inverse condemnation for any of its acts. But see *Baker v Burbank-Glendale-Pasadena Airport Auth.* (1985) 39 C3d 862, 218 CR 293, discussed in Supp §13.3, which permitted an inverse condemnation action against an entity that did not have the power to condemn.

Six regional commissions and the California Coastal Zone Conservation Commission were established by the former California Coastal Zone Conservation Act of 1972 (Pub Res C §§27000–27650). No development after February 1, 1973, is allowed in the permit area of the coastal zone without a permit granted by the regional commission with jurisdiction over the particular area. Pub Res C §27400. See generally California Zoning Practice Supp §§3.87–3.94. The California Coastal Act of 1976 (Pub Res C §§30000–30900) continues the major provisions of the 1972 Act and sets out a comprehensive coastal land use policy.

The California Supreme Court held that denial of a building permit on the ground that the land proposed to be developed may ultimately be designated for public use in a coastal zone plan to be adopted in the near future by the California Coastal Zone Conservation Commission did not constitute a taking. *State v Superior Court* (Veta) (1974) 12 C3d 237, 115 CR 497. The court concluded that, under the California Coastal Zone Conservation Act, determination of whether an applicant qualifies for a permit is entrusted to the commission's discretion; the commission must balance the effect of each proposed development on the coastal environment before a permit may be issued.

See also *Briggs v State ex rel Dep't of Parks & Recreation* (1979) 98 CA3d 190, 159 CR 390, discussed in Supp §4.7A, in which the court denied damages for inverse condemnation when the Coastal Commission refused a development permit because of the interest of the California Department of Parks and Recreation in acquiring the property. Compare *People ex rel State Pub. Works Bd. v Talleur* (1978) 79 CA3d 690, 145 CR 150, discussed in Supp §4.12, which considered the effect of the Coastal Zone Conservation Act on value.

As in *Candlestick Props. v San Francisco Bay Conserv. & Dev. Comm'n, supra,* the court in *State v Superior Court* (Veta), *supra,* relied on the compelling public interest of protecting a valuable natural resource to sustain restrictions imposed by the commission. At the same time, the court observed that the law was a temporary measure to maintain the status quo, pending adoption of a comprehensive plan for California's coast (see Supp §13.22K).

The court in *Morshead v California Regional Water Quality Control Bd.* (1975) 45 CA3d 442, 119 CR 586, held that the Regional Water Control Board acted properly, after notice and hearings, in enforcing orders that sanitation districts refrain from discharging untreated sewage into San Francisco Bay and that they not authorize any further sewer connections until the board's water quality standards were met. Such orders were not a taking or a damaging of the property of persons adversely affected.

When the grazing habits of wild horses and burros protected by the Wild Free-Roaming Horses and Burros Act (16 USC §§1331–1340) diminished the value of private property, the reduction in value did not constitute a taking, because the property owners were not deprived of all economic viable use of their lands. *Mountain States Legal Found. v Hodel* (10th Cir 1986) 799 F2d 1423.

[§13.22K] Temporary Regulations

Interim controls that are more restrictive than might be permitted under permanent ordinances have been upheld to meet an emergency or to further a plan or ordinance that is under study. There are two types of these ordinances: urgency measures enacted under Govt C §65858 and interim ordinances. See generally 2 Broadhead & Rosenfeld, *How To Implement Open Space Plans for the San Francisco Bay Area,* 105–113 (ABAG 1973).

Urgency measures may be enacted without a public hearing by a four-fifths vote of the legislative body, but they are limited to 45 days. An additional extension for 10 months and 15 days and a subsequent one-year extension may each be obtained after notice and a public hearing. Ten days before the expiration of the measure or extension, the legislative body must make a written report of the measures taken to alleviate the conditions that led to the adoption of the ordinance. A 1982 amendment added this report requirement and changed the time periods from an initial four months without a prior public hearing and an eight-month first extension. However, as of January 1, 1989, the former time periods again become law and no such report will be required. The measure may prohibit any land use that would conflict with a contemplated zoning proposal under study or intended for study within a reasonable time.

Under a prior version of Govt C §65858, it was held that the statute does not authorize adoption of interim ordinances that permit a formerly prohibited use or increase the intensity of development. The purpose of this code section is to preserve the status quo, pending establishment of a permanent zoning plan. *Silvera v City of South Lake Tahoe* (1970) 3 CA3d 554, 83 CR 698.

Interim control measures other than those enacted under Govt C §65858 require adherence to all prescribed procedures for adopting zoning ordinances and must have a reasonable duration. The court in *Miller v Board of Pub. Works* (1925) 195 C 477, 234 P 381, first ruled in favor of such an interim zoning ordinance. The court reasoned that zoning plans require time, and during the period of preparation parties should not be permitted to undertake development that would defeat the ultimate execution of the plan. A temporary freeze or moratorium on issuance of building permits in an area established as a redevelopment project is also a valid exercise of police power, based on the need to preserve the status quo, pending a redevelopment plan. *Hunter v Adams* (1960) 180 CA2d 511, 4 CR 776. See also *State v Superior Court* (Veta) (1974) 12 C3d 237, 115 CR 497; *Anderson v City Council* (1964) 229 CA2d 79, 40 CR 41; *Metro Realty v County of El Dorado* (1963) 222 CA2d 508, 35 CR 480.

The court in *Frisco Land & Mining Co. v State* (1977) 74 CA3d 736, 141 CR 820, denied damages for losses incurred by a subdivider due to the moratorium placed on development of unimproved lots during the three-month period immediately following the effective date of the former California Coastal Zone Conservation Act of 1972 (former Pub Res C §§27000–27650; superseded by the California Coastal Act of 1976, Pub Res C §§30000–30900). The subdivider had failed to file forms that were made available for property owners claiming an exemption from the provisions of the Act. But when land development had been prevented for eight years by withholding access in anticipation of freeway construction, a taking had occurred. *Jones v People ex rel Dep't of Transp.* (1978) 22 C3d 144, 148 CR 640.

Interim damages are required for a temporary period preceding the court's invalidation of regulation found to be excessive. *First English Evangelical Lutheran Church v County of Los Angeles* (1987) 482 US 304. In that case, the church owned a campground in a river that had suffered considerable property damage from flooding. The county, based on public safety considerations, banned construction within an interim flood protection area as an urgency measure. Following Justice Brennan's dissent in *San Diego Gas & Elec. Co. v City of San Diego* (1981) 450 US 621, the Supreme Court concluded that invalidation of the ordinance would not be a sufficient remedy and that the temporary taking that deprives the property owner of all use of his property requires compensation as does a permanent taking. However, the Supreme Court did state that, on remand, the trial court could evaluate the county's defense that the ordinance was enacted as a safety regulation.

The *First English* case raises the question of how to assess damages for a temporary taking. One means is the approach used in *Klopping v City of Whittier* (1972) 8 C3d 39, 104 CR 1 (see Supp §4.7A), involving precondemnation damages for unreasonable delay in filing a condemnation action. In that case, the loss of rental income because tenants were driven away by the cloud of condemnation over a redevelopment area was the measure of compensation. Guidance is also available from cases involving abandonment of condemnation proceedings when loss of use and loss of opportunity damages are possible. See Supp §§8.31–8.33.

[§13.22L] Emergency Regulations

Damage done under a police power response to an emergency situation was recognized to be an exception to the rule of compensation for property damage done for a public purpose in *Holtz v Superior Court* (1970) 3 C3d 296, 304, 90 CR 345, 350. In *Teresi v State* (1986) 180 CA3d 239, 225 CR 517 (citing *Holtz*), a medfly eradication program, which caused damage to a pepper crop, was held to qualify for this exception. See also *Farmers Ins. Exch. v State* (1985) 175 CA3d 494, 221 CR 225 (damage to automobile paint finishes by aerial spraying was considered incidental to exercise of police power and not a taking).

Demolition of a building damaged by an earthquake supported a claim in inverse condemnation when the official structural safety report showed that the building was repairable. The municipality acted in the absence of emergency or compelling necessity without according the owner due process. *Rose v City of Coalinga* (1987) 190 CA3d 1627, 236 CR 124. See also *Smith v County of Los Angeles* (1989) 214 CA3d 266, 262 CR 754, which held that removal of slide debris in order to keep a road open to traffic when alternative routes were available is not an emergency under the police power that can justify the taking of private property without compensation.

[§13.22M] Abatement of Nuisance

Demolition to abate a nuisance was a valid exercise of the city's police power. In this case, the property owner had been engaged in a 15-year dispute over whether the maintenance of an unfinished structure constituted a nuisance and had been given ample time to correct the problem. *Duffy v City of Long Beach* (1988) 201 CA3d 1352, 247 CR 715.

[§13.22N] Conditions of Development

As a condition to a building permit or subdivision approval, the governing body may require an owner to dedicate a portion of his land for widening existing roads, new streets, utilities, parks, or open space plans. See §4.64.

Compensation is not necessary in these situations, because the landowner's development both creates the need for the required dedication and receives the economic benefit from the dedication. *Southern Pac. Co. v City of Los Angeles* (1966) 242 CA2d 38, 51 CR 197. This judicial justification to uphold the police power is referred to as the "economic benefit theory."

For the theory to be applied, the dedication must be reasonably related to the improvement for which governmental approval is requested. Govt C §65909; *Ayres v City Council* (1949) 34 C2d 31, 207 P2d 1. In *Mid-Way Cabinet Fixture Mfg. v County of San Joaquin* (1967) 257 CA2d 181,

65 CR 37, a writ of mandate was proper to compel a county to grant a use permit to construct a small addition to an existing structure without the requirement of dedicating and improving part of the firm's property for widening of the street; the addition was not shown to generate any significant increase in traffic. See *Selby Realty Co. v City of San Buenaventura* (1973) 10 C3d 110, 109 CR 799.

In view of the urgent need for open space, however, the court in *Associated Home Builders, Inc. v City of Walnut Creek* (1971) 4 C3d 633, 94 CR 630, ruled that the government does not need to show that the amount of land dedicated for park purposes corresponds to the recreational needs solely attributable to development of a new subdivision. Furthermore, *People ex rel Dep't of Pub. Works v Curtis* (1967) 255 CA2d 378, 63 CR 138, extends the *Southern Pacific* ruling. The court cited *Southern Pacific* for the proposition that a dedication for street-widening purposes, required by a planning body, will not be reversed by the court even when it appears that the dedication related to the general growth of the community. The *Curtis* court, however, failed to consider the findings in *Southern Pacific* that the proposed construction would increase traffic in the area and that the developer would benefit economically from a widened road.

See *Terminal Plaza Corp. v City & County of San Francisco* (1986) 177 CA3d 892, 223 CR 379, in which a city ordinance was not invalid because it placed a disproportionate share of the cost of providing low cost housing on owners of residential hotel units seeking to convert such property to other uses. The ordinance required the owners to provide relocation assistance to hotel residents and choose among several prescribed methods for making "one-for-one replacement" for the units being converted. See also §§4.64–4.66.

It was held unreasonable in *Liberty v California Coastal Comm'n* (1980) 113 CA3d 491, 170 CR 247, for the Coastal Commission to require, as a condition for the permit for construction of a restaurant, that the property owner agree to make his parking lot available for free public parking every day until 5 p.m. for 30 years from the date of his permit. Requiring off-street parking for the public who will use the land involved is a legitimate exercise of police power, but the burden of providing the cost of a general public benefit cannot be shifted to a private party.

The court in *Georgia-Pacific Corp. v California Coastal Comm'n* (1982) 132 CA3d 678, 183 CR 395, ruled that the scope and extent of easements of access required by the commission for new development are reasonably related to a principal purpose of the California Coastal Act of 1976, ¶16 (Pub Res C §§30000–30900), *i.e.,* to provide maximum access to the coast by the general public. This dedication requirement does not depend on showing that the project has created a need for it. Later, in *Pacific Legal Found. v California Coastal Comm'n* (1982) 33 C3d 158, 188 CR 104, the California Supreme Court declined to rule on the constitutionality of beach access guidelines used by the Coastal Commission, on the ground that the suit did not challenge any specific individual permit condition, only general policy guidelines.

The extent of justifying dedication requirements under the Coastal Act of 1976 is illustrated by the following cases. In *Remmenga v California Coastal Comm'n* (1985) 163 CA3d 623, 209 CR 628, the commissioner's conditioning a development permit on the payment of a $5000 in-lieu fee for purchasing public access rights at another coastal development was sustained on the ground that it is proper to look at not only the needs of the project but also the cumulative impact of similar projects and the needs that could be created or increased in the future.

In *Whaler's Village Club v California Coastal Comm'n* (1985) 173 CA3d 240, 220 CR 2, the court held that it was proper to require a homeowners' association to dedicate a public access easement along a beach as a requirement for a permit to allow the association to construct a revetment to protect the association members' beach-front homes from erosion and storm damage.

In *Grupe v California Coastal Comm'n* (1985) 166 CA3d 148, 212 CR 578, a condition to a new development permit for a single family dwelling that required the property owner to dedicate a lateral public access easement along the beach fronting the parcel and affecting nearly 2/3 of the total area of the parcel was held not to deprive the property owner of all reasonable use and economic value of the property. The court noted the fact that the owner had received the benefit of being allowed to proceed with the development of the property and thus increase its value.

In *Nollan v California Coastal Comm'n* (1987) 483 US 825, 107 S Ct 3141, 97 L Ed 2d 677, dedication of a public access easement to the beach as a requirement for a permit to remove one structure and replace it with a new larger structure, when the dedication constituted about a third of the lot in question, was an unconstitutional taking of property. The court emphasized that there must be a connection or "nexus" between the condition of dedication of access and a legitimate governmental interest—here, the preservation of the view of the coast. The direct relationship between the condition imposed by the regulatory agency and the burdens created by the development in *Nollan* appear to contrast with the indirect relationship found in *Associated Home Builders, Whalers Village Club,* and *Grupe,* all of which are discussed above. See Best, *New Constitutional Standards For Land Use Regulation: Portents of Nollan and First English Church,* 1 Hofstra Prop L J 145 (1988).

In *Moore v City of Costa Mesa* (CD Cal 1987) 678 F Supp 1448, the plaintiff successfully obtained a state court declaration that a dedication requirement for street widening was invalid in regard to a variance to build a commercial building. Plaintiff was precluded from pursuing damages in federal court under 42 USC §1983 because (1) the claim was barred by res judicata and (2) any taking claim cannot show that he was deprived of all use of his land. Note, however, that this court's explanation in footnote 8 of *Nollan* is incorrect: The Nollans were not deprived of the use of their property.

A dedication requirement for realignment of the street was ruled invalid on the finding that there was no reasonable relationship between the dedication and the proposed use of the property. Evidence showed that the real purpose was to remedy a poorly planned intersection in its original development and to provide for the city's future growth needs. *Rohn v City of Visalia* (1989) 214 CA3d 1463, 263 CR 319. The city staff report itself concluded that no significant traffic problems would result from the development of the parcel.

Certain municipal exactions, principally fees, are designed for cost recovery of local government to process development permits. At the national level, the United States Supreme Court in *U.S. v Sperry Corp.* (Nov 28, 1989) 110 S Ct 387, 107 L Ed 2d 290, reviewed the imposition of a "user fee" by the United States Government on an award received by an American company from Iran as a result of government-created arbitration. The user fee was challenged as an unconstitutional taking of private property; the Court ruled that a reasonable user fee does not constitute a taking if it is imposed to reimburse the government for the cost of services.

Beginning January 1, 1989, Govt C §66001 established requirements that a local agency must meet to establish, impose, or increase a fee as a condition of approving a development. The agency must (1) identify the fee's purpose, (2) identify the use to which the fee will be put, (3) determine whether there is a reasonable relationship between the fee's use and the type of development project on which the fee is imposed, and (4) determine whether there is a reasonable relationship between the need for the public facility and the type of development project on which the fee is levied.

[§13.22O] Answer to Police Power Defense: Vested Rights

A party who proceeds to do substantial work or expends large sums of money in good faith reliance on a permit issued by an administrative agency acquires a vested right in the permit. Subsequent adoption of more restrictive land use regulations will not affect these properties by precluding completion or modification of the project. *Griffin v County of Marin* (1958) 157 CA2d 507, 321 P2d 148. However, an owner does not have a vested right in a particular zoning classification. *HFH, Ltd. v Superior Court* (1975) 15 C3d 508, 125 CR 365.

In *Burger v County of Mendocino* (1975) 45 CA3d 322, 119 CR 568, a $6500 expenditure for an 80-unit motel was held not substantial.

The opinion in *Spindler Realty Corp. v Monning* (1966) 243 CA2d 255, 53 CR 7, is often asserted for the proposition that, if a project requires several permits, no vested right accrues until all permits have been granted and substantial expenditures are made in reliance on them. In that case, the court held that expenditure of more than $500,000 after issuance of a grading permit did not vest any right to construct the project because a building permit had not been obtained before rezoning of the property.

Spindler was approved by the supreme court in *AVCO Community Developers, Inc. v South Coast Regional Comm'n* (1976) 17 C3d 785, 132 CR 386. In *AVCO* the developer had spent more than $2 million and incurred liabilities of more than $750,000 before its project came under the jurisdiction of the California Coastal Zone Commission. The company had partially completed rough grading, had made street improvements, and had installed some utilities, all with the proper permits and with assurances that they would be allowed to complete the development. However, they had not been granted a building permit. The supreme court reiterated the rule that vested rights are not acquired until substantial expenditures have been made under the authority of a building permit. Until that time the developer takes the risk that subsequent regulations may halt the project. The court did state that the label of building permit might not be critical if the authorizing body had approved specific structures in some other fashion, but that had not occurred in *AVCO*. Under this dictum it is possible that the court would hold that substantial expenditures under a conditional use or similar permit might create vested rights if the permit was granted after the authorizing body had reviewed and approved the proposed structures as to size, type, placement, and number of buildings.

Obtaining a building permit, even when coupled with the delivery of prefabricated housing units to the property, is not sufficient to vest the right to develop because these units are interchangeable and usable on other property. *South Coast Regional Comm'n v Higgins* (1977) 68 CA3d 636, 137 CR 551.

In *Youngblood v Board of Supervisors* (1978) 22 C3d 644, 150 CR 242, a developer acquired a vested right to have its final subdivision map approved despite a change in the general plan's density requirement following approval of the tentative map. Because the final map was in substantial compliance with the tentative map, the local board's approval was a ministerial act under Bus & P C §11549.6 (now Govt C §66474.1). The supreme court dissolved an injunction issued by the appellate court that restrained the county from granting additional building and grading permits under the subdivision map. This action suggests that the court will not permit a government agency to subvert the rule of *Youngblood* by subsequently denying a building permit.

Later cases, however, take a narrow view of the *Youngblood* rule.

In *Hazon-Iny Dev. v City of Santa Monica* (1982) 128 CA3d 1, 179 CR 860, the court held that, when plaintiffs received tentative maps for conversion of rental units to condominiums, they knew that local laws required them to reduce the number of units by combining or removing units. Therefore, when a new rent control ordinance was enacted before plaintiffs received final map approval or building permits, and this new law required additional "removal" or "conversion" permits to be obtained, plaintiffs could not complain that new conditions were being imposed. The court stated that the new permit requirement of the new ordinance was "conceptually" included in the original conditions of the tentative map. The fact that the city could now refuse to grant the removal permit and thus frustrate fulfilling the map conditions was not mentioned in the opinion. In *McMullan v Santa Monica Rent Control Bd.* (1985) 168 CA3d 960, 214 CR 617, a rent control ordinance requiring that a permit be obtained for removal of rental housing from the market, adopted by initiative between tentative subdivision map approval and final map approval, was properly applied to conversion of four apartment units to a condominium.

Subdivision tentative map approvals granted under an invalid general plan cannot be saved by the *Youngblood* rule or by the extension provisions of the State Office of Planning and Research under Govt C §65302.6 if the subdivision approvals were gained before the county sought an extension to revise certain plan elements. *Resource Defense Fund v County of Santa Cruz* (1982) 133 CA3d 800, 184 CR 371. The rule of *Youngblood* was also held not to apply in a Coastal Commission case, *South Cent. Coast Regional Comm'n v Charles A. Pratt Constr. Co.* (1982) 128 CA3d 830, 180 CR 555. Vested rights to an exemption from permit requirements of the Coastal Act arise only when the subdivider is entitled to final map approval according to the requirements of the Subdivision Map Act. Inasmuch as the landowners in *Pratt* had not obtained final map approval before the passage of the Coastal Act, *Youngblood* did not apply. The *Pratt* court stated that *Youngblood* stands only for the proposition that a local governing body does not have absolute discretion to approve or disapprove a final subdivision map when the developer has relied on a tentative map approval with conditions, and has produced a final tract map that satisfies the conditions. The court reasoned that "the overriding environmental policies of the Coastal Act, including a narrow scrutiny of claims of exemption, support our holding that more is required to obtain a vested right than mere tentative map approval." 128 CA3d at 846, 180 CR at 563.

See also *Leroy Land Dev. Corp. v Tahoe Regional Planning Agency* (D Nev 1982) 543 F Supp 277 (developer, who had completed two or three phases of a condominium development and obtained almost all necessary approvals for phase three but had no building permit, did not obtain vested right); *Palmer v Board of Supervisors* (1983) 145 CA3d 779, 193

CR 669 (tentative map that was wrongfully denied based on misrepresentation of the law did not vest rights in zoning at time of denial; the map must conform with new zoning because the denial of subdivision was not in bad faith).

In *Courthouse Plaza Co. v City of Palo Alto* (1981) 117 CA3d 871, 173 CR 161, the court held that a developer did not obtain a vested right to complete the upper six stories of a ten-story building. It was originally approved for construction in two phases, under a planned community zoning district. The expenditures of materials and plans in reliance on the original building and use permits relating to phase one (even though overbuilt to accommodate phase two) were not sufficient to create a vested right when the time to begin construction of phase two had ultimately expired under the original zoning and no permit had been issued for phase two.

In *San Diego Coast Regional Comm'n v See The Sea, Ltd.* (1973) 9 C3d 888, 109 CR 377, the California Coastal Zone Conservation Act of 1972 (former Pub Res C §§27000–27650; superseded by the California Coastal Act of 1976, Pub Res C §§30000–30900) required a coastal permit for construction begun after February 1, 1973. The court applied the vested rights principle and stated that a coastal permit was not required for projects for which a building permit had been granted and on which substantial work had been done before that date.

In *Gisler v County of Madera* (1974) 38 CA3d 303, 112 CR 919, a paper subdivision of agricultural land into 2.5-acre lots was not sufficient to preclude subsequent rezoning of the property by the county to a minimum lot size of 18 acres. The court observed, however, that if actual construction had occurred in the subdivision or money had been spent, there would be limitations on the application of a subsequently enacted zoning ordinance. In *Great W. Sav. & Loan Ass'n v City of Los Angeles* (1973) 31 CA3d 403, 411, 107 CR 359, 364, the court held that substantial expenditure of funds in reliance on the tentative map was sufficient to vest rights. See also *People v County of Kern* (1974) 39 CA3d 830, 115 CR 67.

In *Environmental Coalition v AVCO Community Developers, Inc.* (1974) 40 CA3d 513, 115 CR 59, the court, following *San Diego Coast Regional Comm'n v See The Sea, Ltd., supra,* held that grading under a grading permit for a subdivision could continue because it was begun before the effective date of the Coastal Zone Conservation Act. It concluded that the right to develop the property in toto without a coastal permit was a question to be determined by the trial court on its merits (the issue having been presented to the appellate court on an order granting a preliminary injunction).

The 1974 *AVCO* case concerned the same development as did the 1976 *AVCO* case discussed above. The trial court determined that a permit was required, but it was reversed by the court of appeal. The supreme court granted a hearing in the 1976 case with the result discussed above. With this history in mind, the 1974 court of appeal decision should be cited with caution.

When a property owner converted a building from a first floor supermarket and second floor storage area into 16 retail shops and a small restaurant in reliance on a Coastal Commission agent's statement that no permit would be necessary, the property owner acquired a fundamental vested right on grounds of estoppel. Therefore, in an administrative mandamus proceeding (CCP §1094.5) that arose when the Regional Commission decided that a coastal development permit was necessary, the trial court had to apply the independent judgment test. *Stanson v San Diego Coast Regional Comm'n* (1980) 101 CA3d 38, 161 CR 392. On the independent judgment test, see California Administrative Mandamus §§4.127–4.136, 4.154–4.159 (2d ed Cal CEB 1989).

See also *Billings v California Coastal Comm'n* (1980) 103 CA3d 729, 163 CR 288, in which the court held in an administrative mandamus proceeding that the commission's decision to deny property owners a permit for a minor subdivision was not supported by the law.

Merely applying for a permit does not create any vested rights. A permit application may be denied even though the applicant was entitled to it under existing law and the applicable ordinance was then changed. Unless this action is arbitrary, discriminatory, or confiscatory under the circumstances of the particular case, the applicant has no basis for contesting the action. If litigation follows, the appellate court will look to the law at the time of its decision, rather than at the time of the application. It will not issue an order in conflict with an existing ordinance. *Atlantic Richfield Co. v Board of Supervisors* (1974) 40 CA3d 1059, 115 CR 731.

A landowner who is aware of pending legislation that could require changes in his project does not have a vested fundamental right to be awarded permits when, allegedly in reliance on demolition and foundation permits, he rushes to tear down an old building and begin a new one before a new land use ordinance can become effective. The court in *McCarthy v California Tahoe Regional Planning Agency* (1982) 129 CA3d 222, 180 CR 866, found, as a matter of law, that sums expended under those circumstances were not spent in good faith reliance on the permits.

See Note, *The Effect of Pending Legislation on Applications For Building Permits in California*, 3 U San Francisco L Rev 124 (1968).

In *Southwest Diversified, Inc. v City of Brisbane* (ND Cal 1986) 652 F Supp 788, the court held that a federal permit which included a habitat conservation plan to protect an endangered species of butterfly inhabiting the development site may be sufficiently like a building permit under California law to warrant assertion of vested rights in a prior approval; but the federal court abstained, pending a California court's resolution of state law issues. But, when the Port of Oakland approved a proposed development in principle but did not create a lease or contract, the court held that no property right was created. *Storek & Storek, Inc. v Port of Oakland* (9th Cir 1989) 869 F2d 1322.

[§13.23] Estoppel by Judgment or Deed

Estoppel is a question of fact on which the appellate court will defer to the conclusion of the trier of fact unless the record contains no evidence to support it.

A standard waiver clause in a state right-of-way agreement for freeway acquisition did not preclude a subsequent owner from asserting damages resulting from a discharge of excess water from a drainage system when the state's plan to include it in the freeway project had not been disclosed to the previous owner. *Mehl v People ex rel Dep't of Pub. Works* (1975) 13 C3d 710, 716, 119 CR 625, 628. In *Ellena v State* (1977) 69 CA3d 245, 138 CR 110, however, an owner had been granted compensation under a stipulated judgment for construction of a freeway and accompanying drains across his vineyards. He was precluded from seeking further damages when heavy rains two years later caused the drains to clog and seriously damage his land and crop. The court concluded that the property owner had actual and constructive knowledge of the plans for the project before entering the stipulation and that the subsequent damage was reasonably foreseeable. This decision imposes on the property owner the burden of fully investigating the impact of project plans. It would be advisable to refer to those plans in any agreement or stipulated judgment. See *City of Salinas v Homer* (1980) 106 CA3d 307, 165 CR 65, discussed in Supp §5.12.

Generally, a landowner who accepts and complies with the conditions of a building permit cannot later sue the issuing public entity for inverse condemnation for the cost of compliance. In *Salton Bay Marina v Imperial Irrig. Dist.* (1985) 172 CA3d 914, 218 CR 839, however, the rule was held not to apply. The court held that the building permit condition was contrary to public policy because it purported to absolve an irrigation district from all liability for flooding from a reservoir, whether due to natural causes or to the district's own negligence. Because the condition concerned only a future possibility, the court held that the landowners should not be estopped from seeking damages once the actual taking occurred.

In *California Coastal Comm'n v Superior Court* (1989) 210 CA3d 1488, 258 CR 567, a landowner who brought an inverse action for compensation because the Coastal Commission had imposed a dedication of a public access easement as a condition of a building permit, was denied relief under the doctrine of res judicata because of a failure to first petition for administrative mandamus in a timely manner.

[§13.25] Public Use as Defense to Injunctive Relief

An increased use of a property owner's ditch due to the construction of a public improvement cannot be enjoined; the proper remedy is a suit in inverse condemnation unless this remedy is shown to be inadequate. An injunction is proper, however, to order a public entity to cease its negligent maintenance of an inadequate drainage system. *Sheffet v County of Los Angeles* (1970) 3 CA3d 720, 84 CR 11.

On the other hand, the court in *Kachadoorian v Calwa County Water Dist.* (1979) 96 CA3d 741, 158 CR 223, held that when an alleyway under which a public utility had maintained a water pipeline was abandoned, the alleyway easement was terminated. However, 50 years of use of that pipeline as a part of a community water system was sufficient to establish the necessity of maintaining the pipeline use and thus prevent the property owner from quieting title or seeking injunctive relief. The owner could seek damages only on the theory of inverse condemnation.

[§13.27] Exhaustion of Administrative Remedies and Ripeness

In cases of excessive dedication, refusal to issue permits, revocation of a permit, or failure to exhaust available administrative remedies will foreclose a plaintiff from invoking judicial relief. *Igna v City of Baldwin Park* (1970) 9 CA3d 909, 88 CR 581. See Supp §13.22N; California Administrative Mandamus §§2.25–2.52 (2d ed Cal CEB 1989). However, a party challenging the constitutionality of a legislative act under which an administrative agency functions may not need to exhaust administrative remedies before that agency. See Admin Mandamus §2.44.

When a property owner did not seek a permit before repairing washouts on his property, he could not pursue a subsequent claim in inverse condemnation. *Rutherford v State* (1987) 188 CA3d 1267, 233 CR 781.

A landowner was required to present a claim before the Coastal Commission that he was exempt from the provisions of the former Coastal Zone Conservation Act (Pub Res C §§27000–27650) as a condition to raising that claim in the trial court. *South Coast Regional Comm'n v Gordon* (1977) 18 C3d 832, 135 CR 781. Property owners could not sustain an inverse condemnation action on certain coastal property targeted as high priority for public acquisition when they failed to test the acquisition plan by seeking a building permit. Until the acquisition plan was so tested, it was merely a plan subject to change. *People ex rel Pub. Works Bd. v Superior Court* (Tidwell) (1979) 91 CA3d 95, 154 CR 54.

Public Resources Code §30801 allows any aggrieved person to seek judicial review of a decision of the Coastal Commission by filing a petition for writ of mandate under CCP §1094.5 within 60 days after the decision has become final. In *Walter H. Leimert Co. v California Coastal Comm'n* (1983) 149 CA3d 222, 196 CR 739, the developer had entered into a contract with a water district for delivery of water to its subdivision when it was completed. The Coastal Commission, however, conditioned its approval of a permit for the water district to fix its water system and to develop new ones on the district's not delivering water to the subdivision unless a development permit was granted by the commission. The court held that the developer was precluded from seeking judicial review of damage claims without first pursuing administrative mandamus.

When a subdivider withdrew his application for a permit before the Coastal Commission and instead instituted an action seeking damages in inverse condemnation and challenging the constitutionality of the Act, the subdivider was denied relief for failure to exhaust his administrative remedies. The court could not assume that any invalid conditions would have been approved after review. *Frisco Land & Mining Co. v State* (1977) 74 CA3d 736, 141 CR 820. See also *Pan Pac. Props. v County of Santa Cruz* (1978) 81 CA3d 244, 146 CR 428, in which the failure of the property owner to seek a variance was said to have deprived the county of an opportunity to correct an alleged constitutional infirmity.

A party challenging the constitutionality on its face of a legislative act under which an administrative agency functions does not need to exhaust administrative remedies before that agency as to that issue. The constitutionality of the manner in which the act was applied, however, cannot be challenged without first raising the objections before the administrative agency. *State v Superior Court* (Veta) (1974) 12 C3d 237, 115 CR 497. See also *City of Santa Barbara v Adamson* (1980) 27 C3d 123, 135, 164 CR 539, 545, suggesting that it is not necessary to exhaust administrative remedies when the underlying ordinance is unconstitutional. Note that the Public Utilities Commission has the authority to determine the constitutionality of statutes it is called on to apply. Thus the constitutionality of a statute should be raised at the administrative level when dealing with the PUC. *Southern Pac. Transp. Co. v PUC* (1976) 18 C3d 308, 134 CR 189.

To be excused from exhausting administrative remedies, the aggrieved party must demonstrate positively that the administrative agency's decision in the particular case was predeterminable. *Taper v City of Long Beach* (1982) 129 CA3d 590, 181 CR 169; *Ogo Assocs. v City of Torrance* (1974) 37 CA3d 830, 834, 112 CR 761, 763.

In the United States Supreme Court's decision of *Agins v City of Tiburon* (1980) 447 US 255, discussed in Supp §13.22B, the Court refused to hold that a zoning regulation was an unconstitutional taking on its face, when the ordinance indicated that as many as one to five residential units could be developed on a five-acre parcel and the property owner had not sought permits to develop the property under the ordinance in question.

A landowner was not required to submit a development plan before pursuing an action alleging that public entities had impaired his property by unreasonably delaying condemnation in *Martino v Santa Clara Valley*

Water Dist. (9th Cir 1983) 703 F2d 1141. When a city general plan was adopted prohibiting development in floodway areas, an affected property owner was informed that dedication of one third of his property would be required if that development was sought but that acquisition of the property by the water district was several years away. In addition, the city stated that it would impose the same requirement on any development proposal. Allowing the owner to bring suit against the municipalities absent a development proposal, the court distinguished *Agins* based on *San Diego Gas & Elec. Co. v City of San Diego* (1981) 450 US 621, which suggested that failure to pursue an administrative procedure was not a bar to an attack on the facial validity or effect of an ordinance.

Two United States Supreme Court decisions focus on the issue of ripeness, *MacDonald, Sommer & Frates v County of Yolo* (1986) 477 US 340, and *Williamson County Regional Planning Comm'n v Hamilton Bank* (1985) 473 US 172, both discussed in Supp §13.22B. These cases require a final determination regarding the type and intensity of development that the governmental agency will allow before the court will determine whether regulation constitutes a taking of the property.

In *Kinzli v City of Santa Cruz* (9th Cir 1987) 818 F2d 1449, 1454, modified at 830 F2d 968, the court held that a "final decision" requires "(1) a rejected development plan, and (2) a denial of a variance." Further, a property owner cannot rely on the futility exception until at least one meaningful application has been made to the governmental agency. 818 F2d at 1454. The *Kinzli* developer did not make a meaningful development application because it was abandoned early in the application process.

See also *Lake Nacimiento Ranch Co. v County of San Luis Obispo* (9th Cir 1987) 830 F2d 977, modified at 841 F2d 872; *St. Clair v City of Chico* (9th Cir 1989) 880 F2d 199; *Austin v City & County of Honolulu* (9th Cir 1988) 840 F2d 678; *Shelter Creek Dev. Corp. v City of Oxnard* (9th Cir 1988) 838 F2d 375; *Moore v City of Costa Mesa* (CD Cal 1987) 678 F Supp 1448; Berger, *"Ripeness" Test For Land Use Cases Needs Reform: Reconciling Leading Ninth Circuit Decisions Is An Exercise In Futility,* 11 Zoning & Plan L Rep 57 (1988).

In contrast, in *Herrington v County of Sonoma* (9th Cir 1987) 834 F2d 1488, modified at 857 F2d 567, the denial of a residential subdivision plan based on inconsistency with the general plan did not require the property owner to seek a variance. Government Code §66474(a) requires a county to reject a development proposal that is inconsistent with the general plan; consequently, this section would prohibit a variance for an inconsistent development. Furthermore, there was uncontradicted testimony by county officials at the trial that the subdivision could never have obtained approval. The property owner in this case had met the final decision requirement, but an award of compensation for the taking of the land was set aside and the case remanded for a new trial on damages because the loss of value was based on the rejection of a 32-lot subdivision, although the property owner was allowed to retain the property and presumably could obtain approval for some level of development of the land. See also *Hall v City of Santa Barbara* (9th Cir 1986) 833 F2d 1270, which did not find premature a challenge to an ordinance requiring mobilehome park operators to offer their tenants leases of unlimited duration and transferability.

In a case of downzoning commercial property to open space, a summary judgment in favor of the municipality was reversed on the ground that a triable issue of fact was presented on whether the seeking of a variance would be futile. The question was whether an apparent administrative remedy was really available because the municipality initiating the downzoning which, in itself, was a response to a lot split application for land that was submitted without an accompanying development proposal. *Twain Harte Assocs., Ltd. v County of Tuolomne* (1990) 217 CA3d 71, 265 CR 737.

In *Hoehne v County of San Benito* (9th Cir 1989) 870 F2d 529, a variance or rezoning was not required when the County Board of Supervisors made a clear policy statement by changing five-acre minimum size for single family dwellings on a 60-acre parcel to 40-acre minimum lot size. The property owners initially proposed, to the planning commission, to subdivide into four 15-acre lots meeting the five acre minimum lot size. On appeal, the property owners had reduced the proposed subdivision to three lots, but approval was denied again by the Board of Supervisors. The Board of Supervisors then amended the General Plan and zoning ordinance to impose the 40-acre minimum lot size requirement. It was clear that no subdivision would be allowed.

[§13.28] Availability of Less Drastic Remedies

In the area of land use regulation (see Supp §§13.22A–13.22M) a cause of action in inverse condemnation is often coupled with other causes for mandamus or prohibition, injunctive relief, and declaratory relief. See, e.g., *Selby Realty Co. v City of San Buenaventura* (1973) 10 C3d 110, 109 CR 799. If other less drastic remedies giving adequate protection to plaintiff are available, the court may not allow that party to pursue a remedy for an unlawful taking. In *Selby,* an inverse condemnation cause of action was dismissed on the judicial conclusion that a traditional administrative mandamus proceeding (CCP §1094.5) would be a more appropriate remedy. The supreme court viewed the specter of inverse condemnation as having a serious adverse effect on land use planning because it failed to consider a policy of orderly growth and environmental protection.

The California Supreme Court extended the *Selby* rule in *Agins v City of Tiburon* (1979) 24 C3d 266, 157 CR 372, by declaring inverse condemnation inappropriate in cases in which unconstitutional regulation is alleged; rather, the appropriate remedy was said to be declaratory relief or a mandamus action. However, the Supreme Court in *First English Evangelical Lutheran Church v County of Los Angeles* (1987) 482 US 304, determined that inverse condemnation can be asserted for the over-regulation of land. See Supp §13.22B for discussion of these cases.

In *Viso v State* (1979) 92 CA3d 15, 154 CR 580, allegations that the plaintiff's land had been zoned more restrictively (reclassified from low density residential to general forest) than surrounding land entitled the property owner to test the validity of the zoning action by declaratory relief. The plaintiff had not alleged that the property as rezoned had no use or value, so the court ruled that plaintiff did not state a cause of action in inverse condemnation. See also *Burns v City Council* (1973) 31 CA3d 999, 107 CR 787, in which the appellate court dismissed an action for general, special, and punitive damages (not in inverse condemnation) against a city council for alleged wrongful denial of a building permit on the bases that administrative mandamus was also available to the plaintiff and legislative immunity (see Supp §13.5) was applicable.

Generally, the proper method used to test the validity of conditions in a building permit is a proceeding in mandamus under CCP §1094.5. *Pfeiffer v City of La Mesa* (1977) 69 CA3d 74, 137 CR 804. Likewise, the proper remedy for denial of a building permit for land under the jurisdiction of the Coastal Zone Conservation Commission is mandamus, not inverse condemnation. *Marina Plaza v California Coastal Zone Conserv. Comm'n* (1977) 73 CA3d 311, 140 CR 725. See also *Briggs v State ex rel Dep't of Parks & Recreation* (1979) 98 CA3d 190, 159 CR 390, and the related discussion of choice of action in Supp §13.5.

In *Nollan v California Coastal Comm'n* (1987) 483 US 825, 107 S Ct 3141, 97 L Ed 2d 677, the United States Supreme Court reviewed a petition for a writ of administrative mandamus challenging an access condition imposed on a permit to remove an existing residence and replace it with a larger structure. There is language in that decision that supports a cause of action in inverse condemnation. Specifically, the Court found the condition to be an unreasonable requirement but stated that, if the Coastal Commission wanted the easement "it must pay for it." This, together with the rule of *First English Evangelical Lutheran Church v County of Los Angeles, supra,* recognizing inverse condemnation as a valid remedy for excessive regulation of land, supports pleading an inverse cause of action as part of a mandamus proceeding.

In *California Coastal Comm'n v Superior Court* (1989) 210 CA3d 1488, 258 CR 567, a landowner who brought an inverse condemnation action for compensation, because the Coastal Commission had imposed a dedication of a public access easement as a condition of a building permit, was denied relief under the doctrine of res judicata because of a failure to first petition for administrative mandamus in a timely manner. To recover compensation for inverse condemnation a property owner must first establish the invalidity of the condition imposed. Under Pub Res

C §30801, an administrative mandamus action must be filed within 60 days of the Commission's action. The failure to seek such relief within that statute of limitations precludes the inverse condemnation action. The ruling in *Rossco Holdings, Inc. v State* (1989) 212 CA3d 642, 260 CR 736, has the same effect because the court noted that *Nollan* did not change the rule on challenging a condition and *First English* did not eliminate the need to comply with the appropriate procedural route.

[§13.29] Legislative Immunity for Permit Activities

Government Code §818.4 grants immunity to a public entity for an injury caused by the issuance, denial, suspension, or revocation, or the refusal to do the same, of "any permit, license, certificate, approval, order, or similar authorization where the public entity . . . is authorized by enactment to determine whether or not such authorization should be issued, denied, suspended or revoked." See also Govt C §§815.2(b), 820.2, 821.2. However, the immunities provided by California statutes to protect public entities from monetary damages from the consequences of land use regulations are not applied by the courts to inverse condemnation, which is based on the guaranty of Cal Const art I, §19. See *Sanfilippo v County of Santa Cruz* (ND Cal 1976) 415 F Supp 1340, 1343, which discusses that point but relies on the federal Constitution.

Thus, in mandamus and administrative mandamus actions, California has used these Government Code sections to protect a public entity from liability. See, *e.g.*, *HFH, Ltd. v Superior Court* (1975) 15 C3d 508, 125 CR 365; *State v Superior Court* (Veta) (1974) 12 C3d 237, 115 CR 497; *Selby Realty Co. v City of San Buenaventura* (1973) 10 C3d 110, 109 CR 799; *O'Hagan v Board of Zoning Adjustment* (1974) 38 CA3d 722, 113 CR 501. Now, the rule of these cases must be considered under *First English Evangelical Lutheran Church v County of Los Angeles* (1987) 482 US 304, in which the Supreme Court declared inverse condemnation to be an available remedy for the temporary taking of land by an excessive land use regulation. Under this decision, whether damages can be based on the improper refusal to issue a permit turns on the question of whether there is unreasonable delay in the land use processing.

See also *Zisk v City of Roseville* (1976) 56 CA3d 41, 127 CR 896, in which plaintiffs in an inverse condemnation action attempted to set forth a cause of action under the federal Civil Rights Act (42 USC §1983 or §1985, or both) to reach the individual council members who voted against their land development project. The court concluded that plaintiffs were required to show the absence of any reasonable basis on which to characterize the council's action as being in good faith. Two United States Supreme Court decisions on the pursuit of civil rights remedies are (1) *Owen v City of Independence* (1980) 445 US 622, in which a municipality was held not to be immune from a Civil Rights Act (42

USC §1983) suit for constitutional violation of rights merely because
it had acted in good faith, and (2) *Maine v Thiboutot* (1980) 448 US
1, in which the court ruled that an action could be maintained in state
court for violation of any federal law under the Civil Rights Act.

The court in *Flavin v Board of Educ.* (D Conn 1982) 553 F Supp
827, noted that the United States Supreme Court has narrowed the reach
of the *Thiboutot* case in two recent decisions: In *Pennhurst State School
& Hosp. v Halderman* (1981) 451 US 1, the Supreme Court held that
a Civil Rights Act remedy would not be available when the governing
statute provides an exclusive remedy for violation of its terms (in a subsequent decision in the same case the court ruled that the 11th amendment
prohibits the federal district court from ordering state officials to conform
their conduct to state law; *Pennhurst State School & Hosp. v Halderman*
(1984) 465 US 89); and in *Middlesex County Sewerage Auth. v National
Sea Clammers Ass'n* (1981) 453 US 1, the Court held that statutes that
contain comprehensive enforcement mechanisms cannot be the basis for
a suit under the Civil Rights Act. See also *Clallam County v Department
of Transp.* (9th Cir 1988) 849 F2d 424.

Both the municipality and individual council members were liable under
42 USC §1983 for refusal to issue a building permit to a property owner
who satisfied all requirements made on his property. Denial of substantive
due process does not require proof that all use of the property has been
denied; rather, the interference with property rights was arbitrary. *Bateson
v Geisse* (9th Cir 1988) 857 F2d 1300.

The court in *Hernandez v City of Lafayette* (5th Cir 1981) 643 F2d
1188, held that oppressive land regulation can give rise to a civil rights
claim.

[§13.29A] Equitable Indemnity

A public agency that is sued in inverse condemnation for the approval
and acceptance of certain public improvements constructed by a developer
(see Supp §13.3) may cross-complain for equitable indemnity against the
developer for fraudulent preparation and submission of various permits.
County of San Mateo v Berney (1988) 199 CA3d 1489, 245 CR 738.
Furthermore, the county that has entered into a subdivision agreement
may seek damages against the developer for defective construction under
that agreement. *County of Mariposa v Yosemite W. Assocs.* (1988) 202
CA3d 791, 248 CR 778.

[§13.29B] Collateral Source Rule

The collateral source rule in California provides that, if an injured
party receives some compensation for injuries from a source wholly independent of the tortfeasor, the payment will not be deducted from the
damages that the plaintiff would otherwise collect from the tortfeasor.

Helfend v Southern Cal. Rapid Transit Dist. (1970) 2 C3d 1, 84 CR 173. The rule, however, did not apply in an inverse condemnation action in the case of a landslide damaging a residence when the lender reconveyed its deed of trust, thereby forgiving its debt. *Smith v County of Los Angeles* (1989) 214 CA3d 266, 262 CR 754.

CONCLUSION OF CASE

[§13.30] Recovery of Costs

In any unlawful taking case, "the court rendering judgment for the plaintiff . . . or the attorney representing the public entity who effects a settlement of such proceeding, shall determine and award or allow to such plaintiff, as a part of such judgment or settlement" reimbursement for plaintiff's reasonable costs and expenses, including reasonable attorney appraisal and engineering fees necessary to the proceeding. CCP §1036 (former CCP §1246.3). Under this section, the court in *Parker v City of Los Angeles* (1974) 44 CA3d 556, 118 CR 687, held that an award of attorneys' fees in the amount of one third of the actual damages awarded was reasonable. Compensation to the attorney based on a contingency fee is appropriate because plaintiff bears the burden of first establishing its legal right to damages.

Aetna Life & Cas. Co. v City of Los Angeles (1985) 170 CA3d 865, 216 CR 831, however, held that an award of attorney's fees should not be based solely on the contingency fee arrangement. The trial court should consider factors such as number of hours actually spent on the case, reasonable amount of hourly compensation, difficulty of the issues, the fee, skill of the attorney in dealing with the issues, and extent to which the litigation precluded other employment. See also *Salton Bay Marina, Inc. v Imperial Irrig. Dist.* (1985) 172 CA3d 914, 218 CR 839.

Property owners who are unsuccessful in proving that a local agency has taken or damaged their property are not entitled to costs in inverse condemnation actions (*Crum v Mt. Shasta Power Corp.* (1932) 124 CA 90, 12 P2d 134) but courts have allowed plaintiffs who succeeded in recovering damages in principle but not in fact to be reimbursed costs. In *City of Los Angeles v Ricards* (1973) 10 C3d 385, 110 CR 489, the court awarded plaintiff both trial and appeal costs when there was a taking or damaging, even though it was minimal. Plaintiff recovered no damages compensation because the city replaced the bridge that had been washed out by a water diversion caused by the city's upstream construction work, depriving plaintiff's property of access, and the property owner could not show any loss of use or rental value during the two years between the flooding and replacement of the bridge. See also *Collier v Merced Irrig. Dist.* (1931) 213 C 554, 2 P2d 790, in which the court awarded costs, although benefits from the public project offset the monetary damages for the taking.

When property owners who brought an inverse condemnation action against two defendants prevailed against one but not the other, the public agency that successfully defended itself is entitled to costs against the plaintiff. Property owners are not constitutionally entitled to costs in an inverse condemnation action if they are unable to prove there has been a taking or damaging. *Smith v County of Los Angeles* (1989) 214 CA3d 266, 262 CR 754.

In *Klopping v City of Whittier* (1972) 8 C3d 39, 104 CR 1, both plaintiffs in a consolidated appeal proceeding were allowed their costs, although one was not successful in reversing the judgment of dismissal of his action. After the unsuccessful plaintiff instituted his inverse condemnation suit, the public entity brought its own condemnation action, which proceeded to judgment first. The damages sought in inverse condemnation could have been claimed as a part of the eminent domain award. Consequently, plaintiff was barred from seeking those damages in the inverse condemnation action once the direct proceeding became final (see §8.24 for discussion of cross-complaints in condemnation proceedings). It was the first final judgment, not the final judgment in the first suit, that raised the defense of res judicata. The *Klopping* court relied on *People ex rel Dep't of Pub. Works v International Tel. & Tel. Corp.* (1972) 26 CA3d 549, 103 CR 63, a direct condemnation action that approved a cost award on appeal to an unsuccessful property owner when the appeal involved the failure to apply correct legal principles and not the amount of damages (see Book §10.30); the opinion thus is not clearly authority for recovery of costs other than those on appeal.

In *City of Los Angeles v Beck* (1974) 40 CA3d 763, 115 CR 569, the court refused to extend *Klopping* to allow recovery of attorney's fees and appraiser's fees in a direct condemnation action that was filed after institution of an inverse condemnation suit concerning the same property, but proceeded to final judgment before termination of the inverse condemnation action. Code of Civil Procedure §1036 (former CCP §1246.3) applies only to inverse condemnation. The appellate court hinted that a different result might have been reached if the two actions had been consolidated. The property owners did move to do so, but the motion was denied by the trial court, and the denial of this motion was not raised as an issue on appeal.

When direct and inverse condemnation actions were consolidated, but the direct action was abandoned, litigation expenses were recoverable. *City of Los Angeles v Tilem* (1983) 142 CA3d 694, 191 CR 229. However, under CCP §1036, the owner could not also recover in state court costs for prosecuting a federal civil rights action in federal court, even though the federal action would not have been brought but for the city's allegedly illegal precondemnation activity. Those costs can only be recovered in federal court, if at all.

Even though the pleadings of a particular case do not express the claim as one in condemnation, when the evidence warrants converting it into a suit for inverse condemnation, the plaintiffs who were unsuccessful in the trial court were entitled to costs in litigating the issue of whether development of a public street caused damage to their real property. *Blau v City of Los Angeles* (1973) 32 CA3d 77, 107 CR 727. It was not necessary to apportion attorney's fees awarded a successful plaintiff in an inverse condemnation action to causes of action for negligence and nuisance, in which attorney's fees were not allowable, because most of the time spent preparing the negligence and nuisance cases was relevant to establish only the inverse condemnation action. *Salton Bay Marina v Imperial Irrig. Dist.* (1985) 172 CA3d 914, 218 CR 839.

Attorneys' fees and expenses incurred by defendants in legal proceedings after an award in an eminent domain action, arising out of their attempts to extend their possession of the condemned property beyond an agreed time period and to avoid being held in contempt for holding over, are not recoverable. Former CCP §1246.3 (now CCP §1036) had no application to the proceedings. *Parking Auth. v Nicovich* (1973) 32 CA3d 420, 108 CR 137.

The court in *Stone v City of Los Angeles* (1975) 51 CA3d 987, 124 CR 822, refused to grant litigation expenses to plaintiff in a precondemnation damage inverse condemnation case, because the statute allows those costs only for a taking. See also *People ex rel Dep't of Pub. Works v Peninsula Enters.* (1979) 91 CA3d 332, 153 CR 895. The supreme court in *Holtz v San Francisco BART Dist.* (1976) 17 C3d 648, 131 CR 646, agreed that the distinction between taking and damaging is called for by the statute. However, the court held that a "taking" as used in the statute is less restrictive than a "taking" under Cal Const art I, §19. The court held that defendants' actions (withdrawal of lateral support) amounted to a taking for purposes of the statute, although not a constitutional taking.

The extension of the term "taking" as used in CCP §1036, to damage and destruction of land, was applied to temporary flooding in *Orme v State ex rel Dep't of Water Resources* (1978) 83 CA3d 178, 147 CR 735; to temporary loss of access in *Jones v People ex rel Dep't of Transp.* (1978) 22 C3d 144, 148 CR 640; and to economic damage, such as precondemnation damages, in *City of Los Angeles v Tilem* (1983) 142 CA3d 694, 191 CR 229. The distinction between "taking" and "damaging" for the purpose of recovering litigation expenses appears to have dissolved.

Code of Civil Procedure §998 provides that a party cannot recover costs if, after the party refuses to accept a compromise settlement, the judgment is not more favorable to the refusing party than was the offer. Code of Civil Procedure §998(g) specifically voids the rule when the plaintiff makes the offer in a condemnation action. In *Orpheum Bldg. Co. v San Francisco BART Dist.* (1978) 80 CA3d 863, 146 CR 5, the court interpreted the exemption to apply to inverse condemnation, and in that context "plaintiff" refers to a governmental entity. When a property owner does not succeed in inverse condemnation, the constitutional doctrine of full compensation, which underlies the award of costs, plainly does not apply. *City of Los Angeles v Ricards* (1973) 10 C3d 385, 391, 110 CR 489, 492.

Litigation expenses to the successful plaintiff may not be reduced on the basis that the property owner's appraiser took more time than the public agency's expert and the property owner had been represented at trial by two attorneys, only one of whom took an active role. The appellate court noted that the property owner has a greater burden in a complex inverse condemnation case and the ultimate results reflected the efforts of counsel. *San Gabriel Valley Water Co. v City of Montebello* (1978) 84 CA3d 757, 148 CR 830.

When an attorney acts on his or her own behalf in prosecuting an inverse condemnation action, the attorney is entitled to recover the reasonable value of the professional services that were necessarily rendered during the pretrial and trial proceedings. *Leaf v City of San Mateo* (1984) 150 CA3d 1184, 198 CR 447.

Code of Civil Procedure §1036 does not require the state to segregate a specific sum of the settlement for the payment of attorneys' fees. Thus, a probate court can properly determine the reasonable amount of attorneys' fees for an attorney who handled an inverse condemnation action on behalf of an estate against the State of California. *Estate of Baum* (1989) 209 CA3d 744, 257 CR 566.

[§13.31] Interest

In any condemnation proceeding in which interest is awarded, the interest must be computed as prescribed by CCP §1268.350. CCP §1268.311. See Supp §10.24 for discussion of calculation of interest under CCP §1268.350.

Prejudgment interest accrues in both taking and injury situations. See *Holtz v San Francisco BART Dist.* (1976) 17 C3d 648, 131 CR 646, concluding that "interest must be computed from the date the taking or damaging was sustained." 17 C3d at 651, 131 CR at 648. In *Smith v County of Los Angeles* (1989) 214 CA3d 266, 262 CR 754, interest was allowed from the time damage first occurred to the residents rather than from the date property was actually destroyed on the basis that interest should be awarded from the date property damage reaches the level that substantially interferes with the owner's use and enjoyment of the property.

[§13.32] Attorneys' Fees on Appeal

The award of attorneys' fees to plaintiff on appeal of an inverse condemnation action is not permissible under CCP §1036 (former CCP §1246.3;

see Supp §13.30). That section is concerned only with the trial or pretrial level. *Holtz v San Francisco BART Dist.* (1976) 17 C3d 648, 131 CR 646.

[§13.33] Jury Instructions for Inverse Condemnation Actions

The following proposed jury instructions have been recommended by the State Bar Committee on Eminent Domain for use in inverse condemnation actions and are reprinted here with the committee's permission. Citations have been edited to conform to CEB style. Additional instructions concerning land regulation cases were prepared by the committee in 1978, but they were withdrawn in view of the California Supreme Court decision in *Agins v City of Tiburon* (1979) 24 C3d 266, 157 CR 372, which held that inverse condemnation was an inappropriate remedy for downzoning. That ruling has now been set aside in *First English Evangelical Lutheran Church v County of Los Angeles* (1987) 482 US 304, See discussion in Supp §13.22B.

INSTRUCTION NO. 1

A Plaintiff otherwise entitled to recover will be barred if that Plaintiff failed to commence his lawsuit within the time period provided by law. An inverse condemnation lawsuit must be commenced no later than _ _ years after the cause of action accrued. This lawsuit was commenced by filing a Complaint on _ _ _ _, 19_ _.

Authority:
CCP §319
CCP §338
Britt v Superior Court (1978) 20 C3d 844, 143 CR 695

NOTE: The question of whether a Complaint or other document commencing an action has been filed in a timely manner will not be presented to a jury in every case. This instruction is to be utilized if the Court submits it to the jury.

INSTRUCTION NO. 2

A cause of action in inverse condemnation accrues when the act(s), omission(s) or event(s) which cause(s) the taking or damage have occurred and the effect has stabilized so that the nature and the amount of damage incurred, and the benefits conferred, if any, are ascertained or readily ascertainable.

Authority:
U.S. v Dickinson (1947) 331 US 745
Pierpont Inn, Inc. v State (1969) 70 C2d 282, 74 CR 521

INSTRUCTION NO. 3

When the taking or damage results from a series or sequence of acts, omissions, or events, then the cause of action from the entire series or sequence accrues at the time of stabilization of damages following the last act, omission or event in the sequence or series. A property owner is not required to file piecemeal lawsuits, but may await completion of the series or sequence of acts, omissions or events.

Authority:
U.S. v Dickinson (1947) 331 US 745
Pierpont Inn, Inc. v State (1969) 70 C2d 282, 74 CR 521

INSTRUCTION NO. 4

To recover compensation in inverse condemnation, the Plaintiff must prove:

(1) That he had an interest in real property;

(2) That Defendant approved, constructed, or operated a public project, or was otherwise engaged in an activity for public use and benefit;

(3) That Plaintiff's interest in real property has been taken or damaged;

(4) That Defendant's project, act, or omission was a substantial and proximate cause of the damage.

Authority:
Stoney Creek Orchards v State (1970) 12 CA3d 903, 91 CR 139
Condemnation Practice in California §13.3 (Cal CEB 1973).

INSTRUCTION NO. 5

Whether the Defendant has monies appropriated or otherwise available to pay damages is irrelevant, and should not be considered by you in your deliberations.

INSTRUCTION NO. 7

The compensation to be paid to an owner is measured by the loss of market value of the property interest and not the value of the property interest to the public entity.

INSTRUCTION NO. 11

Certain matters may be considered by you in determining whether or not Plaintiff's property has been taken or damaged and, if so, the extent thereof.

Among those matters are:

1. The nature and extent of the property interest alleged by the Plaintiffs.

2. The geographic limits or legal description of the property or property interest allegedly taken or damaged.

3. The nature of the alleged taking or the damaging, that is, whether it is permanent or limited.

4. The effect of the taking or damaging on the property interest alleged by the Plaintiffs.

In *Aetna Life & Cas. Co. v City of Los Angeles* (1985) 170 CA3d 865, 216 CR 831, the court approved application of BAJI No. 11.80 and the holdings in *People v McCullough* (1950) 100 CA2d 101, 223 P2d 37, and *Redevelopment Agency v Modell* (1960) 177 CA2d 321, 2 CR 245, to an inverse condemnation case. The court thus held that the jury hearing an inverse condemnation action must determine the fair market value of the subject property only from the opinions of qualified witnesses and the property owner. Further, the court held that the jury "may not disregard the evidence as to value and render a verdict which either exceeds or falls below the limits established by the testimony of the witnesses." 170 CA3d at 877, 216 CR at 838.

Appendix A: Legislation on Condemnation

The following changes to Book Appendix A, Parts IA and IB should be made as follows:

Part IA: Constitutional Provisions

Replace Art I, §14 with Art I, §19.
Delete reference to Art I, §14 1/2.
Delete reference to Art XII, §8.
Replace Art XII, §23a with Art XII, §5.
Replace Art XV, §1 with Art X, §1.

Part IB: Statutes of General Application

Delete reference to CCP §170(6) (effective 7/1/87).
Replace CCP §§1237–1273.06 with CCP §§1230.010–1273.050.
Replace Evid C §§810–822 with Evid C §§810–823.
Replace CC §730.03(b)(2) with Prob C §16303(b)(2).
Replace Govt C §§7000–7001 with Govt C §§7000–7002.
After CC §1001, replace "Condemnor may take as agent of state" with "Right of eminent domain provided to private persons for limited purpose of making utility connections."
Delete reference to Govt C §§190–196.
After Health & S C §33398, replace CCP §1243.1 with CCP §1245.60.
Replace Pub Res C §§21000–21151 with Pub Res C §§21000–21177; replace "Environmental Quality Act of 1970" with "California Environmental Quality Act."

Replace Pub Util C §§1503–1505 with Pub Util C §§1503–1505.5.

Substitute the code sections listed below for those listed in Book Appendix A, Parts IC-IE, IIB, as indicated:

Part IC: Express Purposes for Which Power of Eminent Domain May Be Exercised:

Purpose	Code Section Entity Having Power (no changes)
Airports	Pub Util C §21652
Armories	Mil & V C §437 Str & H C §2380
Community college	Ed C §81903 districts
Fire protection	(delete entire reference to fire protection)
School facilities	Ed C §§35720.5, 70902(b)(13)
Sewerage systems	Health & S C §§4740, 4760
Sewers, drains, and conduits	Govt C §§40404, 55003 Str & H C §§5100–5102, 5023–5023.1
Urban renewal	Health & S C §§33719–33720

Part ID: Types of Public Entities Having General Power of Eminent Domain:

Name	Code Section
Education, board of (county)	Ed C §1793
Fire protection districts	Health & S C §13861(c)
Highway districts, joint	Str & H C §§25050(d), 25280
Irrigation districts	Wat C §§22456–22458
Replace junior college governing boards with community college districts	Ed C §§70902(b)(13), 81903
Memorial districts	Mil & V C §1191(a)
Park districts, regional	Pub Res C §§5540, 5542, 5544.1
Pest abatement districts	(delete entire reference)

Public utility districts	Pub Util C §16404
School districts	Ed C §§35270, 35270.5
Water storage districts	Wat C §43530

Part IE: Governmental Entities Expressly Named

Name	*Code Section*
Aeronautics, Department of	Pub Util C §21633
Alameda County Flood Control & Water Conservation District	Deering's act 205, §§5(4), (9), (13), West's §§55–5(4), (9), (13)
Alpine County Water Agency	Deering's act 270, §7, West's §102–7
Amador County Water Agency	Deering's act 276, §3.4, West's §95–3.4
American River Flood Control District	Deering's act 320, §2(f), West's §37–2(f)
Bighorn Mountains Water Agency	Deering's act 9099d, §15(9), West's §112–15(9).
Castaic Lake Water Agency	Deering's act 9099b, §15(g), West's §103–15(g)
Colleges, California State University and (Trustees)	(delete entire reference)
Crestline-Lake Arrowhead Water Agency	Deering's act 9099a, §11(9), West's §104–11(9)
Desert Water Agency	Deering's act 9097, §15(9), West's §100–15(9)
El Dorado County Water Agency	Deering's act 2245, §8, West's §96–8
Fresno Metropolitan Transit Authority	Pub Util C App 1, §§6.3, 6.6, 6.15
General Services, Department of (Director)	Govt C §14662
Hunters Point Reclamation Area	(legislation repealed)
Kern County Water Agency	Deering's act 9098, §3.4, West's §99–3.4

Los Angeles County Flood Control District	Deering's act 4463, §16, West's §28–16
Marin County Transit District	Pub Util C §§70165, 70175, 70176
Mariposa County Water Agency	Deering's act 4613, §3.4, West's §85–3.4
Nevada County Water Agency	Deering's act 5449, §7, West's §90.7
Parks & Recreation, Department of (to establish parkways and scenic easments)	(delete entire reference)
Public Works, Department of (to construct freeways and highways)	Str & H C §§102, 103.5, 104, 104.6
Riverside County Flood Control Water Conservation District	Deering's act 6642, §§9(9), (10), & West's §§48–9(9), (10)
Sacramento Regional Transit District	Pub Util C §§102240, 102242–102243
San Diego County Flood Control District	Deering's act 6914a, §§6(4), (12), West's §§105–64(4, (12)
San Francisco Bay Area Rapid Transit District	Pub Util C §28953, 28955, 28970, 29010
San Joaquin County Flood Control & Water Conservation District	Deering's act 7150, §§5(4), (9), (13), West's §§79–5(4), (9), (13)
San Mateo County Flood Control District	Deering's act 7261, §§3(4), (8)–(9), West's §§87–3(4), (8)–(9)
Santa Clara County Flood Control & Water Conservation District	Deering's act 7335, §§5(4), (7), West's §§60–5(4), (7), 60–6
Shasta County Water Agency, Zone 2	Deering's act 7580, §§42, 47, 65, West's §§83–42, 83–47, 83–65
Solano County Flood Control & Water Conservation District	Deering's act 7733, §3.4, West's §64–3.4
Southern California Rapid Transit District	Pub Util C §§30503, 30530, 30600

Sutter County Water Agency	Deering's act 9096, §§3.4, West's §86–3.4.
Vallejo Sanitation & Flood Control District	Deering's act 8934, §2(f), West's §67–2(f)
West Bay Rapid Transit Authority	Change cite from Pub Util C App 3 §6.6 to Pub Util C App 2 §6.6
Yuba-Bear River Basin Authority	Deering's act 9380, §8, West's §93–8
Yuba County Water Agency	Deering's act 9407, §3.4, West's §84–3.4

Part IIB: Federal Statutes

Entity/Subject Matter	United States Code	Provisions
delete Atomic Energy Commission and replace with Nuclear Regulatory Commission	no change	no change
Cemeteries	38 USC §§1004, 1006	
Defense facilities and housing	delete 42 USC §1594a (repealed)	delete corresponding text
Endangered Species	16 USC §1534	no change
Highways	23 USC §107 42 USC §§4601-4655 (23 USC §§501-511 were repealed)	no change no change

Appendix C: California/Federal Tax Conformity Chart

The following Revenue and Taxation Code sections cited in Book chap 12 have been repealed and renumbered by Stats 1983, ch 488. When the renumbering was intended to emphasize conformity with federal law, the Internal Revenue Code section is also listed below. State statutes that are in variance with federal law are listed as exceptions.

Old Rev & T C Section	Action	New Rev & T C Section	Comparable IRC Section
17062-17063.11	Exception	[No change in 1983, repealed effective Sept. 25, 1987]	
17064	Repealed		
17064.5	Exception	17064.5	
17071	Conform	17071	IRC §61
17154	Repealed		
17155	Conform	17131	IRC §121
17206	Conform	17201	IRC §165
170206.5	Conform	17201	IRC §165(h)
17208	Exception	17250	
17211.6	Conform	17201	IRC §167
17211.7	Conform	17201	IRC §167
17264	Conform	17201	IRC §216
17265	Conform	17201	IRC §216
17401	Conform	17321	IRC §331
17431	Conform	17321	IRC §351
17432	Conform	17321	IRC §354
17461	Conform	17321	IRC §368(a)
17580.1	Conform	17551	IRC §453
18044	Exception	[§18032 repealed, effective July 8, 1985]	
18081	Conform	18031	IRC §1031
18082	Conform	18031	IRC §1033(a)
18083	Conform	18031	IRC §1033(a)(2)(A)
18084	Conform	18031	IRC §1033(a)(2)(B)
18085	Conform	18031	IRC §1033(a)(2)(C)
18086	Conform	18031	IRC §1033(a)(2)(D)
18087	Repealed		

Old Rev & T C Section	Action	New Rev & T C Section	Comparable IRC Section
18088	Conform	18031	IRC §1033(b)
18089	Conform	18031	IRC §1033(c)
18090	Conform	18031	IRC §1033(d)
18090.1	Conform	18031	IRC §1033(e)
18090.2	Exception	18037	
18091-18100.1	Conform	18031	IRC §1034(a)-(k)
18161	Conform	18151	IRC §1221
18163	Conform	18151	IRC §1223(1)
18164	Conform	18151	IRC §1223(2)
18181	Conform	18151	IRC §1231(a)
18182	Exception	[§18169 repealed, effective Sept. 25, 1987]	
18211	Exception	[§18170 repealed, effective January 1, 1986]	
18212	Exception	[§18173 repealed, effective Sept. 25, 1987]	
18213	Exception	18171	
18214	Conform	18151	IRC §1250(c)
18215	Exception	[§18172 repealed, effective Sept. 25, 1987]	
18215.1	Exception	[§18173 repealed, effective Sept. 25, 1987]	
18216	Exception	[§18172 repealed, effective Sept. 25, 1987]	
18217	Conform	18151	IRC §1250(f)-(g)
18218	Conform	18151	IRC §1250(h)

Table of References

The following titles are additions or replacements to the Book Table of References. Sections indicate where references are found in Supplement.

American Institute of Real Estate Appraisers. The Appraisal of Real Estate. 9th ed. Chicago: American Institute of Real Estate Appraisers, 1987: §§4.43, 10.3

Anderson, Paul E. Tax Factors in Real Estate Operations. 7th ed. Englewood Cliffs, N.J.: Prentice-Hall, 1990: §12.36

_____. Tax Planning of Real Estate. 7th ed. Philadelphia: ALI/ABA, 1977: §12.21

Anderson, Robert M. American Law of Zoning. 3d ed. Rochester, N.Y.: Lawyer's Co-operative, 1986: §13.22B

California Administrative Mandamus (2d ed Cal CEB 1989) (replacing the 1966 edition): §§6.20, 13.22O, 13.27

1–3 California Civil Procedure Before Trial (3d ed Cal CEB 1990) (replacing the 1977–78 edition): §§8.4–8.5, 8.22–8.23, 8.25, 9.6, 9.22

1, 2 California Civil Procedure During Trial (Cal CEB 1982, 1984) (replacing the 1960 edition): §§8.25, 9.22, 9.26, 10.28

California Government Tort Liability Practice (Cal CEB 1980) (replacing California Government Tort Liability (Cal CEB 1964): §§13.5, 13.7

California Mortgage and Deed of Trust Practice (2d ed Cal CEB 1990) (replacing the 1979 edition that replaced California Real Estate Secured Transactions (Cal CEB 1970)): §§2.10, 10.14

1 California Taxes (2d ed Cal CEB 1988): §2.15

California Trial Objections (2d ed Cal CEB 1984) (replacing the 1967 edition): §9.26

California Zoning Practice (Cal CEB 1969): §§2.20A, 4.8, 4.12, 4.14A, 13.22A–13.22B, 13.22E, 13.22G, 13.22J

Friedman, Edith J., ed. Encyclopedia of Real Estate Appraising. 3d ed. Englewood Cliffs, N.J.: Prentice-Hall, 1978.

Kahn, Sanders A., Case, Frederick E. & Schimmel, Alfred. Real Estate Appraisal & Investment. 2d ed. New York: John Wiley & Sons, 1977.

Landslide and Subsidence Liability (Cal CEB 1974): §13.19

McMichael, Stanley L. McMichael's Appraising Manual. 4th ed. Englewood Cliffs, N.J.: Prentice-Hall, 1951:

Mertens, Jacob, Mertens Law of Federal Income Taxation. 18 vols, looseleaf. Chicago, Ill.: Callaghan & Co., 1942–1990: §12.1

Miller, George H., Mercer, H. Glenn & Gilbeau, Kenneth. California Real Estate Appraisal: Residential Properties. 3d ed. Englewood Cliffs, N.J.: Prentice-Hall, 1987.

Nierenberg, Gerard I. The Art of Negotiating. Old Tappan, N.J.: Prentice-Hall, 1989.

Robinson, Gerald J. Federal Income Taxation of Real Estate. 5th ed. Boston: Warren, Gorham & Lamont, 1988: §12.1

Society of Real Estate Appraisers. Real Estate Appraisal Principle & Terminology. 2d ed. Chicago: Society of Real Estate Appraisers, 1971:

Witkin, B.E. California Procedure. 10 vols. 3d ed. San Francisco: Bancroft-Whitney, 1985 (replacing the 1971 edition): §10.28

Table of Statutes, Regulations, and Rules

Regulations and Rulings

CALIFORNIA CODE OF REGULATIONS
Title 14
15000: §2.20A
15000–15387: §4.8
Title 18
18081 (former): §12.21
Title 25
6000–6198: §4.53

LEGAL RULINGS
329 (July 25, 1968): Note, ch 12

Rules

CALIFORNIA RULES OF COURT
26: §1.8
135: §1.8
228: §9.26
331–337: §2.26
870: §1.8
App §8(d): §9.26

STATE BAR RULES OF PROFESSIONAL CONDUCT
5–310(B): §9.33

Jury Instructions

CIVIL (BAJI)
11.77: §4.5
11.79: §4.7A
11.80: §§9.68, 13.33
11.81: §4.33
11.82: §4.33
11.98: §9.19

UNITED STATES

Constitution

Art III: §11.5
Amend V: §§11.16, 11.23, 13.22B
Amend VI, Cl 2: §11.5
Amend XI: §§11.29, 13.21, 13.29
Amend XIV: §13.21

Statutes

INTERNAL REVENUE CODE
1: Note, ch 12, §§12.2–12.4
11: Note, ch 12, §§12.2–12.4
46(a)(2)(A): §12.6
48(a)(1)(E): §12.6
49(a): §§12.6, 12.25
56(c): §12.1
56(f): §12.1
61: App C
121: §12.31, App C
121(a)(2): §12.31
121(b): §12.31
121(d)(4): §12.31
163: §12.2
163(h): Note, ch 12, §§12.23, 12.41
163(h)(3): §12.31
165: Note, ch 12, §§12.4, 12.13, App C
165(h): Note, ch 12, §12.4, App C
165(i): Note, ch 12
165(k): §12.4
167: App C
168(c): Note, ch 12
170: §12.13
170(e): §12.13
170(e)(2): §12.13
216: App C
263: §12.2
280B: §12.29
301(a)(1): §12.14
331: App C
331(a): §12.26
331(a)(1) (former): §12.26
332: Note, ch 12, §12.26
334(b)(2): §12.26
336: Note, ch 12, §12.26
336(d)(3): §12.26
337: Note, ch 12, §12.26
351: §12.27, App C
354: App C
368(a): App C
453: App C
453(b)(2): Note, ch 12
453C (former): Note, ch 12
465: Note, ch 12
469: Note, ch 12

Court Rules

Table of Cases

Blau v City of Los Angeles (1973)
32 CA3d 77, 107 CR 727:
§§13.3–13.5, 13.13, 13.19, 13.30

Blue Chip Props. v Permanent Rent
Control Bd. (1985) 170 CA3d
648, 216 CR 492: §13.22I

Bodcaw Co., U.S. v (1979) 440 US
202: §11.23

Bohannan v City of San Diego
(1973) 30 CA3d 416, 106 CR
333: §§13.3, 13.22E

Brandenburg v Los Angeles County
Flood Control Dist. (1941) 45
CA2d 306, 114 P2d 14: §13.13

Bratton v Roundtree (MD Tenn
1976) 76–1 USTC ¶9198, 37
AFTR2d ¶76–438: §12.18

Breidert v Southern Pac. Co. (1964)
61 C2d 659, 39 CR 903: §13.1

Briarwood Props. v City of Los
Angeles (1985) 171 CA3d 1020,
217 CR 849: §13.22I

Briggs v State ex rel Dep't of Parks
& Recreation (1979) 98 CA3d
190, 159 CR 390: §§4.13A,
13.22J, 13.28

Britt v Superior Court (1978) 20
C3d 844, 143 CR 695: §13.33

Brock, M.J., & Sons v City of Davis
(ND Cal 1975) 401 F Supp 354:
§11.30

Brown v Critchfield (1980) 100
CA3d 858, 161 CR 342: §13.3

Brown v U.S. (1923) 263 US 78:
§11.16

Brylawski, Edward F., TC Memo
1983–622: §12.3

Buena Park School Dist. v Metrim
Corp. (1959) 176 CA2d 255, 1
CR 250: §§4.7, 4.33

Buffalo Wire Works Co. (1980) 74
TC 925: §12.24

Bunch v Coachella Valley Water
Dist. (1989) 214 CA3d 203, 262
CR 513: §13.17

Burger v County of Mendocino
(1975) 45 CA3d 322, 119 CR
568: §13.22O

Burns v City Council (1973) 31
CA3d 999, 107 CR 787: §13.28

Burrows v City of Keene (NH 1981)
432 A2d 15: §13.22B

C

California Cent. Coast Regional
Coastal Zone Conserv. Comm'n v
McKeon Constr. (1974) 38 CA3d
154, 112 CR 903: §4.14A

California Cent. Ry. v Hooper (1888)
76 C 404, 18 P 599: §8.2

California Coastal Comm'n v
Superior Court (1989) 210 CA3d
1488, 258 CR 567: §§13.23,
13.28

Cambria Spring Co. v City of Pico
Rivera (1985) 171 CA3d 1080,
217 CR 69: §13.21

Campbell v U.S. (1924) 266 US 368:
§11.20

Candlestick Props. v San Francisco
Bay Conserv. & Dev. Comm'n
(1970) 11 CA3d 557, 89 CR 897:
§§13.22C, 13.22J

Cantu v PG&E (1987) 189 CA3d
160, 234 CR 365: §§6.4–6.5,
6.6B, 13.3–13.4

Carlstrom v Lyon Van & Storage Co.
(1957) 152 CA2d 625, 313 P2d
645: §4.58

Carson Mobilehome Park Owners'
Ass'n v City of Carson (1983) 35
C3d 184, 197 CR 284: §13.22I

Carson Redev. Agency v Adam
(1982) 136 CA3d 608, 186 CR
615: §§2.10, 10.14

Carson Redev. Agency v Wolf
(1979) 99 CA3d 239, 160 CR
213: §4.61

Casalina Corp. (1973) 60 TC 694:
§12.28

Cash v Southern Pac. R.R. (1981)
123 CA3d 974, 177 CR 474:
§8.32

Cavanaugh v State (1978) 85 CA3d
354, 149 CR 453: §4.53

Department of Pub. Works, People
ex rel v Amsden Corp. (1973) 33
CA3d 89, 109 CR 1: §§4.55–4.57,
9.49, 9.54, 10.7, 10.30

Department of Pub. Works, People
ex rel v Bosio (1975) 47 CA3d
495, 121 CR 375: §§6.16, 8.19

Department of Pub. Works, People
ex rel v Buellton Dev. Co. (1943)
58 CA2d 178, 136 P2d 793:
§10.29A

Department of Pub. Works, People
ex rel v Curtis (1967) 255 CA2d
378, 63 CR 138: §13.22N

Department of Pub. Works, People
ex rel v Forster (1962) 58 C2d
257, 23 CR 582: §9.49

Department of Pub. Works, People
ex rel v Glen Arms Estate, Inc.
(1964) 230 CA2d 841, 41 CR
303: §9.49

Department of Pub. Works, People
ex rel v Hurd (1962) 205 CA2d
16, 23 CR 67: §5.6

Department of Pub. Works, People
ex rel v International Tel. & Tel.
Corp. (1972) 26 CA3d 549, 103
CR 63: §13.30

Department of Pub. Works, People
ex rel v Metcalf (1978) 79 CA3d
1, 144 CR 657: §8.33

Department of Pub. Works, People
ex rel v Ocean Shore R.R. (1949)
90 CA2d 464, 203 P2d 579:
§10.12

Department of Pub. Works, People
ex rel v Peninsula Enters. (1979)
91 CA3d 332, 153 CR 895:
§§1.9, 4.7A, 4.31, 4.49, 8.17–8.18

Department of Pub. Works, People
ex rel v Reardon (1971) 4 C3d
507, 93 CR 852: §§4.33, 9.49

Department of Pub. Works, People
ex rel v Romano (1971) 18 CA3d
63, 94 CR 839: §13.3

Department of Pub. Works, People
ex rel v Schultz Co. (1954) 123
CA2d 925, 268 P2d 117: §5.12

Department of Pub. Works, People
ex rel v Shasta Pipe & Supply
Co. (1968) 264 CA2d 520, 70 CR
618: §8.20

Department of Pub. Works, People
ex rel v Simon Newman Co.
(1974) 37 CA3d 398, 112 CR
298: §§4.19–4.22, 5.25, 5.28, 5.30

Department of Pub. Works, People
ex rel v Southern Pac. Transp.
Co. (1973) 33 CA3d 960, 109 CR
525: §§4.13A, 7.11, 9.49, 13.22F

Department of Pub. Works, People
ex rel v Superior Court (1968) 68
C2d 206, 65 CR 342: §6.10

Department of Pub. Works, People
ex rel v Symons (1960) 54 C2d
855, 9 CR 363: §§5.1, 5.6

Department of Pub. Works, People
ex rel v Union Mach. Co. (1955)
133 CA2d 167, 284 P2d 72:
§9.49

Department of Pub. Works, People
ex rel v Williams (1973) 30 CA3d
980, 106 CR 795: §§4.71, 8.10,
8.24, 10.25

Department of Transp., People ex rel
v Callahan Bros. (1977) 69 CA3d
541, 138 CR 239: §§9.14A–9.14B

Department of Transp., People ex rel
v Gardella Square (1988) 200
CA3d 559, 246 CR 139: §§9.14A,
10.23A, 10.25

Department of Transp., People ex rel
v Muller (1984) 36 C3d 263, 203
CR 772: §4.61

Department of Transp., People ex rel
v Patton Mission Props. (1979) 89
CA3d 204, 152 CR 485: §§9.14B,
10.23A

Department of Transp., People ex rel
v Redwood Baseline, Ltd. (1978)
84 CA3d 662, 149 CR 11: §10.14

Department of Transp., People ex rel
v Societa Di Unione E
Beneficenza Italiana (1978) 87
CA3d 14, 150 CR 706: §§9.14B,
10.23A

Griffin v County of Marin (1958) 157 CA2d 507, 321 P2d 148: §13.22O

Group W Cable, Inc. v City of Santa Cruz (ND Cal 1988) 679 F Supp 977: §13.3

Grupe v California Coastal Comm'n (1985) 166 CA3d 148, 212 CR 578: §13.22N

Guinnane v City & County of San Francisco (1987) 197 CA3d 862, 241 CR 787: §§13.21, 13.22G

H

HFH, Ltd. v Superior Court (1975) 15 C3d 508, 125 CR 365: §§13.22B–13.22C, 13.22O, 13.29

Haas & Co. v City & County of San Francisco (9th Cir 1979) 605 F2d 1117: §13.22E

Hadacheck v Sebastian (1915) 239 US 394: §13.22B

Hall v City of Santa Barbara (9th Cir 1986) 833 F2d 1270: §§13.22I, 13.27

Hans v Louisiana (1890) 134 US 1: §13.21

Harding v State ex rel Dep't of Transp. (1984) 159 CA3d 359, 205 CR 561: §5.22

Harry A. Gregg, Estate of (1977) 69 TC 468: §12.26

Harsh Inv. Corp. v U.S. (D Ore 1970) 323 F Supp 409: §12.23

Hawaii Hous. Auth. v Midkiff (1984) 467 US 229: §6.5

Hazon-Iny Dev. v City of Santa Monica (1982) 128 CA3d 1, 179 CR 860: §13.22O

Hecton v People ex rel Dep't of Transp. (1976) 58 CA3d 653, 130 CR 230: §13.21

Helfend v Southern Cal. Rapid Transit Dist. (1970) 2 C3d 1, 84 CR 173: §13.29B

Helix Land Co. v City of San Diego (1978) 82 CA3d 932, 147 CR 683: §§13.22D, 13.22G

Hernandez v City of Lafayette (5th Cir 1981) 643 F2d 1188: §§13.22B, 13.29

Herrington v County of Sonoma (9th Cir 1987) 834 F2d 1488, modified at 857 F2d 567: §13.27

Herrold, Redevelopment Agency v (1978) 86 CA3d 1024, 150 CR 621: §4.70

Hilltop Props., Inc. v State (1965) 233 CA2d 349, 43 CR 605: §1.4

Hladek v City of Merced (1977) 69 CA3d 585, 138 CR 194: §13.5

Hodel v Irving (1987) 481 US 704, 107 S Ct 2076, 95 L Ed 2d 668: §13.22B

Hodel v Virginia Surface Mining & Reclamation Ass'n (1981) 452 US 264: §13.22B

Hoehne v County of San Benito (9th Cir 1989) 870 F2d 529: §13.27

Hollister Park Inv. Co. v Goleta County Water Dist. (1978) 82 CA3d 290, 147 CR 91: §13.18

Holtz v San Francisco BART Dist. (1976) 17 C3d 648, 131 CR 646: §§1.9, 3.8, 10.27, 13.30–13.32

Holtz v Superior Court (1970) 3 C3d 296, 90 CR 345: §13.22L

Honig v Doe (1988) 484 US 305, 108 S Ct 592, 98 L Ed 2d 686: §11.29

Hoohuli v Ariyoshi (9th Cir 1984) 741 F2d 1169: §11.29

Hunter v Adams (1960) 180 CA2d 511, 4 CR 776: §13.22K

Huntington Park Redev. Agency v Duncan (1983) 142 CA3d 17, 190 CR 744: §§4.70, 6.4

I

Igna v City of Baldwin Park (1970) 9 CA3d 909, 88 CR 581: §13.27

Imperial Cattle Co. v Imperial Irrig. Dist. (1985) 167 CA3d 263, 213 CR 622: §13.17

Improved Premises, U.S. v (SD NY 1973) 359 F Supp 528: §11.19

In re Air Crash in Bali, Indonesia (9th Cir 1982) 684 F2d 1301: §13.22B

Inaja Land Co. v Commissioner (1947) 9 TC 727: §12.32

Ingram v City of Redondo Beach (1975) 45 CA3d 628, 119 CR 688: §§13.4–13.5, 13.17

Institoris v City of Los Angeles (1989) 210 CA3d 10, 258 CR 418: §13.5

Institoris v City of Los Angeles (1989) 210 CA3d 10, 258 CR 418: §13.10

Institoris v City of Los Angeles (1989) 210 CA3d 10, 258 CR 418: §13.20

Iske, James, TC Memo 1980–61: §12.32

Ivey, Charles, TC Memo 1983–273: §12.24

J

J. Robert King, Jr. (1981) 77 TC 1113: §§12.14, 12.33

Jack M. Short, TC Memo 1988–40: §12.4

James Iske, TC Memo 1980–61: §12.32

James Mosby (1986) 86 TC 190: §12.2

James Pryor, TC Memo 1987–80: §12.4

Javidzad v City of Santa Monica (1988) 204 CA3d 524, 251 CR 350: §13.22I

Jayne, George W., Estate of (1974) 61 TC 744: §12.26

Jerome K. Goldstein, Estate of, TC Memo 1976–19: §12.28

John E. Morris, Estate of (1971) 55 TC 636: §12.26

John L. Connell, TC Memo 1986–333: §12.13

John McShain (1976) 65 TC 686: §12.29

Johnson v State (1979) 90 CA3d 195, 153 CR 185: §4.7A

Jones v City of Los Angeles (1979) 88 CA3d 965, 152 CR 256: §§4.7A, 13.21

Jones v People ex rel Dep't of Transp. (1978) 22 C3d 144, 148 CR 640: §§1.9, 3.8, 4.7A, 5.20, 13.21, 13.22G, 13.22K, 13.30

Joseph P. Balistrieri, TC Memo 1979–115: §12.14

K

Kachadoorian v Calwa County Water Dist. (1979) 96 CA3d 741, 158 CR 223: §§6.18, 13.5, 13.25

Kahl, Lester Howard, TC Memo 1986–240: §12.27

Kaiser Aetna v U.S. (1979) 444 US 164: §13.22B

Keys v Romley (1966) 64 C2d 396, 50 CR 273: §13.14

Keystone Bituminous Coal Ass'n v DeBenedictis (1987) 480 US 470, 107 S Ct 1232, 94 L Ed 2d 472: §§13.22B, 13.22D

Kiewit, Peter, Sons' Co. v Richmond Redev. Agency (1986) 178 CA3d 435, 223 CR 728: §§4.52–4.53, 4.58

Kimball Laundry Co. v U.S. (1949) 338 US 1: §6.6

King, Jr., J. Robert (1981) 77 TC 1113: §§12.14, 12.33

Kinzli v City of Santa Cruz (9th Cir 1987) 818 F2d 1449, modified at 830 F2d 968: §§13.22B, 13.27

Kinzli v City of Santa Cruz (ND Cal 1985) 620 F Supp 609: §13.22C

Kinzli v City of Santa Cruz (ND Cal 1982) 539 F Supp 887: §13.22C

Kirby Forest Indus. v U.S. (1984) 467 US 1: §11.23A

Kissinger v City of Los Angeles (1958) 161 CA2d 454, 327 P2d 10: §13.22F

Klopp, Benjamin, TC Memo 1960–185: §12.13

Mager v U.S. (MD Pa 1980) 80–1
   USTC ¶9236, 45 AFTR2d
   ¶80–503: §12.31
Magneson v Commissioner (9th Cir
   1985) 753 F2d 1490: §12.17
Maine v Thiboutot (1980) 448 US 1:
   §13.29
Marco S. Marinello Assocs. v
   Commissioner (1st Cir 1976) 535
   F2d 147: §12.28
Marin v City of San Rafael (1980)
   111 CA3d 591, 168 CR 750:
   §§13.3–13.4
Marin Mun. Water Dist. v City of
   Mill Valley (1988) 202 CA3d
   1161, 249 CR 469: §13.3
Marina Plaza v California Coastal
   Zone Conserv. Comm'n (1977) 73
   CA3d 311, 140 CR 725: §13.28
Marinello, Marco S., Assocs. v
   Commissioner (1st Cir 1976) 535
   F2d 147: §12.28
Marshall v Department of Water &
   Power (1990) 219 CA3d 1124,
   268 CR 559: §13.12A
Martino v Santa Clara Valley Water
   Dist. (9th Cir 1983) 703 F2d
   1141: §13.27
McCarthy v California Tahoe
   Regional Planning Agency (1982)
   129 CA3d 222, 180 CR 866:
   §13.22O
McCarthy v City of Manhattan
   Beach (1953) 41 C2d 879, 264
   P2d 932: §13.22C
McCullough, People v (1950) 100
   CA2d 101, 223 P2d 37: §§9.68,
   13.33
McDougald v Southern Pac. R.R.
   (1912) 162 C 1, 120 P 766:
   §13.10A
McKeon v Hastings College of the
   Law (1986) 185 CA3d 877, 230
   CR 176: §4.53
McMahan's of Santa Monica v City
   of Santa Monica (1983) 146
   CA3d 683, 194 CR 582: §§4.52A,
   13.3–13.4, 13.14

McMullan v Santa Monica Rent
   Control Bd. (1985) 168 CA3d
   960, 214 CR 617: §§13.22I,
   13.22O
McShain, John (1976) 65 TC 686:
   §12.29
Mehl v People ex rel Dep't of Pub.
   Works (1975) 13 C3d 710, 119
   CR 625: §§5.12, 5.23, 9.7, 9.11,
   13.10A, 13.23
Merced Irrig. Dist. v Woolstenhulme
   (1971) 4 C3d 478, 93 CR 833:
   §4.5
Merz, U.S. v (1964) 376 US 192:
   §11.22
Metro Realty v County of El Dorado
   (1963) 222 CA2d 508, 35 CR
   480: §13.22K
Metromedia, Inc. v City of San
   Diego (1981) 453 US 490:
   §13.22E
Metromedia, Inc. v City of San
   Diego (1982) 32 C3d 180, 185
   CR 260: §13.22E
Metromedia, Inc. v City of San
   Diego (1980) 26 C3d 848, 164
   CR 510: §13.22E
Meyer, State v (1985) 174 CA3d
   1061, 220 CR 884: §§1.16, 4.7A,
   8.33
Mid-Way Cabinet Fixture Mfg. v
   County of San Joaquin (1967)
   257 CA2d 181, 65 CR 37:
   §13.22N
Middlesex County Sewerage Auth. v
   National Sea Clammers Ass'n
   (1981) 453 US 1: §13.29
Miller v Board of Pub. Works (1925)
   195 C 477, 234 P 381: §§13.22B,
   13.22K
Miller v City of Burbank (1972) 25
   CA3d 1144, 102 CR 559: §§13.5,
   13.17
Miller v Los Angeles County Flood
   Control Dist. (1973) 8 C3d 689,
   106 CR 1: §§13.5, 13.17
Miller, U.S. v (1943) 317 US 369:
   §11.17

Orange County Flood Control Dist. v
Sunny Crest Dairy, Inc. (1978) 77
CA3d 742, 143 CR 803: §§4.7,
4.19–4.22, 4.53, 5.13, 5.20

Orme v State ex rel Dep't of Water
Resources (1978) 83 CA3d 178,
147 CR 735: §§1.9, 13.30

Orpheum Bldg. Co. v San Francisco
BART Dist. (1978) 80 CA3d 863,
146 CR 5: §§13.12A, 13.30

Orsetti v City of Fremont (1978) 80
CA3d 961, 146 CR 75: §§13.22C,
13.22G

Osburn v Department of Transp.
(1990) 221 CA3d 1339, 270 CR
761: §4.53

Owen v City of Independence (1980)
445 US 622: §13.29

P

PG&E v Dame Constr. Co. (1987)
191 CA3d 233, 236 CR 351:
§4.53

PG&E v Hay (1977) 68 CA3d 905,
137 CR 613: §6.9

PG&E v Hufford (1957) 49 C2d
545, 319 P2d 1033: §5.32

PG&E v Parachini (1972) 29 CA3d
159, 105 CR 477: §§5.8, 6.9,
8.2A

PG&E v Superior Court (1986) 180
CA3d 770, 225 CR 768: §§8.2,
8.23

PG&E v Superior Court (1973) 33
CA3d 321, 109 CR 10: §10.19

PG&E v Zuckerman (1987) 189
CA3d 1113, 234 CR 630: §§4.1,
4.30–4.31, 4.68A, 5.8, 9.33,
9.49

Pacific Legal Found. v California
Coastal Comm'n (1982) 33 C3d
158, 188 CR 104: §13.22N

Pacific Outdoor Advertising Co. v
City of Burbank (1978) 86 CA3d
5, 149 CR 906: §4.52

Pacific Tel. & Tel. Co. v
Redevelopment Agency (1978)
87 CA3d 296, 151 CR 68:
§4.53

Palmer v Board of Supervisors
(1983) 145 CA3d 779, 193 CR
669: §13.22O

Pan Pac. Props. v County of Santa
Cruz (1978) 81 CA3d 244, 146
CR 428: §§13.22C, 13.27

Parker v City of Los Angeles (1974)
44 CA3d 556, 118 CR 687: §§4.6,
13.20, 13.30

Parking Auth. v Nicovich (1973) 32
CA3d 420, 108 CR 137: §§4.53,
13.30

Peacock v County of Sacramento
(1969) 271 CA2d 845, 77 CR
391: §§4.13A, 13.13, 13.21,
13.22F–13.22G

Peerless Stages, Inc. v Santa Cruz
Metropolitan Transit Dist. (1977)
67 CA3d 343, 136 CR 567:
§13.5

Peninsula Enters., People ex rel
Dep't of Public Works v (1979)
91 CA3d 332, 153 CR 895: §9.20

Penn Cent. Transp. Co. v New York
City (1978) 438 US 104: §13.22E

Pennell v City of San Jose (Feb. 24,
1988) 108 S Ct 849, 99 L Ed 2d
1: §13.22I

Pennell v City of San Jose (1986) 42
C3d 365, 228 CR 726: §13.22I

Pennhurst State School & Hosp. v
Halderman (1984) 465 US 89:
§§11.29, 13.29

Pennhurst State School & Hosp. v
Halderman (1981) 451 US 1:
§13.29

Pennsylvania Coal Co. v Mahon
(1922) 260 US 393: §13.22D

People ex rel _____ (*see* name of
relator)

People v _____ (*see* name of
defendant)

Peter Kiewit Sons' Co. v Richmond
Redev. Agency (1986) 178 CA3d
435, 223 CR 728: §§4.52–4.53,
4.58

Pfeiffer v City of La Mesa (1977)
69 CA3d 74, 137 CR 804:
§13.28

Ricciardi, People v (1943) 23 C2d
390, 144 P2d 799: §§11.29,
13.12A

Richardson v Koshiba (9th Cir 1982)
693 F2d 911: §11.30

Richmond Elks Hall Ass'n v
Richmond Redev. Agency (9th Cir
1977) 561 F2d 1327: §§4.7A,
11.17, 13.2, 13.21

Richmond Ramblers Motorcycle
Club v Western Title Guar. Co.
(1975) 47 CA3d 747, 121 CR
308: §§2.9, 4.66

Richmond Redev. Agency v Western
Title Guar. Co. (1975) 48 CA3d
343, 122 CR 434: §§4.7A, 8.18A,
9.7, 9.54

Rippley v City of Lincoln (ND
1983) 330 NW2d 505: §13.22B

Rohn v City of Visalia (1989) 214
CA3d 1463, 263 CR 319:
§13.22N

Romero v Department of Pub. Works
(1941) 17 C2d 189, 109 P2d 662:
§10.13

Rose v City of Coalinga (1987) 190
CA3d 1627, 236 CR 124:
§§13.22D, 13.22L

Ross v City of Berkeley (ND Cal
1987) 655 F Supp 820:
§13.22I

Rossco Holdings, Inc. v State (1989)
212 CA3d 642, 260 CR 736:
§13.28

Roy P. Varner, TC Memo 1973–027:
§12.27

Rubin v HUD (ED Pa 1972) 347 F
Supp 555: §11.3

Ruckelshaus v Monsanto Co. (1984)
467 US 986: §11.5

Rutherford v State (1987) 188 CA3d
1267, 233 CR 781: §13.27

S

Sacramento S. R.R. v Heilbron
(1909) 156 C 408, 104 P 979:
§4.1

Salton Bay Marina, Inc. v Imperial
Irrig. Dist. (1985) 172 CA3d 914,
218 CR 839: §§8.33, 13.17,
13.23, 13.30

Salvaty v Falcon Cable Television
(1985) 165 CA3d 798, 212 CR
31: §13.3

San Bernardino County Flood
Control Dist. v Grabowski (1988)
205 CA3d 885, 252 CR 676:
§§6.19–6.20, 6.25, 8.19, 8.24,
10.24

San Bernardino Valley Mun. Water
Dist. v Meeks & Daley Water Co.
(1964) 226 CA2d 216, 38 CR 51:
§13.18

San Diego Coast Regional Comm'n
v See The Sea, Ltd. (1973) 9 C3d
888, 109 CR 377: §13.22O

San Diego Gas & Elec. Co. v City
of San Diego (1981) 450 US 621:
§§13.22B, 13.22G, 13.22K, 13.27

San Diego Gas & Elec. Co. v Daley
(1988) 205 CA3d 1334, 253 CR
144: §§5.22A, 5.32, 9.67A,
10.23A

San Diego Gas & Elec. Co. v
Moreland Inv. Co. (1986) 186
CA3d 1151, 231 CR 274: §9.14A

San Diego Gas & Elec. Co. v 3250
Corp. (1988) 205 CA3d 1075, 252
CR 853: §§4.33, 5.22A, 6.25,
8.22, 9.49

San Diego Unified Port Dist. v
Superior Court (1977) 67 CA3d
361, 136 CR 557: §§13.5, 13.20

San Francisco Unified School Dist. v
Hong Mow (1954) 123 CA2d
668, 267 P2d 349: §10.29A

San Gabriel Valley Water Co. v City
of Montebello (1978) 84 CA3d
757, 148 CR 830: §§4.38, 5.24,
13.30

San Leandro Rock Co. v City of San
Leandro (1982) 136 CA3d 25,
185 CR 829: §13.22B

Santa Clara Valley Water Dist. v
Gross (1988) 200 CA3d 1363,
246 CR 580: §9.14A

Santa Clarita Water Co. v Lyons
(1984) 161 CA3d 450, 207 CR
698: §8.33

Santa Monica Airport Ass'n v City
of Santa Monica (9th Cir 1981)
659 F2d 100: §13.20

Santa Monica Unified School Dist. v
Persh (1970) 5 CA3d 945, 85 CR
463: §§1.4, 7.7

Sayre v City of Cleveland (6th Cir
1974) 493 F2d 64: §§4.7A, 4.70,
13.21

Scolari v Commissioner (9th Cir
1974) 497 F2d 962: §12.28

Scolari, Lino, TC Memo 1973–116:
§12.28

Searle v City of Berkeley Rent
Stabilization Bd. (1988) 197
CA3d 1251, 243 CR 449: §13.22I

Selby Realty Co. v City of San
Buenaventura (1973) 10 C3d 110,
109 CR 799: §§4.7A, 13.21,
13.22G, 13.22N, 13.28–13.29

Seltzer, Benjamin F., Estate of, TC
Memo 1987–568: §12.5

760.807 Acres of Land, U.S. v (9th
Cir 1984) 731 F2d 1443: §11.17

Shaeffer v State (1972) 22 CA3d
1017, 99 CR 861: §13.17

Sheerr v Township of Evesham (NJ
Super 1982) 445 A2d 46: §13.22B

Sheffet v County of Los Angeles
(1970) 3 CA3d 720, 84 CR 11:
§§13.3–13.4, 13.13, 13.25

Shelter Creek Dev. Corp. v City of
Oxnard (9th Cir 1988) 838 F2d
375: §13.27

Short, Jack M., TC Memo 1988–40:
§12.4

Sierra Terreno v Tahoe Regional
Planning Agency (1978) 79 CA3d
439, 144 CR 776: §§13.22C,
13.22G, 13.22J

Silvera v City of South Lake Tahoe
(1970) 3 CA3d 554, 83 CR 698:
§13.22K

633.07 Acres of Land, U.S. v (MD
Pa 1973) 362 F Supp 451: §9.62

Smart v City of Los Angeles (1980)
112 CA3d 232, 169 CR 174:
§13.10

Smith v County of Los Angeles
(1989) 214 CA3d 266, 262 CR
754: §§10.24, 13.4, 13.7, 13.19,
13.22D, 13.22L, 13.29B–13.31

Smith v County of Santa Barbara
(1966) 243 CA2d 126, 52 CR
292: §13.22F

Smith v State (1975) 50 CA3d 529,
123 CR 745: §§4.7A–4.8, 13.21

Sneed v County of Riverside (1963)
218 CA2d 205, 32 CR 318:
§13.22F

South Bay Irrig. Dist. v
California-American Water Co.
(1976) 61 CA3d 944, 133 CR
166: §§4.1, 4.38, 4.47

South Cent. Coast Regional Comm'n
v Charles A. Pratt Constr. Co.
(1982) 128 CA3d 830, 180 CR
555: §13.22O

South Coast Regional Comm'n v
Gordon (1977) 18 C3d 832, 135
CR 781: §13.27

South Coast Regional Comm'n v
Higgins (1977) 68 CA3d 636, 137
CR 551: §13.22O

Southerly Portion of Bodie Island,
U.S. v (ED NC 1953) 114 F Supp
427: §11.5

Southern Cal. Edison Co. v
Bourgerie (1973) 9 C3d 169,
107 CR 76: §§2.11, 4.62, 10.14,
13.13

Southern Cal. Edison Co. v Rice
(9th Cir 1982) 685 F2d 354:
§6.14

Southern Pac. Co. v City of Los
Angeles (1966) 242 CA2d 38, 51
CR 197: §13.22N

Southern Pac. Transp. Co. v PUC
(1976) 18 C3d 308, 134 CR 189:
§13.27

Southern Ry. v South Carolina
Highway Dep't (ED SC 1965)
246 F Supp 435: §13.21

Table of Forms: Book

Table of Forms: Supplement

Index

Make sure you are using the latest supplement

For your convenience, the following list identifies the most recent publication date of each CEB supplement (as of December, 1990).

Supplement Title	Product Number	Publication Date
Advising California Employers	BU-35514	3/90
Advising California Nonprofit Corporations	BU-36625	6/90
Advising California Partnerships, 2d Edition	BU-35632	3/90
Appeals and Writs in Criminal Cases	CR-33484	12/90
Attorney's Guide to California Professional Corporations, 4th Edition	TX-30932	10/89
Attorney's Guide to Pension and Profit-Sharing Plans, 3d Edition	TX-30732	2/89
Attorney's Guide to the Law of Competitive Business Practices	BU-35566	2/90
Attorney's Guide to Trade Secrets	BU-30038	3/90
Business Buy-Out Agreements	BU-32007	10/87
California Administrative Hearing Practice	CP-35655	6/90
California Administrative Mandamus, 2d Edition	CP-38811	6/90
California Attorney's Damages Guide	CP-31437	3/90
California Attorney's Fees Award Practice	CP-30395	4/90
California Automobile Insurance Law Guide	TO-30751	11/89
California Breach of Contract Remedies	CP-34461	11/90
California Civil Appellate Practice, 2d Edition	CP-32327	5/90
California Civil Litigation Forms Manual	CP-34471	9/90
California Civil Procedure During Trial, Volume 1	CP-36656	11/89
California Civil Procedure During Trial, Volume 2	CP-38825	1/90

Supplement Title	Product Number	Publication Date
California Civil Writ Practice, 2d Edition	CP-30642	11/89
California Commercial Law (I, II)	BU-30042	1/89
California Condominium and Planned Development Practice	RE-38875	1/90
California Criminal Law Procedure and Practice	CR-30783	12/90
California Decedent Estate Practice 1, 2	ES-35663	12/90
California Decedent Estate Practice 3	ES-30863	8/90
California Eviction Defense Manual	RE-30457	4/90
California Evidence Benchbook, 2d Edition	CP-32371	6/90
California Expert Witness Guide	CP-30694	4/89
California Government Tort Liability Practice	TO-34429	10/90
California Juvenile Court Practice, Volume 1	CR-35527	2/90
California Juvenile Court Practice, Volume 2	CR-35536	6/90
California Lis Pendens Practice	RE-30596	12/90
California Local Probate Rules, 11th Edition	ES-39661	2/90
California Marital Dissolution Practice, Volume 1	FA-35576	6/90
California Marital Dissolution Practice, Volume 2	FA-37786	5/90
California Marital Termination Agreements	FA-30872	6/90
California Mechanics' Liens and Other Remedies, 2d Edition	RE-30992	10/90
California Personal Injury Proof	TO-30563	4/90
California Probate Code Annotated to CEB Publications	ES-31191	2/90
California Probate Workflow Manual	ES-31561	8/90
California Real Property Financing, Volume 1	RE-30971	3/90
California Real Property Practice Forms Manual	RE-30921	2/90
California Real Property Remedies Practice	RE-38868	5/90
California Real Property Sales Transactions	RE-36619	4/90
California Residential Landlord-Tenant Practice	RE-37734	6/90
California Search and Seizure Practice, 2d Edition	CR-31328	11/89

Supplement Title	Product Number	Publication Date
Operating Problems of California Corporations	BU-31157	6/89
Organizing Corporations in California, 2d Edition	BU-37766	8/90
Personal Tax Planning for Professionals and Owners of Small Businesses	TX-36635	6/90
Persuasive Opening Statements and Closing Arguments	CP-39651	3/90
Practicing California Judicial Arbitration	CP-30666	6/90
Real Property Exchanges	RE-34535	1/90
Secured Transactions in California Commercial Law Practice	BU-32312	4/90
Tax Aspects of California Partnerships	TX-37745	8/90
Tax Aspects of Marital Dissolutions, 2d Edition	TX-31331	5/90
Tax Practice in California	TX-30494	9/90
Taxation of Real Property Transfers	RE-37756	10/90
Trial Attorney's Evidence Code Notebook, 3d Edition	CP-30296	5/90
Wrongful Employment Termination Practice	CP-30902	1/90

Not Yet Supplemented	Product Number
Attorney's Guide to California Construction Contracts and Disputes, 2d Edition	RE-31440
California Civil Procedure Before Trial, 3d Edition	CP-3154*
California Conservatorships and Guardianships	ES-3150*
California Mortgage and Deed of Trust Practice, 2d Edition	RE-3134*
California Real Property Financing, Volume 2	RE-3098*
Counseling California Corporations	BU-3923*
Effective Introduction of Evidence	CP-3135*
Fee Agreement Forms Manual	MI-3044*
Jefferson's Synopsis of California Evidence Law	CP-3079*